3rd Workshop on Asian Translation (WAT 2016)

Osaka, Japan
11 - 16 December 2016

ISBN: 978-1-5108-3326-5

Preface

Many Asian countries are rapidly growing these days and the importance of communicating and exchanging the information with these countries has intensified. To satisfy the demand for communication among these countries, machine translation technology is essential.

Machine translation technology has rapidly evolved recently and it is seeing practical use especially between European languages. However, the translation quality of Asian languages is not that high compared to that of European languages, and machine translation technology for these languages has not reached a stage of proliferation yet. This is not only due to the lack of the language resources for Asian languages but also due to the lack of techniques to correctly transfer the meaning of sentences from/to Asian languages. Consequently, a place for gathering and sharing the resources and knowledge about Asian language translation is necessary to enhance machine translation research for Asian languages.

The Workshop on Machine Translation (WMT), the world's largest machine translation workshop, mainly targets on European languages and does not include Asian languages. The International Workshop on Spoken Language Translation (IWSLT) has spoken language translation tasks for some Asian languages using TED talk data, but these is no task for written language.

The Workshop on Asian Translation (WAT) is an open machine translation evaluation campaign focusing on Asian languages. WAT gathers and shares the resources and knowledge of Asian language translation to understand the problems to be solved for the practical use of machine translation technologies among all Asian countries. WAT is unique in that it is an "open innovation platform": the test data is fixed and open, so participants can repeat evaluations on the same data and confirm changes in translation accuracy over time. WAT has no deadline for the automatic translation quality evaluation (continuous evaluation), so participants can submit translation results at any time.

Following the success of the previous WAT workshops (WAT2014, WAT2015), WAT2016 brings together machine translation researchers and users to try, evaluate, share and discuss brand-new ideas about machine translation. For the 3rd WAT, we proudly include new Asian languages: Hindi and Indonesian in addition to Japanese, Chinese and Korean for the machine translation evaluation shared tasks. We had 15 teams who submitted their translation results, and more than 500 submissions in total.

In addition to the shared tasks, WAT2016 also feature scientific papers on topics related to the machine translation, especially for Asian languages. The program committee accepted 7 papers that cover wide variety of topics such as neural machine translation, simultaneous interpretation, southeast Asian languages and so on.

We are indebted to Hideto Kazawa (Google) who gave an invited talk. We are grateful to "SunFlare Co., Ltd.", "TOIN Corporation", "Baobab, Inc". "Asia-Pacific Association for Machine Translation (AAMT)" and "PostEdit.Tokyo Co., Ltd." for partially sponsoring the workshop. We would like to thank all the authors who submitted papers. We express our deepest gratitude to the committee members for their timely reviews. We also thank the COLING 2016 organizers for their help with administrative matters.

WAT2016 Organizers

Organisers

Toshiaki Nakazawa, Japan Science and Technology Agency (JST), Japan

Hideya Mino, National Institute of Information and Communications Technology (NICT), Japan

Chenchen Ding, National Institute of Information and Communications Technology (NICT), Japan

Isao Goto, Japan Broadcasting Corporation (NHK), Japan

Graham Neubig, Nara Institute of Science and Technology (NAIST), Japan

Sadao Kurohashi, Kyoto University, Japan

Ir. Hammam Riza, Agency for the Assessment and Application of Technology (BPPT), Indonesia

Pushpak Bhattacharyya, Indian Institute of Technology Bombay (IIT), India

Programme Committee

Rafael E. Banchs, Institute for Infocomm Research, Singapore

Hailong Cao, Harbin Institute of Technology, China

Michael Carl, Copenhagen Business School, Denmark

Marine Carpuat, University of Maryland, USA

Chenhui Chu, JST, Japan

Fabien Cromières, JST, Japan

Hideto Kazawa, Google, Japan

Anoop Kunchookuttan, IIT Bombay, India

Jong-Hyeok Lee, Pohang University of Science and Technology, Korea

Gurpreet Singh Lehal, Punjabi University, Patiala, India

Haizhou Li, Institute for Infocomm Research, Singapore

Qun Liu, Dublin City University, Ireland

Liling Tan, Universität des Saarlandes, Germany

Masao Utiyama, NICT, Japan

Andy Way, Dublin City University, Ireland

Dekai Wu, HKUST, Hong Kong

Deyi Xiong, Soochow University, China

Dongdong Zhang, Microsoft Research Asia, China

Jiajun Zhang, Chinese Academy of Sciences, China

Technical Collaborators

Luis Fernando D'Haro, Institute for Infocomm Research, Singapore

Rafael E. Banchs, Institute for Infocomm Research, Singapore

Haizhou Li, Institute for Infocomm Research, Singapore

Invited Speaker

Hideto Kazawa, Senior Engineering Manager, Google, Japan

Google's Neural Machine Translation System: Training and Serving a Very Large Neural MT Models

Abstract

Recently Neural Machine Translation (NMT) systems are reported to outperform other approaches in machine translation. However, NMT systems are known to be computationally expensive both in training and in translation inference – sometimes prohibitively so in the case of very large data sets and large models. Several authors have also charged that NMT systems lack robustness, particularly when input sentences contain rare words. These issues have hindered NMT's use in practical deployments and services, where both accuracy and speed are essential. In this talk, I present GNMT, Google's Neural Machine Translation system, which attempts to address many of these issues. Our model consists of a deep LSTM network with 8 encoder and 8 decoder layers using residual connections as well as attention connections from the decoder network to the encoder. To improve parallelism and therefore decrease training time, our attention mechanism connects the bottom layer of the decoder to the top layer of the encoder. To accelerate the final translation speed, we employ low-precision arithmetic during inference computations. To improve handling of rare words, we divide words into a limited set of common sub-word units ("wordpieces") for both input and output. On the WMT'14 English-to-French and English-to-German benchmarks, GNMT achieves competitive results to state-of-the-art. Using a human side-by-side evaluation on a set of isolated simple sentences, it reduces translation errors by an average of 60phrase-based production system.

Short bio

Hideto Kazawa received M.Sc from University of Tokyo and Dr. Eng. from Nara Adavanced Institute of Science and Technology. He is now a Senior Engineering Manager of Google Translate team.

Conference Program

December 12, 2016

December 12, 2016 (continued)

12:00–14:00   **Lunch**

14:00–14:45   **Invited talk**

Google's Neural Machine Translation System: Training and Serving a Very Large Neural MT Models
Hideto Kazawa

14:45–15:45   **Research paper II**

An Efficient and Effective Online Sentence Segmenter for Simultaneous Interpretation
Xiaolin Wang, Andrew Finch, Masao Utiyama and Eiichiro Sumita

Similar Southeast Asian Languages: Corpus-Based Case Study on Thai-Laotian and Malay-Indonesian
Chenchen Ding, Masao Utiyama and Eiichiro Sumita

Integrating empty category detection into preordering Machine Translation
Shunsuke Takeno, Masaaki Nagata and Kazuhide Yamamoto

15:45–16:00   **System description II**

Kyoto University Participation to WAT 2016
Fabien Cromieres, Chenhui Chu, Toshiaki Nakazawa and Sadao Kurohashi

16:00–16:05   **Commemorative photo**

December 12, 2016 (continued)

16:05–17:00   **Poster presentation II (System description)**

Kyoto University Participation to WAT 2016
Fabien Cromieres, Chenhui Chu, Toshiaki Nakazawa and Sadao Kurohashi

Character-based Decoding in Tree-to-Sequence Attention-based Neural Machine Translation
Akiko Eriguchi, Kazuma Hashimoto and Yoshimasa Tsuruoka

Faster and Lighter Phrase-based Machine Translation Baseline
Liling Tan

Improving Patent Translation using Bilingual Term Extraction and Re-tokenization for Chinese–Japanese
Wei Yang and Yves Lepage

Controlling the Voice of a Sentence in Japanese-to-English Neural Machine Translation
Hayahide Yamagishi, Shin Kanouchi, Takayuki Sato and Mamoru Komachi

Chinese-to-Japanese Patent Machine Translation based on Syntactic Pre-ordering for WAT 2016
Katsuhito Sudoh and Masaaki Nagata

IITP English-Hindi Machine Translation System at WAT 2016
Sukanta Sen, Debajyoty Banik, Asif Ekbal and Pushpak Bhattacharyya

Residual Stacking of RNNs for Neural Machine Translation
Raphael Shu and Akiva Miura

17:00–   **Closing**

Overview of the 3rd Workshop on Asian Translation

Toshiaki Nakazawa
Japan Science and
Technology Agency
`nakazawa@pa.jst.jp`

Chenchen Ding and **Hideya Mino**
National Institute of
Information and
Communications Technology
`{chenchen.ding, hideya.mino}@nict.go.jp`

Isao Goto
NHK
`goto.i-es@nhk.or.jp`

Graham Neubig
Carnegie Mellon University
`gneubig@cs.cmu.edu`

Sadao Kurohashi
Kyoto University
`kuro@i.kyoto-u.ac.jp`

Abstract

This paper presents the results of the shared tasks from the 3rd workshop on Asian translation (WAT2016) including J↔E, J↔C scientific paper translation subtasks, C↔J, K↔J, E↔J patent translation subtasks, I↔E newswire subtasks and H↔E, H↔J mixed domain subtasks. For the WAT2016, 15 institutions participated in the shared tasks. About 500 translation results have been submitted to the automatic evaluation server, and selected submissions were manually evaluated.

1 Introduction

The Workshop on Asian Translation (WAT) is a new open evaluation campaign focusing on Asian languages. Following the success of the previous workshops WAT2014 (Nakazawa et al., 2014) and WAT2015 (Nakazawa et al., 2015), WAT2016 brings together machine translation researchers and users to try, evaluate, share and discuss brand-new ideas of machine translation. We are working toward the practical use of machine translation among all Asian countries.

For the 3rd WAT, we adopt new translation subtasks with English-Japanese patent description, Indonesian-English news description and Hindi-English and Hindi-Japanese mixed domain corpus in addition to the subtasks that were conducted in WAT2015. Furthermore, we invited research papers on topics related to the machine translation, especially for Asian languages. The submissions of the research papers were peer reviewed by at least 2 program committee members and the program committee accepted 7 papers that cover wide variety of topics such as neural machine translation, simultaneous interpretation, southeast Asian languages and so on.

WAT is unique for the following reasons:

- Open innovation platform
  The test data is fixed and open, so evaluations can be repeated on the same data set to confirm changes in translation accuracy over time. WAT has no deadline for automatic translation quality evaluation (continuous evaluation), so translation results can be submitted at any time.

- Domain and language pairs
  WAT is the world's first workshop that uses scientific papers as the domain, and Chinese ↔ Japanese, Korean ↔ Japanese and Indonesian ↔ English as language pairs. In the future, we will add more Asian languages, such as Vietnamese, Thai, Burmese and so on.

- Evaluation method
  Evaluation is done both automatically and manually. For human evaluation, WAT uses pairwise evaluation as the first-stage evaluation. Also, JPO adequacy evaluation is conducted for the selected submissions according to the pairwise evaluation results.

Proceedings of the 3rd Workshop on Asian Translation,
pages 1–46, Osaka, Japan, December 11-17 2016.

LangPair	Train	Dev	DevTest	Test
ASPEC-JE	3,008,500	1,790	1,784	1,812
ASPEC-JC	672,315	2,090	2,148	2,107

Table 1: Statistics for ASPEC.

2 Dataset

WAT uses the Asian Scientific Paper Excerpt Corpus (ASPEC) [1], JPO Patent Corpus (JPC) [2], BPPT Corpus [3] and IIT Bombay English-Hindi Corpus (IITB Corpus) [4] as the dataset.

2.1 ASPEC

ASPEC is constructed by the Japan Science and Technology Agency (JST) in collaboration with the National Institute of Information and Communications Technology (NICT). It consists of a Japanese-English scientific paper abstract corpus (ASPEC-JE), which is used for J↔E subtasks, and a Japanese-Chinese scientific paper excerpt corpus (ASPEC-JC), which is used for J↔C subtasks. The statistics for each corpus are described in Table1.

2.1.1 ASPEC-JE

The training data for ASPEC-JE was constructed by the NICT from approximately 2 million Japanese-English scientific paper abstracts owned by the JST. Because the abstracts are comparable corpora, the sentence correspondences are found automatically using the method from (Utiyama and Isahara, 2007). Each sentence pair is accompanied by a similarity score and the field symbol. The similarity scores are calculated by the method from (Utiyama and Isahara, 2007). The field symbols are single letters A-Z and show the scientific field for each document [5]. The correspondence between the symbols and field names, along with the frequency and occurrence ratios for the training data, are given in the README file from ASPEC-JE.

The development, development-test and test data were extracted from parallel sentences from the Japanese-English paper abstracts owned by JST that are not contained in the training data. Each data set contains 400 documents. Furthermore, the data has been selected to contain the same relative field coverage across each data set. The document alignment was conducted automatically and only documents with a 1-to-1 alignment are included. It is therefore possible to restore the original documents. The format is the same as for the training data except that there is no similarity score.

2.1.2 ASPEC-JC

ASPEC-JC is a parallel corpus consisting of Japanese scientific papers from the literature database and electronic journal site J-STAGE of JST that have been translated to Chinese with permission from the necessary academic associations. The parts selected were abstracts and paragraph units from the body text, as these contain the highest overall vocabulary coverage.

The development, development-test and test data are extracted at random from documents containing single paragraphs across the entire corpus. Each set contains 400 paragraphs (documents). Therefore, there are no documents sharing the same data across the training, development, development-test and test sets.

2.2 JPC

JPC was constructed by the Japan Patent Office (JPO). It consists of a Chinese-Japanese patent description corpus (JPC-CJ), Korean-Japanese patent description corpus (JPC-KJ) and English-Japanese patent description corpus (JPC-EJ) with four sections, which are Chemistry, Electricity, Mechanical engineering, and Physics, based on International Patent Classification (IPC). Each corpus is separated into

---

[1] http://lotus.kuee.kyoto-u.ac.jp/ASPEC/

[2] http://lotus.kuee.kyoto-u.ac.jp/WAT/patent/index.html

[3] http://orchid.kuee.kyoto-u.ac.jp/WAT/bppt-corpus/index.html

[4] http://www.cfilt.iitb.ac.in/iitb_parallel/index.html

[5] http://opac.jst.go.jp/bunrui/index.html

LangPair	Train	Dev	DevTest	Test
JPC-CJ	1,000,000	2,000	2,000	2,000
JPC-KJ	1,000,000	2,000	2,000	2,000
JPC-EJ	1,000,000	2,000	2,000	2,000

Table 2: Statistics for JPC.

LangPair	Train	Dev	DevTest	Test
BPPT-IE	50,000	400	400	400

Table 3: Statistics for BPPT Corpus.

training, development, development-test and test data, which are sentence pairs. This corpus was used for patent subtasks C↔J, K↔J and E↔J. The statistics for each corpus are described in Table2.

The Sentence pairs in each data were randomly extracted from a description part of comparable patent documents under the condition that a similarity score between sentences is greater than or equal to the threshold value 0.05. The similarity score was calculated by the method from (Utiyama and Isahara, 2007) as with ASPEC. Document pairs which were used to extract sentence pairs for each data were not used for the other data. Furthermore, the sentence pairs were extracted to be same number among the four sections. The maximize number of sentence pairs which are extracted from one document pair was limited to 60 for training data and 20 for the development, development-test and test data. The training data for JPC-CJ was made with sentence pairs of Chinese-Japanese patent documents published in 2012. For JPC-KJ and JPC-EJ, the training data was extracted from sentence pairs of Korean-Japanese and English-Japanese patent documents published in 2011 and 2012. The development, development-test and test data for JPC-CJ, JPC-KJ and JPC-EJ were respectively made with 100 patent documents published in 2013.

2.3 BPPT Corpus

BPPT Corpus was constructed by Badan Pengkajian dan Penerapan Teknologi (BPPT). This corpus consists of a Indonesian-English news corpus (BPPT-IE) with five sections, which are Finance, International, Science and Technology, National, and Sports. These data come from Antara News Agency. This corpus was used for newswire subtasks I↔E. The statistics for each corpus are described in Table3.

2.4 IITB Corpus

IIT Bombay English-Hindi corpus contains English-Hindi parallel corpus (IITB-EH) as well as monolingual Hindi corpus collected from a variety of existing sources and corpora developed at the Center for Indian Language Technology, IIT Bombay over the years. This corpus was used for mixed domain subtasks H↔E. Furthermore, mixed domain subtasks H↔J were added as a pivot language task with a parallel corpus created using openly available corpora (IITB-JH) [6]. Most sentence pairs in IITB-JH come from the Bible corpus. The statistics for each corpus are described in Table4.

3 Baseline Systems

Human evaluations were conducted as pairwise comparisons between the translation results for a specific baseline system and translation results for each participant's system. That is, the specific baseline system was the standard for human evaluation. A phrase-based statistical machine translation (SMT) system was adopted as the specific baseline system at WAT 2016, which is the same system as that at WAT 2014 and WAT 2015.

In addition to the results for the baseline phrase-based SMT system, we produced results for the baseline systems that consisted of a hierarchical phrase-based SMT system, a string-to-tree syntax-based

---

[6] http://lotus.kuee.kyoto-u.ac.jp/WAT/Hindi-corpus/WAT2016-Ja-Hi.zip

LangPair	Train	Dev	Test	Monolingual Corpus (Hindi)
IITB-EH	1,492,827	520	2,507	45,075,279
IITB-JH	152,692	1,566	2,000	-

Table 4: Statistics for IITB Corpus.

SMT system, a tree-to-string syntax-based SMT system, seven commercial rule-based machine translation (RBMT) systems, and two online translation systems. The SMT baseline systems consisted of publicly available software, and the procedures for building the systems and for translating using the systems were published on the WAT web page[7]. We used Moses (Koehn et al., 2007; Hoang et al., 2009) as the implementation of the baseline SMT systems. The Berkeley parser (Petrov et al., 2006) was used to obtain syntactic annotations. The baseline systems are shown in Table 5.

The commercial RBMT systems and the online translation systems were operated by the organizers. We note that these RBMT companies and online translation companies did not submit themselves. Because our objective is not to compare commercial RBMT systems or online translation systems from companies that did not themselves participate, the system IDs of these systems are anonymous in this paper.

---

[7]http://lotus.kuee.kyoto-u.ac.jp/WAT/

System ID	System	Type	ASPEC				JPC						IITB		BPPT		pivot	
			JE	EJ	JC	CJ	JE	EJ	JC	CJ	JK	KJ	HE	EH	IE	EI	HJ	JH
SMT Phrase	Moses' Phrase-based SMT	SMT	✓	✓	✓	✓	✓	✓	✓	✓	✓	✓	✓	✓	✓	✓	✓	✓
SMT Hiero	Moses' Hierarchical Phrase-based SMT	SMT	✓	✓	✓	✓	✓	✓	✓	✓	✓	✓	✓	✓	✓	✓		
SMT S2T	Moses' String-to-Tree Syntax-based SMT and Berkeley parser	SMT	✓		✓		✓		✓				✓		✓			
SMT T2S	Moses' Tree-to-String Syntax-based SMT and Berkeley parser	SMT		✓		✓		✓		✓				✓		✓		
RBMT X	The Honyaku V15 (Commercial system)	RBMT	✓	✓			✓	✓										
RBMT X	ATLAS V14 (Commercial system)	RBMT	✓	✓			✓	✓										
RBMT X	PAT-Transer 2009 (Commercial system)	RBMT	✓	✓			✓	✓										
RBMT X	J-Beijing 7 (Commercial system)	RBMT			✓	✓			✓	✓								
RBMT X	Hohrai 2011 (Commercial system)	RBMT			✓	✓				✓								
RBMT X	J Soul 9 (Commercial system)	RBMT									✓	✓						
RBMT X	Korai 2011 (Commercial system)	RBMT									✓	✓						
Online X	Google translate (July and August, 2016 or August, 2015)	(SMT)	✓	✓	✓	✓	✓	✓	✓	✓	✓	✓	✓	✓	✓	✓	✓	✓
Online X	Bing translator (July and August, 2016 or August and September, 2015)	(SMT)	✓	✓	✓	✓	✓	✓	✓	✓	✓	✓	✓	✓	✓	✓	✓	✓

Table 5: Baseline Systems

3.1 Training Data

We used the following data for training the SMT baseline systems.

- Training data for the language model: All of the target language sentences in the parallel corpus.
- Training data for the translation model: Sentences that were 40 words or less in length. (For ASPEC Japanese–English training data, we only used train-1.txt, which consists of one million parallel sentence pairs with high similarity scores.)
- Development data for tuning: All of the development data.

3.2 Common Settings for Baseline SMT

We used the following tools for tokenization.

- Juman version 7.0[8] for Japanese segmentation.
- Stanford Word Segmenter version 2014-01-04[9] (Chinese Penn Treebank (CTB) model) for Chinese segmentation.
- The Moses toolkit for English and Indonesian tokenization.
- Mecab-ko[10] for Korean segmentation.
- Indic NLP Library[11] for Hindi segmentation.

To obtain word alignments, GIZA++ and grow-diag-final-and heuristics were used. We used 5-gram language models with modified Kneser-Ney smoothing, which were built using a tool in the Moses toolkit (Heafield et al., 2013).

3.3 Phrase-based SMT

We used the following Moses configuration for the phrase-based SMT system.

- distortion-limit
  - 20 for JE, EJ, JC, and CJ
  - 0 for JK, KJ, HE, and EH
  - 6 for IE and EI
- msd-bidirectional-fe lexicalized reordering
- Phrase score option: GoodTuring

The default values were used for the other system parameters.

3.4 Hierarchical Phrase-based SMT

We used the following Moses configuration for the hierarchical phrase-based SMT system.

- max-chart-span = 1000
- Phrase score option: GoodTuring

The default values were used for the other system parameters.

3.5 String-to-Tree Syntax-based SMT

We used the Berkeley parser to obtain target language syntax. We used the following Moses configuration for the string-to-tree syntax-based SMT system.

- max-chart-span = 1000
- Phrase score option: GoodTuring
- Phrase extraction options: MaxSpan = 1000, MinHoleSource = 1, and NonTermConsecSource.

The default values were used for the other system parameters.

---

[8] http://nlp.ist.i.kyoto-u.ac.jp/EN/index.php?JUMAN
[9] http://nlp.stanford.edu/software/segmenter.shtml
[10] https://bitbucket.org/eunjeon/mecab-ko/
[11] https://bitbucket.org/anoopk/indic_nlp_library

3.6 Tree-to-String Syntax-based SMT

We used the Berkeley parser to obtain source language syntax. We used the following Moses configuration for the baseline tree-to-string syntax-based SMT system.

- max-chart-span = 1000
- Phrase score option: GoodTuring
- Phrase extraction options: MaxSpan = 1000, MinHoleSource = 1, MinWords = 0, NonTermConsecSource, and AllowOnlyUnalignedWords.

The default values were used for the other system parameters.

4 Automatic Evaluation

4.1 Procedure for Calculating Automatic Evaluation Score

We calculated automatic evaluation scores for the translation results by applying three metrics: BLEU (Papineni et al., 2002), RIBES (Isozaki et al., 2010) and AMFM (Banchs et al., 2015). BLEU scores were calculated using *multi-bleu.perl* distributed with the Moses toolkit (Koehn et al., 2007); RIBES scores were calculated using *RIBES.py* version 1.02.4 [12]; AMFM scores were calculated using scripts created by technical collaborators of WAT2016. All scores for each task were calculated using one reference. Before the calculation of the automatic evaluation scores, the translation results were tokenized with word segmentation tools for each language.

For Japanese segmentation, we used three different tools: Juman version 7.0 (Kurohashi et al., 1994), KyTea 0.4.6 (Neubig et al., 2011) with Full SVM model [13] and MeCab 0.996 (Kudo, 2005) with IPA dictionary 2.7.0 [14]. For Chinese segmentation we used two different tools: KyTea 0.4.6 with Full SVM Model in MSR model and Stanford Word Segmenter version 2014-06-16 with Chinese Penn Treebank (CTB) and Peking University (PKU) model [15] (Tseng, 2005). For Korean segmentation we used mecab-ko [16]. For English and Indonesian segmentations we used tokenizer.perl [17] in the Moses toolkit. For Hindi segmentation we used Indic NLP Library [18].

Detailed procedures for the automatic evaluation are shown on the WAT2016 evaluation web page [19].

4.2 Automatic Evaluation System

The participants submit translation results via an automatic evaluation system deployed on the WAT2016 web page, which automatically gives evaluation scores for the uploaded results. Figure 1 shows the submission interface for participants. The system requires participants to provide the following information when they upload translation results:

- Subtask:

    - Scientific papers subtask ($J \leftrightarrow E, J \leftrightarrow C$);
    - Patents subtask ($C \leftrightarrow J, K \leftrightarrow J, E \leftrightarrow J$);
    - Newswire subtask ($I \leftrightarrow E$)
    - Mixed domain subtask ($H \leftrightarrow E, H \leftrightarrow J$)

- Method (SMT, RBMT, SMT and RBMT, EBMT, NMT, Other);

---

[12] http://www.kecl.ntt.co.jp/icl/lirg/ribes/index.html

[13] http://www.phontron.com/kytea/model.html

[14] http://code.google.com/p/mecab/downloads/detail?
name=mecab-ipadic-2.7.0-20070801.tar.gz

[15] http://nlp.stanford.edu/software/segmenter.shtml

[16] https://bitbucket.org/eunjeon/mecab-ko/

[17] https://github.com/moses-smt/mosesdecoder/tree/
RELEASE-2.1.1/scripts/tokenizer/tokenizer.perl

[18] https://bitbucket.org/anoopk/indic_nlp_library

[19] http://lotus.kuee.kyoto-u.ac.jp/WAT/evaluation/index.html

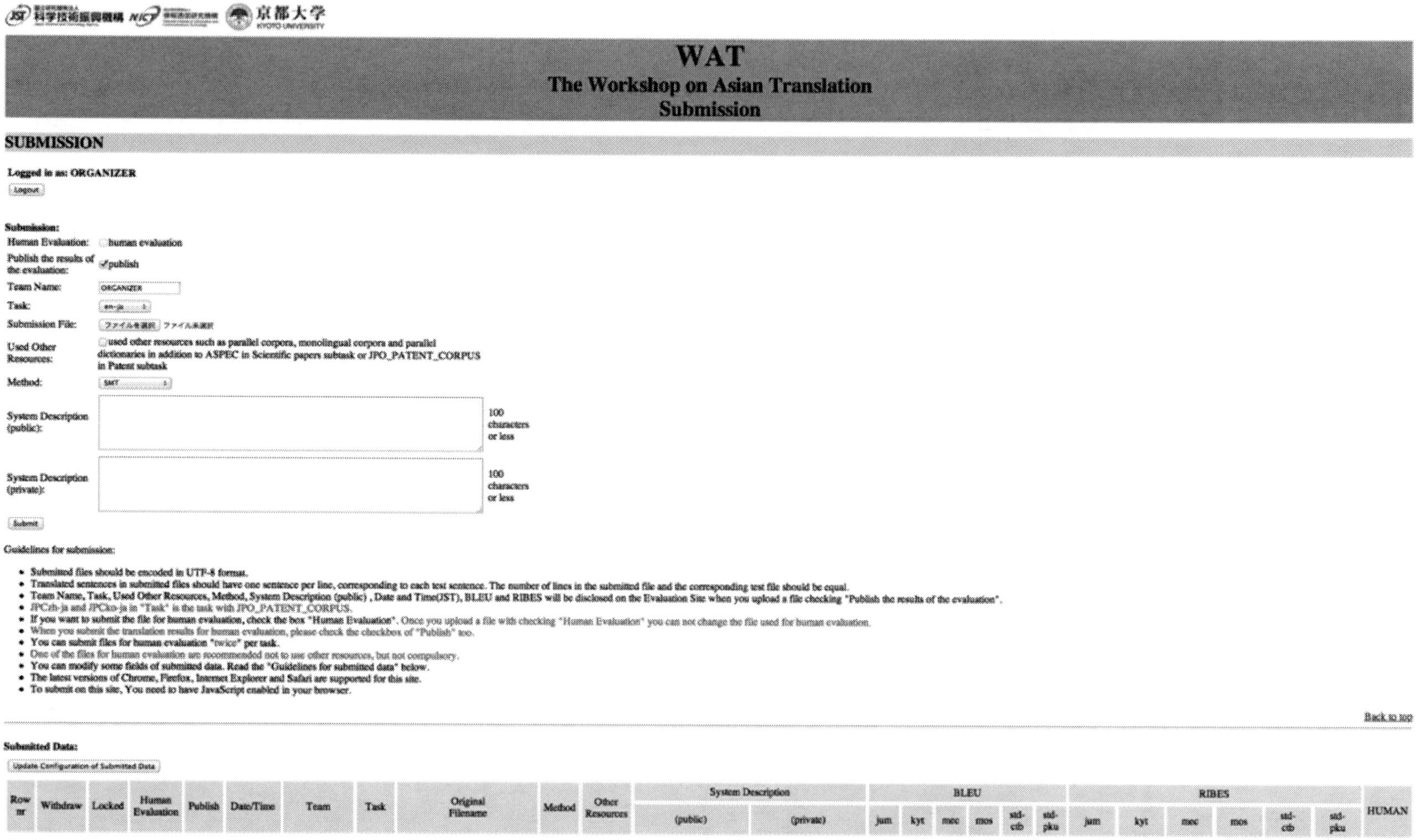

Row nr	Withdraw	Locked	Human Evaluation	Publish	Date/Time	Team	Task	Original Filename	Method	Other Resources	System Description		BLEU						RIBES						HUMAN
											(public)	(private)	jum	kyt	mec	mos	std-ctb	std-pku	jum	kyt	mec	mos	std-ctb	std-pku	

Figure 1: The submission web page for participants

- Use of other resources in addition to ASPEC / JPC / BPPT Corpus / IITB Corpus;

- Permission to publish the automatic evaluation scores on the WAT2016 web page.

The server for the system stores all submitted information, including translation results and scores, although participants can confirm only the information that they uploaded. Information about translation results that participants permit to be published is disclosed on the web page. In addition to submitting translation results for automatic evaluation, participants submit the results for human evaluation using the same web interface. This automatic evaluation system will remain available even after WAT2016. Anybody can register to use the system on the registration web page [20].

5　Human Evaluation

In WAT2016, we conducted 2 kinds of human evaluations: *pairwise evaluation* and *JPO adequacy evaluation*.

5.1　Pairwise Evaluation

The pairwise evaluation is the same as the last year, but not using the crowdsourcing this year. We asked professional translation company to do pairwise evaluation. The cost of pairwise evaluation per sentence is almost the same to that of last year.

We randomly chose 400 sentences from the Test set for the pairwise evaluation. We used the same sentences as the last year for the continuous subtasks. Each submission is compared with the baseline translation (Phrase-based SMT, described in Section 3) and given a *Pairwise* score[21].

5.1.1　Pairwise Evaluation of Sentences

We conducted pairwise evaluation of each of the 400 test sentences. The input sentence and two translations (the baseline and a submission) are shown to the annotators, and the annotators are asked to judge which of the translation is better, or if they are of the same quality. The order of the two translations are at random.

5.1.2　Voting

To guarantee the quality of the evaluations, each sentence is evaluated by 5 different annotators and the final decision is made depending on the 5 judgements. We define each judgement $j_i (i = 1, \cdots, 5)$ as:

$$j_i = \begin{cases} 1 & \text{if better than the baseline} \\ -1 & \text{if worse than the baseline} \\ 0 & \text{if the quality is the same} \end{cases}$$

The final decision D is defined as follows using $S = \sum j_i$:

$$D = \begin{cases} win & (S \geq 2) \\ loss & (S \leq -2) \\ tie & (otherwise) \end{cases}$$

5.1.3　Pairwise Score Calculation

Suppose that W is the number of *wins* compared to the baseline, L is the number of *losses* and T is the number of *ties*. The Pairwise score can be calculated by the following formula:

$$Pairwise = 100 \times \frac{W - L}{W + L + T}$$

From the definition, the Pairwise score ranges between -100 and 100.

---

[20] http://lotus.kuee.kyoto-u.ac.jp/WAT/registration/index.html
[21] It was called HUMAN score in WAT2014 and Crowd score in WAT2015.

5	All important information is transmitted correctly. (100%)
4	Almost all important information is transmitted correctly. (80%–)
3	More than half of important information is transmitted correctly. (50%–)
2	Some of important information is transmitted correctly. (20%–)
1	Almost all important information is NOT transmitted correctly. (–20%)

Table 6: The JPO adequacy criterion

5.1.4 Confidence Interval Estimation

There are several ways to estimate a confidence interval. We chose to use bootstrap resampling (Koehn, 2004) to estimate the 95% confidence interval. The procedure is as follows:

1. randomly select 300 sentences from the 400 human evaluation sentences, and calculate the Pairwise score of the selected sentences

2. iterate the previous step 1000 times and get 1000 Pairwise scores

3. sort the 1000 scores and estimate the 95% confidence interval by discarding the top 25 scores and the bottom 25 scores

5.2 JPO Adequacy Evaluation

The participants' systems, which achieved the top 3 highest scores among the pairwise evaluation results of each subtask[22], were also evaluated with the JPO adequacy evaluation. The JPO adequacy evaluation was carried out by translation experts with a quality evaluation criterion for translated patent documents which the Japanese Patent Office (JPO) decided. For each system, two annotators evaluate the test sentences to guarantee the quality.

5.2.1 Evaluation of Sentences

The number of test sentences for the JPO adequacy evaluation is 200. The 200 test sentences were randomly selected from the 400 test sentences of the pairwise evaluation. The test sentence include the input sentence, the submitted system's translation and the reference translation.

5.2.2 Evaluation Criterion

Table 6 shows the JPO adequacy criterion from 5 to 1. The evaluation is performed subjectively. "Important information" represents the technical factors and their relationships. The degree of importance of each element is also considered to evaluate. The percentages in each grade are rough indications for the transmission degree of the source sentence meanings. The detailed criterion can be found on the JPO document (in Japanese) [23].

6 Participants List

Table 7 shows the list of participants for WAT2016. This includes not only Japanese organizations, but also some organizations from outside Japan. 15 teams submitted one or more translation results to the automatic evaluation server or human evaluation.

---

[22]The number of systems varies depending on the subtasks.

[23]http://www.jpo.go.jp/shiryou/toushin/chousa/tokkyohonyaku_hyouka.htm

Team ID	Organization	ASPEC				JPC						BPPT		IITBC		pivot	
		JE	EJ	JC	CJ	JE	EJ	JC	CJ	JK	KJ	IE	EI	HE	EH	HJ	JH
NAIST (Neubig, 2016)	Nara Institute of Science and Technology	✓															
Kyoto-U (Cromieres et al., 2016)	Kyoto University	✓	✓	✓	✓												
TMU (Yamagishi et al., 2016)	Tokyo Metropolitan University	✓															
bjtu_nlp (Li et al., 2016)	Beijing Jiaotong University	✓	✓	✓	✓	✓	✓	✓	✓								
Sense (Tan, 2016)	Saarland University											✓	✓				
NICT-2 (Imamura and Sumita, 2016)	National Institute of Information and Communication Technology	✓	✓	✓	✓	✓	✓	✓	✓								
WASUIPS (Yang and Lepage, 2016)	Waseda University								✓								
EHR (Ehara, 2016)	Ehara NLP Research Laboratory		✓		✓				✓		✓				✓	✓	
ntt (Sudoh and Nagata, 2016)	NTT Communication Science Laboratories								✓								
TOKYOMT (Shu and Miura, 2016)	Weblio, Inc.		✓														
IITB-EN-ID (Singh et al., 2016)	Indian Institute of Technology Bombay											✓	✓				
JAPIO (Kinoshita et al., 2016)	Japan Patent Information Organization		✓		✓	✓			✓		✓						
IITP-MT (Sen et al., 2016)	Indian Institute of Technology Patna														✓		
UT-KAY (Hashimoto et al., 2016)	University of Tokyo				✓												
UT-AKY (Eriguchi et al., 2016)	University of Tokyo		✓														

Table 7: List of participants who submitted translation results to WAT2016 and their participation in each subtasks.

7 Evaluation Results

In this section, the evaluation results for WAT2016 are reported from several perspectives. Some of the results for both automatic and human evaluations are also accessible at the WAT2016 website[24].

7.1 Official Evaluation Results

Figures 2, 3, 4 and 5 show the official evaluation results of ASPEC subtasks, Figures 6, 7, 8, 9 and 10 show those of JPC subtasks, Figures 11 and 12 show those of BPPT subtasks and Figures 13 and 14 show those of IITB subtasks. Each figure contains automatic evaluation results (BLEU, RIBES, AM-FM), the pairwise evaluation results with confidence intervals, correlation between automatic evaluations and the pairwise evaluation, the JPO adequacy evaluation result and evaluation summary of top systems.

The detailed automatic evaluation results for all the submissions are shown in Appendix A. The detailed JPO adequacy evaluation results for the selected submissions are shown in Table 8. The weights for the weighted κ (Cohen, 1968) is defined as $|Evaluation1 - Evaluation2|/4$.

From the evaluation results, the following can be observed:

- Neural network based translation models work very well also for Asian languages.

- None of the automatic evaluation measures perfectly correlate to the human evaluation result (JPO adequacy).

- The JPO adequacy evaluation result of IITB E→H shows an interesting tendency: the system which achieved the best average score has the lowest ratio of the perfect translations and vice versa.

7.2 Statistical Significance Testing of Pairwise Evaluation between Submissions

Tables 9, 10, 11 and 12 show the results of statistical significance testing of ASPEC subtasks, Tables 13, 14, 15, 16 and 17 show those of JPC subtasks, 18 shows those of BPPT subtasks and 19 shows those of JPC subtasks. $\ggg$, $\gg$ and $>$ mean that the system in the row is *better* than the system in the column at a significance level of $p < 0.01$, 0.05 and 0.1 respectively. Testing is also done by the bootstrap resampling as follows:

1. randomly select 300 sentences from the 400 pairwise evaluation sentences, and calculate the Pairwise scores on the selected sentences for both systems

2. iterate the previous step 1000 times and count the number of wins (W), losses (L) and ties (T)

3. calculate $p = \frac{L}{W+L}$

Inter-annotator Agreement

To assess the reliability of agreement between the workers, we calculated the Fleiss' κ (Fleiss and others, 1971) values. The results are shown in Table 20. We can see that the κ values are larger for X → J translations than for J → X translations. This may be because the majority of the workers are Japanese, and the evaluation of one's mother tongue is much easier than for other languages in general.

7.3 Chronological Evaluation

Figure 15 shows the chronological evaluation results of 4 subtasks of ASPEC and 2 subtasks of JPC. The Kyoto-U (2016) (Cromieres et al., 2016), ntt (2016) (Sudoh and Nagata, 2016) and naver (2015) (Lee et al., 2015) are NMT systems, the NAIST (2015) (Neubig et al., 2015) is a forest-to-string SMT system, Kyoto-U (2015) (Richardson et al., 2015) is a dependency tree-to-tree EBMT system and JAPIO (2016) (Kinoshita et al., 2016) system is a phrase-based SMT system.

What we can see is that in ASPEC-JE and EJ, the overall quality is improved from the last year, but the ratio of grade 5 is decreased. This is because the NMT systems can output much fluent translations

---

[24]http://lotus.kuee.kyoto-u.ac.jp/WAT/evaluation/index.html

but the adequacy is worse. As for ASPEC-JC and CJ, the quality is very much improved. Literatures (Junczys-Dowmunt et al., 2016) say that Chinese receives the biggest benefits from NMT.

The translation quality of JPC-CJ does not so much varied from the last year, but that of JPC-KJ is much worse. Unfortunately, the best systems participated last year did not participate this year, so it is not directly comparable.

8   Submitted Data

The number of published automatic evaluation results for the 15 teams exceeded 400 before the start of WAT2016, and 63 translation results for pairwise evaluation were submitted by 14 teams. Furthermore, we selected maximum 3 translation results from each subtask and evaluated them for JPO adequacy evaluation. We will organize the all of the submitted data for human evaluation and make this public.

9   Conclusion and Future Perspective

This paper summarizes the shared tasks of WAT2016. We had 15 participants worldwide, and collected a large number of useful submissions for improving the current machine translation systems by analyzing the submissions and identifying the issues.

For the next WAT workshop, we plan to include newspaper translation tasks for Japanese, Chinese and English where the context information is important to achieve high translation quality, so it is a challenging task.

We would also be very happy to include other languages if the resources are available.

Appendix A   Submissions

Tables 21 to 36 summarize all the submissions listed in the automatic evaluation server at the time of the WAT2016 workshop (12th, December, 2016). The OTHER RESOURCES column shows the use of resources such as parallel corpora, monolingual corpora and parallel dictionaries in addition to ASPEC, JPC, BPPT Corpus, IITB Corpus.

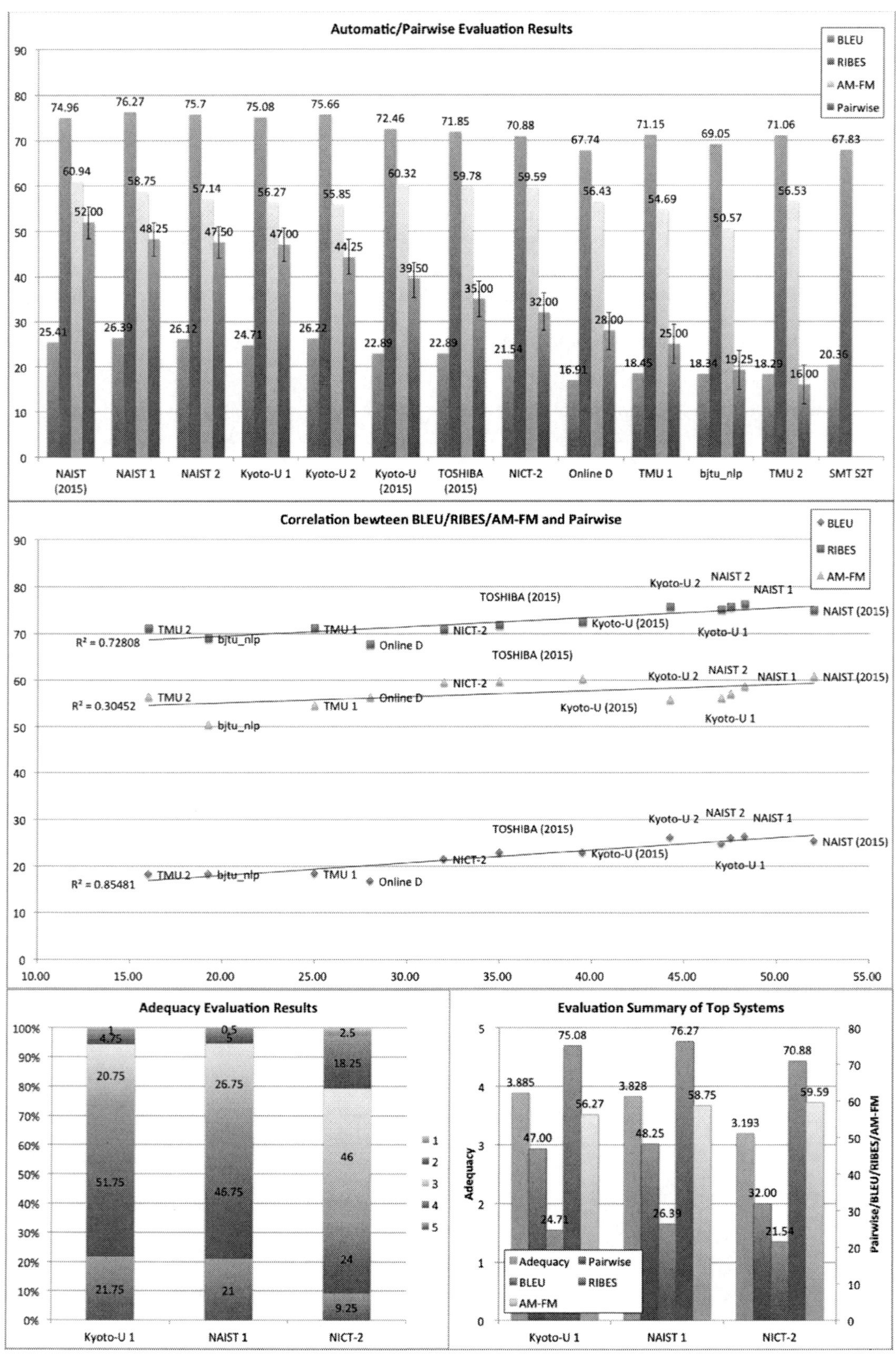

Figure 2: Official evaluation results of ASPEC-JE.

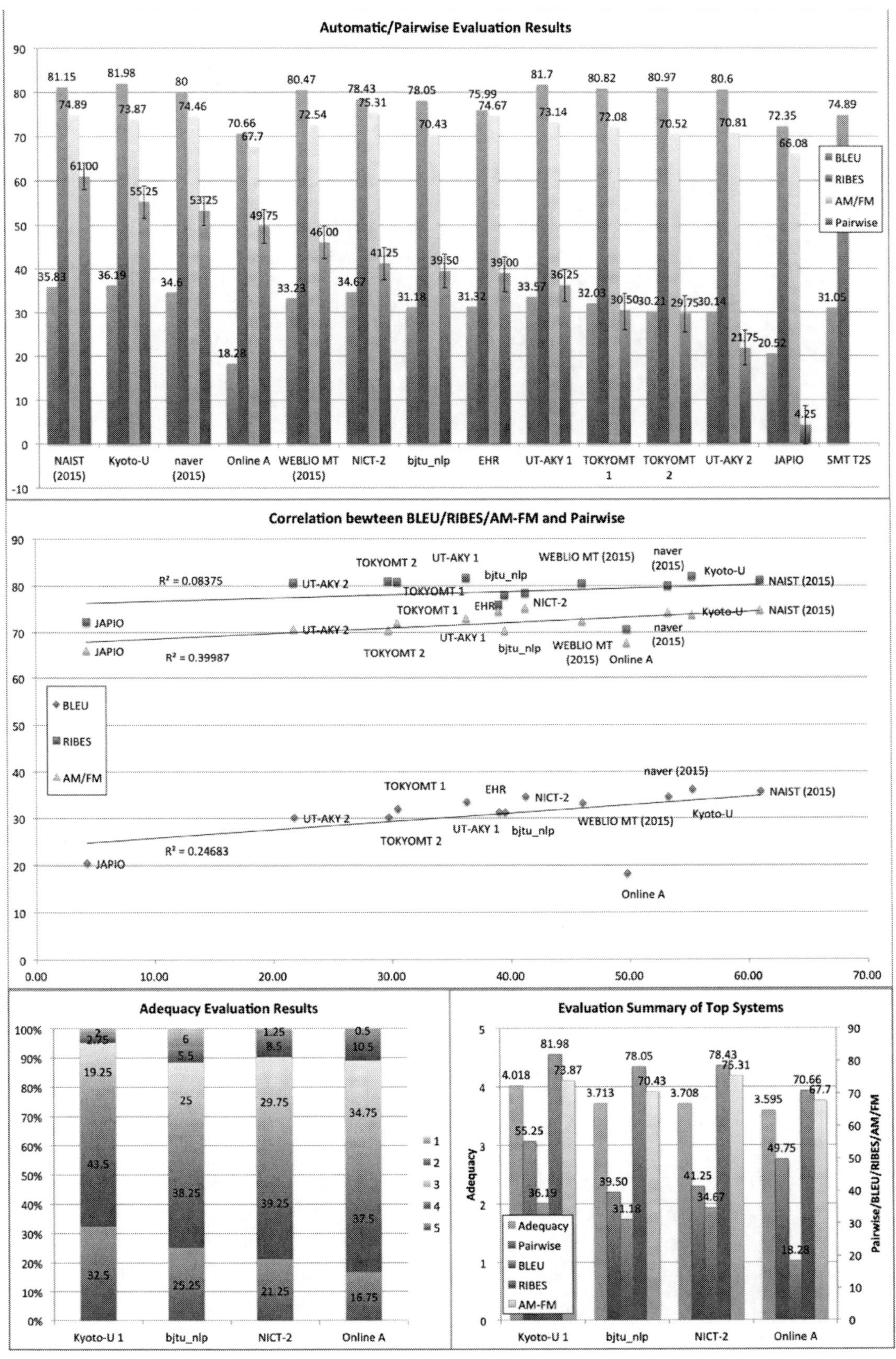

Figure 3: Official evaluation results of ASPEC-EJ.

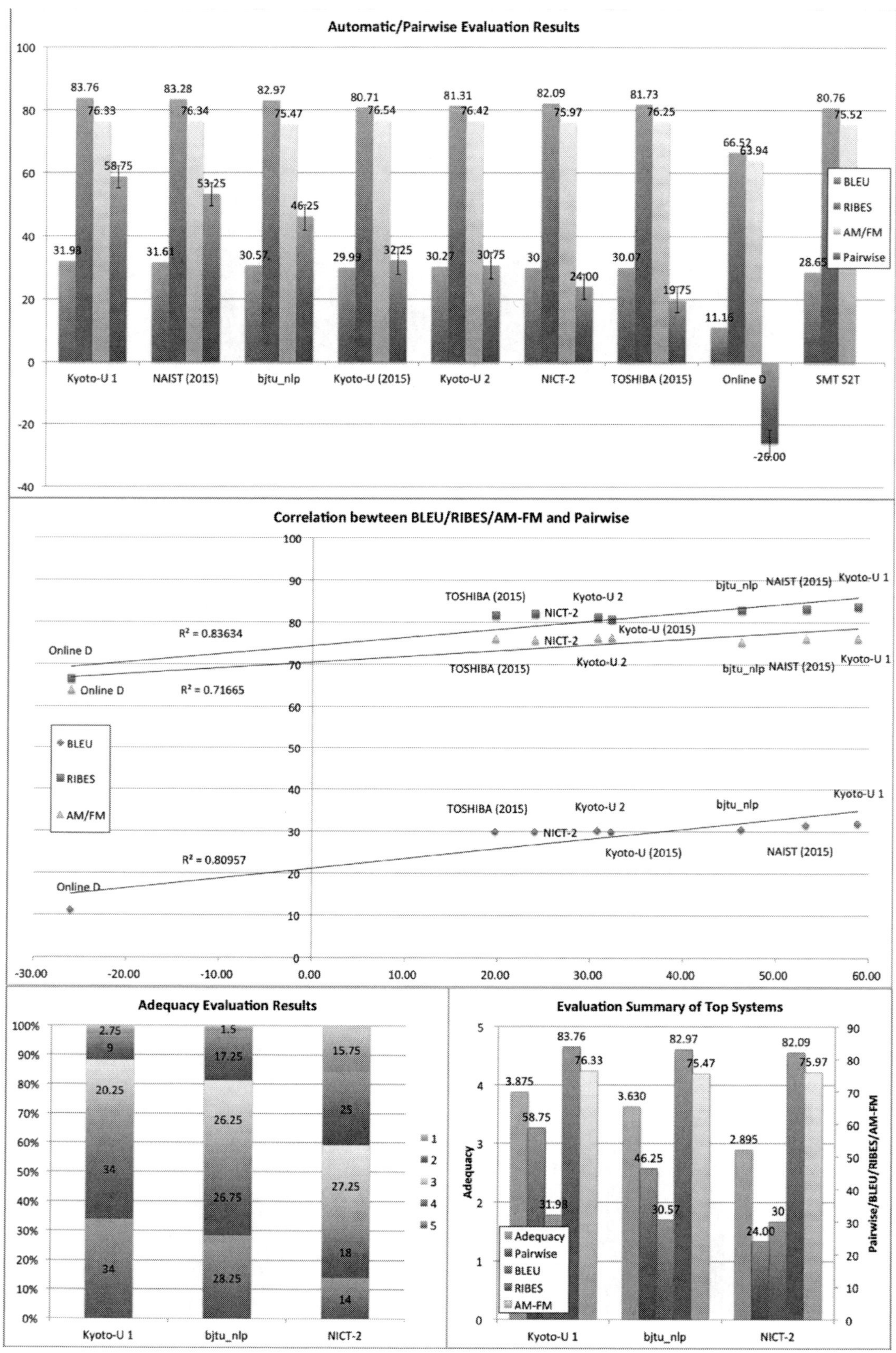

Figure 4: Official evaluation results of ASPEC-JC.

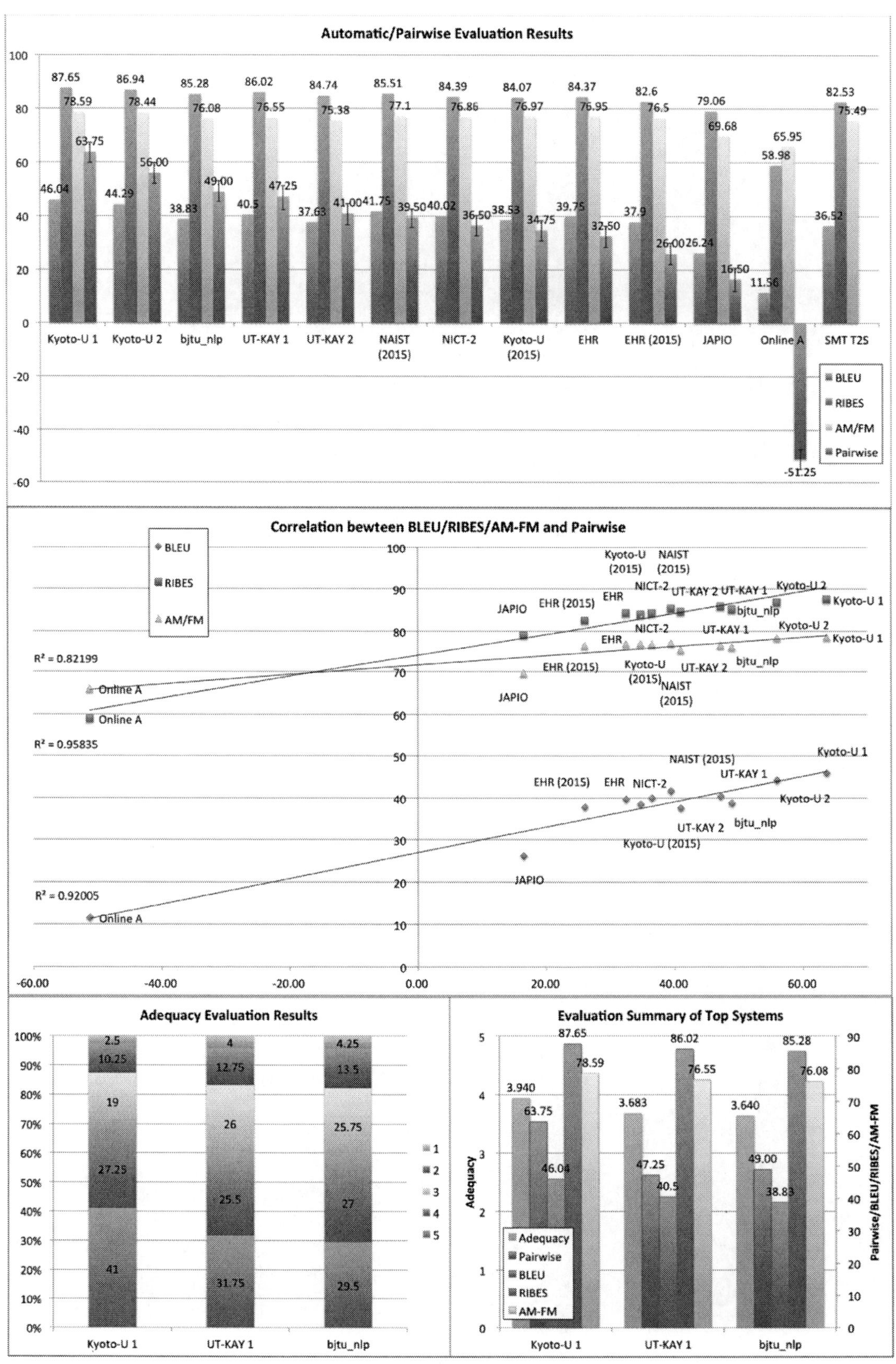

Figure 5: Official evaluation results of ASPEC-CJ.

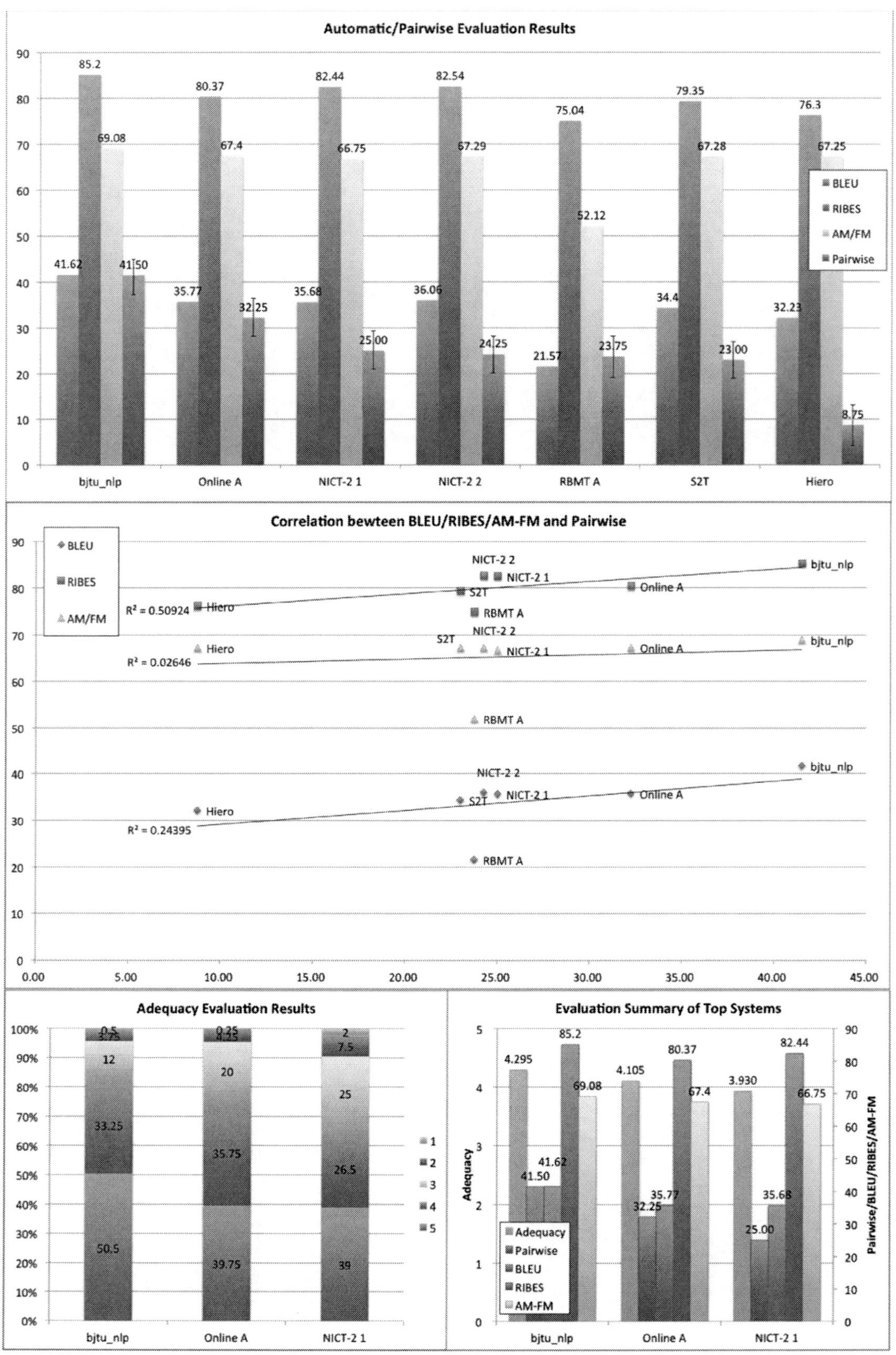

Figure 6: Official evaluation results of JPC-JE.

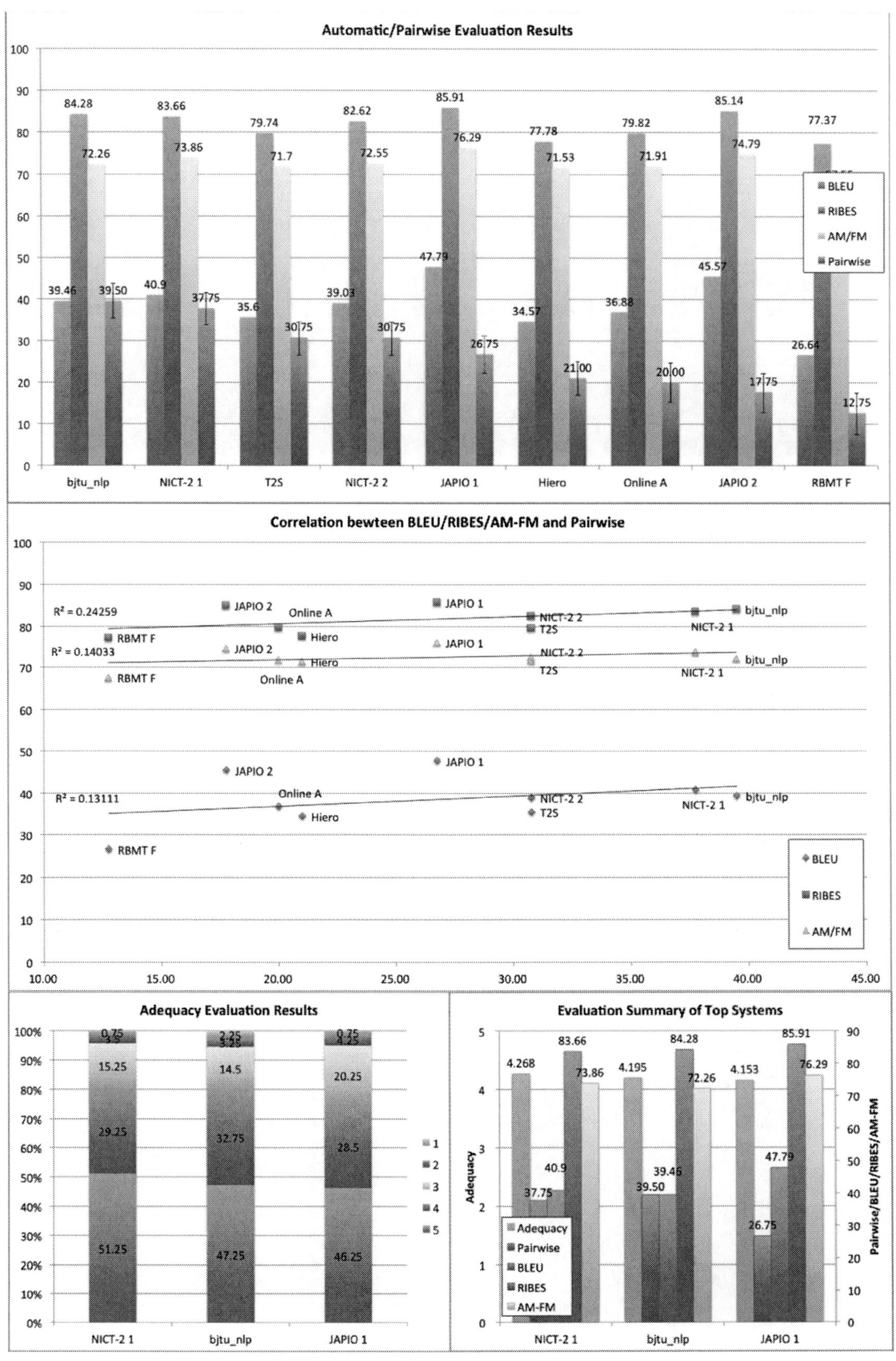

Figure 7: Official evaluation results of JPC-EJ.

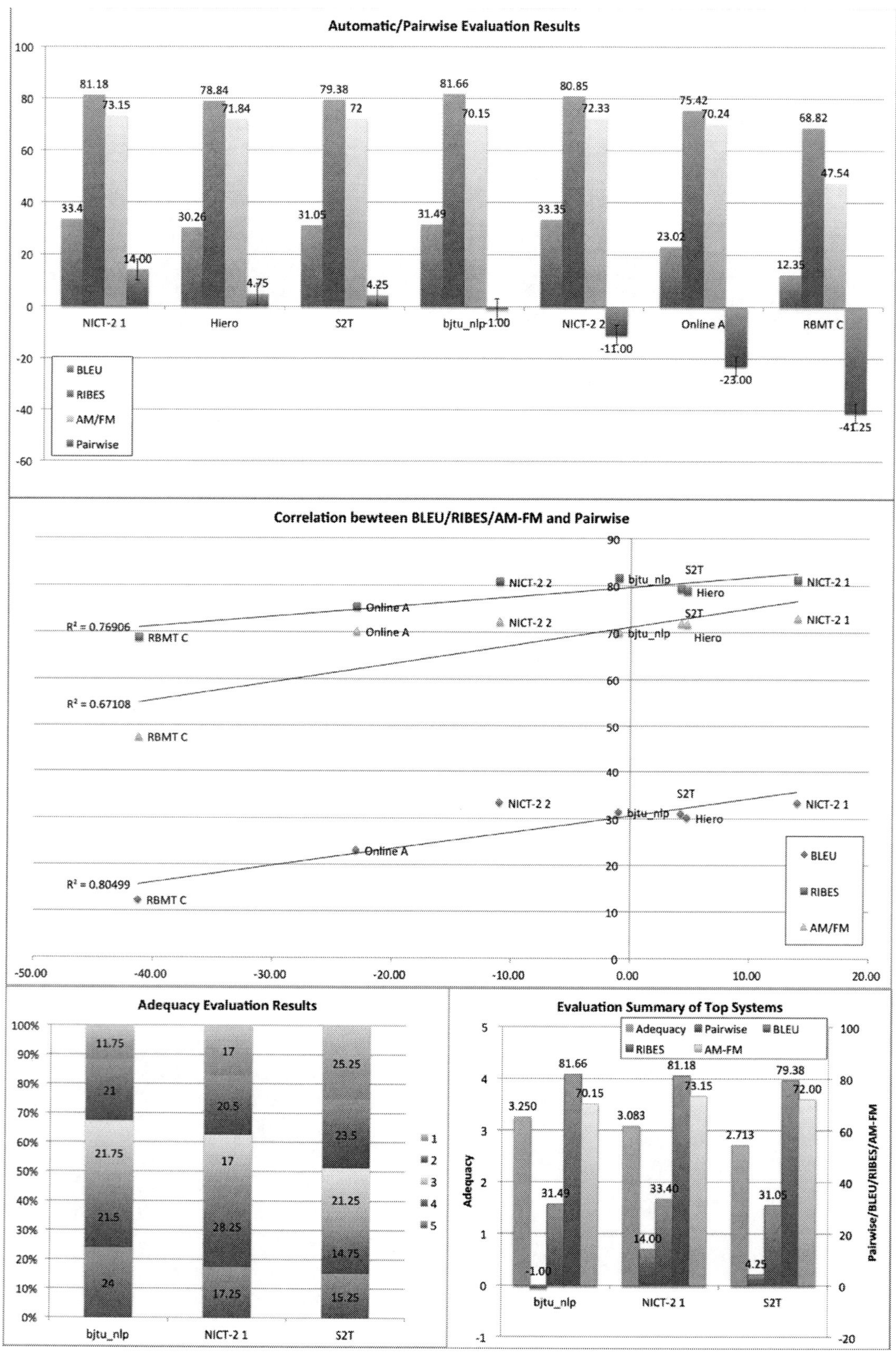

Figure 8: Official evaluation results of JPC-JC.

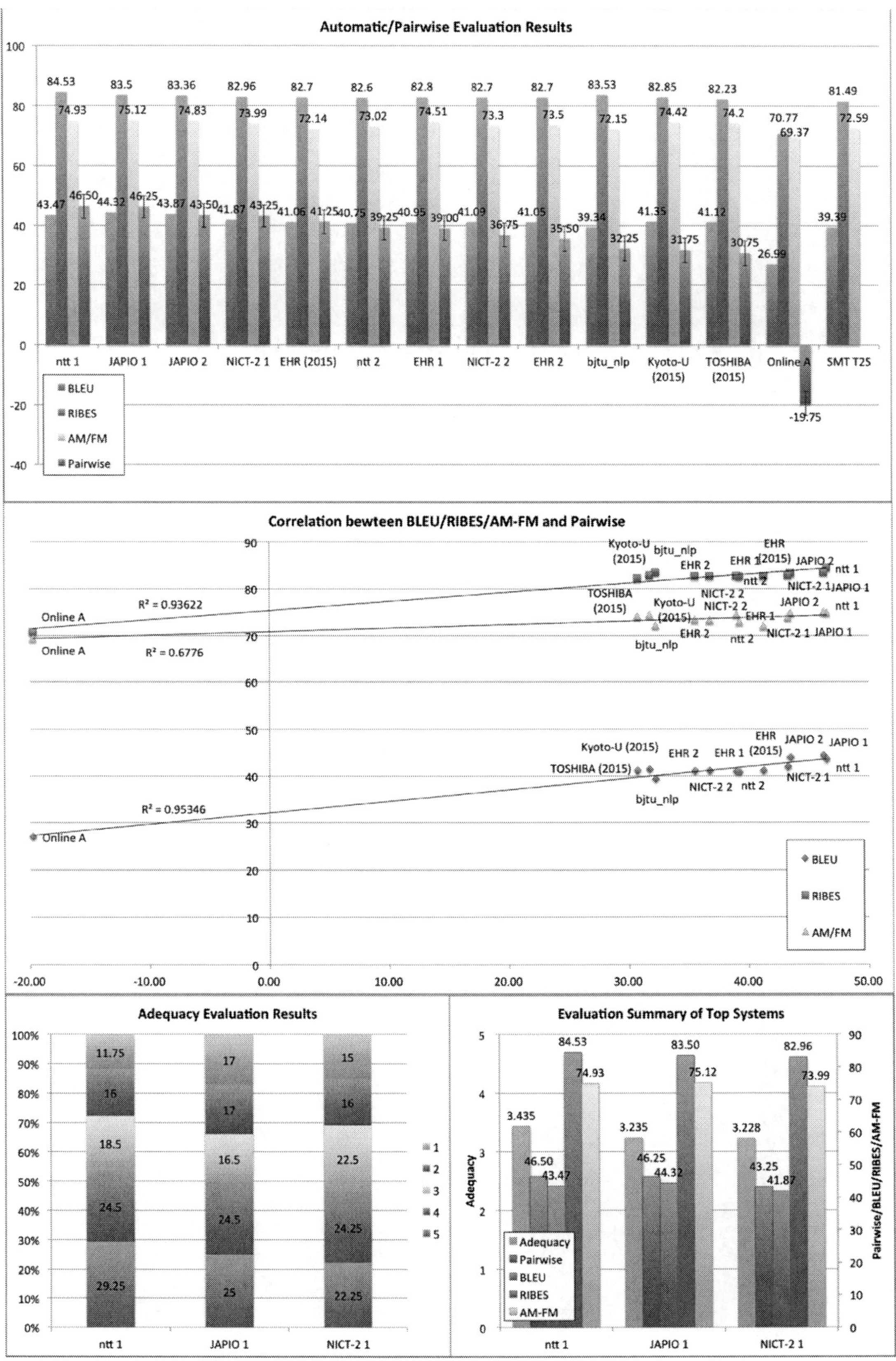

Figure 9: Official evaluation results of JPC-CJ.

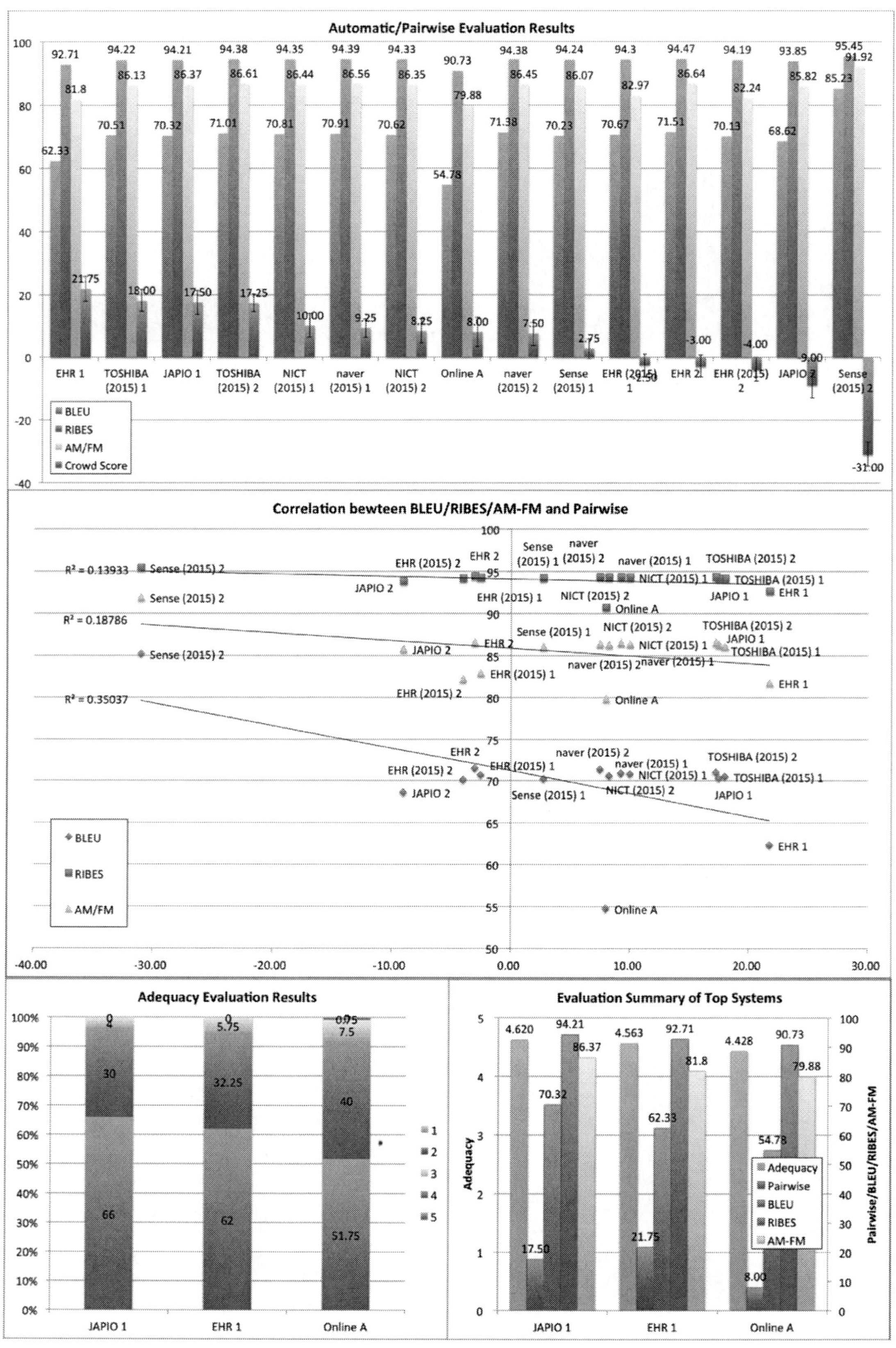

Figure 10: Official evaluation results of JPC-KJ.

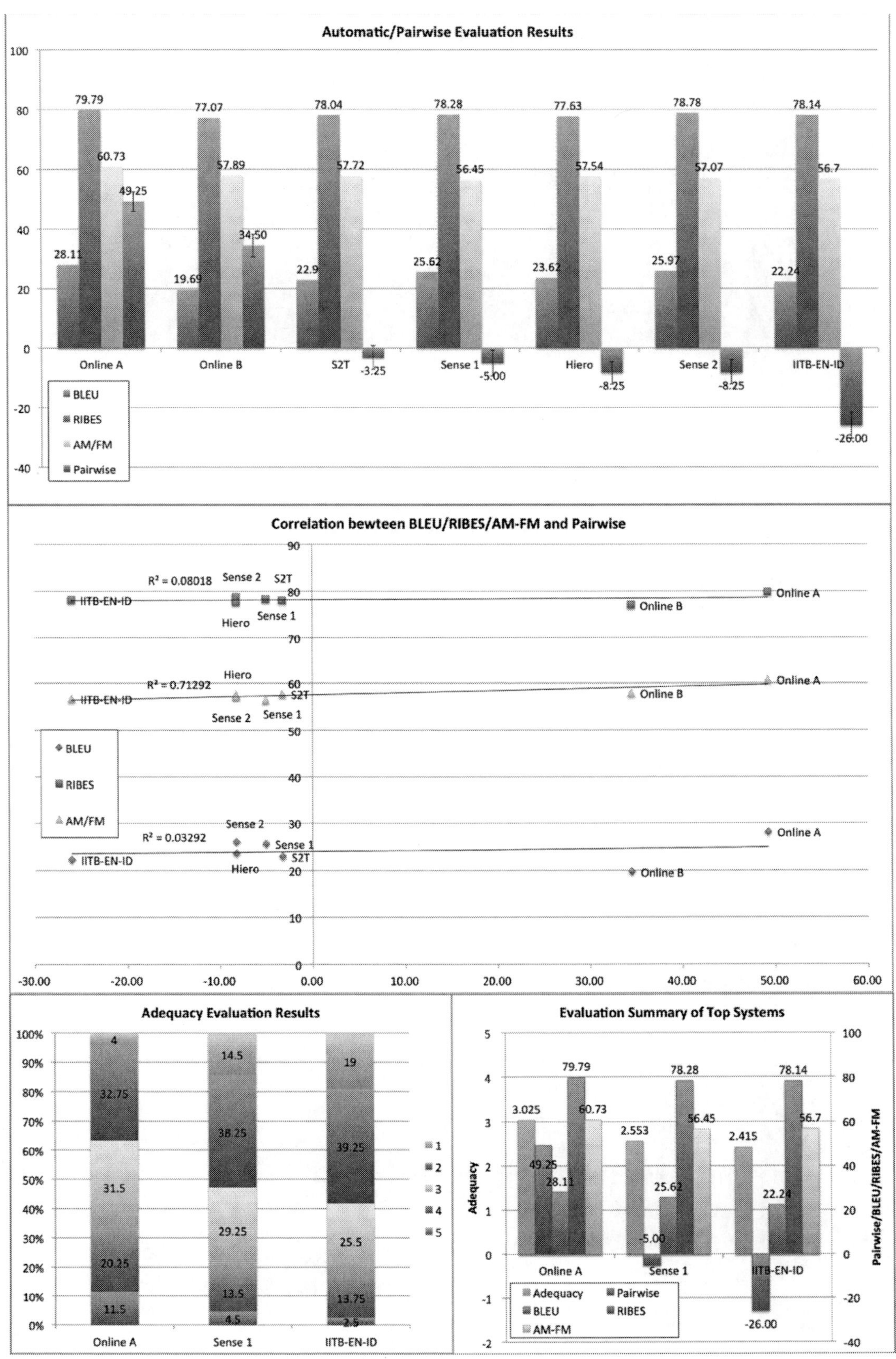

Figure 11: Official evaluation results of BPPT-IE.

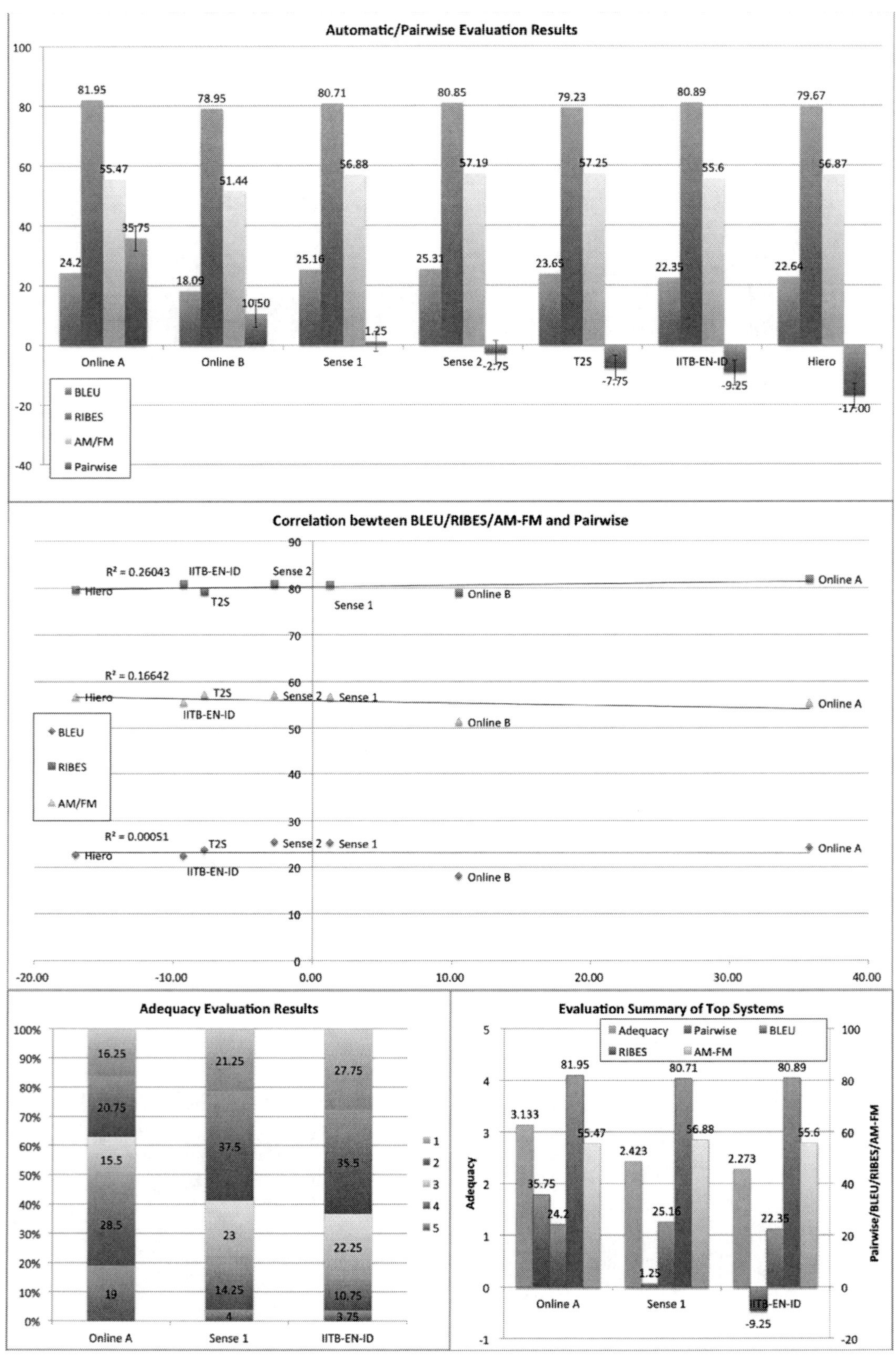

Figure 12: Official evaluation results of BPPT-EI.

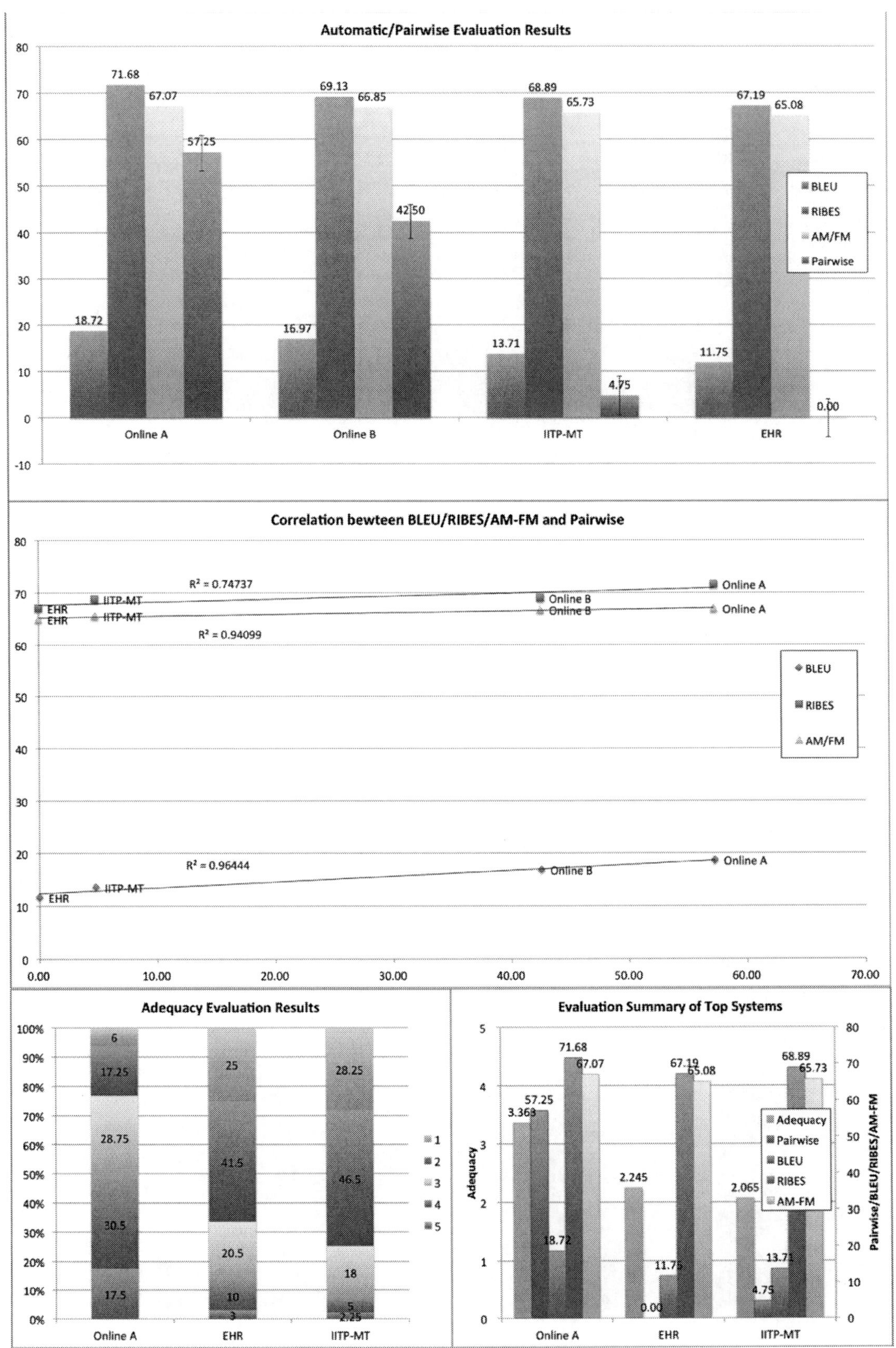

Figure 13: Official evaluation results of IITB-EH.

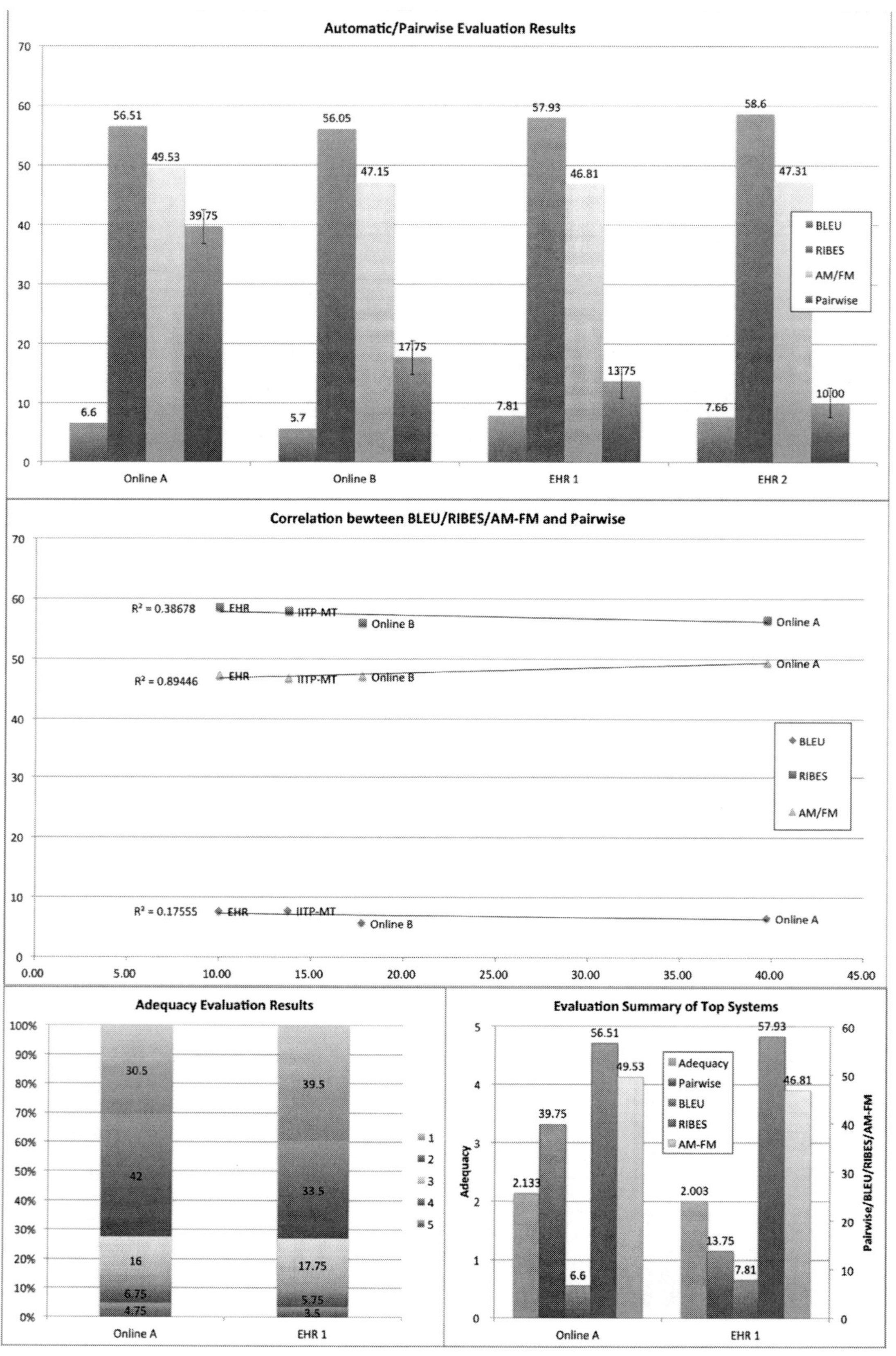

Figure 14: Official evaluation results of IITB-HJ.

| SYSTEM ID | Annotator A | | Annotator B | | all | | weighted |
	average	variance	average	variance	average	κ	κ
ASPEC-JE							
Kyoto-U 1	3.760	0.682	4.010	0.670	3.885	0.205	0.313
NAIST 1	3.705	0.728	3.950	0.628	3.828	0.257	0.356
NICT-2	3.025	0.914	3.360	0.740	3.193	0.199	0.369
ASPEC-EJ							
Kyoto-U 1	3.970	0.759	4.065	0.851	4.018	0.346	0.494
bjtu_nlp	3.800	0.980	3.625	1.364	3.713	0.299	0.509
NICT-2	3.745	0.820	3.670	0.931	3.708	0.299	0.486
Online A	3.600	0.770	3.590	0.862	3.595	0.273	0.450
ASPEC-JC							
Kyoto-U 1	3.995	1.095	3.755	1.145	3.875	0.203	0.362
bjtu_nlp	3.920	1.054	3.340	1.244	3.630	0.154	0.290
NICT-2	2.940	1.846	2.850	1.368	2.895	0.237	0.477
ASPEC-CJ							
Kyoto-U 1	4.245	1.045	3.635	1.232	3.940	0.234	0.341
UT-KAY 1	3.995	1.355	3.370	1.143	3.683	0.152	0.348
bjtu_nlp	3.950	1.278	3.330	1.221	3.640	0.179	0.401
JPC-JE							
bjtu_nlp	4.085	0.798	4.505	0.580	4.295	0.254	0.393
Online A	3.910	0.652	4.300	0.830	4.105	0.166	0.336
NICT-2 1	3.705	1.118	4.155	1.011	3.930	0.277	0.458
JPC-EJ							
NICT-2 1	4.025	0.914	4.510	0.570	4.268	0.234	0.412
bjtu_nlp	3.920	0.924	4.470	0.749	4.195	0.151	0.340
JAPIO 1	4.055	0.932	4.250	0.808	4.153	0.407	0.562
JPC-JC							
bjtu_nlp	3.485	1.720	3.015	1.755	3.250	0.274	0.507
NICT-2 1	3.230	1.867	2.935	1.791	3.083	0.307	0.492
S2T	2.745	2.000	2.680	1.838	2.713	0.305	0.534
JPC-CJ							
ntt 1	3.605	1.889	3.265	1.765	3.435	0.263	0.519
JAPIO 1	3.385	1.947	3.085	2.088	3.235	0.365	0.592
NICT-2 1	3.410	1.732	3.045	1.883	3.228	0.322	0.518
JPC-KJ							
JAPIO 1	4.580	0.324	4.660	0.304	4.620	0.328	0.357
EHR 1	4.510	0.380	4.615	0.337	4.563	0.424	0.478
Online A	4.380	0.466	4.475	0.409	4.428	0.517	0.574
BPPT-IE							
Online A	2.675	0.489	3.375	1.564	3.025	0.048	0.187
Sense 1	2.685	0.826	2.420	1.294	2.553	0.242	0.408
IITB-EN-ID	2.485	0.870	2.345	1.216	2.415	0.139	0.324
BPPT-EI							
Online A	2.890	1.778	3.375	1.874	3.133	0.163	0.446
Sense 1	2.395	1.059	2.450	1.328	2.423	0.305	0.494
IITB-EN-ID	2.185	1.241	2.360	1.130	2.273	0.246	0.477
IITB-EH							
Online A	3.200	1.330	3.525	1.189	3.363	0.103	0.155
EHR	2.590	1.372	1.900	0.520	2.245	0.136	0.263
IITP-MT	2.350	1.198	1.780	0.362	2.065	0.066	0.164
IITB-HJ							
Online A	1.955	1.563	2.310	0.664	2.133	0.120	0.287
EHR 1	1.530	1.049	2.475	0.739	2.003	0.055	0.194

Table 8: JPO adequacy evaluation results in detail.

	NAIST 1	NAIST 2	Kyoto-U 1	Kyoto-U 2	Kyoto-U (2015)	TOSHIBA (2015)	NICT-2	Online D	TMU 1	bjtu_nlp	TMU 2
NAIST (2015)	>>	>>>	>>>	>>>	>>>	>>>	>>>	>>>	>>>	>>>	>>>
NAIST 1		-	-	>>	>>>	>>>	>>>	>>>	>>>	>>>	>>>
NAIST 2			-	>>	>>>	>>>	>>>	>>>	>>>	>>>	>>>
Kyoto-U 1				>	>>>	>>>	>>>	>>>	>>>	>>>	>>>
Kyoto-U 2					>>	>>>	>>>	>>>	>>>	>>>	>>>
Kyoto-U (2015)						>>	>>>	>>>	>>>	>>>	>>>
TOSHIBA (2015)							>	>>>	>>>	>>>	>>>
NICT-2								>>	>>>	>>>	>>>
Online D									-	>>>	>>>
TMU 1										>>	>>>
bjtu_nlp											-

Table 9: Statistical significance testing of the ASPEC-JE Pairwise scores.

	Kyoto-U	naver (2015)	Online A	WEBLIO_MT (2015)	NICT-2	bjtu_nlp	EHR	UT-AKY 1	TOKYOMT 1	TOKYOMT 2	UT-AKY 2	JAPIO
NAIST (2015)	>>>	>>>	>>>	>>>	>>>	>>>	>>>	>>>	>>>	>>>	>>>	>>>
Kyoto-U		-	>>	>>>	>>>	>>>	>>>	>>>	>>>	>>>	>>>	>>>
naver (2015)			>>	>>>	>>>	>>>	>>>	>>>	>>>	>>>	>>>	>>>
Online A				>	>>>	>>>	>>>	>>>	>>>	>>>	>>>	>>>
WEBLIO_MT (2015)					>	>>>	>>>	>>>	>>>	>>>	>>>	>>>
NICT-2						-	-	>>	>>>	>>>	>>>	>>>
bjtu_nlp							-	>	>>>	>>>	>>>	>>>
EHR								-	>>>	>>>	>>>	>>>
UT-AKY 1									>>>	>>>	>>>	>>>
TOKYOMT 1										-	>>>	>>>
TOKYOMT 2											>>>	>>>
UT-AKY 2												>>>

Table 10: Statistical significance testing of the ASPEC-EJ Pairwise scores.

	NAIST (2015)	bjtu_nlp	Kyoto-U (2015)	Kyoto-U 2	NICT-2	TOSHIBA (2015)	Online D
Kyoto-U 1	>>>	>>>	>>>	>>>	>>>	>>>	>>>
NAIST (2015)		>>>	>>>	>>>	>>>	>>>	>>>
bjtu_nlp			>>>	>>>	>>>	>>>	>>>
Kyoto-U (2015)				-	>>>	>>>	>>>
Kyoto-U 2					>>>	>>>	>>>
NICT-2						>>	>>>
TOSHIBA (2015)							>>>

Table 11: Statistical significance testing of the ASPEC-JC Pairwise scores.

	Kyoto-U 2	bjtu_nlp	UT-KAY 1	UT-KAY 2	NAIST (2015)	NICT-2	Kyoto-U (2015)	EHR	EHR (2015)	JAPIO	Online A
Kyoto-U 1	≫	≫	≫	≫	≫	≫	≫	≫	≫	≫	≫
Kyoto-U 2		≫	≫	≫	≫	≫	≫	≫	≫	≫	≫
bjtu_nlp			-	≫	≫	≫	≫	≫	≫	≫	≫
UT-KAY 1				≫	≫	≫	≫	≫	≫	≫	≫
UT-KAY 2					-	≫	≫	≫	≫	≫	≫
NAIST (2015)						>	≫	≫	≫	≫	≫
NICT-2							-	≫	≫	≫	≫
Kyoto-U (2015)								-	≫	≫	≫
EHR									≫	≫	≫
EHR (2015)										≫	≫
JAPIO											≫

Table 12: Statistical significance testing of the ASPEC-CJ Pairwise scores.

	Online A	NICT-2 1	NICT-2 2	RBMT A	S2T	SMT Hiero
bjtu_nlp	≫	≫	≫	≫	≫	≫
Online A		≫	≫	≫	≫	≫
NICT-2 1			-	-	-	≫
NICT-2 2				-	-	≫
RBMT A					-	≫
SMT S2T						≫

Table 13: Statistical significance testing of the JPC-JE Pairwise scores.

	NICT-2 1	SMT T2S	NICT-2 2	JAPIO 1	SMT Hiero	Online A	JAPIO 2	RBMT F
bjtu_nlp	-	≫	≫	≫	≫	≫	≫	≫
NICT-2 1		≫	≫	≫	≫	≫	≫	≫
SMT T2S			-	>	≫	≫	≫	≫
NICT-2 2				>	≫	≫	≫	≫
JAPIO 1					≫	≫	≫	≫
SMT Hiero						-	>	≫
Online A							-	≫
JAPIO 2								≫

Table 14: Statistical significance testing of the JPC-EJ Pairwise scores.

	SMT Hiero	SMT S2T	bjtu_nlp	NICT-2 2	Online A	RBMT C
NICT-2 1	≫	≫	≫	≫	≫	≫
SMT Hiero		-	>	≫	≫	≫
SMT S2T			>	≫	≫	≫
bjtu_nlp				≫	≫	≫
NICT-2 2					≫	≫
Online A						≫

Table 15: Statistical significance testing of the JPC-JC Pairwise scores.

	JAPIO 1	JAPIO 2	NICT-2 1	EHR (2015)	ntt 2	EHR 1	NICT-2 2	EHR 2	bjtu_nlp	Kyoto-U (2015)	TOSHIBA (2015)	Online A
ntt 1	-	>	>	>>	>>>	>>>	>>>	>>>	>>>	>>>	>>>	>>>
JAPIO 1		>>	>	>>>	>>>	>>>	>>>	>>>	>>>	>>>	>>>	>>>
JAPIO 2			-	-	>>	>>	>>>	>>>	>>>	>>>	>>>	>>>
NICT-2 1				-	>>	>>	>>>	>>>	>>>	>>>	>>>	>>>
EHR (2015)					-	-	>>	>>>	>>>	>>>	>>>	>>>
ntt 2						-	-	>>	>>>	>>>	>>>	>>>
EHR 1							-	-	>	>>>	>>>	>>>
NICT-2 2								-	>>	>>	>>	>>>
EHR 2									-	>	>>	>>>
bjtu_nlp										-	-	>>>
Kyoto-U (2015)											-	>>>
TOSHIBA (2015)												>>>

Table 16: Statistical significance testing of the JPC-CJ Pairwise scores.

	TOSHIBA (2015) 1	JAPIO 1	TOSHIBA (2015) 2	NICT (2015) 1	naver (2015) 1	NICT (2015) 2	Online A	naver (2015) 2	Sense (2015) 1	EHR (2015) 1	EHR 2	EHR (2015) 2	JAPIO 2	Sense (2015) 2
EHR 1	>	>	>	>>>	>>>	>>>	>>>	>>>	>>>	>>>	>>>	>>>	>>>	>>>
TOSHIBA (2015) 1		-	-	>>>	>>>	>>>	>>>	>>>	>>>	>>>	>>>	>>>	>>>	>>>
JAPIO 1			-	>>>	>>>	>>>	>>>	>>>	>>>	>>>	>>>	>>>	>>>	>>>
TOSHIBA (2015) 2				>>>	>>>	>>>	>>>	>>>	>>>	>>>	>>>	>>>	>>>	>>>
NICT (2015) 1					-	-	-	-	>>>	>>>	>>>	>>>	>>>	>>>
naver (2015) 1						-	-	-	>>>	>>>	>>>	>>>	>>>	>>>
NICT (2015) 2							-	-	>>>	>>>	>>>	>>>	>>>	>>>
Online A								-	>	>>>	>>>	>>>	>>>	>>>
naver (2015) 2									>>>	>>>	>>>	>>>	>>>	>>>
Sense (2015) 1										>	>>>	>>>	>>>	>>>
EHR (2015) 1											-	-	>>>	>>>
EHR 2												-	>>>	>>>
EHR (2015) 2													>	>>>
JAPIO 2														>>>

Table 17: Statistical significance testing of the JPC-KJ Pairwise scores.

	Online B	SMT S2T	Sense 1	SMT Hiero	Sense 2	IITB-EN-ID
Online A	>>>	>>>	>>>	>>>	>>>	>>>
Online B		>>>	>>>	>>>	>>>	>>>
SMT S2T			-	>	>	>>>
Sense 1				>	>	>>>
SMT Hiero					-	>>>
Sense 2						>>>

	Online B	Sense 1	Sense 2	SMT T2S	IITB-EN-ID	SMT Hiero
Online A	>>>	>>>	>>>	>>>	>>>	>>>
Online B		>>>	>	>>>	>>>	>>>
Sense 1			>	>>>	>>>	>>>
Sense 2				>>>	>>>	>>>
SMT T2S					-	>>>
IITB-EN-ID						>>>

Table 18: Statistical significance testing of the BPPT-IE (left) and BPPT-EI (right) Pairwise scores.

	Online B	IITP-MT	EHR
Online A	≫	≫	≫
Online B		≫	≫
IITP-MT			≫

	Online B	EHR 1	EHR 2
Online A	≫	≫	≫
Online B		≫	≫
EHR 1			≫

Table 19: Statistical significance testing of the IITB-EH (left) and IITB-HJ (right) Pairwise scores.

ASPEC-JE		ASPEC-EJ		ASPEC-JC		ASPEC-CJ	
SYSTEM ID	κ	SYSTEM ID	κ	SYSTEM ID	κ	SYSTEM ID	κ
NAIST (2015)	0.078	NAIST (2015)	0.239	Kyoto-U 1	0.177	Kyoto-U 1	0.195
NAIST 1	0.081	Kyoto-U	0.215	NAIST (2015)	0.221	Kyoto-U 2	0.151
NAIST 2	0.091	naver (2015)	0.187	bjtu_nlp	0.187	bjtu_nlp	0.168
Kyoto-U 1	0.106	Online A	0.181	Kyoto-U (2015)	0.197	UT-KAY 1	0.172
Kyoto-U 2	0.148	WEBLIO MT (2015)	0.193	Kyoto-U 2	0.251	UT-KAY 2	0.156
Kyoto-U (2015)	0.066	NICT-2	0.177	NICT-2	0.190	NAIST (2015)	0.089
TOSHIBA (2015)	0.068	bjtu_nlp	0.247	TOSHIBA (2015)	0.214	NICT-2	0.168
NICT-2	0.106	EHR	0.195	Online D	0.180	Kyoto-U (2015)	0.144
Online D	0.081	UT-AKY 1	0.204	ave.	0.202	EHR	0.152
TMU 1	0.060	TOKYOMT 1	0.189			EHR (2015)	0.190
bjtu_nlp	0.146	TOKYOMT 2	0.200			JAPIO	0.185
TMU 2	0.072	UT-AKY 2	0.201			Online A	0.207
ave.	0.092	JAPIO	0.183			ave.	0.165
		ave	0.201				

JPC-JE		JPC-EJ		JPC-JC		JPC-CJ		JPC-KJ	
SYSTEM ID	κ	SYSTEM ID	κ	SYSTEM ID	κ	SYSTEM ID	κ	SYSTEM ID	κ
bjtu_nlp	0.256	bjtu_nlp	0.339	NICT-2 1	0.076	ntt 1	0.169	EHR 1	0.256
Online A	0.242	NICT-2 1	0.367	Hiero	0.127	JAPIO 1	0.121	TOSHIBA (2015) 1	0.221
NICT-2 1	0.280	T2S	0.378	S2T	0.133	JAPIO 2	0.160	JAPIO 1	0.228
NICT-2 2	0.293	NICT-2 2	0.346	bjtu_nlp	0.085	NICT-2 1	0.150	TOSHIBA (2015) 2	0.176
RBMT A	0.179	JAPIO 1	0.323	NICT-2 2	0.068	EHR (2015)	0.123	NICT (2015) 1	0.351
S2T	0.296	Hiero	0.383	Online A	0.055	ntt 2	0.114	naver (2015) 1	0.469
Hiero	0.324	Online A	0.403	RBMT C	0.116	EHR 1	0.155	NICT (2015) 2	0.345
ave.	0.267	JAPIO 2	0.336	ave.	0.094	NICT-2 2	0.151	Online A	0.232
		RBMT F	0.323			EHR 2	0.150	naver (2015) 2	0.299
		ave.	0.355			bjtu_nlp	0.200	Sense (2015) 1	0.522
						Kyoto-U (2015)	0.096	EHR (2015) 1	0.363
						TOSHIBA (2015)	0.131	EHR 2	0.399
						Online A	0.116	EHR (2015) 2	0.373
						ave.	0.141	JAPIO 2	0.260
								Sense (2015) 2	0.329
								ave.	0.322

BPPT-IE		BPPT-EI		IITB-EH		IITB-HJ	
SYSTEM ID	κ	SYSTEM ID	κ	SYSTEM ID	κ	SYSTEM ID	κ
Online A	-0.083	Online A	0.094	Online A	0.141	Online A	0.285
Online B	-0.051	Online B	0.063	Online B	0.110	Online B	0.488
S2T	0.025	Sense 1	0.135	IITP-MT	0.215	EHR 1	0.452
Sense 1	0.145	Sense 2	0.160	EHR	0.196	EHR 2	0.510
Hiero	0.057	T2S	0.089	ave.	0.166	ave.	0.434
Sense 2	0.102	IITB-EN-ID	0.115				
IITB-EN-ID	0.063	Hiero	0.165				
ave.	0.037	ave.	0.117				

Table 20: The Fleiss' kappa values for the pairwise evaluation results.

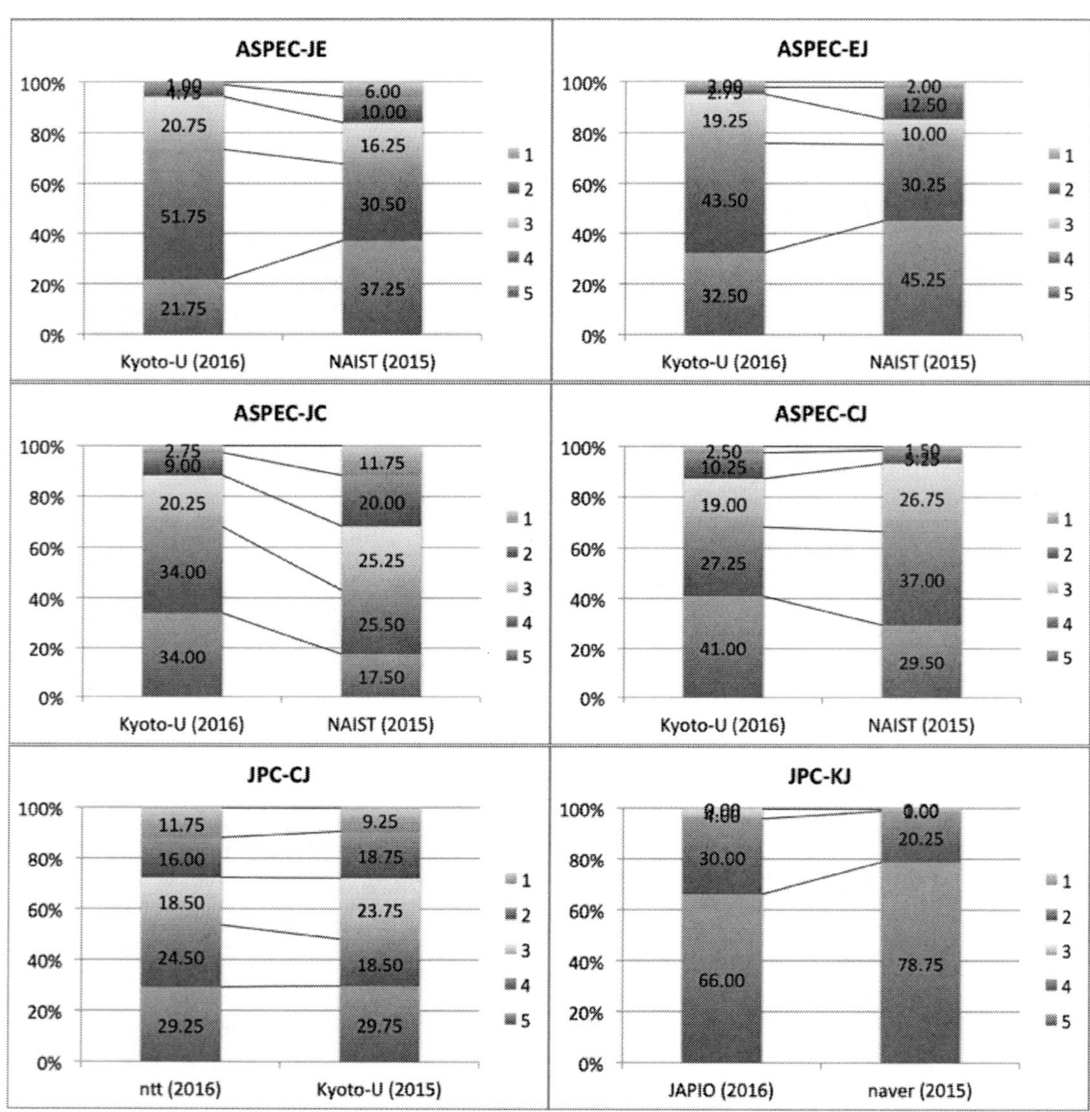

Figure 15: The chronological evaluation results of JPO adequacy evaluation.

SYSTEM ID	ID	METHOD	OTHER RESOURCES	BLEU	RIBES	AMFM	Pair	SYSTEM DESCRIPTION
SMT Hiero	2	SMT	NO	18.72	0.651066	0.588880	——	Hierarchical Phrase-based SMT
SMT Phrase	6	SMT	NO	18.45	0.645137	0.590950	——	Phrase-based SMT
SMT S2T	877	SMT	NO	20.36	0.678253	0.593410	+7.00	String-to-Tree SMT
RBMT D	887	Other	YES	15.29	0.683378	0.551690	+16.75	RBMT D
RBMT E	76	Other	YES	14.82	0.663851	0.561620	——	RBMT E
RBMT F	79	Other	YES	13.86	0.661387	0.556840	——	RBMT F
Online C (2014)	87	Other	YES	10.64	0.624827	0.466480	——	Online C (2014)
Online D (2014)	35	Other	YES	15.08	0.643588	0.564170	——	Online D (2014)
Online D (2015)	775	Other	YES	16.85	0.676609	0.562270	+0.25	Online D (2015)
Online D	1042	Other	YES	16.91	0.677412	0.564270	+28.00	Online D (2016)
NAIST 1	1122	SMT	NO	26.39	0.762712	0.587450	+48.25	Neural MT w/ Lexicon and MinRisk Training 4 Ensemble
NAIST 2	1247	SMT	NO	26.12	0.756956	0.571360	+47.50	Neural MT w/ Lexicon 6 Ensemble
Kyoto-U 1	1182	NMT	NO	26.22	0.756601	0.558540	+44.25	Ensemble of 4 single-layer model (30k voc)
Kyoto-U 2	1246	NMT	NO	24.71	0.750802	0.562650	+47.00	voc src:200k voc tgt: 52k + BPE 2-layer self-ensembling
TMU 1	1222	NMT	NO	18.29	0.710613	0.565270	+16.00	2016 our proposed method to control output voice
TMU 2	1234	NMT	NO	18.45	0.711542	0.546880	+25.00	6 ensemble
BJTU-nlp 1	1168	NMT	NO	18.34	0.690455	0.505730	+19.25	RNN Encoder-Decoder with attention mechanism, single model
NICT-2 1	1104	SMT	YES	21.54	0.708808	0.595930	——	Phrase-based SMT with Preordering + Domain Adaptation (JPC and ASPEC) + Google 5-gram LM

Table 21: ASPEC-JE submissions

SYSTEM ID	ID	METHOD	OTHER RESOURCES	BLEU			RIBES			AMFM			Pair	SYSTEM DESCRIPTION
				juman	kytea	mecab	juman	kytea	mecab	juman	kytea	mecab		
SMT Phrase	5	SMT	NO	27.48	29.80	28.27	0.683735	0.691926	0.695390	0.736380	0.736380	0.736380	——	Phrase-based SMT
SMT Hiero	367	SMT	NO	30.19	32.56	30.94	0.734705	0.746978	0.747722	0.743900	0.743900	0.743900	+31.50	Hierarchical Phrase-based SMT
SMT T2S	875	SMT	NO	31.05	33.44	32.10	0.748883	0.758031	0.760516	0.744370	0.744370	0.744370	+30.00	Tree-to-String SMT
RBMT A	68	Other	YES	12.86	14.43	13.16	0.670167	0.676464	0.678934	0.626940	0.626940	0.626940	——	RBMT A
RBMT B	883	Other	YES	13.18	14.85	13.48	0.671958	0.680748	0.682683	0.622930	0.622930	0.622930	+9.75	RBMT B
RBMT C	95	Other	YES	12.19	13.32	12.14	0.668372	0.672645	0.676018	0.594380	0.594380	0.594380	——	RBMT C
Online A (2014)	34	Other	YES	19.66	21.63	20.17	0.718019	0.723486	0.725848	0.695420	0.695420	0.695420	——	Online A (2014)
Online A (2015)	774	Other	YES	18.22	19.77	18.46	0.705882	0.713960	0.718150	0.677200	0.677200	0.677200	+34.25	Online A (2015)
Online A (2016)	1041	Other	YES	18.28	19.81	18.51	0.706639	0.715222	0.718559	0.677020	0.677020	0.677020	+49.75	Online A (2016)
Online B (2014)	91	Other	YES	17.04	18.67	17.36	0.687797	0.693390	0.698126	0.643070	0.643070	0.643070	——	Online B (2014)
Online B (2015)	889	Other	YES	17.80	19.52	18.11	0.693359	0.701966	0.703859	0.646160	0.646160	0.646160	——	Online B (2015)
Kyoto-U 1	1172	NMT	NO	36.19	38.20	36.78	0.819836	0.823878	0.828956	0.738700	0.738700	0.738700	+55.25	BPE tgt/src: 52k 2-layer lstm self-ensemble of 3
EHR 1	1140	SMT	NO	31.32	33.58	32.28	0.759914	0.771427	0.775023	0.746720	0.746720	0.746720	+39.00	PBSMT with preordering (DL=6)
BJTU-nlp 1	1143	NMT	NO	31.18	33.47	31.80	0.780510	0.787497	0.791088	0.704340	0.704340	0.704340	+39.50	RNN Encoder-Decoder with attention mechanism, single model char 1 , ens 2 , version 1
TOKYOMT 1	1131	NMT	NO	30.21	33.38	31.24	0.809691	0.817258	0.819951	0.705210	0.705210	0.705210	+29.75	
TOKYOMT 2	1217	NMT	NO	32.03	34.77	32.98	0.808189	0.814452	0.818130	0.720810	0.720810	0.720810	+30.50	Combination of NMT and T2S
JAPIO 1	1165	SMT	YES	20.52	22.56	21.05	0.723467	0.728584	0.731474	0.660790	0.660790	0.660790	+4.25	Phrase-based SMT with Preordering + JAPIO corpus + rule-based posteditor
NICT-2 1	1097	SMT	YES	34.67	36.86	35.37	0.784335	0.790993	0.793409	0.753080	0.753080	0.753080	+41.25	Phrase-based SMT with Preordering + Domain Adaptation (JPC and ASPEC) + Google 5-gram LM
UT-AKY 1	1224	NMT	NO	30.14	33.20	31.09	0.806025	0.814490	0.815836	0.708140	0.708140	0.708140	+21.75	tree-to-seq NMT model (character-based decoder)
UT-AKY 2	1228	NMT	NO	33.57	36.95	34.65	0.816984	0.824456	0.827647	0.731440	0.731440	0.731440	+36.25	tree-to-seq NMT model (word-based decoder)

Table 22: ASPEC-EJ submissions

SYSTEM ID	ID	METHOD	OTHER RESOURCES	BLEU			RIBES			AMFM			Pair	SYSTEM DESCRIPTION
				kytea	stanford (ctb)	stanford (pku)	kytea	stanford (ctb)	stanford (pku)	kytea	stanford (ctb)	stanford (pku)		
SMT Phrase	7	SMT	NO	27.96	28.01	27.68	0.788961	0.790263	0.790937	0.749450	0.749450	0.749450	——	Phrase-based SMT
SMT Hiero	3	SMT	NO	27.71	27.70	27.35	0.809128	0.809561	0.811394	0.745100	0.745100	0.745100	——	Hierarchical Phrase-based SMT
SMT S2T	881	SMT	NO	28.65	28.65	28.35	0.807606	0.809457	0.808417	0.755230	0.755230	0.755230	+7.75	String-to-Tree SMT
RBMT B	886	Other	YES	17.86	17.75	17.49	0.744818	0.745885	0.743794	0.667960	0.667960	0.667960	-11.00	RBMT B
RBMT C	244	Other	NO	9.62	9.96	9.59	0.642278	0.648758	0.645385	0.594900	0.594900	0.594900	——	RBMT C
Online C (2014)	216	Other	YES	7.26	7.01	6.72	0.612808	0.613075	0.611563	0.587820	0.587820	0.587820	——	Online C (2014)
Online C (2015)	891	Other	YES	7.44	7.05	6.75	0.611964	0.615048	0.612158	0.566060	0.566060	0.566060	——	Online C (2015)
Online D (2014)	37	Other	YES	9.37	8.93	8.84	0.606905	0.606328	0.604149	0.625430	0.625430	0.625430	——	Online D (2014)
Online D (2015)	777	Other	YES	10.73	10.33	10.08	0.660484	0.660847	0.660482	0.634090	0.634090	0.634090	-14.75	Online D (2015)
Online D (2016)	1045	Other	YES	11.16	10.72	10.54	0.665185	0.667382	0.666953	0.639440	0.639440	0.639440	-26.00	Online D (2016)
Kyoto-U 1	1071	NMT	NO	31.98	32.08	31.72	0.837579	0.839354	0.835932	0.763290	0.763290	0.763290	+58.75	2 layer lstm dropout 0.5 200k source voc unk replaced
Kyoto-U 2	1109	EBMT	NO	30.27	29.94	29.92	0.813114	0.813581	0.813054	0.764230	0.764230	0.764230	+30.75	KyotoEBMT 2016 w/o reranking
BJTU-nlp 1	1120	NMT	NO	30.57	30.49	30.31	0.829679	0.829113	0.827637	0.754690	0.754690	0.754690	+46.25	RNN Encoder-Decoder with attention mechanism, single model
NICT-2 1	1105	SMT	YES	30.00	29.97	29.78	0.820891	0.820069	0.821090	0.759670	0.759670	0.759670	+24.00	Phrase-based SMT with Preordering + Domain Adaptation (JPC and ASPEC)

Table 23: ASPEC-JC submissions

SYSTEM ID	ID	METHOD	OTHER RESOURCES	BLEU			RIBES			AMFM			Pair	SYSTEM DESCRIPTION
				juman	kytea	mecab	juman	kytea	mecab	juman	kytea	mecab		
SMT Phrase	8	SMT	NO	34.65	35.16	34.77	0.772498	0.766384	0.771005	0.753010	0.753010	0.753010	——	Phrase-based SMT
SMT Hiero	4	SMT	NO	35.43	35.91	35.64	0.810406	0.798726	0.807665	0.750950	0.750950	0.750950	——	Hierarchical Phrase-based SMT
SMT T2S	879	SMT	NO	36.52	37.07	36.64	0.825292	0.820490	0.825025	0.754870	0.754870	0.754870	+17.25	Tree-to-String SMT
RBMT A	885	Other	YES	9.37	9.87	9.35	0.666277	0.652402	0.661730	0.626070	0.626070	0.626070	-28.00	RBMT A
RBMT D	242	Other	NO	8.39	8.70	8.30	0.641189	0.626400	0.633319	0.586790	0.586790	0.586790	——	RBMT D
Online A (2014)	36	Other	YES	11.63	13.21	11.87	0.595925	0.598172	0.598573	0.658060	0.658060	0.658060	——	Online A (2014)
Online A (2015)	776	Other	YES	11.53	12.82	11.68	0.588285	0.590393	0.592887	0.649860	0.649860	0.649860	-19.00	Online A (2015)
Online A (2016)	1043	Other	YES	11.56	12.87	11.69	0.589802	0.589397	0.593361	0.659540	0.659540	0.659540	-51.25	Online A (2016)
Online B (2014)	215	Other	YES	10.48	11.26	10.47	0.600733	0.596006	0.600706	0.636930	0.636930	0.636930	——	Online B (2014)
Online B (2015)	890	Other	YES	10.41	11.03	10.36	0.597355	0.592841	0.597298	0.628290	0.628290	0.628290	——	Online B (2015)
Kyoto-U 1	1255	NMT	NO	44.29	45.05	44.32	0.869360	0.864748	0.869913	0.784380	0.784380	0.784380	+56.00	src: 200k tgt: 50k 2-layers self-ensembling
Kyoto-U 2	1256	NMT	NO	46.04	46.70	46.05	0.876531	0.872904	0.876946	0.785910	0.785910	0.785910	+63.75	voc: 30k ensemble of 3 independent model + reverse rescoring
EHR 1	1063	SMT	YES	39.75	39.85	39.40	0.843723	0.836156	0.841952	0.769490	0.769490	0.769490	+32.50	LM-based merging of outputs of preordered word-based PB-SMT(DL=6) and preordered character-based PBSMT(DL=6).
BJTU-nlp 1	1138	NMT	NO	38.83	39.25	38.68	0.852818	0.846301	0.852298	0.760840	0.760840	0.760840	+49.00	RNN Encoder-Decoder with attention mechanism, single model
JAPIO 1	1208	SMT	YES	26.24	27.87	26.37	0.790553	0.780637	0.785917	0.696770	0.696770	0.696770	+16.50	Phrase-based SMT with Preordering + JAPIO corpus + rule-based posteditor
NICT-2 1	1099	SMT	YES	40.02	40.45	40.29	0.843941	0.837707	0.842513	0.768580	0.768580	0.768580	+36.50	Phrase-based SMT with Preordering + Domain Adaptation (JPC and ASPEC) + Google 5-gram LM
UT-KAY 1	1220	NMT	NO	37.63	39.07	37.82	0.847407	0.842055	0.848040	0.753820	0.753820	0.753820	+41.00	An end-to-end NMT with 512 dimensional single-layer LSTMs, UNK replacement, and domain adaptation
UT-KAY 2	1221	NMT	NO	40.50	41.81	40.67	0.860214	0.854690	0.860449	0.765530	0.765530	0.765530	+47.25	Ensemble of our NMT models with and without domain adaptation

Table 24: ASPEC-CJ submissions

SYSTEM ID	ID	METHOD	OTHER RESOURCES	BLEU	RIBES	AMFM	Pair	SYSTEM DESCRIPTION
SMT Phrase	977	SMT	NO	30.80	0.730056	0.664830	—	Phrase-based SMT
SMT Hiero	979	SMT	NO	32.23	0.763030	0.672500	+8.75	Hierarchical Phrase-based SMT
SMT S2T	980	SMT	NO	34.40	0.793483	0.672760	+23.00	String-to-Tree SMT
RBMT A	1090	Other	YES	21.57	0.750381	0.521230	+23.75	RBMT A
RBMT B	1095	Other	YES	18.38	0.710992	0.518110	—	RBMT B
RBMT C	1088	Other	YES	21.00	0.755017	0.519210	—	RBMT C
Online A (2016)	1035	Other	YES	35.77	0.803661	0.673950	+32.25	Online A (2016)
Online B (2016)	1051	Other	YES	16.00	0.688004	0.486450	—	Online B (2016)
BJTU-nlp 1	1149	NMT	NO	41.62	0.851975	0.690750	+41.50	RNN Encoder-Decoder with attention mechanism, single model
NICT-2 1	1080	SMT	NO	35.68	0.824398	0.667540	+25.00	Phrase-based SMT with Preordering + Domain Adaptation
NICT-2 2	1103	SMT	YES	36.06	0.825420	0.672890	+24.25	Phrase-based SMT with Preordering + Domain Adaptation (JPC and ASPEC) + Google 5-gram LM

Table 25: JPC-JE submissions

SYSTEM ID	ID	METHOD	OTHER RESOURCES	BLEU			RIBES			AMFM			Pair	SYSTEM DESCRIPTION
				juman	kytea	mecab	juman	kytea	mecab	juman	kytea	mecab		
SMT Phrase	973	SMT	NO	32.36	34.26	32.52	0.728539	0.728281	0.729077	0.711900	0.711900	0.711900	—	Phrase-based SMT
SMT Hiero	974	SMT	NO	34.57	36.61	34.79	0.777759	0.778657	0.779049	0.715300	0.715300	0.715300	+21.00	Hierarchical Phrase-based SMT
SMT T2S	975	SMT	NO	35.60	37.65	35.82	0.797353	0.796783	0.798025	0.717030	0.717030	0.717030	+30.75	Tree-to-String SMT
RBMT D	1085	Other	YES	23.02	24.90	23.45	0.761224	0.757341	0.760325	0.647730	0.647730	0.647730	—	RBMT D
RBMT E	1087	Other	YES	21.35	23.17	21.53	0.743484	0.741985	0.742300	0.646930	0.646930	0.646930	—	RBMT E
RBMT F	1086	Other	YES	26.64	28.48	26.84	0.773673	0.769244	0.773344	0.675470	0.675470	0.675470	+12.75	RBMT F
Online A (2016)	1036	Other	YES	36.88	37.89	36.83	0.798168	0.792471	0.796308	0.719110	0.719110	0.719110	+20.00	Online A (2016)
Online B (2016)	1073	Other	YES	21.57	22.62	21.65	0.743083	0.735203	0.740962	0.659950	0.659950	0.659950	—	Online B (2016)
BJTU-nlp 1	1112	NMT	NO	39.46	41.16	39.45	0.842762	0.840148	0.842669	0.722560	0.722560	0.722560	+39.50	RNN Encoder-Decoder with attention mechanism, single model
JAPIO 1	1141	SMT	YES	45.57	46.40	45.74	0.851376	0.848580	0.849513	0.747910	0.747910	0.747910	+17.75	Phrase-based SMT with Preordering + JAPIO corpus
JAPIO 2	1156	SMT	YES	47.79	48.57	47.92	0.859139	0.856392	0.857422	0.762850	0.762850	0.762850	+26.75	Phrase-based SMT with Preordering + JPC/JAPIO corpora
NICT-2 1	1078	SMT	NO	39.03	40.74	38.98	0.826228	0.823582	0.824428	0.725540	0.725540	0.725540	+30.75	Phrase-based SMT with Preordering + Domain Adaptation
NICT-2 2	1098	SMT	YES	40.90	42.51	40.66	0.836556	0.832401	0.832622	0.738630	0.738630	0.738630	+37.75	Phrase-based SMT with Preordering + Domain Adaptation (JPC and ASPEC) + Google 5-gram LM

Table 26: JPC-EJ submissions

SYSTEM ID	ID	METHOD	OTHER RESOURCES	BLEU			RIBES			AMFM			Pair	SYSTEM DESCRIPTION
				kytea	stanford (ctb)	stanford (pku)	kytea	stanford (ctb)	stanford (pku)	kytea	stanford (ctb)	stanford (pku)		
SMT Phrase	966	SMT	NO	30.60	32.03	31.25	0.787321	0.797888	0.794388	0.710940	0.710940	0.710940	——	Phrase-based SMT
SMT Hiero	967	SMT	NO	30.26	31.57	30.91	0.788415	0.799118	0.796685	0.718360	0.718360	0.718360	+4.75	Hierarchical Phrase-based SMT
SMT S2T	968	SMT	NO	31.05	32.35	31.70	0.793846	0.802805	0.800848	0.720030	0.720030	0.720030	+4.25	String-to-Tree SMT
RBMT C	1118	Other	YES	12.35	13.72	13.17	0.688240	0.708681	0.700210	0.475430	0.475430	0.475430	-41.25	RBMT C
Online A	1038	Other	YES	23.02	23.57	23.29	0.754241	0.760672	0.760148	0.702350	0.702350	0.702350	-23.00	Online A (2016)
Online B	1069	Other	YES	9.42	9.59	8.79	0.642026	0.651070	0.643520	0.527180	0.527180	0.527180	——	Online B (2016)
BJTU-nlp 1	1150	NMT	NO	31.49	32.79	32.51	0.816577	0.822978	0.820820	0.701490	0.701490	0.701490	-1.00	RNN Encoder-Decoder with attention mechanism, single model
NICT-2 1	1081	SMT	NO	33.35	34.64	33.81	0.808513	0.817996	0.815322	0.723270	0.723270	0.723270	-11.00	Phrase-based SMT with Preordering + Domain Adaptation
NICT-2 2	1106	SMT	YES	33.40	34.64	33.83	0.811788	0.820320	0.818701	0.731520	0.731520	0.731520	+14.00	Phrase-based SMT with Preordering + Domain Adaptation (JPC and ASPEC)

Table 27: JPC-JC submissions

SYSTEM ID	ID	METHOD	OTHER RESOURCES	BLEU			RIBES			AMFM			Pair	SYSTEM DESCRIPTION
				juman	kytea	mecab	juman	kytea	mecab	juman	kytea	mecab		
SMT Phrase	431	SMT	NO	38.34	38.51	38.22	0.782019	0.778921	0.781456	0.723110	0.723110	0.723110	——	Phrase-based SMT
SMT Hiero	430	SMT	NO	39.22	39.52	39.14	0.806058	0.802059	0.804523	0.729370	0.729370	0.729370	——	Hierarchical Phrase-based SMT
SMT T2S	432	SMT	NO	39.39	39.90	39.39	0.814919	0.811350	0.813595	0.725920	0.725920	0.725920	+20.75	Tree-to-String SMT
RBMT A	759	Other	NO	10.49	10.72	10.35	0.674060	0.664098	0.667349	0.557130	0.557130	0.557130	-39.25	RBMT A
RBMT B	760	Other	NO	7.94	8.07	7.73	0.596200	0.581837	0.586941	0.502100	0.502100	0.502100	——	RBMT B
Online A (2015)	647	Other	YES	26.80	27.81	26.89	0.712242	0.707264	0.711273	0.693840	0.693840	0.693840	-7.00	Online A (2015)
Online A (2016)	1040	Other	YES	26.99	27.91	27.02	0.707739	0.702718	0.706707	0.693720	0.693720	0.693720	-19.75	Online A (2016)
Online B (2015)	648	Other	YES	12.33	12.72	12.44	0.648996	0.641255	0.648742	0.588380	0.588380	0.588380	——	Online B (2015)
EHR 1	1007	SMT	YES	40.95	41.20	40.51	0.828040	0.824502	0.826864	0.745080	0.745080	0.745080	+39.00	Combination of word-based PB-SMT and character-based PBSMT with DL=6.
EHR 2	1009	SMT and RBMT	YES	41.05	41.05	40.52	0.827048	0.821940	0.824852	0.735010	0.735010	0.735010	+35.50	Combination of word-based PB-SMT, character-based PBSMT and RBMT+PBSPE with DL=6.
ntt 1	1193	SMT	NO	40.75	41.05	40.68	0.825985	0.822125	0.824840	0.730190	0.730190	0.730190	+39.25	PBMT with pre-ordering on dependency structures
ntt 2	1200	NMT	NO	43.47	44.27	43.53	0.845271	0.843105	0.844968	0.749270	0.749270	0.749270	+46.50	NMT with pre-ordering and attention over bidirectional LSTMs (pre-ordering module is the same as the PBMT submission)
BJTU-nlp 1	1128	NMT	NO	39.34	39.72	39.30	0.835314	0.830505	0.833216	0.721460	0.721460	0.721460	+32.25	RNN Encoder-Decoder with attention mechanism, single model
JAPIO 1	1180	SMT	YES	43.87	44.47	43.66	0.833586	0.829360	0.831534	0.748330	0.748330	0.748330	+43.50	Phrase-based SMT with Preordering + JAPIO corpus
JAPIO 2	1192	SMT	YES	44.32	45.12	44.09	0.834959	0.830164	0.832955	0.751200	0.751200	0.751200	+46.25	Phrase-based SMT with Preordering + JAPIO corpus
NICT-2 1	1079	SMT	NO	41.09	41.27	41.24	0.827009	0.822664	0.825323	0.733020	0.733020	0.733020	+36.75	Phrase-based SMT with Preordering + Domain Adaptation
NICT-2 2	1100	SMT	YES	41.87	42.39	42.13	0.829640	0.826744	0.828107	0.739890	0.739890	0.739890	+43.25	Phrase-based SMT with Preordering + Domain Adaptation (JPC and ASPEC) + Google 5-gram LM

Table 28: JPC-CJ submissions

SYSTEM ID	ID	METHOD	OTHER RESOURCES	BLEU	RIBES	AMFM	Pair	SYSTEM DESCRIPTION
SMT Phrase	1020	SMT	NO	67.09	0.933825	0.844950	——	Phrase-based SMT
SMT Hiero	1021	SMT	NO	66.52	0.932391	0.844550	-3.50	Hierarchical Phrase-based SMT
RBMT C	1083	Other	YES	43.26	0.872746	0.766520	——	RBMT C
RBMT D	1089	Other	YES	45.59	0.877411	0.765530	-53.25	RBMT D
Online A	1037	Other	YES	48.75	0.898976	0.791320	-21.00	Online A (2016)
Online B	1068	Other	YES	28.21	0.827843	0.692980	——	Online B (2016)

Table 29: JPC-JK submissions

SYSTEM ID	ID	METHOD	OTHER RESOURCES	BLEU			RIBES			AMFM			Pair	SYSTEM DESCRIPTION
				juman	kytea	mecab	juman	kytea	mecab	juman	kytea	mecab		
SMT Phrase	438	SMT	NO	69.22	70.36	69.73	0.941302	0.939729	0.940756	0.856220	0.856220	0.856220	——	Phrase-based SMT
SMT Hiero	439	SMT	NO	67.41	68.65	68.00	0.937162	0.935903	0.936570	0.850560	0.850560	0.850560	+2.75	Hierarchical Phrase-based SMT
RBMT A	653	Other	YES	42.00	43.97	42.45	0.876396	0.873734	0.875146	0.712020	0.712020	0.712020	-7.25	RBMT A
RBMT B	654	Other	YES	34.74	37.51	35.54	0.845712	0.849014	0.846228	0.643150	0.643150	0.643150	——	RBMT B
Online A (2015)	652	Other	YES	55.05	56.84	55.46	0.909152	0.909385	0.908838	0.800460	0.800460	0.800460	+38.75	Online A (2015)
Online A (2016)	1039	Other	YES	54.78	56.68	55.14	0.907320	0.907652	0.906743	0.798750	0.798750	0.798750	+8.00	Online A (2016)
Online B (2015)	651	Other	YES	36.41	38.72	37.01	0.851745	0.852263	0.851945	0.728750	0.728750	0.728750	——	Online B (2015)
EHR 1	1005	SMT	YES	71.51	72.32	71.77	0.944651	0.943514	0.944606	0.866370	0.866370	0.866370	-3.00	Combination of word-based PB-SMT and character-based PBSMT with DL=0. Parentheses surrounding number in Korean sentences are deleted.
EHR 2	1006	SMT	YES	62.33	64.17	62.75	0.927065	0.927215	0.927017	0.818030	0.818030	0.818030	+21.75	Combination of word-based PB-SMT and character-based PBSMT with DL=0. Parentheses in Korean side and not in Japanese side are added to Japanese for training and dev sets.
JAPIO 1	1206	SMT	YES	68.62	69.49	68.90	0.938474	0.937066	0.938230	0.858190	0.858190	0.858190	-9.00	Phrase-based SMT + JAPIO corpus + rule-based posteditor
JAPIO 2	1209	SMT	YES	70.32	71.07	70.52	0.942137	0.940544	0.941746	0.863660	0.863660	0.863660	+17.50	Phrase-based SMT + JPC/JAPIO corpora + rule-based posteditor

Table 30: JPC-KJ submissions

SYSTEM ID	ID	METHOD	OTHER RESOURCES	BLEU	RIBES	AMFM	Pair	SYSTEM DESCRIPTION
SMT Phrase	971	SMT	NO	24.57	0.779545	0.578310	0.00	Phrase-based SMT
SMT Hiero	981	SMT	NO	23.62	0.776309	0.575450	-8.25	Hierarchical Phrase-based SMT
SMT S2T	982	SMT	NO	22.90	0.780436	0.577210	-3.25	String-to-Tree SMT
Online A	1033	Other	YES	28.11	0.797852	0.607290	+49.25	Online A
Online B	1052	Other	YES	19.69	0.770690	0.578920	+34.50	Online B
Sense 1	1171	SMT	NO	25.62	0.782761	0.564500	-5.00	Baseline-C50-PBMT
Sense 2	1173	SMT	NO	25.97	0.787768	0.570710	-8.25	Clustercat-PBMT

Table 31: BPPT-IE submissions

SYSTEM ID	ID	METHOD	OTHER RESOURCES	BLEU	RIBES	AMFM	Pair	SYSTEM DESCRIPTION
SMT Phrase	972	SMT	NO	23.95	0.808362	0.559800	0.00	Phrase-based SMT
SMT Hiero	983	SMT	NO	22.64	0.796701	0.568660	-17.00	Hierarchical Phrase-based SMT
SMT T2S	984	SMT	NO	23.65	0.792346	0.572520	-7.75	Tree-to-String SMT
Online A	1034	Other	YES	24.20	0.819504	0.554720	+35.75	Online A
Online B	1050	Other	YES	18.09	0.789499	0.514430	+10.50	Online B
Sense 1	1170	SMT	NO	25.16	0.807097	0.568780	+1.25	Baseline-C50-PBMT
Sense 2	1174	SMT	NO	25.31	0.808484	0.571890	-2.75	Clustercat-C50-PBMT
ITTB-EN-ID 1	1239	SMT	NO	22.35	0.808943	0.555970	-9.25	BLNLM

Table 32: BPPT-EI submissions

SYSTEM ID	ID	METHOD	OTHER RESOURCES	BLEU	RIBES	AMFM	Pair	SYSTEM DESCRIPTION
Online A	1031	Other	YES	21.37	0.714537	0.621100	+44.75	Online A (2016)
Online B	1048	Other	YES	15.58	0.683214	0.590520	+14.00	Online B (2016)
SMT Phrase	1054	SMT	NO	10.32	0.638090	0.574850	0.00	Phrase-based SMT

Table 33: IITB-HE submissions

SYSTEM ID	ID	METHOD	OTHER RESOURCES	BLEU	RIBES	AMFM	Pair	SYSTEM DESCRIPTION
SMT Phrase	1252	SMT	NO	10.790000	0.651166	0.660860	——	Phrase-based SMT
Online A	1032	Other	YES	18.720000	0.716788	0.670660	+57.25	Online A (2016)
Online B	1047	Other	YES	16.970000	0.691298	0.668450	+42.50	Online B (2016)
EHR 1	1166	SMT	NO	11.750000	0.671866	0.650750	0.00	PBSMT with preordering (DL=6)
IITP-MT 1	1185	SMT	YES	13.710000	0.688913	0.657330	+4.75	IITP-MT System1

Table 34: IITB-EH submissions

SYSTEM ID	ID	METHOD	OTHER RESOURCES	BLEU			RIBES			AMFM			Pair	SYSTEM DESCRIPTION
				juman	kytea	mecab	juman	kytea	mecab	juman	kytea	mecab		
SMT Phrase	1251	SMT	NO	2.05	4.17	2.42	0.440122	0.496402	0.461763	0.360910	0.360910	0.360910	——	Phrase-based SMT
Online A	1064	Other	YES	6.60	10.42	7.47	0.565109	0.597863	0.576725	0.495270	0.495270	0.495270	+39.75	Online A (2016)
Online B	1065	Other	YES	5.70	8.91	6.38	0.560486	0.589558	0.571670	0.471450	0.471450	0.471450	+17.75	Online B (2016)
EHR 1	1167	SMT	YES	7.81	10.12	8.11	0.579285	0.617098	0.588723	0.468140	0.468140	0.468140	+13.75	PBSMT with phrase table pivoting and pivot language (en) reordering. User dictionary and TED based LM are used.
EHR 2	1179	SMT	YES	7.66	9.80	7.95	0.585953	0.618106	0.597490	0.473120	0.473120	0.473120	+10.00	PBSMT with sentence level pivoting and pivot language (en) reordering. User dictionary and TED based LM are used.

Table 35: IITB-HJ submissions

SYSTEM ID	ID	METHOD	OTHER RESOURCES	BLEU	RIBES	AMFM	Pair	SYSTEM DESCRIPTION
SMT Phrase	1253	SMT	NO	1.590000	0.399448	0.467980	——	Phrase-based SMT
Online B	1066	Other	YES	4.210000	0.488631	0.528220	+51.75	Online B (2016)
Online A	1067	Other	YES	4.430000	0.495349	0.525690	+54.50	Online A (2016)

Table 36: IITB-JH submissions

References

Rafael E. Banchs, Luis F. D'Haro, and Haizhou Li. 2015. Adequacy-fluency metrics: Evaluating mt in the continuous space model framework. *IEEE/ACM Trans. Audio, Speech and Lang. Proc.*, 23(3):472–482, March.

Jacob Cohen. 1968. Weighted kappa: Nominal scale agreement with provision for scaled disagreement or partial credit. *Psychological Bulletin*, 70(4):213 – 220.

Fabien Cromieres, Chenhui Chu, Toshiaki Nakazawa, and Sadao Kurohashi. 2016. Kyoto university participation to wat 2016. In *Proceedings of the 3rd Workshop on Asian Translation (WAT2016)*, pages 166–174, Osaka, Japan, December. The COLING 2016 Organizing Committee.

Terumasa Ehara. 2016. Translation systems and experimental results of the ehr group for wat2016 tasks. In *Proceedings of the 3rd Workshop on Asian Translation (WAT2016)*, pages 111–118, Osaka, Japan, December. The COLING 2016 Organizing Committee.

Akiko Eriguchi, Kazuma Hashimoto, and Yoshimasa Tsuruoka. 2016. Character-based decoding in tree-to-sequence attention-based neural machine translation. In *Proceedings of the 3rd Workshop on Asian Translation (WAT2016)*, pages 175–183, Osaka, Japan, December. The COLING 2016 Organizing Committee.

J.L. Fleiss et al. 1971. Measuring nominal scale agreement among many raters. *Psychological Bulletin*, 76(5):378–382.

Kazuma Hashimoto, Akiko Eriguchi, and Yoshimasa Tsuruoka. 2016. Domain adaptation and attention-based unknown word replacement in chinese-to-japanese neural machine translation. In *Proceedings of the 3rd Workshop on Asian Translation (WAT2016)*, pages 75–83, Osaka, Japan, December. The COLING 2016 Organizing Committee.

Kenneth Heafield, Ivan Pouzyrevsky, Jonathan H. Clark, and Philipp Koehn. 2013. Scalable modified kneser-ney language model estimation. In *Proceedings of the 51st Annual Meeting of the Association for Computational Linguistics (Volume 2: Short Papers)*, pages 690–696, Sofia, Bulgaria, August. Association for Computational Linguistics.

Hieu Hoang, Philipp Koehn, and Adam Lopez. 2009. A unified framework for phrase-based, hierarchical, and syntax-based statistical machine translation. In *Proceedings of the International Workshop on Spoken Language Translation*, pages 152–159.

Kenji Imamura and Eiichiro Sumita. 2016. Nict-2 translation system for wat2016: Applying domain adaptation to phrase-based statistical machine translation. In *Proceedings of the 3rd Workshop on Asian Translation (WAT2016)*, pages 126–132, Osaka, Japan, December. The COLING 2016 Organizing Committee.

Hideki Isozaki, Tsutomu Hirao, Kevin Duh, Katsuhito Sudoh, and Hajime Tsukada. 2010. Automatic evaluation of translation quality for distant language pairs. In *Proceedings of the 2010 Conference on Empirical Methods in Natural Language Processing*, EMNLP '10, pages 944–952, Stroudsburg, PA, USA. Association for Computational Linguistics.

Marcin Junczys-Dowmunt, Tomasz Dwojak, and Hieu Hoang. 2016. Is neural machine translation ready for deployment? a case study on 30 translation directions.

Satoshi Kinoshita, Tadaaki Oshio, Tomoharu Mitsuhashi, and Terumasa Ehara. 2016. Translation using japio patent corpora: Japio at wat2016. In *Proceedings of the 3rd Workshop on Asian Translation (WAT2016)*, pages 133–138, Osaka, Japan, December. The COLING 2016 Organizing Committee.

Philipp Koehn, Hieu Hoang, Alexandra Birch, Chris Callison-Burch, Marcello Federico, Nicola Bertoldi, Brooke Cowan, Wade Shen, Christine Moran, Richard Zens, Chris Dyer, Ondrej Bojar, Alexandra Constantin, and Evan Herbst. 2007. Moses: Open source toolkit for statistical machine translation. In *Annual Meeting of the Association for Computational Linguistics (ACL), demonstration session*.

Philipp Koehn. 2004. Statistical significance tests for machine translation evaluation. In Dekang Lin and Dekai Wu, editors, *Proceedings of EMNLP 2004*, pages 388–395, Barcelona, Spain, July. Association for Computational Linguistics.

T. Kudo. 2005. Mecab : Yet another part-of-speech and morphological analyzer. *http://mecab.sourceforge.net/*.

Sadao Kurohashi, Toshihisa Nakamura, Yuji Matsumoto, and Makoto Nagao. 1994. Improvements of Japanese morphological analyzer JUMAN. In *Proceedings of The International Workshop on Sharable Natural Language*, pages 22–28.

Hyoung-Gyu Lee, JaeSong Lee, Jun-Seok Kim, and Chang-Ki Lee. 2015. NAVER Machine Translation System for WAT 2015. In *Proceedings of the 2nd Workshop on Asian Translation (WAT2015)*, pages 69–73, Kyoto, Japan, October.

Shaotong Li, JinAn Xu, Yufeng Chen, and Yujie Zhang. 2016. System description of bjtu_nlp neural machine translation system. In *Proceedings of the 3rd Workshop on Asian Translation (WAT2016)*, pages 104–110, Osaka, Japan, December. The COLING 2016 Organizing Committee.

Toshiaki Nakazawa, Hideya Mino, Isao Goto, Sadao Kurohashi, and Eiichiro Sumita. 2014. Overview of the 1st Workshop on Asian Translation. In *Proceedings of the 1st Workshop on Asian Translation (WAT2014)*, pages 1–19, Tokyo, Japan, October.

Toshiaki Nakazawa, Hideya Mino, Isao Goto, Graham Neubig, Sadao Kurohashi, and Eiichiro Sumita. 2015. Overview of the 2nd Workshop on Asian Translation. In *Proceedings of the 2nd Workshop on Asian Translation (WAT2015)*, pages 1–28, Kyoto, Japan, October.

Graham Neubig, Yosuke Nakata, and Shinsuke Mori. 2011. Pointwise prediction for robust, adaptable japanese morphological analysis. In *Proceedings of the 49th Annual Meeting of the Association for Computational Linguistics: Human Language Technologies: Short Papers - Volume 2*, HLT '11, pages 529–533, Stroudsburg, PA, USA. Association for Computational Linguistics.

Graham Neubig, Makoto Morishita, and Satoshi Nakamura, 2015. *Proceedings of the 2nd Workshop on Asian Translation (WAT2015)*, chapter Neural Reranking Improves Subjective Quality of Machine Translation: NAIST at WAT2015, pages 35–41. Workshop on Asian Translation.

Graham Neubig. 2016. Lexicons and minimum risk training for neural machine translation: Naist-cmu at wat2016. In *Proceedings of the 3rd Workshop on Asian Translation (WAT2016)*, pages 119–125, Osaka, Japan, December. The COLING 2016 Organizing Committee.

Kishore Papineni, Salim Roukos, Todd Ward, and Wei-Jing Zhu. 2002. Bleu: a method for automatic evaluation of machine translation. In *ACL*, pages 311–318.

Slav Petrov, Leon Barrett, Romain Thibaux, and Dan Klein. 2006. Learning accurate, compact, and interpretable tree annotation. In *Proceedings of the 21st International Conference on Computational Linguistics and 44th Annual Meeting of the Association for Computational Linguistics*, pages 433–440, Sydney, Australia, July. Association for Computational Linguistics.

John Richardson, Raj Dabre, Fabien Cromières, Toshiaki Nakazawa, and Sadao Kurohashi. 2015. KyotoEBMT System Description for the 2nd Workshop on Asian Translation. In *Proceedings of the 2nd Workshop on Asian Translation (WAT2015)*, pages 54–60, Kyoto, Japan, October.

Sukanta Sen, Debajyoty Banik, Asif Ekbal, and Pushpak Bhattacharyya. 2016. Iitp english-hindi machine translation system at wat 2016. In *Proceedings of the 3rd Workshop on Asian Translation (WAT2016)*, pages 216–222, Osaka, Japan, December. The COLING 2016 Organizing Committee.

Raphael Shu and Akiva Miura. 2016. Residual stacking of rnns for neural machine translation. In *Proceedings of the 3rd Workshop on Asian Translation (WAT2016)*, pages 223–229, Osaka, Japan, December. The COLING 2016 Organizing Committee.

Sandhya Singh, Anoop Kunchukuttan, and Pushpak Bhattacharyya. 2016. Iit bombay ' s english-indonesian submission at wat: Integrating neural language models with smt. In *Proceedings of the 3rd Workshop on Asian Translation (WAT2016)*, pages 68–74, Osaka, Japan, December. The COLING 2016 Organizing Committee.

Katsuhito Sudoh and Masaaki Nagata. 2016. Chinese-to-japanese patent machine translation based on syntactic pre-ordering for wat 2016. In *Proceedings of the 3rd Workshop on Asian Translation (WAT2016)*, pages 211–215, Osaka, Japan, December. The COLING 2016 Organizing Committee.

Liling Tan. 2016. Faster and lighter phrase-based machine translation baseline. In *Proceedings of the 3rd Workshop on Asian Translation (WAT2016)*, pages 184–193, Osaka, Japan, December. The COLING 2016 Organizing Committee.

Huihsin Tseng. 2005. A conditional random field word segmenter. In *In Fourth SIGHAN Workshop on Chinese Language Processing*.

Masao Utiyama and Hitoshi Isahara. 2007. A japanese-english patent parallel corpus. In *MT summit XI*, pages 475–482.

Hayahide Yamagishi, Shin Kanouchi, Takayuki Sato, and Mamoru Komachi. 2016. Controlling the voice of a sentence in japanese-to-english neural machine translation. In *Proceedings of the 3rd Workshop on Asian Translation (WAT2016)*, pages 203–210, Osaka, Japan, December. The COLING 2016 Organizing Committee.

Wei Yang and Yves Lepage. 2016. Improving patent translation using bilingual term extraction and re-tokenization for chinese–japanese. In *Proceedings of the 3rd Workshop on Asian Translation (WAT2016)*, pages 194–202, Osaka, Japan, December. The COLING 2016 Organizing Committee.

Translation of Patent Sentences with a Large Vocabulary
of Technical Terms Using Neural Machine Translation

Zi Long
Takehito Utsuro
Grad. Sc. Sys. & Inf. Eng.,
University of Tsukuba,
sukuba, 305-8573, Japan

Tomoharu Miitsuhashi
Japan Patent
Information Organization,
4-1-7, Tokyo, Koto-ku,
Tokyo, 135-0016, Japan

Mikio Yamamoto
Grad. Sc. Sys. & Inf. Eng.,
University of Tsukuba,
Tsukuba, 305-8573, Japan

Abstract

Neural machine translation (NMT), a new approach to machine translation, has achieved promising results comparable to those of traditional approaches such as statistical machine translation (SMT). Despite its recent success, NMT cannot handle a larger vocabulary because training complexity and decoding complexity proportionally increase with the number of target words. This problem becomes even more serious when translating patent documents, which contain many technical terms that are observed infrequently. In NMTs, words that are out of vocabulary are represented by a single unknown token. In this paper, we propose a method that enables NMT to translate patent sentences comprising a large vocabulary of technical terms. We train an NMT system on bilingual data wherein technical terms are replaced with technical term tokens; this allows it to translate most of the source sentences except technical terms. Further, we use it as a decoder to translate source sentences with technical term tokens and replace the tokens with technical term translations using SMT. We also use it to rerank the 1,000-best SMT translations on the basis of the average of the SMT score and that of the NMT rescoring of the translated sentences with technical term tokens. Our experiments on Japanese-Chinese patent sentences show that the proposed NMT system achieves a substantial improvement of up to 3.1 BLEU points and 2.3 RIBES points over traditional SMT systems and an improvement of approximately 0.6 BLEU points and 0.8 RIBES points over an equivalent NMT system without our proposed technique.

1 Introduction

Neural machine translation (NMT), a new approach to solving machine translation, has achieved promising results (Kalchbrenner and Blunsom, 2013; Sutskever et al., 2014; Cho et al., 2014; Bahdanau et al., 2015; Jean et al., 2014; Luong et al., 2015a; Luong et al., 2015b). An NMT system builds a simple large neural network that reads the entire input source sentence and generates an output translation. The entire neural network is jointly trained to maximize the conditional probability of a correct translation of a source sentence with a bilingual corpus. Although NMT offers many advantages over traditional phrase-based approaches, such as a small memory footprint and simple decoder implementation, conventional NMT is limited when it comes to larger vocabularies. This is because the training complexity and decoding complexity proportionally increase with the number of target words. Words that are out of vocabulary are represented by a single unknown token in translations, as illustrated in Figure 1. The problem becomes more serious when translating patent documents, which contain several newly introduced technical terms.

There have been a number of related studies that address the vocabulary limitation of NMT systems. Jean el al. (2014) provided an efficient approximation to the softmax to accommodate a very large vocabulary in an NMT system. Luong et al. (2015b) proposed annotating the occurrences of a target unknown word token with positional information to track its alignments, after which they replace the tokens with their translations using simple word dictionary lookup or identity copy. Li et al. (2016) proposed to replace out-of-vocabulary words with similar in-vocabulary words based on a similarity model learnt from monolingual data. Sennrich et al. (2016) introduced an effective approach based on encoding rare and unknown words as sequences of subword units. Luong and Manning (2016) provided a character-level

47

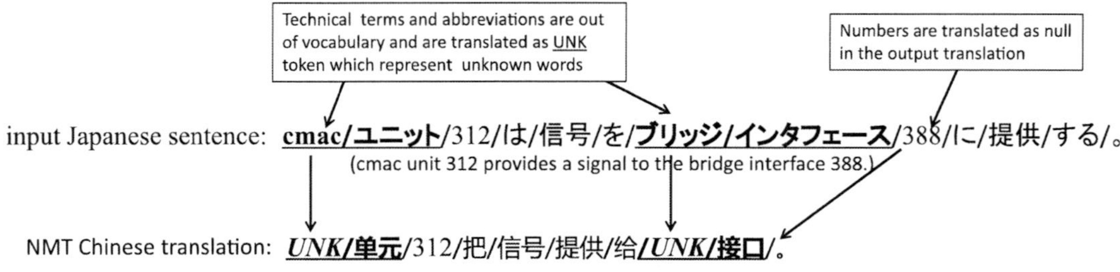

Figure 1: Example of translation errors when translating patent sentences with technical terms using NMT

and word-level hybrid NMT model to achieve an open vocabulary, and Costa-jussà and Fonollosa (2016) proposed a NMT system based on character-based embeddings.

However, these previous approaches have limitations when translating patent sentences. This is because their methods only focus on addressing the problem of unknown words even though the words are parts of technical terms. It is obvious that a technical term should be considered as one word that comprises components that always have different meanings and translations when they are used alone. An example is shown in Figure1, wherein Japanese word "ブリッジ"(bridge) should be translated to Chinese word "桥架" when included in technical term "bridge interface"; however, it is always translated as "桥".

In this paper, we propose a method that enables NMT to translate patent sentences with a large vocabulary of technical terms. We use an NMT model similar to that used by Sutskever et al. (2014), which uses a deep long short-term memories (LSTM) (Hochreiter and Schmidhuber, 1997) to encode the input sentence and a separate deep LSTM to output the translation. We train the NMT model on a bilingual corpus in which the technical terms are replaced with technical term tokens; this allows it to translate most of the source sentences except technical terms. Similar to Sutskever et al. (2014), we use it as a decoder to translate source sentences with technical term tokens and replace the tokens with technical term translations using statistical machine translation (SMT). We also use it to rerank the 1,000-best SMT translations on the basis of the average of the SMT and NMT scores of the translated sentences that have been rescored with the technical term tokens. Our experiments on Japanese-Chinese patent sentences show that our proposed NMT system achieves a substantial improvement of up to 3.1 BLEU points and 2.3 RIBES points over a traditional SMT system and an improvement of approximately 0.6 BLEU points and 0.8 RIBES points over an equivalent NMT system without our proposed technique.

2 Japanese-Chinese Patent Documents

Japanese-Chinese parallel patent documents were collected from the Japanese patent documents published by the Japanese Patent Office (JPO) during 2004-2012 and the Chinese patent documents published by the State Intellectual Property Office of the People's Republic of China (SIPO) during 2005-2010. From the collected documents, we extracted 312,492 patent families, and the method of Utiyama and Isahara (2007) was applied[1] to the text of the extracted patent families to align the Japanese and Chinese sentences. The Japanese sentences were segmented into a sequence of morphemes using the Japanese morphological analyzer MeCab[2] with the morpheme lexicon IPAdic,[3] and the Chinese sentences were segmented into a sequence of words using the Chinese morphological analyzer Stanford Word Segment (Tseng et al., 2005) trained using the Chinese Penn Treebank. In this study, Japanese-Chinese parallel patent sentence pairs were ordered in descending order of sentence-alignment score and we used the topmost 2.8M pairs, whose Japanese sentences contain fewer than 40 morphemes and

---

[1] Herein, we used a Japanese-Chinese translation lexicon comprising around 170,000 Chinese entries.
[2] http://mecab.sourceforge.net/
[3] http://sourceforge.jp/projects/ipadic/

Chinese sentences contain fewer than 40 words.[4]

3 Neural Machine Translation (NMT)

NMT uses a single neural network trained jointly to maximize the translation performance (Kalchbrenner and Blunsom, 2013; Sutskever et al., 2014; Cho et al., 2014; Bahdanau et al., 2015; Luong et al., 2015a). Given a source sentence $x = (x_1, \ldots, x_N)$ and target sentence $y = (y_1, \ldots, y_M)$, an NMT system uses a neural network to parameterize the conditional distributions

$$p(y_l \mid y_{<l}, x)$$

for $1 \leq l \leq M$. Consequently, it becomes possible to compute and maximize the log probability of the target sentence given the source sentence

$$\log p(y \mid x) = \sum_{l=1}^{M} \log p(y_l | y_{<l}, x) \tag{1}$$

In this paper, we use an NMT model similar to that used by Sutskever et al. (2014). It uses two separate deep LSTMs to encode the input sequence and output the translation. The encoder, which is implemented as a recurrent neural network, reads the source sentence one word at a time and then encodes it into a large vector that represents the entire source sentence. The decoder, another recurrent neural network, generates a translation on the basis of the encoded vector one word at a time.

One important difference between our NMT model and the one used by Sutskever et al. (2014) is that we added an attention mechanism. Recently, Bahdanau et al. (2015) proposed an attention mechanism, a form of random access memory, to help NMT cope with long input sequences. Luong et al. (2015a) proposed an attention mechanism for different scoring functions in order to compare the source and target hidden states as well as different strategies for placing the attention. In this paper, we utilize the attention mechanism proposed by Bahdanau et al. (2015), wherein each output target word is predicted on the basis of not only a recurrent hidden state and the previously predicted word but also a context vector computed as the weighted sum of the hidden states.

4 NMT with a Large Technical Term Vocabulary

4.1 NMT Training after Replacing Technical Term Pairs with Tokens

Figure 2 illustrates the procedure of the training model with parallel patent sentence pairs, wherein technical terms are replaced with technical term tokens "TT_1", "TT_2", ….

In the step 1 of Figure 2, we align the Japanese technical terms, which are automatically extracted from the Japanese sentences, with their Chinese translations in the Chinese sentences.[5] Here, we introduce the following two steps to identify technical term pairs in the bilingual Japanese-Chinese corpus:

1. According to the approach proposed by Dong et al. (2015), we identify Japanese-Chinese technical term pairs using an SMT phrase translation table. Given a parallel sentence pair $\langle S_J, S_C \rangle$ containing a Japanese technical term t_J, the Chinese translation candidates collected from the phrase translation table are matched against the Chinese sentence S_C of the parallel sentence pair. Of those found in S_C, t_C with the largest translation probability $P(t_C \mid t_J)$ is selected, and the bilingual technical term pair $\langle t_J, t_C \rangle$ is identified.

---

[4]In this paper, we focus on the task of translating patent sentences with a large vocabulary of technical terms using the NMT system, where we ignore the translation task of patent sentences that are longer than 40 morphemes in Japanese side or longer than 40 words in Chinese side.

[5]In this work, we approximately regard all the Japanese compound nouns as Japanese technical terms. These Japanese compound nouns are automatically extracted by simply concatenating a sequence of morphemes whose parts of speech are either nouns, prefixes, suffixes, unknown words, numbers, or alphabetical characters. Here, morpheme sequences starting or ending with certain prefixes are inappropriate as Japanese technical terms and are excluded. The sequences that include symbols or numbers are also excluded. In Chinese side, on the other hand, we regard Chinese translations of extracted Japanese compound nouns as Chinese technical terms, where we do not regard other Chinese phrases as technical terms.

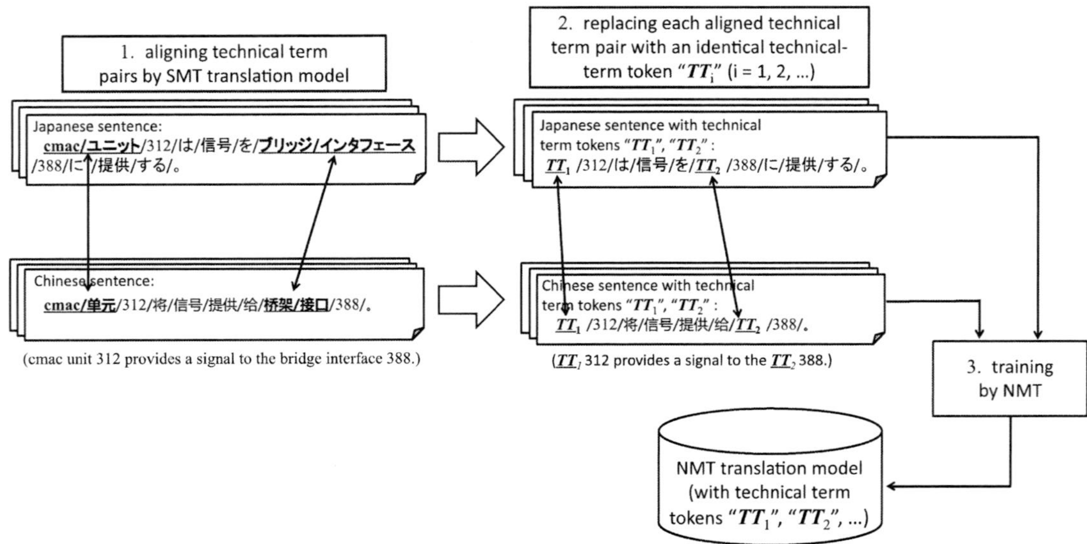

Figure 2: NMT training after replacing technical term pairs with technical term tokens "TT_i" ($i = 1, 2, \ldots$)

2. For the Japanese technical terms whose Chinese translations are not included in the results of Step 1, we then use an approach based on SMT word alignment. Given a parallel sentence pair $\langle S_J, S_C \rangle$ containing a Japanese technical term t_J, a sequence of Chinese words is selected using SMT word alignment, and we use the Chinese translation t_C for the Japanese technical term t_J.[6]

As shown in the step 2 of Figure 2, in each of Japanese-Chinese parallel patent sentence pairs, occurrences of technical term pairs $\langle t_J^1, t_C^1 \rangle$, $\langle t_J^2, t_C^2 \rangle$, …, $\langle t_J^k, t_C^k \rangle$ are then replaced with technical term tokens $\langle TT_1, TT_1 \rangle$, $\langle TT_2, TT_2 \rangle$, …, $\langle TT_k, TT_k \rangle$. Technical term pairs $\langle t_J^1, t_C^1 \rangle$, $\langle t_J^2, t_C^2 \rangle$, …, $\langle t_J^k, t_C^k \rangle$ are numbered in the order of occurrence of Japanese technical terms t_J^i ($i = 1, 2, \ldots, k$) in each Japanese sentence S_J. Here, note that in all the parallel sentence pairs $\langle S_J, S_C \rangle$, technical term tokens "TT_1", "TT_2", … that are identical throughout all the parallel sentence pairs are used in this procedure. Therefore, for example, in all the Japanese patent sentences S_J, the Japanese technical term t_J^1 which appears earlier than other Japanese technical terms in S_J is replaced with TT_1. We then train the NMT system on a bilingual corpus, in which the technical term pairs is replaced by "TT_i" ($i = 1, 2, \ldots$) tokens, and obtain an NMT model in which the technical terms are represented as technical term tokens.[7]

4.2 NMT Decoding and SMT Technical Term Translation

Figure 3 illustrates the procedure for producing Chinese translations via decoding the Japanese sentence using the method proposed in this paper. In the step 1 of Figure 3, when given an input Japanese sentence, we first automatically extract the technical terms and replace them with the technical term tokens "TT_i" ($i = 1, 2, \ldots$). Consequently, we have an input sentence in which the technical term tokens "TT_i" ($i = 1, 2, \ldots$) represent the positions of the technical terms and a list of extracted Japanese technical terms. Next, as shown in the step 2-N of Figure 3, the source Japanese sentence with technical term tokens is translated using the NMT model trained according to the procedure described in Section 4.1, whereas the extracted Japanese technical terms are translated using an SMT phrase translation table in the step 2-S of Figure 3.[8] Finally, in the step 3, we replace the technical term tokens "TT_i" ($i = 1, 2, \ldots$)

---

[6]We discard discontinuous sequences and only use continuous ones.

[7]We treat the NMT system as a black box, and the strategy we present in this paper could be applied to any NMT system (Kalchbrenner and Blunsom, 2013; Sutskever et al., 2014; Cho et al., 2014; Bahdanau et al., 2015; Luong et al., 2015a).

[8]We use the translation with the highest probability in the phrase translation table. When an input Japanese technical term has multiple translations with the same highest probability or has no translation in the phrase translation table, we apply a compositional translation generation approach, wherein Chinese translation is generated compositionally from the constituents

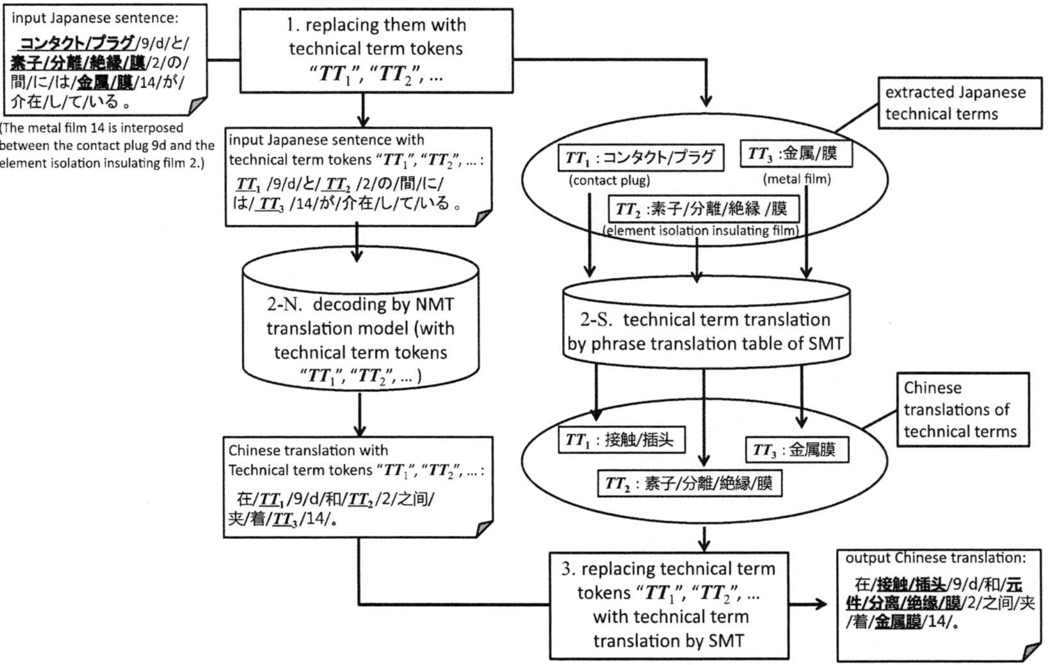

Figure 3: NMT decoding with technical term tokens "TT_i" ($i = 1, 2, \ldots$) and SMT technical term translation

of the sentence translation with SMT the technical term translations.

4.3 NMT Rescoring of 1,000-best SMT Translations

As shown in the step 1 of Figure 4, similar to the approach of NMT rescoring provided in Sutskever et al.(2014), we first obtain 1,000-best translation list of the given Japanese sentence using the SMT system. Next, in the step 2, we then replace the technical terms in the translation sentences with technical term tokens "TT_i" ($i = 1, 2, 3, \ldots$), which must be the same with the tokens of their source Japanese technical terms in the input Japanese sentence. The technique used for aligning Japanese technical terms with their Chinese translations is the same as that described in Section 4.1. In the step 3 of Figure 4, the 1,000-best translations, in which technical terms are represented as tokens, are rescored using the NMT model trained according to the procedure described in Section 4.1. Given a Japanese sentence S_J and its 1,000-best Chinese translations S_C^n ($n = 1, 2, \ldots, 1,000$) translated by the SMT system, NMT score of each translation sentence pair $\langle S_J, S_C^n \rangle$ is computed as the log probability $\log p(S_C^n \mid S_J)$ of Equation (1). Finally, we rerank the 1,000-best translation list on the basis of the average SMT and NMT scores and output the translation with the highest final score.

5 Evaluation

5.1 Training and Test Sets

We evaluated the effectiveness of the proposed NMT system in translating the Japanese-Chinese parallel patent sentences described in Section 2. Among the 2.8M parallel sentence pairs, we randomly extracted 1,000 sentence pairs for the test set and 1,000 sentence pairs for the development set; the remaining sentence pairs were used for the training set.

According to the procedure of Section 4.1, from the Japanese-Chinese sentence pairs of the training set, we collected 6.5M occurrences of technical term pairs, which are 1.3M types of technical term pairs with 800K unique types of Japanese technical terms and 1.0M unique types of Chinese technical terms.

of Japanese technical terms.

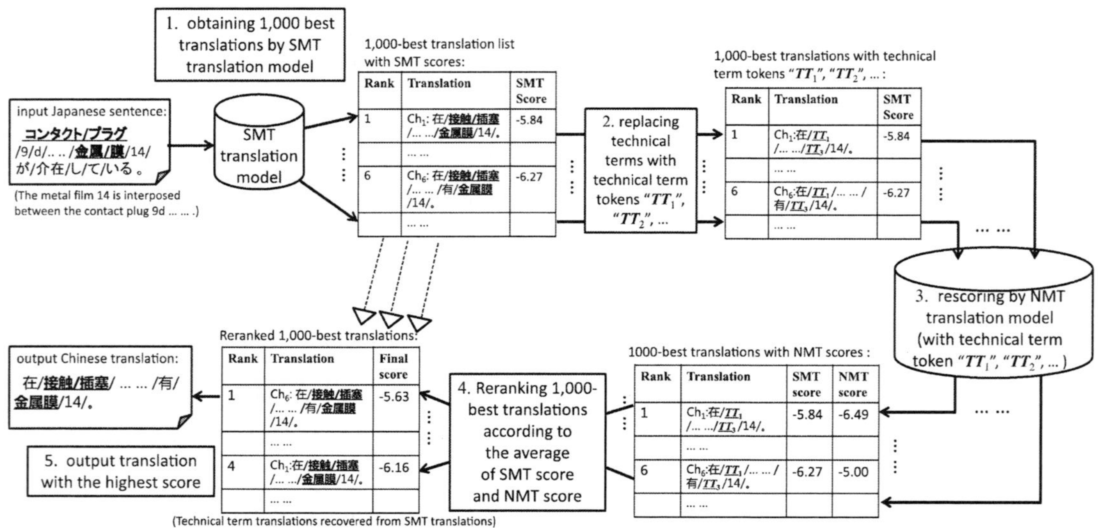

Figure 4: NMT rescoring of 1,000-best SMT translations with technical term tokens "TT_i" ($i = 1, 2, \ldots$)

Out of the total 6.5M occurrences of technical term pairs, 6.2M were replaced with technical term tokens using the phrase translation table, while the remaining 300K were replaced with technical term tokens using the word alignment.[9] We limited both the Japanese vocabulary (the source language) and the Chinese vocabulary (the target language) to 40K most frequently used words.

Within the total 1,000 Japanese patent sentences in the test set, 2,244 occurrences of Japanese technical terms were identified, which correspond to 1,857 types.

5.2 Training Details

For the training of the SMT model, including the word alignment and the phrase translation table, we used Moses (Koehn et al., 2007), a toolkit for a phrase-based SMT models.

For the training of the NMT model, our training procedure and hyperparameter choices were similar to those of Sutskever et al. (2014). We used a deep LSTM neural network comprising three layers, with 512 cells in each layer, and a 512-dimensional word embedding. Similar to Sutskever et al. (2014), we reversed the words in the source sentences and ensure that all sentences in a minibatch are roughly the same length. Further training details are given below:

- All of the LSTM's parameter were initialized with a uniform distribution ranging between -0.06 and 0.06.

- We set the size of a minibatch to 128.

- We used the stochastic gradient descent, beginning at a learning rate of 0.5. We computed the perplexity of the development set using the currently produced NMT model after every 1,500 minibatches were trained and multiplied the learning rate by 0.99 when the perplexity did not decrease with respect to the last three perplexities. We trained our model for a total of 10 epoches.

- Similar to Sutskever et al. (2014), we rescaled the normalized gradient to ensure that its norm does not exceed 5.

---

[9]There are also Japanese technical terms (3% of all the extracted terms) for which Chinese translations can be identified using neither the SMT phrase translation table nor the SMT word alignment.

Table 1: Automatic evaluation results

System	NMT decoding and SMT technical term translation		NMT rescoring of 1,000-best SMT translations	
	BLEU	RIBES	BLEU	RIBES
Baseline SMT (Koehn et al., 2007)	52.5	88.5	-	-
Baseline NMT	53.5	90.0	55.0	89.1
NMT with technical term translation by SMT	55.3	**90.8**	**55.6**	89.3

Table 2: Human evaluation results (the score of pairwise evaluation ranges from -100 to 100 and the score of JPO adequacy evaluation ranges from 1 to 5)

System	NMT decoding and SMT technical term translation		NMT rescoring of 1,000-best SMT translations	
	pairwise evaluation	JPO adequacy evaluation	pairwise evaluation	JPO adequacy evaluation
Baseline SMT (Koehn et al., 2007)	-	3.5	-	-
Baseline NMT	5.0	3.8	28.5	4.1
NMT with technical term translation by SMT	**36.5**	**4.3**	31.0	4.1

We implement the NMT system using TensorFlow,[10] an open source library for numerical computation. The training time was around two days when using the described parameters on an 1-GPU machine.

5.3 Evaluation Results

We calculated automatic evaluation scores for the translation results using two popular metrics: BLEU (Papineni et al., 2002) and RIBES (Isozaki et al., 2010). As shown in Table 1, we report the evaluation scores, on the basis of the translations by Moses (Koehn et al., 2007), as the baseline SMT[11] and the scores based on translations produced by the equivalent NMT system without our proposed approach as the baseline NMT. As shown in Table 1, the two versions of the proposed NMT systems clearly improve the translation quality when compared with the baselines. When compared with the baseline SMT, the performance gain of the proposed system is approximately 3.1 BLEU points if translations are produced by the proposed NMT system of Section 4.3 or 2.3 RIBES points if translations are produced by the proposed NMT system of Section 4.2. When compared with the result of decoding with the baseline NMT, the proposed NMT system of Section 4.2 achieved performance gains of 0.8 RIBES points. When compared with the result of reranking with the baseline NMT, the proposed NMT system of Section 4.3 can still achieve performance gains of 0.6 BLEU points. Moreover, when the output translations produced by NMT decoding and SMT technical term translation described in Section 4.2 with the output translations produced by decoding with the baseline NMT, the number of unknown tokens included in output translations reduced from 191 to 92. About 90% of remaining unknown tokens correspond to numbers, English words, abbreviations, and symbols.[12]

In this study, we also conducted two types of human evaluation according to the work of Nakazawa et al. (2015): pairwise evaluation and JPO adequacy evaluation. During the procedure of pairwise eval-

---

[10] https://www.tensorflow.org/

[11] We train the SMT system on the same training set and tune it with development set.

[12] In addition to the two versions of the proposed NMT systems presented in Section 4, we evaluated a modified version of the propsed NMT system, where we introduce another type of token corresponding to unknown compound nouns and integrate this type of token with the technical term token in the procedure of training the NMT model. We achieved a slightly improved translation performance, BLEU/RIBES scores of 55.6/90.9 for the proposed NMT system of Section 4.2 and those of 55.7/89.5 for the proposed NMT system of Section 4.3.

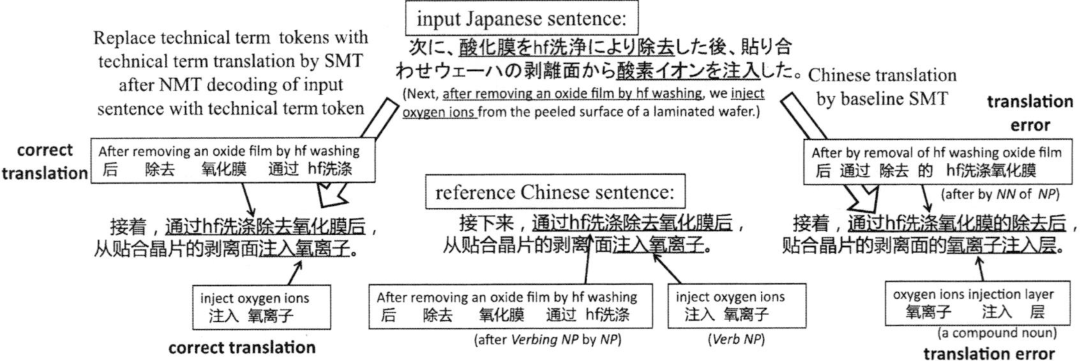

Figure 5: Example of correct translations produced by the proposed NMT system with SMT technical term translation (compared with baseline SMT)

uation, we compare each of translations produced by the baseline SMT with that produced by the two versions of the proposed NMT systems, and judge which translation is better, or whether they are with comparable quality. The score of pairwise evaluation is defined by the following formula, where W is the number of better translations compared to the baseline SMT, L the number of worse translations compared to the baseline SMT, and T the number of translations having their quality comparable to those produced by the baseline SMT:

$$score = 100 \times \frac{W - L}{W + L + T}$$

The score of pairwise evaluation ranges from -100 to 100. In the JPO adequacy evaluation, Chinese translations are evaluated according to the quality evaluation criterion for translated patent documents proposed by the Japanese Patent Office (JPO).[13] The JPO adequacy criterion judges whether or not the technical factors and their relationships included in Japanese patent sentences are correctly translated into Chinese, and score Chinese translations on the basis of the percentage of correctly translated information, where the score of 5 means all of those information are translated correctly, while that of 1 means most of those information are not translated correctly. The score of the JPO adequacy evaluation is defined as the average over the whole test sentences. Unlike the study conducted Nakazawa et al. (Nakazawa et al., 2015), we randomly selected 200 sentence pairs from the test set for human evaluation, and both human evaluations were conducted using only one judgement. Table 2 shows the results of the human evaluation for the baseline SMT, the baseline NMT, and the proposed NMT system. We observed that the proposed system achieved the best performance for both pairwise evaluation and JPO adequacy evaluation when we replaced technical term tokens with SMT technical term translations after decoding the source sentence with technical term tokens.

Throughout Figure 5~Figure 7, we show an identical source Japanese sentence and each of its translations produced by the two versions of the proposed NMT systems, compared with translations produced by the three baselines, respectively. Figure 5 shows an example of correct translation produced by the proposed system in comparison to that produced by the baseline SMT. In this example, our model correctly translates the Japanese sentence into Chinese, whereas the translation by the baseline SMT is a translation error with several erroneous syntactic structures. As shown in Figure 6, the second example highlights that the proposed NMT system of Section 4.2 can correctly translate the Japanese technical term "貼り合わせウェーハ"(laminated wafer) to the Chinese technical term "贴合晶片". The translation by the baseline NMT is a translation error because of not only the erroneously translated unknown token but also the Chinese word "贴合的", which is not appropriate as a component of a Chinese technical term. Another example is shown in Figure 7, where we compare the translation of a reranking SMT 1,000-best

---

[13]https://www.jpo.go.jp/shiryou/toushin/chousa/pdf/tokkyohonyaku_hyouka/01.pdf　(in Japanese)

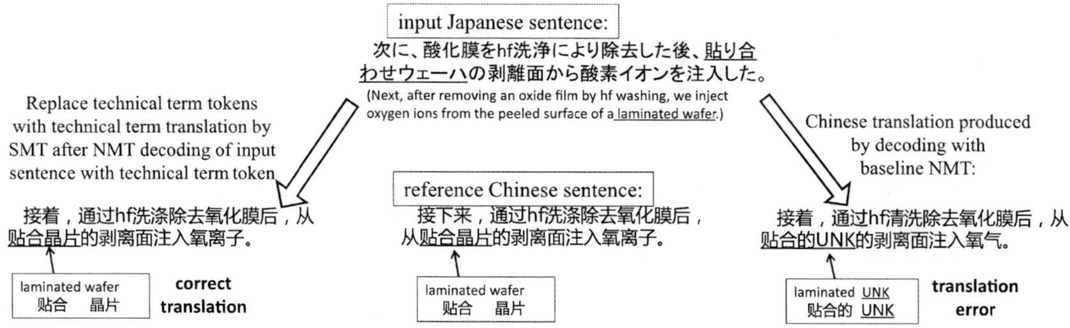

Figure 6: Example of correct translations produced by the proposed NMT system with SMT technical term translation (compared to decoding with the baseline NMT)

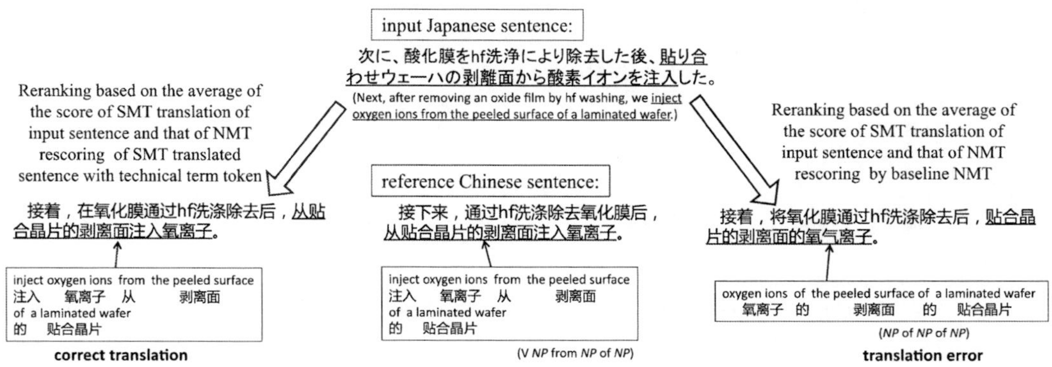

Figure 7: Example of correct translations produced by reranking the 1,000-best SMT translations with the proposed NMT system (compared to reranking with the baseline NMT)

translation produced by the proposed NMT system with that produced by reranking with the baseline NMT. It is interesting to observe that compared with the baseline NMT, we obtain a better translation when we rerank the 1,000-best SMT translations using the proposed NMT system, in which technical term tokens represent technical terms. It is mainly because the correct Chinese translation "晶片"(wafter) of Japanese word "ウェーハ" is out of the 40K NMT vocabulary (Chinese), causing reranking with the baseline NMT to produce the translation with an erroneous construction of "noun phrase of noun phrase of noun phrase". As shown in Figure 7, the proposed NMT system of Section 4.3 produced the translation with a correct construction, mainly because Chinese word "晶片"(wafter) is a part of Chinese technical term "贴合晶片"(laminated wafter) and is replaced with a technical term token and then rescored by the NMT model (with technical term tokens "TT_1", "TT_2", . . .).

6   Conclusion

In this paper, we proposed an NMT method capable of translating patent sentences with a large vocabulary of technical terms. We trained an NMT system on a bilingual corpus, wherein technical terms are replaced with technical term tokens; this allows it to translate most of the source sentences except the technical terms. Similar to Sutskever et al. (2014), we used it as a decoder to translate the source sentences with technical term tokens and replace the tokens with technical terms translated using SMT. We also used it to rerank the 1,000-best SMT translations on the basis of the average of the SMT score and that of NMT rescoring of translated sentences with technical term tokens. For the translation of Japanese patent sentences, we observed that our proposed NMT system performs better than the phrase-based SMT system as well as the equivalent NMT system without our proposed approach.

One of our important future works is to evaluate our proposed method in the NMT system proposed by Bahdanau et al. (2015), which introduced a bidirectional recurrent neural network as encoder and is the state-of-the-art of pure NMT system recently. However, the NMT system proposed by Bahdanau et al. (2015) also has a limitation in addressing out-of-vocabulary words. Our proposed NMT system is expected to improve the translation performance of patent sentences by applying approach of Bahdanau et al. (2015). Another important future work is to quantitatively compare our study with the work of Luong et al. (2015b). In the work of Luong et al. (2015b), they replace low frequency single words and translate them in a post-processing Step using a dictionary, while we propose to replace the whole technical terms and post-translate them with phrase translation table of SMT system. Therefore, our proposed NMT system is expected to be appropriate to translate patent documents which contain many technical terms comprised of multiple words and should be translated together. We will also evaluate the present study by reranking the n-best translations produced by the proposed NMT system on the basis of their SMT rescoring. Next, we will rerank translations from both the n-best SMT translations and n-best NMT translations. As shown in Section 5.3, the decoding approach of our proposed NMT system achieved the best RIBES performance and human evaluation scores in our experiments, whereas the reranking approach achieved the best performance with respect to BLEU. A translation with the highest average SMT and NMT scores of the n-best translations produced by NMT and SMT, respectively, is expected to be an effective translation.

References

D. Bahdanau, K. Cho, and Y. Bengio. 2015. Neural machine translation by jointly learning to align and translate. In *Proc. 3rd ICLR*.

K. Cho, B. van Merriënboer, C. Gulcehre, F. Bougares, H. Schwenk, and Y. Bengio. 2014. Learning phrase representations using rnn encoder-decoder for statistical machine translation. In *Proc. EMNLP*.

M. R. Costa-jussà and J. A. R. Fonollosa. 2016. Character-based neural machine translation. In *Proc. 54th ACL*, pages 357–361.

L. Dong, Z. Long, T. Utsuro, T. Mitsuhashi, and M. Yamamoto. 2015. Collecting bilingual technical terms from Japanese-Chinese patent families by SVM. In *Proc. PACLING*, pages 71–79.

S. Hochreiter and J. Schmidhuber. 1997. Long short-term memory. *Neural computation*, 9(8):1735–1780.

H. Isozaki, T. Hirao, K. Duh, K. Sudoh, and H. Tsukada. 2010. Automatic evaluation of translation quality for distant language pairs. In *Proc. EMNLP*, pages 944–952.

S. Jean, K. Cho, Y. Bengio, and R. Memisevic. 2014. On using very large target vocabulary for neural machine translation. In *Proc. 28th NIPS*, pages 1–10.

N. Kalchbrenner and P. Blunsom. 2013. Recurrent continous translation models. In *Proc. EMNLP*, pages 1700–1709.

P. Koehn, H. Hoang, A. Birch, C. Callison-Burch, M. Federico, N. Bertoldi, B. Cowan, W. Shen, C. Moran, R. Zens, C. Dyer, O. Bojar, A. Constantin, and E. Herbst. 2007. Moses: Open source toolkit for statistical machine translation. In *Proc. 45th ACL, Companion Volume*, pages 177–180.

X. Li, J. Zhang, and C. Zong. 2016. Towards zero unknown word in neural machine translation. In *Proc. 25th IJCAI*, pages 2852–2858.

M. Luong and C. D. Manning. 2016. Achieving open vocabulary neural machine translation with hybrid word-character models. In *Proc. 54th ACL*, pages 1054–1063.

M. Luong, H. Pham, and C. D. Manning. 2015a. Effective approaches to attention-based neural machine translation. In *Proc. EMNLP*.

M. Luong, I. Sutskever, O. Vinyals, Q. V. Le, and W. Zaremba. 2015b. Addressing the rare word problem in neural machine translation. In *Proc. 53rd ACL*, pages 11–19.

T. Nakazawa, H. Mino, I. Goto, G. Neubig, S. Kurohashi, and E. Sumita. 2015. Overview of the 2nd workshop on asian translation. In *Proc. 2nd WAT*, pages 1–28.

K. Papineni, S. Roukos, T. Ward, and W.-J. Zhu. 2002. BLEU: a method for automatic evaluation of machine translation. In *Proc. 40th ACL*, pages 311–318.

R. Sennrich, B. Haddow, and A. Birch. 2016. Neural machine translation of rare words with subword units. In *Proc. 54th ACL*, pages 1715–1725.

I. Sutskever, O. Vinyals, and Q. V. Le. 2014. Sequence to sequence learning with neural machine translation. In *Proc. 28th NIPS*.

H. Tseng, P. Chang, G. Andrew, D. Jurafsky, and C. Manning. 2005. A conditional random field word segmenter for Sighan bakeoff 2005. In *Proc. 4th SIGHAN Workshop on Chinese Language Processing*, pages 168–171.

M. Utiyama and H. Isahara. 2007. A Japanese-English patent parallel corpus. In *Proc. MT Summit XI*, pages 475–482.

Japanese-English Machine Translation of Recipe Texts

Takayuki Sato
Tokyo Metropolitan University
Tokyo, Japan
sato-takayuki@ed.tmu.ac.jp

Jun Harashima
Cookpad Inc.
Tokyo, Japan
jun-harashima@cookpad.com

Mamoru Komachi
Tokyo Metropolitan University
Tokyo, Japan
komachi@tmu.ac.jp

Abstract

Concomitant with the globalization of food culture, demand for the recipes of specialty dishes has been increasing. The recent growth in recipe sharing websites and food blogs has resulted in numerous recipe texts being available for diverse foods in various languages. However, little work has been done on machine translation of recipe texts. In this paper, we address the task of translating recipes and investigate the advantages and disadvantages of traditional phrase-based statistical machine translation and more recent neural machine translation. Specifically, we translate Japanese recipes into English, analyze errors in the translated recipes, and discuss available room for improvements.

1 Introduction

In recent years, an increasing amount of recipe data has become available on the web. For example, as of September 2016, more than 2.45 million recipes are available on cookpad, 1 million on Yummly, and 0.3 million on Allrecipes, to name a few. These recipes are from all over the world, and are written in various languages, including English and Japanese. However, language barriers may prevent the users from discovering recipes of local specialities.

Many researchers have focused on various tasks such as recipe analysis (Maeta et al., 2015), information retrieval (Yasukawa et al., 2014), summarization (Yamakata et al., 2013), and recommendation (Forbes and Zhu, 2011). However, to date, little work has been done on machine translation of recipe texts. In particular, Japanese foods are gaining popularity because they are considered healthy. We believe that many people would be able to use cooking recipes currently available only in Japanese if those Japanese recipes were translated into other languages.

In this study, we translated recipes via machine translation and investigated the advantages and disadvantages of machine translation in the recipe domain. First, we translated Japanese recipes into English using phrase-based statistical machine translation (PBSMT) and neural machine translation (NMT). Then, we classified translation errors into several categories in accordance with Multidimensional Quality Metrics (MQM) (Burchardt and Lommel, 2014). Finally, we analyzed the classified errors and discussed how to mitigate them.

2 Recipe Parallel Corpus

As described in the previous section, we focused on translating Japanese recipe texts into English, because almost all of the recipe texts on cookpad, which is one of the largest recipe sharing services in the world, are written in Japanese. We used a Japanese-English parallel corpus provided by Cookpad Inc. that includes $16,283$ recipes. Each recipe mainly consists of a title, ingredients, and steps. Examples of a title, an ingredient, and a step are shown in Table 1.[1] Unlike general parallel corpora, a translation pair of a step does not always consist of one parallel sentence. Examples of step texts in Table 1 show the case where there are two sentences in the translation pair.

---

[1] In this paper, we use the abbreviation of the cases: NOM (nominative), ACC (accusative), and TOP (topic marker).

Proceedings of the 3rd Workshop on Asian Translation,
pages 58–67, Osaka, Japan, December 11-17 2016.

Table 1: Examples of title, ingredient and step.

Title	簡単 シンプル！ふわふわ 卵 の オムライス easy simple ！ fluffy egg of omurice Easy and Simple Fluffy Omurice
Ingredient	ご飯（冷や ご飯 でも 可） rice (cold rice also available) Rice (or cold rice)
Step	ケチャップと　ソースを　混ぜ 合わせます．味見 しながら 比率 は　調節 してください． ketchup and sauce ACC mix ． taste while ratio TOP adjust please ． Mix the ketchup and Japanese Worcestershire-style sauce. Taste and adjust the ratio.

Table 2: Number of sentences and words in each field.

	Language	Title	Ingredient	Step	Total
sentence		$16,170$	$131,938$	$124,771$	$272,879$
word	Japanese	$115,336$	$322,529$	$1,830,209$	$2,268,074$
	English	$100,796$	$361,931$	$1,932,636$	$2,395,363$

These translation pairs were collected through the following two processes: translation and modification. First, a Japanese native speaker fluent in English translated Japanese recipes into English. Then, two native English speakers checked the translation and modified it as necessary. Note that the participants in these two processes were familiar with cooking.

We adopted the following three preprocessing procedures to this corpus in order to easily handle it. First, each Japanese text and its English translation in steps were split into sentences by a period. We used sentences that met the following conditions in our experiments: (1) the number of the split sentences in Japanese is the same as that in English or (2) there are exactly one Japanese and two English sentences. In the sentences in English that met the second condition, the first period was changed into ', and' to join two English sentences. This preprocessing excluded $25,654$ texts where there were $59,282$ Japanese step sentences and $57,016$ English step sentences. Second, we excluded sentence pairs where the longer sentence is more than two times longer than the other. This process is necessary because some English sentences were translated as simple expressions, and hence the ratio of the length of the sentence pairs was sometimes large. An example is shown below.

(1)　　関西 の　　お 店 の　味　！我が家 の　　お好み焼き　．
　　　kansai-style restaurant taste ！ my own home okonomiyaki ．
　　　kansai-style okonomiyaki ．

Third, sentences that contain more than 40 words were excluded from our experiments. Table 2 shows the number of sentences and words in each field after preprocessing. The size of the Japanese vocabulary was $23,519$, while that of the English vocabulary was $17,307$.

After prepossessing, we randomly chose 100 recipes as a development set ($1,706$ sentences) and 100 recipes as a test set ($1,647$ sentences). The former was used to tune our translation models, while the latter was used to analyze translation errors and to evaluate the translation models.

3　Machine Translation Methods

We used two methods in our experiments: PBSMT and NMT. The former has been widely accepted as one of the bases of machine translation systems that we generally use, whereas the latter has been gaining great attention in research community because of its fluency and simplicity.

PBSMT obtains a language model and a translation model (phrase table) from a parallel corpus and translates sentences based on these models (Koehn et al., 2003). The method achieves good performance on any language pair consisting of languages whose word orders are similar to each other, as in the case of English and French. Conversely, it performs poorly when the word orders of the languages differ, as in the case of English and Japanese. In addition, PBSMT often generates ungrammatical sentences because it does not consider syntactic information.

NMT embeds each source word into a d-dimensional vector and generates a target sentence from the vectors (Sutskever et al., 2014). Even though the method does not use any syntactic information, it can generate grammatical sentences. However, due to the execution time it requires, NMT generally limits the size of the vocabulary for a target language. Therefore, compared with PBSMT, which can handle many phrases in the target language, NMT has a disadvantage in that it cannot generate low frequent words. The method also has the disadvantage that it often generates target words that do not correspond to any words in the source sentences (Tu et al., 2016).

The setting for each method in this study was as follows. We used the parallel corpus described in Section 2 as our corpus, Moses (ver.2.1.1) (Koehn et al., 2007) as the PBSMT method, and conducted Japanese word segmentation using MeCab (Kudo et al., 2004) with IPADIC (ver.2.7.0) as the dictionary. Word alignment was obtained by running Giza++. The language model was learned with the English side of the recipe corpus using KenLM (Heafield, 2011) with 5-gram. Other resources in English were not used for training the language model because the style of recipe texts is different from general corpus in that it contains many noun phrases in title and ingredient, and many imperatives in step. The size of the phrase table was approximately 3 million pairs, and we used the development set to tune the weights for all features by minimum error rate training (MERT) (Och, 2003). We used the default parameter 6 for the distortion limit.

We reimplemented the NMT model in accordance with (Bahdanau et al., 2015). Note that we used long short-term memory (LSTM) (Hochreiter and Schmidhuber, 1997) instead of gated recurrent unit (Cho et al., 2014) for each recurrent neural network (RNN) unit of the model. The model had 512-dimensional word embeddings and 512-dimensional hidden units with one layer LSTM. We set the vocabulary size of the model to $30,000$, and we did not perform any unknown word processing during training. Adagrad (Duchi et al., 2011) was used with the initial learning rate of 0.01 as an optimization method. The initial values for word embeddings on both sides were obtained by training word2vec[2] with default setting because better results were shown in our preliminary experiments. The initial word embeddings on the source side were learned with a raw Japanese recipe corpus (Harashima et al., 2016) consisting of approximately 13 million step sentences. Conversely, initial word embeddings on the target side were learned with approximately $120,000$ English step sentences included in the parallel corpus. Title sentences were not used for learning because they were often written with free expression largely different depending on each recipe. Ingredient sentences were also not used because most of them consisted of a few words. The batch size was set to 64 and the number of epochs was set to 10. We selected the model that gave the highest BLEU score in the development set for testing. Beam search for decoding in NMT was not carried out. When testing, the output length was set up to 40 words.

Each output was evaluated via two metrics: bilingual evaluation understudy (BLEU) (Papineni et al., 2002) score and rank-based intuitive bilingual evaluation score (RIBES) (Isozaki et al., 2010). BLEU is more sensitive to word agreement than RIBES, whereas RIBES is more sensitive to word order evaluation. We set two hyper-parameters for RIBES: α was 0.25 and β was 0.10.

4 Error Classification of Recipe Translation

We conducted blackbox analysis on the outputs of PBSMT and NMT. Blackbox analysis is a type of analysis that does not take into account how translation output is obtained. The error classification used for this analysis is based on the MQM ANNOTATION DECISION TREE (Burchardt and Lommel, 2014) because it makes the classification of each error more consistent. The method classifies each error by following a decision tree where each node asks a Yes/No question. If the question is answered with a 'Yes', the corresponding text span is classified as the error specified by the tree node. When a text span is classified as an error at higher priority, that part is not classified as other errors. The same process continues until the lowest priority error is checked.

The error classification defined in MQM is roughly divided into two parts: Accuracy and Fluency. Accuracy addresses the extent to which the target text accurately renders the meaning of the source text. It is usually called 'Adequacy' in the literature. Fluency relates to the monolingual qualities of the target

---

[2]https://radimrehurek.com/gensim/models/word2vec.html

text. In this section, we explain the fine classification of accuracy and fluency metrics in detail and describe how to classify and analyze the errors.

4.1 Accuracy

In terms of accuracy, MQM defines (1) Omission, (2) Untranslated, (3) Addition, (4) Terminology, (5) Mistranslation and (6) General. In this study, we adapted the MQM ANNOTATION DECISION TREE to recipe translation to classify each error. We modified the original MQM ANNOTATION DECISION TREE in three different ways. First, we divided mistranslation errors into substitution and word order and considered them independently. This is because the tendency of substitution and word order is so different in a distant language pair such as Japanese and English that the difference should be reflected. Second, we defined a new order to classify each error, in which substitution and word order are given the highest priority. This makes the classification of substitution easy, especially for NMT, which sometimes outputs completely different target words from source sentences. Third, we excluded terminology because terminology-related errors do not occur when only a single domain, such as food recipes, is considered. Therefore, in this study, the following fine classification was applied: (1) Substitution, (2) Word order, (3) Omission, (4) Untranslated, (5) Addition, (6) General. Here, we explain the definition of each error classification with examples.

Accuracy (Substitution)   The target content does not represent the source content owing to inappropriate words. In the following example, 'Heat' is used for '割る' (break).

(2)   卵 を 割る .
        egg ACC break .
        Heat an egg .

Accuracy (Word order)   The target content does not represent the source content owing to inappropriate word positions. In the following example, 'from step 1' should be placed after 'into a bowl .'.

(3)   1 の 器 に レタスを 入れる .
        1 from bowl into lettuce ACC add   .
        Add the lettuce from step 1 into a bowl .

Accuracy (Omission)   Content in the source sentence is missing from the translation. In the following example, the translation does not contain a word for 'はちみつ' (honey).

(4)   はちみつ 生地 は 1 次 発酵   まで 済ませる .
        honey   dough ACC first fermenatation until finish   .
        Make the dough until the first rising .

Accuracy (Untranslated)   Source words have been left untranslated. From the following example, it can be seen that there is an untranslated word '狭い' (narrow).

(5)   長 さ を 整え , 幅 の 狭いほうで カット する .
        length ACC adjust , width NOM narrow   with cut   .
        Adjust the length , and cut the 狭い into it .

Accuracy (Addition)   The translation includes words or phrases that are not present in the source sentence. In the following example, 'red' and 'into a pot' should not have been added.

(6)   ソース を 加える .
        sauce   ACC add   .
        Add the red sauce into a pot .

Accuracy (General)   It is applied when the translation error is difficult to classify into a certain category in terms of accuracy. The number of errors is counted by phrases in the source that are not represented in the target. In the following example, there are four errors.

(7)   出来上がっ た 時に 倒れ ない ため です ．
       finished   when fall not   for   ．
       It will be hard to cover the cake .

4.2   Fluency

In terms of fluency, MQM defines (1) Word order, (2) Word form, (3) Function words, (4) Grammar general, (5) Fluency general. Here, we explain the definition of each error classes with examples.

Grammar (Word order)   The word order is incorrect. In the following example, the position of the word 'place' is incorrect and is considered to be before the word 'parts'. The number of errors equals the number of content words at wrong positions.

(8)   Parts of the face , place on a baking sheet .

Grammar (Word form)   The wrong form of a word is used. The following example includes one error because 'uses' is incorrect.

(9)   I uses the dough for step 4 .

Grammar (Function Words)   This is a misuse of function words such as preposition, particle, and pronoun. From the following example, it can be seen that the function word 'to' is unnecessary.

(10)   It 's finished to .

Grammar (General)   In addition to the errors identified above, there are other grammatical errors such as insertion and omission of unnecessary content words. In the following example, there is not a verb.

(11)   The honey dough for the first rising .

Fluency (General)   Even when a sentence is grammatically correct, it may have some issues in terms of fluency. The sentence used as the example of this category is unintelligible because of the phrase 'from the cake'. For each unintelligible phrase, we count content words in it as errors (in this case, 'cake' and 'future.').

(12)   I was going to be taken from the cake in the future .

5   Results and Discussion

We translated Japanese sentences in the corpus described in Section 2 into English sentences following the procedure described in Section 3. We then evaluated the outputs with automatic evaluation metrics, BLEU and RIBES. Finally, we discussed the results for each type of sentence, title, ingredient, and step. The outputs were also analyzed following the error classification procedure outlined in Section 4. Note that all the recipes in the test set were used for the automatic evaluation and 25 recipes randomly chosen from the test set were used for error analysis.

5.1   Automatic Evaluation

The results obtained following automatic evaluation by BLEU and RIBES are shown in Table 3.

Title is represented with a relatively large vocabulary and free expression largely different depending on each recipe. In other words, it includes low frequent expressions. The percentage of the number of sentences for which title accounts is very low compared with ingredient and step as shown in Table 2. Hence, the translation of title is more difficult than that of ingredient and step owing to data sparsity.

Table 3: Automatic evaluation BLEU/RIBES results.

Method	Title	Ingredient	Step	Total
PBSMT	**22.15 / 61.85**	**56.10 / 90.03**	25.37 / 74.98	**28.09 / 81.72**
NMT	19.68 / 61.49	55.75 / 89.70	**25.68 / 77.84**	28.01 / 82.79

Table 4: Number of accuracy errors in 25 recipes.

Method	Substitution	Word order	Omission	Untranslated	Addition	General	Total
PBSMT	49 (11.0%)	98 (21.9%)	139 (31.1%)	23 (5.1%)	95 (21.3%)	43 (9.6%)	447
NMT	102 (19.2%)	20 (3.8%)	176 (33.1%)	0 (0.0%)	114 (21.5%)	119 (22.4%)	531

PBSMT shows better performance for title translation than NMT both in BLEU and RIBES, because it is possible for PBSMT to partially translate title using the phrase table created from infrequent expressions. On the other hand, some NMT outputs are very short and do not include any word that corresponds to any source words. It resulted in poor performance of BLEU.

Ingredient has very short sentences, with an average length of 3.0 words. In addition, there are not many translation candidates for each ingredient. Consequently, the BLEU and RIBES scores for both methods are very high. Although the margin between PBSMT and NMT is small, PBSMT exhibited better performance in both metrics. Translating the names of ingredients was similar to translation using a dictionary, at which PBSMT is better.

In the translation of step, NMT shows better performance than PBSMT in BLEU and RIBES. When several nouns are enumerated, the reordering distance tends to be long because the target sentence is usually written in imperative form. However, it appears that NMT does not have any difficulty in translating such sentences. This is because NMT is good at modeling long dependencies owing to the use of RNN. There is also a case where omission occurs in a source sentence and zero-anaphora and/or coreference resolution will be required to generate the omitted word in a target sentence. It appears difficult for both methods to output a word for the omitted word but NMT tended to estimate more words than PBSMT.

Finally, let us look at the results for RIBES. It is possible that RIBES is a metric that can be higher for NMT than for PBSMT. NMT tends to output shorter sentences than the references. Conversely, PBSMT does not output sentences that are as short as those of NMT because it ensures that all the source phrases are translated. However, the default parameter of RIBES optimized for patent translation (Isozaki et al., 2010) does not significantly penalize omission errors that frequently occur in NMT. Instead, it penalizes substitution errors and word order errors, which are abundant in PBSMT. This suggests that we need to investigate a better evaluation metric for assessing the quality of NMT.

5.2 Error Analysis

5.2.1 Accuracy

The number of accuracy errors is shown in Table 4. Compared with NMT, PBSMT has many errors related to the word order. In general, PBSMT exhibits poor results against syntactically different language pairs because reordering words is difficult in such cases. As the sentence length becomes longer, word order errors increase, because reordering words becomes more difficult. The majority of the corpus used in this study comprised short sentences, especially for title and ingredient. Ingredient sentences are very short and title sentences are relatively short. The average length of step sentences is also not so long, and is 14.0 words in Japanese and 15.0 words in English. However, many steps are written in imperative order form in English. Consequently, even when the sentence length is short, inevitably a word order error occurs because word reordering frequently occurs in the case of long distances. The example below is a part of a sentence in which some ingredients are enumerated; thus, PBSMT has difficulty in reordering word positions.

(13)   4 の   鍋 に 1 の   ブリ   & 3 の   大根   & しいたけ   & 生姜 を
          4 from pan to 1 from amberjack and 3 from daikon radish and shiitake mashrooms and ginger ACC
          入れ ,
          add ,
          PBSMT: Amberjack and daikon radish and shiitake mushrooms , and add the ginger from step 1
          to the pan from step 3

This error is frequently seen because the names of ingredients often appear in steps. It appears that the solution in order for PBSMT to handle these errors requires a translation model with a syntactic rule such as a constituent structure or dependency structure.

On the other hand, NMT has many more errors in terms of substitution than with PBSMT. In substitution, there were errors in which the meanings of the source word and the target word were not similar at all. For example, 'sweet potato' was output as the translated word for 'キャベツ' (cabbage). To solve this problem, the use of lexicon probability obtained from a phrase table or a dictionary is considered promising for the NMT model (Arthur et al., 2016).

There were many omission errors and addition errors in both PBSMT and NMT. In particular, omission errors account for a large percentage in both methods. The following example shows that omission errors or addition errors occur in either, or both methods.

(14)   ホーム ベーカリー の 生地 作り コース で   生地 を   作る .
          bread maker   of dough setting   with dough ACC make.
          PBSMT: Make the dough in the bread maker to make the dough.
          NMT: Make the dough using the dough setting.
          Reference: Use the bread dough function on the bread maker to make the bread dough.

In terms of omission or addition errors, PBSMT and NMT output errors occur in the same sentences although the error positions are different. In the example above, omission of '生地 作り コース' (dough setting) and addition of 'to make' and 'the dough' are seen in the PBSMT output. On the other hand, NMT omits the translation of 'ホーム ベーカリー の' (on the bread maker). Thus, it appears that sentences in which machine translation output errors occur in both methods are somewhat similar.

Addition is seen in a sentence where an object in Japanese is omitted. Recipe steps in Japanese tend to omit words that have already appeared in the same recipe. In the translation of such sentences, some words should be inserted in the target sentence. An example is given below.

(15)   紙   に包んで ,
          paper in wrap   ,
          NMT: Wrap the cake in the cake paper,
          Reference: Wrap the cakes in parchment paper,

This sentence does not contain the source word that corresponds to 'the cake', but the word exists in the reference. NMT succeeded in generating 'the cake' in this example. However, in general, performing zero-anaphora resolution for inter-sentential arguments is difficult. NMT is more promising than PBSMT in terms of modeling of long dependency to estimate omitted arguments. It appears important to take into account the ingredients used or the order in which actions are completed in the flow of the recipe.

Although 'untranslated' is considered an error that occurs only in PBSMT, the ratio proves to be very low. The corpus used in this study did not have a large vocabulary; therefore, the words that appeared in the training dataset include almost all of the words in the test set. Therefore, untranslated errors rarely occurred in this dataset.

5.2.2 Fluency

The number of fluency errors is shown in Table 5. Word order errors appear to have occurred for the same reason as word order errors that adversely affect accuracy.

Few word form errors were seen in both methods. There was little ambiguity in tense, because title and ingredient are mostly noun phrases, and most of the steps are written in imperative form. In addition, disagreement between subject and verb or that of tense rarely occurred, because most of the subjects

Table 5: Number of fluency errors in 25 recipes.

| Method | Grammar | | | | Fluency | Total |
	Word order	Word form	Function words	General	General	
PBSMT	18 (14.0%)	2 (1.6%)	24 (18.6%)	73 (56.9%)	12 (9.3%)	129
NMT	4 (4.8%)	1 (1.2%)	6 (7.2%)	17 (20.5%)	55 (66.3%)	83

corresponded to ingredients, which are expressed in third person singular.

More function word errors were seen in PBSMT than in NMT. The main class of word error encountered was the addition of an unnecessary function word. The reason for this appears to be the noise in the phrase extraction process when creating a phrase table. Output consisting of phrases with noise can be avoided by taking syntactic constraints into account. In the following example, 'in' is an inappropriate word:

(16)   PBSMT: Remove the sinew from the chicken tenders and fold <u>in</u> lightly .

The errors in grammar in general were mainly errors related to a content word. In particular, omission and addition of a noun and a verb are observed in many outputs. This appears to have the same cause as function word errors. The following example shows the omission of a verb:

(17)   PBSMT: Basic chiffon cake milk to make the dough .

The output of NMT has many unintelligible sentences that are classified under fluency general. NMT outputs a few grammar-related errors, such as word order, function word, and grammar general. Repetition of the same word and phrase were commonly seen in NMT but never in PBSMT.

(18)   NMT: leave to steam for about 2 hours , and open the pot , <u>and open the pot</u> .

6   Related Work

In machine translation in the recipe domain, solving zero-anaphora analysis problems appears to be essential because some of step sentences have an order relationship in which reference is made to words that have previously appeared, especially ingredients with zero pronouns. In other words, better translation performance can be obtained if ingredients in the flow of the recipe are correctly detected. Mori et al. (2014) annotated a role label for each ingredient in a monolingual recipe corpus to model the recipe flow. If the information is appropriately adapted to the machine translation process well, some problems encountered by the machine translation systems in the recipe domain can be solved.

Bentivogli et al. (2016) conducted error analysis of PBSMT and NMT with the English-German language pair. THe authors were the first to work on error analysis of NMT and also with PBSMT and tree-based statistical machine translation in which they analyzed errors in several ways. The automatic evaluation metrics used in their study were BLEU and two types of modified translation error rate (TER) (Snover et al., 2006): Human-targeted TER and Multi-reference TER. For analysis of linguistic errors, three error categories were used: morphology errors, lexical errors and word order errors. In terms of word order errors, they also conducted fine-grained word order error analysis in which they took part-of-speech tagging and dependency parsing into account.

Ishiwatari et al. (2016) used the same recipe corpus as we used for domain adaptation of SMT without a sentence-aligned parallel corpus. In their research, the MT system was trained only with an out-domain corpus that consisted of words related to Japanese history and the temples of shrines in Kyoto. Then, they adapted the MT system to a recipe corpus in which there were many words that did not appear in the out-domain corpus, using count-based vectors to translate unknown words. Although their method performed well in the translation of the out-domain corpus, it did not focus on recipe translation itself.

7 Conclusion and Future Work

In this paper, we proposed a new task of translating cooking recipes. We translated Japanese recipes into English using PBSMT and NMT and evaluated the outputs with BLEU and RIBES. Further, we discussed the tendency observed by studying the outputs. Each of three parts comprising a recipe (title, ingredient, and step) had its own characteristics. Title proved difficult to translate owing to a relatively large vocabulary despite its limited length. Good performance was achieved in the translation of ingredient because it is very simply written compared with title and step. In translating step, PBSMT and NMT exhibited different tendencies. Many word order errors were found in PBSMT outputs corresponding to step, resulting in a lower score for RIBES in PBSMT than in NMT.

Error analysis of the outputs was also conducted with the error classification expanded from the MQM ANNOTATION DECISION TREE. The results of the error analysis showed that the tendency of each type of errors differs according to the translation method applied. Compared with that of NMT, the output of PBSMT contained many grammatical errors. On the other hand, NMT had more substitution errors than PBSMT. NMT also tended to output target words that differ in meaning form the original source word. In addition, although the outputs of NMT were usually grammatically correct, some of them were unintelligible. Many omission errors and addition errors were found in both methods.

As our future work, we plan to tackle on the machine translation of recipe texts, taking into account the ingredients used and the order in which actions are completed in the flow of the recipe. It may be possible to solve omission errors in either or both sides using the information. To achieve that, we also need to perform machine translation without sentence-alignment, but with the whole document.

Acknowledgement

This research was (partly) supported by Grant-in-Aid for Research on Priority Areas, Tokyo Metropolitan University, "Research on social big data."

References

Philip Arthur, Graham Neubig, and Satoshi Nakamura. 2016. Incorporating Discrete Translation Lexicons into Neural Machine Translation. In *Proceedings of the 2016 Conference on Empirical Methods in Natural Language Processing (EMNLP)*, pages 1557–1667.

Dzmitry Bahdanau, Kyunghyun Cho, and Yoshua Bengio. 2015. Neural Machine Translation by Jointly Learning to Align and Translate. In *5th International Conference on Learning Representations (ICLR)*.

Luisa Bentivogli, Arianna Bisazza, Mauro Cettolo, and Marcello. 2016. Neural versus phrase-based machine translation quality: a case study. In *Proceedings of the 2016 Conference on Empirical Methods in Natural Language Processing (EMNLP)*, pages 257–267.

Aljoscha Burchardt and Arle Lommel. 2014. Practical Guidelines for the Use of MQM in Scientific Research on Translation Quality. Technical report, QTLaunchPad.

Kyunghyun Cho, Bart van Merrienboer, Caglar Gulcehre, Dzmitry Bahdanau, Fethi Bougares, Holger Schwenk, and Yoshua Bengio. 2014. Learning Phrase Representations using RNN Encoder-Decoder for Statistical Machine Translation. In *Proceedings of the 2014 Conference on Empirical Methods in Natural Language Processing (EMNLP)*, pages 1724–1734.

John Duchi, Elad Hazan, and Yoram Singer. 2011. Adaptive Subgradient Methods for Online Learning and Stochastic Optimization. In *Journal of Machine Learning Research 12*, pages 2121–2159.

Peter Forbes and Mu Zhu. 2011. Content-boosted Matrix Factorization for Recommender Systems: Experiments with Recipe Recommendation. In *Proceedings of the 5th ACM Conference on Recommender Systems (RecSys)*, pages 261–264.

Jun Harashima, Michiaki Ariga, Kenta Murata, and Masayuki Ioki. 2016. A Large-Scale Recipe and Meal Data Collection as Infrastructure for Food Research. In *Proceedings of the 10th International Conference on Language Resources and Evaluation (LREC)*, pages 2455–2459.

Kenneth Heafield. 2011. Kenlm: Faster and smaller language model queries. In *Proceedings of the 6th Workshop on Statistical Machine Translation*, pages 187–197.

Sepp Hochreiter and Jurgen Schmidhuber. 1997. LONG SHORT-TERM MEMORY. In *Neural Computation 9*, pages 1735–1780.

Shonosuke Ishiwatari, Naoki Yoshinaga, Masashi Toyoda, and Masaru Kitsuregawa. 2016. Instant Translation Model Adaptation by Translating Unseen Words in Continuous Vector Space. In *The 17th International Conference on Intelligent Text Processing and Computational Linguistics (CICLing)*.

Hideki Isozaki, Tsutom Hirao, Kevin Duh, Katsuhito Sudoh, and Hajime Tsukada. 2010. Automatic Evaluation of Translation Quality for Distant Language Pairs. In *Proceedings of the 2010 Conference on Empirical Methods in Natural Language Processing (EMNLP)*, pages 944–952.

Philipp Koehn, Franz Josef Och, and Daniel Maruc. 2003. Statistical phrase-based translation. In *Proceedings of the 2003 Human Language Technology Conference of the North American Chapter of the Association for Computational Linguistics (HLT-NAACL)*, pages 48–54.

Philipp Koehn, Hieu Hoang, Alexandra Birch, Chris Callison-Burch, Marcello Federico, Nicola Bertoldi, Brooke Cowan, Wade Shen, Christine Moran, and Richard Zens. 2007. Moses: Open Source Toolkit for Statistical Machine Translation. In *Proceedings of the 45th Annual Meeting of the Association for Computational Linguistics Companion Volume Proceedings of the Demo and Poster Sessions*, pages 177–180.

Taku Kudo, Kaoru Yamamoto, and Yuji Matsumoto. 2004. Applying Conditional Random Fields to Japanese Morphological Analysis. In *Proceedings of the 2004 Conference on Empirical Methods in Natural Language Processing (EMNLP)*, pages 230–237.

Hirokuni Maeta, Tetsuro Sasada, and Shinsuke Mori. 2015. A Framework for Procedural Text Understanding. In *Proceedings of the 14th International Conference on Parsing Technologies (IWPT)*, pages 50–60.

Shinsuke Mori, Hirokuni Maeta, Yoko Yamakata, and Tetsuro Sasada. 2014. Flow Graph Corpus from Recipe Texts. In *Proceedings of the 9th International Conference on Language Resources and Evaluation (LREC)*, pages 2370–2377.

Franz Josef Och. 2003. Minimum Error Rate Training in Statistical Machine Translation. In *Proceedings of the 41st Annual Meeting of the Association for Computational Linguistics (ACL)*, pages 160–167.

Kishore Papineni, Salim Roukos, Todd Ward, and Wei-Jing Zhu. 2002. BLEU: A Method for Automatic Evaluation of Machine Translation. In *Proceedings of the 40st Annual Meeting of the Association for Computational Linguistics (ACL)*, pages 138–145.

Matthew Snover, Bonnie Dorr, Richard Schwartz, Linnea Micciulla, and John Makhoul. 2006. A Study of Translation Edit Rate with Targeted Human Annotation. In *Proceedings of the Biennial Conference of the Association for Machine Translation in the Americas (AMTA)*, pages 223–231.

Ilya Sutskever, Oriol Vinyals, and Quoc V. Le. 2014. Sequence to Sequence Learning with Neural Networks. In *In Advances in Neural Information Processing Systems 27 (NIPS)*, pages 3104–3112.

Zhaopeng Tu, Zhengdong Lu, Yang Liu, Xiaohua Liu, and Hang Li. 2016. Modeling Coverage for Neural Machine Translation. In *Proceedings of the 54th Annual Meeting of the Association for Computational Linguistics (ACL)*, pages 177–180.

Yoko Yamakata, Shinji Imahori, Yuichi Sugiyama, Shinsuke Mori, and Katsumi Tanaka. 2013. Feature Extraction and Summarization of Recipes using Flow Graph. In *Proceedings of the 5th International Conference on Social Informatics (SocInfo)*, pages 241–254.

Michiko Yasukawa, Fernando Diaz, Gregory Druck, and Nobu Tsukada. 2014. Overview of the NTCIR-11 Cooking Recipe Search Task. In *Proceedings of the 11th NTCIR Conference (NTCIR-11)*, pages 483–496.

IIT Bombay's English-Indonesian submission at WAT: Integrating Neural Language Models with SMT

Sandhya Singh   **Anoop Kunchukuttan**   **Pushpak Bhattacharyya**
Center for Indian Language Technology
Department of Computer Science & Engineering
Indian Institute of Technology Bombay
{sandhya, anoopk, pb}@cse.iitb.ac.in

Abstract

This paper describes the IIT Bombay's submission as a part of the shared task in WAT 2016 for English–Indonesian language pair. The results reported here are for both the direction of the language pair. Among the various approaches experimented, Operation Sequence Model (OSM) and Neural Language Model have been submitted for WAT. The OSM approach integrates translation and reordering process resulting in relatively improved translation. Similarly the neural experiment integrates Neural Language Model with Statistical Machine Translation (SMT) as a feature for translation. The Neural Probabilistic Language Model (NPLM) gave relatively high BLEU points for Indonesian to English translation system while the Neural Network Joint Model (NNJM) performed better for English to Indonesian direction of translation system. The results indicate improvement over the baseline Phrase-based SMT by 0.61 BLEU points for English-Indonesian system and 0.55 BLEU points for Indonesian-English translation system.

1   Introduction

This paper describes IIT Bombay's submission for the English-Indonesian and Indonesian-English language pairs for the shared task in the 3rd Workshop on Asian Translation[1] (WAT) (Nakazawa et al., 2016).

Every language pair in machine translation brings in new challenges in the form of their linguistic features. The Indonesian language, also known as Bahasa(Indonesia) is the official language of Indonesia. It is the fourth most populous country[2] in the world with approximately 190 million[3] people speaking this language. The language belongs to the Austronesian language family and has a lot of influence from Dutch language. It is also considered mutually intelligible with the Malay language. The script used is Roman/Latin script. The sentence structure followed is similar to English language i.e. Subject Verb Object (SVO). But it is highly agglutinative and morphologically rich as compared to English language. Hence, English-Indonesian is a very important language pair for translation studies.

There is very limited work related to Indonesian language machine translation. Some of the previous work done is discussed here. Yulianti et al. (2011) experimented with a hybrid MT system (HMT) for Indonesian-English translation. They created a pipeline system where the input is first translated using a rule based MT system (RBMT) and the output is further processed with statistical MT system (SMT) to improve the translation quality. The results indicate that a pure SMT system outperforms HMT system in all cases. Larasati (2012) focused on resources and tool preparation for Indonesian-English SMT system as the author described this language pair as under-resourced and

---

[2] http://www.infoplease.com/world/statistics/most-populous-countries.html

[3] https://en.wikipedia.org/wiki/Indonesian_language

Proceedings of the 3rd Workshop on Asian Translation,
pages 68–74, Osaka, Japan, December 11-17 2016.

under-studied. MorphInd, a morphanalyzer was developed as a part of the experiment. The tool could give more morphological information at a word level compared to its previous versions. The author also developed a standard parallel corpus IDENTIC, which could be used by the research community for MT related task. The experiment with preprocessed Indonesian data resulted in an improved SMT system output. Mantoro et al. (2013) attempted to find the optimal parameter for English-Indonesian SMT system by varying the weights of translation model, language model, distortion (reordering) and word penalty. And the optimally tuned SMT system is able to give a BLEU score of 22.14. Above discussed work clearly indicate that there is a lot of scope for experimentation for this language pair.

Recently, Hermanto et al.(2015) performed an experimental study with RNN language model for English-Indonesian MT system. The experiment was done on a very small set of data for neural LM and the output was compared with SMT system trained on same data. The perplexity analysis of both the systems show that RNN model system outperforms SMT system with n-gram LM.

The results of Hermanto et al.(2015) and various other research outcomes on different language pair using neural language model motivated our approach of experimentation using NLM and NNJM as a feature in SMT.

2   System Description

For our participation in WAT 2016 shared task for English ←→ Indonesian language pair, we experimented with the following systems –

1. *Phrase-Based SMT system* : This was our baseline system for the WMT shared task. The standard Moses Toolkit (Koehn et al., 2007) was used with MGIZA++ (Gao and Vogel, 2008) for word alignment on training corpus followed by *grow-diag-final-and* symmetrization heuristics for extracting phrases and lexicalized reordering. Tuning was done using Batch MIRA (Cherry and Foster, 2012) with the default 60 passes over the data and *–return-best-dev* flag to get the highest scoring run into the final moses.ini file. A 5-gram language model using SRILM toolkit (Stolcke, 2002) with Kneser-Ney smoothing was trained.

2. *Use of Neural Language Model* : A neural probabilistic language model was trained and integrated as a feature for the phrase-based translation model. For this, the default NPLM[4] implementation in Moses which is similar to the method described in Vaswani et al. (2013) was used. The goal was to examine if neural language models can improve the fluency for Indonesian-English translation and English-Indonesian translation by making use of distributed representations. We experimented with various word embedding sizes of 700, 750 and 800 for the first hidden layer in the network to get the optimal parameter while decoding.

3. *Use of Bilingual Neural Joint Language Model* : Devlin et al. (2014) have shown that including source side context information in the neural language model can lead to substantial improvement in translation quality. We experimented with Devlin's method which uses NPLM[3] in the back-end to train a neural network joint language model (NNJM) using parallel data and integrated it as a feature for the phrase-based translation as implemented in Moses. A 5-gram language model augmented with 9 source context words and single hidden layer required for fast decoding was used as a parameter to train the joint model.

4. *Use of Operational Sequence Model* : Operation sequence model was trained as it integrates N-gram-based reordering and translation in a single generative process which can result in relatively improved translation over phrase based system. OSM approach as suggested in Durrani et al. (2013) considers both source and target information for generating a translation. It deals with minimum translation units i.e. words, along with context information of source and target sentence which spans across phrasal boundries. A 5-gram OSM was used for the experimentation here.

---

[4] http://nlg.isi.edu/software/nplm/

These 4 systems were trained for both directions of language pair and the test data was decoded and evaluated with BLEU points, RIBES scores, AMFM scores, Pairwise crowdsourcing scores and Adequacy scores for comparative performance evaluation.

3   Experimental Setup

The data provided for the WAT 2016 shared task experiment for English-Indonesian language pair comprised of news domain data with a good mix of finance, international, science, national and sports news. The data was prepared using the scripts available with moses. After extracting the data in individual files for training, tuning and testing purpose, it was tokenized and truecased using the learnt truecased model. The training data was further cleaned for the maximum sentence length of 80 words.

For training the neural language model (Vaswani et al., 2013), additional monolingual data was used for each direction of language pair. For Indonesian-English, additional 2 million sentences of English Europarl data[5] was used for the experimentation. The data was tokenized and truecased for the experiment. For English-Indonesian direction, additional 2 million Indonesian sentences from Commoncrawl[6] was used for experiment. Since Commoncrawl provides raw data by web scraping, the Indonesian data obtained was cleaned for noisy sentences and then tokenized and truecased for training the language model. Table – 1 gives the statistics of the data used for experimentation.

Language	Training Set	Tuning Set	Test Set	For LM
English	44939 sentences	400 sentences	400 sentences	50000 sentences + 2M sentences (Europarl)
Indonesian	44939 sentences	400 sentences	400 sentences	50000 sentences + 2M sentences (Commoncrawl)

Table 1. Data used for the experiments

For training the joint neural language model (Devlin et al., 2014), the parallel data used for training the SMT system was used to train the bilingual neural language model.

4   Results & Analysis

4.1   Indonesian to English MT system

A comparative performance of baseline phrase based system, OSM system and neural LM and with joint neural LM for Indonesian-English MT system have been shown in Table-2. The translated output of all the three systems trained are evaluated for Bilingual Evaluation Understudy (BLEU), Rank-based Intuitive Bilingual Evaluation Score (RIBES) and Adequacy-Fluency Metric (AMFM).

For OSM experiment, a 5-gram operation sequence model was trained with the default settings of phrase based system as discussed in section 2. The BLEU scores shows a relative improvement of 0.21 points over the baseline phrase based system. The output of this system was submitted for human evaluation process for this direction of language pair.

For neural LM system, a 5-gram model with a vocabulary size of 100K and word embedding

---

[5] http://www.statmt.org/europarl/

[6] http://commoncrawl.org/

dimensions of 150 units in second hidden layer was trained with 3 different first hidden layer parameter i.e. 700 units, 750 units , 800 units. The aim was to use the most fitting model for decoding.

The model was optimized for only 5 epochs of stochastic gradient ascent due to time constraint with small batch sizes of 1000 words. The neural model obtained was added to moses.ini file as a feature with a default weight of 0.5. The translation model was tuned further to get better weights for all the parameters required of the translation system.

Approach Used	BLEU score	RIBES score	AMFM score
Phrase based SMT	22.03	0.78032	0.564580
Operation Sequence Model*	22.24	0.781430	0.566950
Neural LM with OE= 700	**22.58**	0.781983	**0.569330**
Neural LM with OE = 750	21.99	0.780901	0.56340
Neural LM with OE = 800	22.15	**0.782302**	0.566470
Joint Neural LM	22.05	0.781268	0.565860

Table 2. Experiment Results for Indonesian-English MT system
(OE – Output Embeddin; * : submitted to WAT)

Similarly, the joint neural LM using the bilingual data was also trained with the source and target vocabulary size of 100K and total n-gram size of 14 comprising of 5-gram target language model and 9-gram source context window with word embedding dimension of 750 units for the single hidden layer. The neural model obtained was included in the moses.ini file as a feature with default weight as 0.5. This decoding model was tuned further to learn the new weights with added feature and then used for translation.

Reference Sentence	Translated Sentence	Error Analysis
Moreover, syariah banking has yet to become a national agenda, Riawan said.	In addition, the banking industry had not so national agenda, said Riawan who also director of the main BMI.	Phrase insertion
Of course, we will adhere to the rules, Bimo said.	We will certainly *patuhi* regulations, Bimo said.	All words not translated
The Indonesian government last year canceled 11 foreign-funded projects across the country for various reasons, the Finance Ministry said.	The government has cancel foreign loans from various creditors to 11 projects in 2006 because various reasons.	Phrase dropped
As the second largest Islamic bank with a 29% market share of the Islamic banking industry's total assets at end-2007 albeit only 0.5% of overall banking industry's total assets, net financing margin NFM on Muamalat's financing operations increased to 7.9% in 2007 from 6.4% in 2004 due to better funding structure.	As the second largest bank of the market by 29 percent of the total assets syariah banking loans at the end of December 2007 although the market only 0.5 percent of the total assets banking industry as a whole, financing profit margin Muamalat rose to 7.9 percent in 2007 from 6.4 percent in 2004 thanks to funding structure.	Phrase dropped

Table 3. Indonesian-English NPLM based MT system output

The scores clearly indicate that both the approaches of LM i.e. neural LM generated from much bigger monolingual corpus or joint neural LM outperforms the baseline phrase-based SMT system. For WAT, the neural LM with word embedding dimensions of 700 units for the first hidden layer is submitted for participation. The BLEU score shows an improvement of 0.55 points over our baseline system. These scores may be improved with further tuning of the neural parameters.

Some translation outputs of relatively better performing NPLM system compared against the reference sentences have been given in Table-3. An analysis of the translation output was done for NPLM based Indonesian-English MT system. The output sentences were adequate and fluent to some extent. The major error found was of dropping and insertion of phrases. In some instances, the Indonesian words could not be translated to English due to lack of vocabulary learnt. Though, OOV word percentage was found to be 5% of the total words in the test set. Another major pattern error was in the choice of function words used for English language. This error might require some linguistic insight on the Indonesian side of the language pair to understand the usage of function words in the source language.

4.2   English to Indonesian MT system

For the reverse direction of language pair i.e. English-Indonesian, similar set of experiments were performed with same parameters as mentioned in section 4.1. The results obtained for the baseline phrase-based system, OSM based system, neural LM with additional monolingual data from commoncrawl with 3 different parameter variations and joint neural LM system have been given in Table-4. Since the authors do not know the Indonesian language, the translated output could not be manualy evaluated for error analysis at authors' end.

For this direction of language pair, the scores of OSM experiment is comaparable to baseline phrase based system with a score of 21.70 BLEU points. However, the joint neural language model has outperformed the neural LM and the baseline system by 0.61 BLEU scores. Joint neural LM output was submitted for manual evaluation.

Approach Used	BLEU score	RIBES score	AMFM score
Phrase based SMT	21.74	0.804986	0.55095
Operation Sequence Model	21.70	0.806182	0.552480
Neural LM with OE = 700	22.12	0.804933	0.5528
Neural LM with OE =750	21.64	0.806033	0.555
Neural LM with OE = 800	22.08	0.806697	0.55188
Joint neural LM*	**22.35**	**0.808943**	**0.55597**

Table 4. Experiment Results for English-Indonesian MT system

(OE – Output Embedding; * : submitted to WAT)

4.3   Human Evaluation Result Analysis

As a part of shared task evaluation process, the translation system performance was human evaluated using two methods: pairwise crowdsourcing evaluation compared against the baseline system and JPO adequacy evaluation for content transmission.

For Indonesian-English system, human evaluation was done on OSM system output. The crowdsourcing results show that 20% of the translations were better than the baseline system, 34% translations were comparable and 46% were worse than the baseline system. The system scored -26.00 in the crowdsourcing evaluation and 2.98 in adequacy evaluation. Table-5 shows the adequacy score distribution as received in JPO adequacy evaluation. However, the automatic evaluation scores are found to be comparable to the baseline system.

Experiment	Approach Followed	Adequacy distribution					Adequacy Score
		5	4	3	2	1	
Indonesian-English	OSM approach	12%	18.75%	31.75%	30.5%	7%	2.98
English-Indonesian	NNJM	17.75%	25.25%	23.25%	16.5%	17.25%	3.10

Table 5. JPO Adequacy scores for English↔Indonesian

The joint neural LM approach for English-Indonesian system was submitted for human evaluation. The human evaluation scores shows that 23% of the translation were better than the baseline system, 44.75% were in tie with baseline system and 32.25% were worse than the baseline system. The crowdsourcing evaluation score is -9.250 and adequacy evaluation score is 3.10. For the JPO adequacy score, we observed that 33% sentences have at least 3 point difference between the annotator scores. The scores received have been given in Table-5.

5   Conclusion and future work

In our research group, we have been working on a usecase related to English-Indonesian Machine Translation. This motivated us to participate in this shared task despite of having no exposure to Indonesian language. Since no member of the team had any previous experience with Indonesian language, not much of the linguistic insight was used in performing the experiments. This was an enriching experience in the terms of using computational ability for machine translation with minimum linguistic insight of one of the language in pair for translation. The BLEU scores show that using neural LM helps in improving the translation quality .

In future , we would like to investigate the hyperparameters for the neural language model. We also plan to look at pure neural machine translation approaches for the English-Indoneian language pair.

Reference

Bahdanau, Dzmitry, Kyunghyun Cho, and Yoshua Bengio. 2015. *"Neural machine translation by jointly learning to align and translate."* In ICLR.

Cherry, Colin, and George Foster. 2012. *"Batch tuning strategies for statistical machine translation."* Proceedings of the 2012 Conference of the North American Chapter of the Association for Computational Linguistics: Human Language Technologies. Association for Computational Linguistics.

Devlin, Jacob, Rabih Zbib, Zhongqiang Huang, Thomas Lamar, Richard M. Schwartz, and John Makhoul. 2014. *"Fast and Robust Neural Network Joint Models for Statistical Machine Translation."* In conference of the Association of Computational Linguistics.

Durrani, Nadir, Helmut Schmid, and Alexander Fraser. 2011. *"A joint sequence translation model with integrated reordering."* Proceedings of the 49th Annual Meeting of the Association for Computational Linguistics: Human Language Technologies-Volume 1. Association for Computational Linguistics.

Durrani, Nadir, Alexander M. Fraser, and Helmut Schmid. 2013. *"Model With Minimal Translation Units, But Decode With Phrases."* HLT-NAACL.

Durrani, N., Fraser, A. M., Schmid, H., Hoang, H., & Koehn, P. 2013. *" Can markov models over minimal translation units help phrase-based smt?. "* In conference of the Association of Computational Linguistics .

Gao, Qin, and Stephan Vogel. 2008. *"Parallel implementations of word alignment tool."* Software Engineering, Testing, and Quality Assurance for Natural Language Processing. Association for Computational Linguistics.

Hermanto, Andi, Teguh Bharata Adji, and Noor Akhmad Setiawan. 2015. *"Recurrent neural network language model for English-Indonesian Machine Translation: Experimental study."* 2015 International Conference on Science in Information Technology (ICSITech). IEEE.

Koehn, Philipp, Hieu Hoang, Alexandra Birch, Chris Callison-Burch, Marcello Federico, Nicola Bertoldi, Brooke Cowan. 2007. *"Moses: Open source toolkit for statistical machine translation."* In Proceedings of the 45th annual meeting of the ACL on interactive poster and demonstration sessions. Association for Computational Linguistics.

Larasati, Septina Dian. 2012. *"Towards an Indonesian-English SMT system: A case study of an understudied and under-resourced language, Indonesian."* WDS'12 Proceedings of Contributed Papers 1.

Mantoro, Teddy, Jelita Asian, Riza Octavian, and Media Anugerah Ayu. 2013. *"Optimal translation of English to Bahasa Indonesia using statistical machine translation system."* In Information and Communication Technology for the Muslim World (ICT4M), 2013 5th International Conference of IEEE.

Nakazawa, Toshiaki and Mino, Hideya and Ding, Chenchen and Goto, Isao and Neubig, Graham and Kurohashi, Sadao and Sumita, Eiichiro. 2016. *"Overview of the 3rd Workshop on Asian Translation."* Proceedings of the 3rd Workshop on Asian Translation (WAT2016), October.

Niehues, Jan, Teresa Herrmann, Stephan Vogel, and Alex Waibel. 2011. *"Wider context by using bilingual language models in machine translation."* InProceedings of the Sixth Workshop on Statistical Machine Translation. Association for Computational Linguistics.

Schwenk, Holger. 2012. *"Continuous Space Translation Models for Phrase-Based Statistical Machine Translation."* COLING (Posters).

Stolcke, Andreas. 2002. *"SRILM-an extensible language modeling toolkit."* Interspeech. Vol. 2002.

Vaswani, Ashish, Yinggong Zhao, Victoria Fossum, and David Chiang. 2013. *"Decoding with Large-Scale Neural Language Models Improves Translation."* In *EMNLP*.

Yulianti, Evi, Indra Budi, Achmad N. Hidayanto, Hisar M. Manurung, and Mirna Adriani. 2011. *"Developing Indonesian-English Hybrid Machine Translation System."* In Advanced Computer Science and Information System (ICACSIS), 2011 International Conference of IEEE.

Domain Adaptation and Attention-Based Unknown Word Replacement in Chinese-to-Japanese Neural Machine Translation

Kazuma Hashimoto, Akiko Eriguchi, and Yoshimasa Tsuruoka

The University of Tokyo, 7-3-1 Hongo, Bunkyo-ku, Tokyo, Japan

`{hassy, eriguchi, tsuruoka}@logos.t.u-tokyo.ac.jp`

Abstract

This paper describes our UT-KAY system that participated in the Workshop on Asian Translation 2016. Based on an Attention-based Neural Machine Translation (ANMT) model, we build our system by incorporating a domain adaptation method for multiple domains and an attention-based unknown word replacement method. In experiments, we verify that the attention-based unknown word replacement method is effective in improving translation scores in Chinese-to-Japanese machine translation. We further show results of manual analysis on the replaced unknown words.

1 Introduction

End-to-end Neural Machine Translation (NMT) with Recurrent Neural Networks (RNNs) is attracting increasing attention (Sutskever et al., 2014). By incorporating attention mechanisms (Bahdanau et al., 2015), NMT models have achieved state-of-the-art results on several translation tasks, such as English-to-German (Luong et al., 2015a) and English-to-Japanese (Eriguchi et al., 2016) tasks.

Although NMT is attractive due to its translation quality and relatively simple architecture, it is known to have some serious problems including unknown (or rare) word problems (Luong et al., 2015b). Thus, there is still room for improvement in many aspects of NMT models. In our UT-KAY system that participated in the Workshop on Asian Translation 2016 (WAT 2016) (Nakazawa et al., 2016a), we investigate the following two issues:

- adaptation with multiple domains, and

- attention-based unknown word replacement.

Our system is based on an Attention-based NMT (ANMT) model (Luong et al., 2015a). To explicitly treat translation pairs from multiple domains, our system extends a domain adaptation method for neural networks (Watanabe et al., 2016), and apply it to the baseline ANMT model. To address the unknown word problems in translated sentences, we investigate the effectiveness of replacing each unknown word according to the attention scores output by the baseline ANMT model.

In experiments, we apply our system to a Chinese-to-Japanese translation task of scientific text. Our experimental results show that the attention-based unknown word replacement method consistently improves the BLEU scores by about 1.0 for the baseline system, the domain adaptation system, and the ensemble of the two systems. Moreover, our manual analysis on the replaced unknown words indicates that the scores can be further improved if a high quality dictionary is available. While the domain adaptation method does not improve upon the baseline system in terms of the automatic evaluation metrics, the ensemble of the systems with and without the domain adaptation method boosts the BLEU score by 2.7. As a result, our UT-KAY system has been selected as one of the top three systems in the Chinese-to-Japanese task at WAT 2016.

2 Related Work

2.1 Domain Adaptation for Sentence Generation Tasks

An NMT model is usually built as a single large neural network and trained using a large parallel corpus. Such a parallel corpus is, in general, constructed by collecting sentence pairs from a variety of domains

Proceedings of the 3rd Workshop on Asian Translation,
pages 75–83, Osaka, Japan, December 11-17 2016.

(or topics), such as computer science and biomedicine. Sentences in different domains have different word distributions, and it has been shown that domain adaption is an effective way of improving image captioning models, which perform sentence generation like NMT models (Watanabe et al., 2016). Luong and Manning (2015) proposed pre-training techniques using a large general domain corpus to perform domain adaptation for NMT models. However, both of these approaches assume that there are only two domains, i.e., the source and target domains. In practice, there exist multiple topics, and thus the explicit use of information about multiple domains in the NMT models is worth investigating.

2.2 Unknown Word Replacement in NMT

Previous approaches to unknown word problems are roughly categorized into three types: character-based, subword-based, and copy-based approaches. The character-based methods aim at building word representations for unknown words by using character-level information (Luong and Manning, 2016). The character-based methods can handle any words and has achieved better results than word-based methods. However, the computational cost grows rapidly.

Recently, Sennrich et al. (2016) have shown that the use of subword units in NMT models is effective. The subword units can treat multiple levels of granularity existing in words and reduce the size of the vocabulary compared with the standard word-based models. However, the rules to use the subword units are built based on the training data, and thus there still remains the problem of treating an infinite number of the unknown words.

The copy-based methods aim at copying relevant source words to replace unknown words. Some use existing alignment tools (Luong et al., 2015b), and others suggest that using attention scores in the ANMT models can be an alternative to using alignment tools (Jean et al., 2015). The copy-based method should be effective in translation tasks where characters and words are shared across different languages. However, to the best of our knowledge, there is no previous work which inspects the replacement results based on the attention mechanism to investigate the relevance of the replacement method in ANMT models.

3 The UT-KAY System at WAT 2016

In this section, we describe our UT-KAY system at WAT 2016. We first describe the baseline method for our system in Section 3.1 and then explain how our system works in Section 3.2, 3.3, and 3.4.

3.1 Baseline Methods

3.1.1 Attention-Based Sequential NMT

We employ an ANMT model presented in Luong et al. (2015a) as our baseline and follow the single-layer setting as in Eriguchi et al. (2016). Let us represent the source sentence of length M by word sequence $\boldsymbol{x} = (x_1, x_2, \ldots, x_M)$ and its corresponding target sentence of length N by word sequence $\boldsymbol{y} = (y_1, y_2, \ldots, y_N)$. For embedding the source word sequence $\boldsymbol{x}$ into a d_h-dimensional vector space, Long Short-Term Memory (LSTM) units are used as follows:

$$s_i = \mathrm{LSTM}(s_{i-1}, v(x_i)), \tag{1}$$

where s_i and $s_{i-1} \in \mathbb{R}^{d_h \times 1}$ are the i-th and $(i-1)$-th hidden states, s_0 is filled with zeros, and $v(x_i) \in \mathbb{R}^{d_e \times 1}$ is the d_e-dimensional word embedding of the i-th source word x_i. The LSTM function is formulated with internal states, called *memory cells*, as follows:

$$
\begin{aligned}
i_i &= \sigma(U_s^i s_{i-1} + V_s^i v(x_i) + b_s^i), &\quad f_i &= \sigma(U_s^f s_{i-1} + V_s^f v(x_i) + b_s^f), \\
o_i &= \sigma(U_s^o s_{i-1} + V_s^o v(x_i) + b_s^o), &\quad u_i &= \tanh(U_s^u s_{i-1} + V_s^u v(x_i) + b_s^u), \\
c_i &= i_t \odot u_i + f_i \odot c_{i-1}, &\quad s_i &= o_i \odot \tanh(c_i),
\end{aligned}
\tag{2}
$$

where $U_s \in \mathbb{R}^{d_h \times d_h}$, $V_s \in \mathbb{R}^{d_h \times d_e}$, $b_s \in \mathbb{R}^{d_h \times 1}$ are the LSTM's weight matrices and bias vectors, and $c_i \in \mathbb{R}^{d_h \times 1}$ is the memory cell. The operator $\odot$ denotes element-wise multiplication and $\sigma(\cdot)$ is the logistic sigmoid function.

Once s_M, which represents the entire source sentence x, is obtained for representing the source sentence x, the ANMT model estimates the conditional probability that the j-th target word y_j is generated given the target word sequence $(y_1, y_2, \ldots, y_{j-1})$ and the source sentence x:

$$p(y_j | y_1, y_2, \ldots, y_{j-1}, x) = \mathrm{softmax}(W_p \tilde{t}_j + b_p), \tag{3}$$

where $W_p \in \mathbb{R}^{|\mathbb{V}_t| \times d_h}$ and $b_p \in \mathbb{R}^{|\mathbb{V}_t| \times 1}$ are an weight matrix and a bias vector, $\mathbb{V}_t$ is the target word vocabulary, and $\tilde{t}_j \in \mathbb{R}^{d_h \times 1}$ is the hidden state for generating the j-th target word. In general, the target word vocabulary $\mathbb{V}_t$ is constructed by a pre-defined number of the most frequent words in the training data, and the other words are mapped to a special token *UNK* to indicate that they are unknown words. $\tilde{t}_j$ is conditioned by the j-the hidden state $t_j \in \mathbb{R}^{d_h \times 1}$ of another LSTM RNN and an attention vector $a_j \in \mathbb{R}^{d_h \times 1}$ as follows:

$$t_j = \mathrm{LSTM}(t_{j-1}, [v(y_{j-1}); \tilde{t}_{j-1}]), \tag{4}$$

$$a_j = \sum_{i=1}^{M} \alpha_{(j,i)} s_i, \tag{5}$$

$$\tilde{t}_j = \tanh(W_t t_j + W_a a_j + b_{\tilde{t}}), \tag{6}$$

where $[v(y_{j-1}); \tilde{t}_{j-1}] \in \mathbb{R}^{(d_e + d_h) \times 1}$ is the concatenation of $v(y_{j-1})$ and $\tilde{t}_{j-1}$, and $W_t \in \mathbb{R}^{d_h \times d_h}$, $W_a \in \mathbb{R}^{d_h \times d_h}$, and $b_{\tilde{t}} \in \mathbb{R}^{d_h \times 1}$ are weight matrices and a bias vector. To use the information about the source sentence, t_1 is set equal to s_M. The attention score $\alpha_{(j,i)}$ is used to estimate how important the i-th source-side hidden state s_i is, for predicting the j-the target word:

$$\alpha_{(j,i)} = \frac{\exp(t_j \cdot s_i)}{\sum_{k=1}^{M} \exp(t_j \cdot s_k)}, \tag{7}$$

where $t_j \cdot s_k$ is the dot-product used to measure the relatedness between the two vectors.

All of the model parameters in the ANMT model are optimized by minimizing the following objective function:

$$J(\theta) = -\frac{1}{|\mathcal{T}|} \sum_{(x,y) \in \mathcal{T}} \sum_{j=1}^{N} \log p(y_j | y_1, y_2, \ldots, y_{j-1}, x), \tag{8}$$

where θ denotes the set of the model parameters, and $\mathcal{T}$ is the set of source and target sentence pairs to train the model.

3.1.2 Domain Adaptation for Neural Networks by Feature Augmentation

To learn translation pairs from multiple domains, we employ a domain adaptation method which has proven to be effective in neural image captioning models (Watanabe et al., 2016). It should be noted that neural image captioning models can be formulated in a similar manner to NMT models. That is, if we use images as source information instead of the source sentences, the task is then regarded as an image captioning task. We use the corresponding equations in Section 3.1.1 to describe the domain adaptation method by assuming that x is a representation of an image.

The method assumes that we have data from two domains: $\mathcal{D}_1$ and $\mathcal{D}_2$. The softmax parameters (W_p, b_p) in Equation (3) are separately assigned to each of the two domains, and the parameters $(W_p^{\mathcal{D}_1}, b_p^{\mathcal{D}_1})$ and $(W_p^{\mathcal{D}_2}, b_p^{\mathcal{D}_2})$ are decomposed into two parts as follows:

$$W_p^{\mathcal{D}_1} = W_p^{\mathcal{G}} + \overline{W}_p^{\mathcal{D}_1}, \quad b_p^{\mathcal{D}_1} = b_p^{\mathcal{G}} + \overline{b}_p^{\mathcal{D}_1}, \quad W_p^{\mathcal{D}_2} = W_p^{\mathcal{G}} + \overline{W}_p^{\mathcal{D}_2}, \quad b_p^{\mathcal{D}_2} = b_p^{\mathcal{G}} + \overline{b}_p^{\mathcal{D}_2}, \tag{9}$$

where $(W_p^{\mathcal{G}}, b_p^{\mathcal{G}})$ is the shared component in $(W_p^{\mathcal{D}_1}, b_p^{\mathcal{D}_1})$ and $(W_p^{\mathcal{D}_2}, b_p^{\mathcal{D}_2})$, and $(\overline{W}_p^{\mathcal{D}_1}, \overline{b}_p^{\mathcal{D}_1})$ and $(\overline{W}_p^{\mathcal{D}_2}, \overline{b}_p^{\mathcal{D}_2})$ are the domain-specific components. Intuitively, the shared component learns general information across multiple domains, and the domain-specific components learn domain-specific information.

The model parameters are optimized by replacing the negative log-likelihood in Equation (8) as follows:

$$-\frac{1}{2}\log p^{\mathcal{G}}(y_j|y_1, y_2, \ldots, y_{j-1}, \boldsymbol{x}) - \frac{1}{2}\log p^{\mathcal{D}_1}(y_j|y_1, y_2, \ldots, y_{j-1}, \boldsymbol{x}), \tag{10}$$

$$-\frac{1}{2}\log p^{\mathcal{G}}(y_j|y_1, y_2, \ldots, y_{j-1}, \boldsymbol{x}) - \frac{1}{2}\log p^{\mathcal{D}_2}(y_j|y_1, y_2, \ldots, y_{j-1}, \boldsymbol{x}), \tag{11}$$

where the first one is used for data from $\mathcal{D}_1$, and the second one is used for data from $\mathcal{D}_2$. The probabilities $p^{\mathcal{G}}, p^{\mathcal{D}_1}, p^{\mathcal{D}_2}$ are computed by replacing $(\boldsymbol{W}_p, \boldsymbol{b}_p)$ in Equation (3) with $(2\boldsymbol{W}_p^{\mathcal{G}}, 2\boldsymbol{b}_p^{\mathcal{G}})$, $(2\overline{\boldsymbol{W}}_p^{\mathcal{D}_1}, 2\overline{\boldsymbol{b}}_p^{\mathcal{D}_1})$, $(2\overline{\boldsymbol{W}}_p^{\mathcal{D}_2}, 2\overline{\boldsymbol{b}}_p^{\mathcal{D}_2})$, respectively. At test time, we only use $(\boldsymbol{W}_p^{\mathcal{D}_1}, \boldsymbol{b}_p^{\mathcal{D}_1})$ and $(\boldsymbol{W}_p^{\mathcal{D}_2}, \boldsymbol{b}_p^{\mathcal{D}_2})$ to compute the output probabilities.

3.2 Adaptation with Multiple Domains

The domain adaptation method described in Section 3.1.2 assumes that we have only two domains, namely, source and target domains, but in practice we can have many domains. In this paper, we extend the domain adaptation method in order to treat data from multiple domains. Assuming that we have data from K domains $\mathcal{D}_1, \mathcal{D}_2, \ldots, \mathcal{D}_K$, we decompose the softmax parameters for the K domains in exactly the same way as Equation (9). That is, we have $K + 1$ softmax parameters: $(\boldsymbol{W}_p^{\mathcal{G}}, \boldsymbol{b}_p^{\mathcal{G}}), (\overline{\boldsymbol{W}}_p^{\mathcal{D}_1}, \overline{\boldsymbol{b}}_p^{\mathcal{D}_1}), \ldots, (\overline{\boldsymbol{W}}_p^{\mathcal{D}_K}, \overline{\boldsymbol{b}}_p^{\mathcal{D}_K})$.

The reformulated objective function in the domain adaptation method can be optimized in the same way as the ANMT model, and to speed up the training, we apply *BlackOut* (Ji et al., 2016), a sampling-based approximation method for large vocabulary language modeling, as in Eriguchi et al. (2016). More specifically, we independently approximate the output probabilities $p^{\mathcal{G}}, p^{\mathcal{D}_1}, \ldots, p^{\mathcal{D}_K}$ using BlackOut sampling. To sample negative examples, we use the global unigram distribution computed by using all data from all the K domains.

3.3 Attention-Based Unknown Word Replacement

As described in Section 3.1.1, the ANMT model computes an attention score $\alpha_{(j,i)}$ to estimate how important the i-th hidden state in the source-side LSTM is for generating the j-th target word. Although the attention mechanism is not designed as word alignment in traditional statistical machine translation, it is observed that high attention scores are often assigned to word-level translation pairs (Bahdanau et al., 2015).

In this paper, we investigate the effectiveness of using the attention scores to replace unknown words in translated sentences with words in source sentences. For each unknown word *UNK* in a translated sentence, we replace it with the source word having the highest attention score. That is, we replace the j-th target word (*UNK*) with the k-th source word when $\alpha_{(j,k)}$ is the highest among $\alpha_{(j,i)}$ $(1 \leq i \leq M)$.

3.4 Ensemble

At test time, we employ two separate ensemble techniques.

3.4.1 Ensemble of Output Probabilities

The first one is a widely-used technique which takes the average of output probabilities for generating target words. Here we can treat each NMT model as a black box to output a word probability distribution and take the average of the probabilities from all of the models:

$$\frac{1}{L}\sum_{k=1}^{L} p_k(y_j|y_1, y_2, \ldots, y_{j-1}, \boldsymbol{x}), \tag{12}$$

where p_k is the probability from the k-th NMT model, and L is the number of NMT models we have.

3.4.2 Ensemble of Attention Scores

When generating target sentences using the ensemble technique described in Section 3.4.1, we have L set of attention scores, assuming that we use the ANMT models. We use the averaged attention scores over the L set of attention scores each time we replace an unknown word by the method described in Section 3.3. It should be noted that the two ensemble techniques in this section are separately used and thus the attention scores are *not* averaged during the sentence generation step.

4 Experimental Settings

4.1 Data

At WAT 2016, there are several tasks for several language pairs. In this work, we choose the ASPEC Chinese-to-Japanese (ASPEC-CJ) translation task[1] (Nakazawa et al., 2016b) as our first step to investigate the effectiveness of our system. The ASPEC-CJ dataset includes sentences from multiple domains with annotations, and the language pair shares the same Chinese characters. There are 10 predefined domain tags: *Abs, AGS, BIO, CHEM, ENE, ENVI, INFO, MATE, MED, SP*. We treated Abs, BIO, and MED as a single domain, and also INFO and SP.[2] Consequently, the number of the domains was 7 in our experiments.

The training data includes 672,315 sentence pairs, the development data includes 2,090 sentence pairs, and the test data includes 2,107 sentence pairs. We used all of the training data to train the ANMT models, and built the source and target vocabularies using the words which appear in the training data more than twice. Consequently, the source vocabulary has 94,961 words and the target vocabulary has 69,580 words, including the UNK token and a special token for representing the end of sentences *EOS* for each vocabulary. The source and target words were obtained using the Kytea tool and the Stanford Core NLP tool, respectively.[3]

4.2 Parameter Optimization and Translation

We set the dimensionality of word embeddings and hidden states to 512 (i.e., $d_e = d_h = 512$), and we used single-layer LSTMs. All of the model parameters, except for the bias vectors and weight matrices of the softmax layer, were initialized with uniform random values from $[-1.0, 1.0]$. The bias vectors and the softmax weight were initialized with zeros. For the BlackOut approximation method, we set the number of negative samples to 2,000, and the objective function was optimized via mini-batch stochastic gradient descent. The mini-batch size was 128 without any constraints, such as lengths of the sentences in each mini-batch. All of the mini-batches were constructed randomly at the beginning of each epoch. For each mini-batch, the gradients were divided by the mini-batch size, and then the L2 norm of the gradients was clipped to 3. The initial learning rate was 1.0 and it was multiplied by 0.75 to decrease the learning rate when the perplexity for the development data did not improve. We checked the perplexity for the development data after each epoch.[4]

To generate the target sentences, we used the beam search strategy based on the statistics of the sentence lengths as in Eriguchi et al. (2016). We set the beam size to 20, and after generating the sentences using the beam search, we applied the attention-based unknown word replacement method to the unknown words output by the system.

5 Results and Discussion

5.1 Main Results

Table 1 shows our experimental results in terms of BLEU and RIBES scores for the development and test data. In the table, the results of the best systems at WAT 2015 and WAT 2016, Neubig et al. (2015) and Kyoto-U, are also shown. These results are the Kytea-based evaluation results. First, we can see

---

[1] http://lotus.kuee.kyoto-u.ac.jp/ASPEC/
[2] The categorization was based on personal communication with the organizer of WAT 2016.
[3] http://www.phontron.com/kytea/ and http://stanfordnlp.github.io/CoreNLP/.
[4] Our system was implemented using our CPU-based neural network library: https://github.com/hassyGo/N3LP.

Method	Dev. data		Test data	
	BLEU	RIBES	BLEU	RIBES
(1) ANMT	38.09	83.67	-	-
(2) ANMT w/ UNK replacement	39.05	83.98	39.06	84.23
(3) ANMT w/ domain adaptation	38.28	83.83	-	-
(4) ANMT w/ domain adaptation and UNK replacement	39.24	84.20	39.07	84.21
(5) Ensemble of (1) and (3)	40.66	84.91	-	-
(6) Ensemble of (1) and (3) w/ UNK replacement	41.72	85.25	41.81	85.47
The best system at WAT 2015 (Neubig et al., 2015)	-	-	42.95	84.77
The best system at WAT 2016 (Kyoto-U, NMT)	-	-	46.70	87.29

Table 1: Kytea-based BLEU and RIBES scores for the development and test data on the ASPEC-CJ task. The results (4) and (6) were submitted to the official evaluation system.

that the attention-based unknown word replacement method (*UNK replacement* in the table) consistently improves the BLEU scores by about 1.0, and the RIBES scores by about 0.3 for the development data. Next, currently we have not observed significant improvement by using the domain adaptation method, in terms of the BLEU and RIBES scores. Finally, the ensemble of the two ANMT models with and without domain adaptation consistently improves the translation scores, and in particular, the BLEU score improves by about 2.7, and the RIBES score improves by about 1.2. In most of previous work on NMT models, the ensemble is performed by using exactly the same models with different parameter initialization settings. By contrast, we performed the ensemble using two different models with different objective functions, and observed large gains for the BLEU scores.

The Kyoto-U system achieved the best results at WAT 2016, and it is also based on NMT. The system's scores are much better than ours. As shown in the system description on the official website, the system seems to be based on sophisticated methods, such as "reverse scoring", which should be helpful in improving our system. In general, results of NMT models highly depend not only on such techniques, but also on their model settings, such as the number of RNN layers and dimensionality of embeddings and hidden states. Thus, it is not surprising that the two NMT-based systems produce such different scores.

5.2 Analysis on Attention-Based Unknown Word Replacement

To inspect the results of the attention-based unknown word replacement method, we manually checked the translated sentences of the development data. In the translated sentences in our best result by the method (6), we found 690 sentences which include unknown words. Among them, we sampled 132 sentences including 250 unknown words. Then we categorized all the cases into five types as follows:

(A) Correct   A replacement case is categorized as (A) if the replaced word is picked up from its relevant position in its source sentence and exactly the same as the corresponding word in its reference translation. Thus, type (A) contributes to improving BLEU scores.

(B) Acceptable   A replacement case is categorized as (B) if the replaced word is picked up from its relevant position, but it is not the same as the reference word while it fits the translated Japanese sentence. That is, type (B) is semantically acceptable, but it does not contribute to improving BLEU scores.

(C) Correct with word translation   A replacement case is categorized as (C) if the replaced word is picked up from its relevant position, but it is a Chinese word which should be translated into its corresponding Japanese words.

(D) Partially correct   A replacement case is categorized as (D) if the replaced word is picked up from its relevant position but some words are missing. Thus, it cannot be regarded as a sufficient translation.

Type	Count	Ratio
(A) Correct	76	30.4%
(B) Acceptable	5	2.0%
(C) Correct with word translation	104	41.6%
(D) Partially correct	50	20.0%
(E) Incorrect	15	6.0%
Total	250	100.0%

Table 2: Analysis on the attention-based unknown word replacement method for 250 replacements in 132 translated sentences of the development data.

R. 1	Yukon や北西領域，Hudson や James 湾，北部ケベック，ラブラドール，グリーンランドの汚染物質に関する情報を，文献，組織，研究者から広範囲に収集した。
T. 1	Yukon(A) と北西分野，Hudson(A) と James(A) 湾，北部の 魁北克(C)，拉布拉多(C)，Greenland(B) の汚染物質の情報について文献，組織，研究者から広範囲の収集を行った。
R. 2	高尾山の環境保全と京王の社会貢献
T. 2	高 尾山(A) の環境保全と 京(D) の社会貢献

Table 3: Examples of the unknown word replacements.

(E) Incorrect   A replacement case is categorized as (E) if the replaced word is picked up from an irrelevant position and it does not make sense in its translated sentence.

Table 2 shows the results of the manual analysis on the 250 cases. We can see that about 30% of the unknown word replacements are categorized as (A), which leads to the improvement of the BLEU score by 1.06 (40.66→41.72) in Table 1. The majority is type (C), and thus it is still room for improvement in the results by combining external resources like word-level dictionaries.[5] These results suggest that the attention-based unknown word replacement method can be a simple way for improving translation results in Chinese-to-Japanese translation, and the method can be used in any attention-based NMT models.

Table 3 shows two examples of the translated sentences which include unknown words, and for each example, its reference translation (**R.**) and its translation result (**T.**) are shown. The replaced unknown words are underlined with their corresponding replacement types. In the first example, there are six unknown words, and all of them are categorized as (A), (B), or (C), which means that the ANMT model can distinguish between different unknown words even though all of them are represented with the special token *UNK*. The replaced Chinese word "魁北克" means "Quebec" and "ケベック" in English and Japanese, respectively, and "拉布拉多" means "Labrador" and "ラブラドール" in English and Japanese, respectively. The two replacements are categorized as (C) because they need to be translated into their corresponding Japanese words. The word "Greenland" means "グリーンランド" in Japanese, and it seems that some English words are also used in the reference sentences. Thus we categorized this case as (B).

In the second example, there are two unknown words, and both of them are related to named entities; "高尾山" is a Japanese mountain and "京王" is a Japanese company. However, as opposed to our expectation, "高尾山" is split into "高" and "尾山", and "京王" is split into "京" and "王". As a result, the unknown word replacement method picks up only a part of the word "京王", which leads to an insufficient translation (categorized as (D)). These results suggest that improving the accuracy of the word segmentation will lead to better translation results by the ANMT models.

5.3   Analysis on Domain Adaptation

We inspected the BLEU scores for development data of each domain. Tabe 4 shows the results of the methods (2), (4), and (6) presented in Table 1 and the number of sentence pairs for each domain. From

---

[5]We tried to automatically build a dictionary using a word alignment tool, but the word segmentation results were so noisy that we could not obtain informative dictionary.

		BIO	CHEM	ENE	ENVI	INFO	MATE
	Method (2)	35.27	37.24	39.74	36.21	41.91	34.92
BLEU	Method (4)	34.86	33.96	40.37	37.16	41.58	37.80
	Method (6)	37.84	42.77	43.64	39.29	44.17	38.65
# of samples in the development data		216	19	37	804	982	32

Table 4: BLEU scores for the development data of each domain.

these results we can see that the domain adaptation method (Method (4)) performs better than the baseline method (Method (2)) in some domains, but not in others. The ensemble result (Method (6)) consistently improves the results for all of the domains.

We expect the domain adaptation method to disambiguate the meaning of a word according to its context. For example in Table 3, both of the Japanese words "領域" and "分野" mean "field" and "area" but their meanings depend on their context. In such a case, the domain or context information should be helpful in disambiguating the meanings. However, none of our methods could successfully output the appropriate word "領域". To investigate the result, we inspected the usage of the Japanese word "領域" in the training data, and found that similar usages to the above example were rare. Therefore, this *rare usage problem* would be addressed, not by the domain adaptation method, but by adding large monolingual data to make the language modeling more accurate.

6   Conclusion

This system description paper presented our UT-KAY system based on an attention-based neural machine translation model. We investigated the effectiveness of a domain adaptation method and an attention-based unknown word replacement method. The domain adaptation method does not currently lead to better results than our baseline model. By contrast, we have found that the attention-based unknown word replacement has potential benefits in Chinese-to-Japanese NMT models, which can be applied to any attention-based models.

Acknowledgments

This work was supported by CREST, JST.

References

Dzmitry Bahdanau, Kyunghyun Cho, and Yoshua Bengio. 2015. Neural Machine Translation by Jointly Learning to Align and Translate. In *Proceedings of the 3rd International Conference on Learning Representations*.

Akiko Eriguchi, Kazuma Hashimoto, and Yoshimasa Tsuruoka. 2016. Tree-to-Sequence Attentional Neural Machine Translation. In *Proceedings of the 54th Annual Meeting of the Association for Computational Linguistics (Volume 1: Long Papers)*, pages 823–833.

Sébastien Jean, Orhan Firat, Kyunghyun Cho, Roland Memisevic, and Yoshua Bengio. 2015. Montreal Neural Machine Translation Systems for WMT ' 15. In *Proceedings of the Tenth Workshop on Statistical Machine Translation*, pages 134–140.

Shihao Ji, S. V. N. Vishwanathan, Nadathur Satish, Michael J. Anderson, and Pradeep Dubey. 2016. BlackOut: Speeding up Recurrent Neural Network Language Models With Very Large Vocabularies. In *Proceedings of the 4th International Conference on Learning Representations*.

Minh-Thang Luong and Christopher D. Manning. 2015. Stanford Neural Machine Translation Systems for Spoken Language Domains. In *Proceedings of the 12th International Workshop on Spoken Language Translation*, pages 76–79.

Minh-Thang Luong and Christopher D. Manning. 2016. Achieving Open Vocabulary Neural Machine Translation with Hybrid Word-Character Models. In *Proceedings of the 54th Annual Meeting of the Association for Computational Linguistics (Volume 1: Long Papers)*, pages 1054–1063.

Minh-Thang Luong, Hieu Pham, and Christopher D. Manning. 2015a. Effective Approaches to Attention-based Neural Machine Translation. In *Proceedings of the 2015 Conference on Empirical Methods in Natural Language Processing*, pages 1412–1421.

Minh-Thang Luong, Ilya Sutskever, Quoc Le, Oriol Vinyals, and Wojciech Zaremba. 2015b. Addressing the Rare Word Problem in Neural Machine Translation. In *Proceedings of the 53rd Annual Meeting of the Association for Computational Linguistics and the 7th International Joint Conference on Natural Language Processing (Volume 1: Long Papers)*, pages 11–19.

Toshiaki Nakazawa, Hideya Mino, Chenchen Ding, Isao Goto, Graham Neubig, Sadao Kurohashi, and Eiichiro Sumita. 2016a. Overview of the 3rd Workshop on Asian Translation. In *Proceedings of the 3rd Workshop on Asian Translation (WAT2016)*.

Toshiaki Nakazawa, Manabu Yaguchi, Kiyotaka Uchimoto, Masao Utiyama, Eiichiro Sumita, Sadao Kurohashi, and Hitoshi Isahara. 2016b. Aspec: Asian scientific paper excerpt corpus. In *Proceedings of the 10th Conference on International Language Resources and Evaluation (LREC2016)*.

Graham Neubig, Makoto Morishita, and Satoshi Nakamura. 2015. Neural Reranking Improves Subjective Quality of Machine Translation: NAIST at WAT2015. In *Proceedings of the 2nd Workshop on Asian Translation (WAT2015)*, pages 35–41.

Rico Sennrich, Barry Haddow, and Alexandra Birch. 2016. Neural Machine Translation of Rare Words with Subword Units. In *Proceedings of the 54th Annual Meeting of the Association for Computational Linguistics (Volume 1: Long Papers)*, pages 1715–1725.

Ilya Sutskever, Oriol Vinyals, and Quoc V Le. 2014. Sequence to Sequence Learning with Neural Networks. In *Advances in Neural Information Processing Systems 27*, pages 3104–3112.

Yusuke Watanabe, Kazuma Hashimoto, and Yoshimasa Tsuruoka. 2016. Domain Adaptation for Neural Networks by Parameter Augmentation. In *Proceedings of the 1st Workshop on Representation Learning for NLP*, pages 249–257.

Global Pre-ordering for Improving Sublanguage Translation

Masaru Fuji[†‡] **Masao Utiyama**[†] **Eiichiro Sumita**[†] **Yuji Matsumoto**[‡]

† National Institute of Information and Communication Technology
3-5 Hikaridai, Seika-cho, Soraku-gun, Kyoto, Japan
{fuji.masaru,mutiyama,eiichiro.sumita}@nict.go.jp

‡ Nara Institute of Science and Technology
8916-5 Takayama-cho, Ikoma, Nara, Japan
{fuji.masaru.fe1,matsu}@is.naist.jp

Abstract

When translating formal documents, capturing the sentence structure specific to the sublanguage is extremely necessary to obtain high-quality translations. This paper proposes a novel global reordering method with particular focus on long-distance reordering for capturing the global sentence structure of a sublanguage. The proposed method learns global reordering models from a non-annotated parallel corpus and works in conjunction with conventional syntactic reordering. Experimental results on the patent abstract sublanguage show substantial gains of more than 25 points in the RIBES metric and comparable BLEU scores both for Japanese-to-English and English-to-Japanese translations.

1 Introduction

Formal documents such as legal and technical documents often form sublanguages. Previous studies have highlighted that capturing the sentence structure specific to the sublanguage is extremely necessary for obtaining high-quality translations especially between distant languages (Buchmann et al., 1984; Luckhardt, 1991; Marcu et al., 2000). Figure 1 illustrates two pairs of bilingual sentences specific to the sublanguage of patent abstracts. In both sentence pairs, the global sentence structure ABC in the source sentences must be reordered to CBA in the target sentences to produce a structurally appropriate translation. Each of the components ABC must then be syntactically reordered to complete the reordering.

Various attempts have been made along this line of research. One such method is the skeleton-based statistical machine translation (SMT) which uses a syntactic parser to extract the global sentence structure, or the *skeleton*, from syntactic trees and uses conventional SMT to train global reordering (Mellebeek et al., 2006; Xiao et al., 2014). However, the performance of this method is limited by syntactic parsing, therefore the global reordering has low accuracy where the accuracy of syntactic parsing is low. Another approach involves manually preparing synchronous context-free grammar rules for capturing the global sentence structure of the target sublanguage (Fuji et al., 2015). However, this method requires manual preparation of rules. Both methods are unsuitable for formal documents such as patent abstracts, because they fail to adapt to sentences with various expressions, for which manual preparation of rules is complex.

This paper describes a novel global reordering method for capturing sublanguage-specific global sentence structure to supplement the performance of conventional syntactic reordering. The method learns a global pre-ordering model from non-annotated corpora without using syntactic parsing and uses this model to perform global pre-ordering on newly inputted sentences. As the global pre-ordering method does not rely on syntactic parsing, it is not affected by the degradation of parsing accuracy, and is readily applicable to new sublanguages. Globally pre-ordered sentence segments are then syntactically reordered before being translated by SMT.

In this empirical study on the patent abstract sublanguage in Japanese-to-English and English-to-Japanese translations, the translation quality of the sublanguage was improved when global pre-ordering

Proceedings of the 3rd Workshop on Asian Translation,
pages 84–93, Osaka, Japan, December 11-17 2016.

Pair 1	Japanese	[[$_A$ アンテナ資源を有効に活用して信頼性の高い通信を行うことができる][$_B$ 通信装置を][$_C$ 提供すること。]]
	Japanese (word-for-word translation)	[[$_A$ Antenna resources effectively utilizing reliability high communication perform capable][$_B$ communication apparatus][$_C$ to provide.]]
	English	[[$_C$ To provide][$_B$ a communication apparatus][$_A$ capable of performing highly reliable communication by effectively utilizing antenna resources.]]

Pair 2	Japanese	[[$_A$ 高画質な画像を形成できる][$_B$ 画像形成装置を][$_C$ 提供する。]]
	Japanese (word-for-word translation)	[[$_A$ High quality images form enable][$_B$ image formation device][$_C$ to provide.]]
	English	[[$_C$ To provide][$_B$ an image formation device][$_A$ which enables high quality images to be formed.]]

Figure 1: Example of sublanguage-specific bilingual sentences requiring global reordering. A, B, C are the sentence segments constituting global sentence structures.

was combined with syntactic pre-ordering. A statistically significant improvement was observed against the syntactic pre-ordering alone, and a substantial gain of more than 25 points in RIBES score against the baseline was observed for both Japanese-to-English and English-to-Japanese translations, and the BLEU scores remained comparable.

2 Related Work

The hierarchical phrase-based method (Chiang, 2005) is one of the early attempts at reordering for SMT. In this method, reordering rules are automatically extracted from non-annotated text corpora during the training phase, and the reordering rules are applied in decoding. As the method does not require syntactic parsing and learns from raw text corpora, it is highly portable. However, this method does not specifically capture global sentence structures.

The tree-to-string and string-to-tree SMTs are the methods which employ syntactic parsing, whenever it is available, either for the source or for the target language to improve the translation of the language pair (Yamada and Knight, 2001; Ambati and Chen, 2007). However, these methods too are not specifically designed for capturing global sentence structures.

The skeleton-based SMT is a method particularly focusing on the reordering of global sentence structure (Mellebeek et al., 2006; Xiao et al., 2014). It uses a syntactic parser to extract the global sentence structure, or the *skeleton*, from syntactic trees, and uses conventional SMT to train global reordering. Another related approach is the reordering method based on predicate-argument structure (Komachi et al., 2006). However, the performance of sentence structure extraction tends to be low when the accuracy of the syntactic parsing is low.

The syntactic pre-ordering is the state-of-the-art method which has substantially improved reordering accuracy, and hence the translation quality (Isozaki et al., 2010b; Goto et al., 2015; de Gispert et al., 2015; Hoshino et al., 2015). However, the adaptation of this method to a new domain requires manually parsed corpora for the target domains. In addition, the method does not have a specific function for capturing global sentence structure. Thus, we apply here our proposed global reordering model as a preprocessor to this syntactic reordering method to ensure the capturing of global sentence structures.

3 Global Pre-ordering Method

We propose a novel global reordering method for capturing sublanguage-specific global sentence structure. On the basis of the finding that sublanguage-specific global structures can be detected using relatively shallow analysis of sentences (Buchmann et al., 1984), we extract from the training set the n-grams frequently occurring in sentences involving global reordering and use these n-grams to detect the global structure of newly inputted sentences.

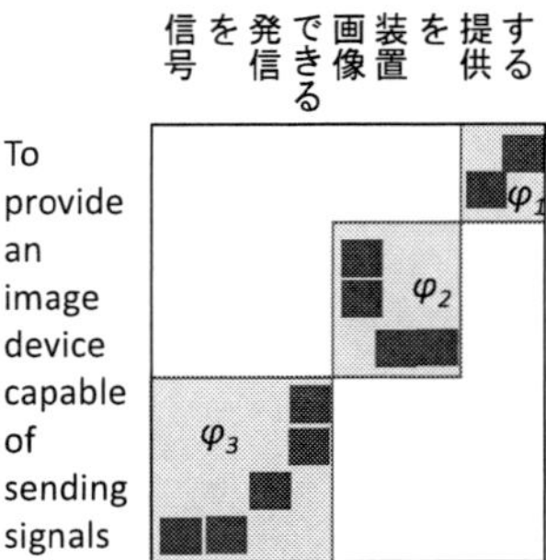

Figure 2: An example of segments arranged in swap orientations for English to Japanese translation

For example, Figure 1 shows two sentence pairs in the training set that contain global reordering, where the segments ABC in the source sentence must be reordered globally to CBA in the target sentence to obtain structurally appropriate translations. With segment boundaries represented by the symbol "|", the extraction of unigrams on both sides of the two segment boundaries of sentence E1 of Figure 1 yields

$$\{provide, |, a\} \quad \{apparatus, |, capable\}.$$

When we input the sentence *"To provide a heating apparatus capable of maintaining the temperature,"* this is matched against the above unigrams. Thus, the segment boundary positions are detected as *"To provide | a heating apparatus | capable of maintaining the temperature."* The detected segments are then reordered globally to yield the sentence *"Capable of maintaining the temperature | a heating apparatus | to provide,"* which has the appropriate global sentence structure for the target Japanese sentence. Each segment is then syntactically reordered before inputting to English-to-Japanese SMT.

The method consists of two steps. Step (i): we extract sentence pairs containing global reordering from the training corpus. We call this subset of the training corpus the *global reordering corpus*. Step (ii): we extract features from the source sentences of the global reordering corpus, and use these features to detect the segments of newly inputted sentences. We then reorder these detected segments globally. In step (ii), we experiment with a detection method based on heuristics, as well as a method based on machine learning. Steps (i) and (ii) are described in the following subsections.

3.1 Extraction of Sentence Pairs Containing Global Reordering

We extract sentences containing global reordering from the training corpus and store them in the global reordering corpus; they can subsequently be used for training and prediction. We consider that a sentence pair contains global reordering if the segments in the target sentence appear in swap orientation (Galley and Manning, 2008) to the source segments, when the sentences are divided into two or three segments each. Figure 2 shows an example of a sentence pair involving global reordering with the sentence divided into three segments. We take the following steps:

1. We divide each source and target sentence into two or three segments. The candidate segments start at all possible word positions in the sentence. Here, a sentence pair consisting of K segments is represented as $(\phi_1, \phi_2 \cdots \phi_K)$, where ϕ_k consists of the kth phrase of the source sentence and $\alpha_k{}^{th}$ phrase of the target sentence. These segments meet the standard phrase extraction constraint.
2. By referring to the alignment table, the source and target phrases of ϕ_k are considered to be in swap orientation if $\alpha_k = \alpha_{k+1} + 1$.
3. From the candidates produced in step1, we select all segments satisfying the conditions of step 2. If there is more than one candidate, we select the segment candidate based on the head directionality of the source sentence. For a head-initial language, such as English, we select the candidate for which ϕ_K has the largest length. For a head-final language, such as Japanese, we select the candidate for which ϕ_1 has the largest length.

ID	n-grams	len	freq
m1	*prevent,* |	1	2217
m2	*To, prevent,* |	2	1002
m3	*To, prevent,* |*, imperfect*	3	120
m4	*To, prevent,* |*, imperfect, coating*	4	18

Figure 3: Example of n-gram matching against an input sentence containing two segments. The input sentence is *"To prevent imperfect coating and painting."*

3.2 Training and Prediction of Global Reordering

3.2.1 Heuristics-based Method

In the heuristics-based method, we extract n-grams from the source sentences of the global reordering corpus and match these n-grams against a newly inputted sentence to perform global reordering. We call this method *heuristics-based*, because automatic learning is not used for optimizing the extraction and matching processes of the n-grams, but rather, we heuristically find the optimal setting for the given training data. Below, we describe the extraction and matching processes.

N-gram extraction We extract n-grams occurring on both sides of the segment boundary between adjacent segments ϕ_k and ϕ_{k+1}. In the heuristic-based method, n can assume different values in the left- and right-hand sides of the segment boundary. Let B be the index of the first word in ϕ_{k+1}, and f be the source sentence. Then the range of n-grams extracted on the left-hand side of f is as follows where nL is the value n of the n-gram.

$$(f_{B-nL}, f_{B-nL+1} \cdots f_{B-1}) \tag{1}$$

Likewise, the range of n-grams extracted from the right-hand side of f is as follows where nR denotes the value n of the n-gram.

$$(f_B \cdots f_{B+nR-2}, f_{B+nR-1}) \tag{2}$$

Decoding The decoding process of our global reordering is based on n-gram matching. We hypothesize that the matching candidate is more reliable (i) when the length of the n-gram matching is larger and/or (ii) when the occurrence frequency of the n-grams is higher. Thus, we heuristically determine the following score where len denotes the length of n-gram matching and $freq$ denotes the occurrence frequency of the n-grams. We calculate the score for all matching candidates and select the candidate that has the highest score.

$$\log(freq) \times len \tag{3}$$

Figure 3 shows an example of the decoding process for an input sentence containing two segments, i.e., $K = 2$, with one segment boundary. $m1$ through $m4$ are the n-grams matching the input sentence *"To prevent imperfect coating and painting,"* where "|" denotes the position of the segment boundary. The matching length is indicated by len which is the sum of nL and nR on both sides of the segment boundary. For example, for $m3$, the occurrence frequency is given as 120 and len is calculated such that $len = nL + nR = 2 + 1 = 3$. A score is calculated using equation 3 for all candidates, $m1$ through $m4$, and the candidate obtaining the highest score is used to determine the segment boundary.

3.2.2 Machine Learning-based Method

As the heuristic method involves intuitive determination of settings, which makes it difficult to optimize the performance of the system, we introduce machine learning to facilitate the optimization of segment detection. We regard segment boundary prediction as a binary classification task and use support vector machine (SVM) models to perform training and prediction. We train an SVM model to predict whether each of the word positions in the input sentence is a segment boundary by providing the features relating to the word in question. We use two types of features, as described below, for SVMs, both for training and prediction.

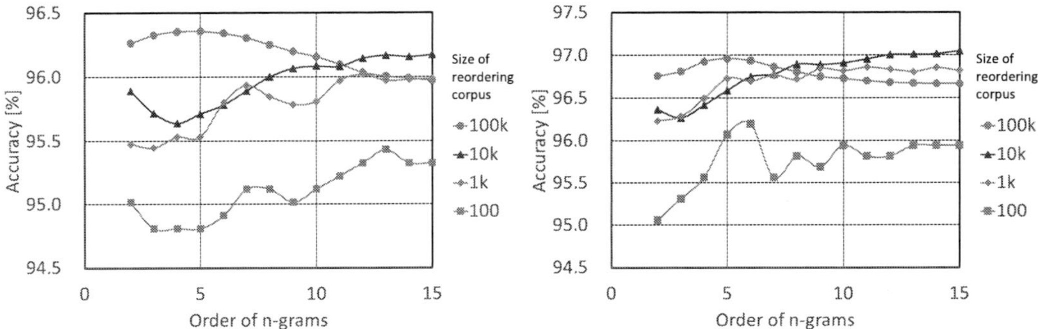

Figure 4: Variation in the boundary prediction accuracy for Japanese input

Figure 5: Variation in the boundary prediction accuracy for English input

- **N-grams**: Here, n-grams are extracted from both sides of the word under training/prediction. In contrast to the heuristics-based method, for simplicity, we use here the same value of n for n-grams in the left- and right-hand sides of the examined word. The n-grams used are as follows, where f is the sentence, i is the index of the word in question, and n is the value n of n-grams.

$$(f_{i-n+1}, f_{i-n+2} \cdots f_i \cdots f_{i+n-1}, f_{i+n}) \tag{4}$$

- **Position in the sentence**: The position of the word under training/prediction is provided as a feature. This feature is introduced to differentiate multiple occurrences of identical n-grams within the same sentence. The position value is calculated as the position of the word counted from the beginning of the sentence divided by the number of words contained in the sentence. This is shown as follows, where i denotes the index of the word in question and F is the number of words contained in the sentence.

$$\frac{i}{F} \tag{5}$$

In the prediction process, we extract the features corresponding to the word position i and then input these features to the SVM model to make a prediction for i. By repeating this prediction process for every i in the sentence, we obtain a sentence with each position i marked either as a segment boundary or as *not* a segment boundary. These predicted segments are then reordered globally to produce the global sentence structure of the target language.

4 Experiments

In this section, we first describe the reordering configuration for depicting the effect of global pre-ordering. We then describe the primary preparation of global reordering, followed by a description of the settings used in our translation experiment.

4.1 Reordering Configuration

To illustrate the effect of introducing global pre-ordering, we evaluate the following four reordering configurations: **(T1)** Baseline SMT without any reordering; **(T2)** T1 with global pre-ordering only. The input sentence is globally pre-ordered, and this reordered sentence is translated and evaluated; **(T3)** T1 with conventional syntactic pre-ordering (Goto et al., 2015). The input sentence is pre-ordered using conventional syntactic pre-ordering and the reordered sentence is translated and evaluated; and **(T4)** T1 with a combination of syntactic and global pre-ordering. The input sentence is globally pre-ordered, each segment is reordered using syntactic pre-ordering and the reordered sentence is translated and evaluated.

4.2 Preparation of Global Reordering

In preparation for global pre-ordering, we calibrated the machine learning-based detection to determine the optimal feature set for detecting segments. To determine the optimal feature set, we plotted the prediction accuracy with respect to the size of the global reordering corpus and value n of n-grams. As our support vector machines, we used liblinear 1.94 (Fan et al., 2008) for training and prediction.

Figure 4 shows the variation in the prediction accuracy with respect to the size of the global reordering corpus and the order of an n-gram for Japanese input. Figure 5 shows the same for English input. The *accuracy* is the average accuracy of a ten-fold cross-validation for the global reordering corpus. From the calibration shown in the tables, we select the settings producing the highest prediction accuracy, namely, a value of $five$ for the n of n-grams and a size of $100k$ for the global reordering corpus, for both Japanese and English inputs.

4.3 Translation Experiment Setup

Data As our experimental data, we use the Patent Abstracts of Japan (PAJ), the English translations of Japanese patent abstracts. We automatically align (Utiyama and Isahara, 2007) PAJ with the corresponding original Japanese abstracts, from which we randomly select 1,000,000 sentence pairs for training, 1,000 for development and 1,000 for testing. This training data for the translation experiment are also used for training global reordering as described in the previous subsection. Out of the 1,000 sentences in the test set, we extract the sentences that show any matching with the n-grams and use these sentences for our evaluation. In our experiments, the number of sentences actually used for evaluation is 300.

Baseline SMT The baseline system for our experiment is Moses phrase-based SMT (Koehn et al., 2007) with the default distortion limit of six. We use KenLM (Heafield et al., 2013) for training language models and SyMGIZA++ (Junczys-Dowmunt and Szal, 2010) for word alignment. The weights of the models are tuned with the n-best batch MIRA (Cherry and Foster, 2012). As variants of the baseline, we also evaluate the translation output of the Moses phrase-based SMT with a distortion limit of 20, as well as that of the Moses hierarchical phrase-based (Chiang, 2005) SMT with the default maximum chart span of ten.

Conventional syntactic pre-ordering Syntactic pre-ordering is implemented on the Berkeley Parser. The input sentences are parsed using the Berkeley Parser, and the binary nodes are swapped by the classifier (Goto et al., 2015). As a variant of conventional reordering, we also use a reordering model based on the top-down bracketing transducer grammar (TDBTG) (Nakagawa, 2015). We use the output of mkcls and SyMGIZA++ obtained during the preparation of the baseline SMT for training TDBTG-based reordering.

Global pre-ordering Global pre-ordering consists of the detection of segment boundaries and the reordering of the detected segments. Out of the 1,000,000 phrase-aligned sentence pairs in the training set for SMT, we use the first 100,000 sentence pairs for extracting the sentence pairs containing global reordering. We only use a portion of the SMT training data due to the slow execution speed of the current implementation of the software program for extracting sentence pairs containing global reordering. We evaluate both the heuristic and the machine learning-based methods for comparison.

Evaluation metrics We use the RIBES (Isozaki et al., 2010a) and the BLEU (Papineni et al., 2002) scores as evaluation metrics. We use both metrics because n-gram-based metrics such as BLEU alone cannot fully illustrate the effects of global reordering. RIBES is an evaluation metric based on rank correlation which measures long-range relationships and is reported to show much higher correlation with human evaluation than BLEU for evaluating document translations between distant languages (Isozaki and Kouchi, 2015).

5 Results

The evaluation results based on the present translation experiment are shown in Tables 1 and 2 for Japanese-to-English and English-to-Japanese translations respectively, listing the RIBES and BLEU scores computed for each of the four reordering configurations. The numbers in the brackets refer to the improvement over the baseline phrase-based SMT with a distortion limit of six.

A substantial gain of more than 25 points in the RIBES scores compared to the baseline is observed for both Japanese-to-English and English-to-Japanese translations, when global pre-ordering is used in con-

Table 1: Evaluation of Japanese-to-English translation where *glob-pre* denotes global pre-ordering and *pre* denotes conventional syntactic pre-ordering, *dl* denotes distortion limit, HPB denotes hierarchical phrase-based SMT and TDBTG denotes reordering based on top-down bracketing transduction grammar. The bold numbers indicate a statistically insignificant difference from the best system performance according to the bootstrap resampling method at $p = 0.05$ (Koehn, 2004).

	Reordering config		Settings			Results	
	glob-pre	pre	SMT	glob-pre	pre	RIBES	BLEU
T1			PB dl=6			44.9	17.9
			PB dl=20			53.7 (+8.8)	21.3 (+3.4)
			HPB			54.9 (+10.0)	23.1 (+5.2)
T2	√		PB dl=6	heuristic		61.7 (+16.8)	19.6 (+1.7)
			PB dl=6	SVM		61.0 (+16.1)	19.3 (+1.4)
T3		√	PB dl=6		TDBTG	64.6 (+19.7)	22.3 (+4.4)
			PB dl=6		syntactic	64.9 (+20.0)	**25.5 (+7.6)**
T4	√	√	PB dl=6	heuristic	syntactic	**71.3 (+26.4)**	**25.3 (+7.4)**
			PB dl=6	SVM	syntactic	**72.1 (+27.2)**	**25.6 (+7.7)**

Table 2: Evaluation of English-to-Japanese translation

	Reordering config		Settings			Results	
	glob-pre	pre	SMT	glob-pre	pre	RIBES	BLEU
T1			PB dl=6			43.2	27.9
			PB dl=20			54.4 (+11.1)	29.0 (+1.1)
			HPB			59.1 (+15.8)	32.1 (+4.2)
T2	√		PB dl=6	heuristic		59.5 (+16.2)	28.4 (+0.5)
			PB dl=6	SVM		65.3 (+22.1)	29.1 (+1.2)
T3		√	PB dl=6		TDBTG	**77.7 (+34.5)**	34.9 (+7.0)
			PB dl=6		syntactic	76.1 (+32.8)	**36.9 (+9.0)**
T4	√	√	PB dl=6	heuristic	syntactic	**77.3 (+34.1)**	**36.5 (+8.6)**
			PB dl=6	SVM	syntactic	**77.7 (+34.5)**	**36.5 (+8.6)**

junction with conventional pre-ordering. Also, the combination of global syntactic pre-ordering performs significantly better than syntactic pre-ordering alone. The BLEU score is not as sensitive to the introduction of global reordering, probably because the improvement is mainly concerned with long-distance reordering. We will further discuss the matter of evaluation metrics in the following section.

Figure 6 shows typical translations of the four reordering configurations: T1, T2, T3 and T4. Compared with the reference, the baseline (T1) fails to produce segment A and fails to output segments B and C in the correct order. In addition, the word order within each segment is not appropriate. The baseline with global pre-ordering (T2) successfully produces all three segments in the correct order, although the quality within each segment is not improved. The translation using conventional pre-ordering alone (T3) improves the local word order, while it fails to arrange the segments in the correct order. The translation with global and syntactic pre-ordering (T4) successfully produces the segments in the correct order, while at the same time improving the word order in each of the segments.

6 Analysis

To evaluate the ability of our proposed method to produce appropriate sentence structures in translated sentences, we count the number of sentences with correct global sentence structures among the translated test sentences. We think this is an important figure because the failure to produce the correct global sentence structure leads to inappropriate translation in most sublanguage-specific translations. We consider

Reference: [A To provide] [B a toner cake layer forming apparatus] [C which forms a toner cake layer having a high solid content and which can be actuated by an electrostatic printing engine.]
T1: [C Solid content of high toner cake layer for generating an electrostatic print engine operates in] [B a toner cake layer forming device.]
T2: [A To provide] [B toner cake layer forming apparatus] [C of the solid content of high toner cake layer for generating an electrostatic print engine can be operated.]
T3: [C For generating toner cake layer having a high solids content and] [A to provide] [B a toner cake layer forming device] [C which can be operated by an electrostatic printing engine.]
T4: [A To provide] [B a toner cake layer forming device] [C for generating toner cake layer having a high solid content, and operable by an electrostatic printing engine.]

Figure 6: Typical translations

Table 3: Number of correct global reordering in 100 test sentences

	Reordering config		Settings			Correct global reordering in 100 test sentences	
	glob-pre	pre	SMT	glob-pre	pre	Japanese-to English	English-to Japanese
T1			PB dl=6			4	6
			PB dl=20			12	15
			HPB			11	28
T2	√		PB dl=6	heuristic		24	23
			PB dl=6	SVM		31	26
T3		√	PB dl=6		TDBTG	21	59
			PB dl=6		syntactic	27	67
T4	√	√	PB dl=6	heuristic	syntactic	46	68
			PB dl=6	SVM	syntactic	58	63

that a translated sentence has a correct global sentence structure if it meets the following two criteria: (a) The translated sentence actually has the sentence structure CBA, where the source sentence structure ABC must be reordered to CBA in the target sentence. All the segments must be present in the correct order in the translated sentence; (b) All the words in each of the ABC segments in the source sentence must appear in an undivided segment in the target sentence. We randomly select a portion of the translated test sentences and manually counted the number of sentences meeting these criteria.

Table 3 shows the number of correct global reordering in Japanese-to-English and English-to-Japanese translations out of the 100 sentences randomly selected from the test set. The table shows that T4, which combines global and syntactic reordering, has a largely improved sentence structure compared with T1 and T2. In case of Japanese-to-English translation, the performance of T4 is much higher than T3, the state-of-the-art reordering alone. In case of an English-to-Japanese translation, the performance of the syntactic reordering is already considerably higher than the baseline and hence the performance of T4 is comparable to that of T3. The prominent improvement in BLEU scores by HPB observed in Tables 1 and 2 do not appear as prominent in Table 3, probably because HPB deals with more local reordering which is reflected well by BLEU score, but does not contribute much to global reordering.

7 Conclusion

In this paper, we proposed a global pre-ordering method that supplements conventional syntactic pre-ordering and improves translation quality for sublanguages. The proposed method learns global reordering models without syntactic parsing from a non-annotated corpus. Our experimental results on the patent abstract sublanguage show substantial gains of more than 25 points in RIBES and comparable BLEU scores for Japanese-to-English and English-to-Japanese translations.

References

Vamshi Ambati and Wei Chen. 2007. *Cross Lingual Syntax Projection for Resource-Poor Languages*. CMU.

Beat Buchmann, Susan Warwick-Armstrong, and Patrick Shane. 1984. Design of a machine translation system for a sublanguage. In *10th International Conference on Computational Linguistics and 22nd Annual Meeting of the Association for Computational Linguistics, Proceedings of COLING '84, July 2-6, 1984, Stanford University, California, USA.*, pages 334–337.

Colin Cherry and George Foster. 2012. Batch tuning strategies for statistical machine translation. In *Proceedings of the 2012 Conference of the North American Chapter of the Association for Computational Linguistics: Human Language Technologies*, NAACL HLT '12, pages 427–436, Stroudsburg, PA, USA. Association for Computational Linguistics.

David Chiang. 2005. A hierarchical phrase-based model for statistical machine translation. In *Proceedings of the 43rd Annual Meeting on Association for Computational Linguistics*, ACL '05, pages 263–270, Stroudsburg, PA, USA. Association for Computational Linguistics.

Adrià de Gispert, Gonzalo Iglesias, and William Byrne. 2015. Fast and accurate preordering for SMT using neural networks. In *Proceedings of the Conference of the North American Chapter of the Association for Computational Linguistics - Human Language Technologies (NAACL HLT 2015)*, June.

Rong-En Fan, Kai-Wei Chang, Cho-Jui Hsieh, Xiang-Rui Wang, and Chih-Jen Lin. 2008. LIBLINEAR: A library for large linear classification. *Journal of Machine Learning Research*, 9:1871–1874.

Masaru Fuji, Atsushi Fujita, Masao Utiyama, Eiichiro Sumita, and Yuji Matsumoto. 2015. Patent claim translation based on sublanguage-specific sentence structure. In *Proceedings of the 15th Machine Translation Summit*, pages 1–16.

Michel Galley and Christopher D. Manning. 2008. A simple and effective hierarchical phrase reordering model. In *Proceedings of the Conference on Empirical Methods in Natural Language Processing*, EMNLP '08, pages 848–856, Stroudsburg, PA, USA. Association for Computational Linguistics.

Isao Goto, Masao Utiyama, Eiichiro Sumita, and Sadao Kurohashi. 2015. Preordering using a target-language parser via cross-language syntactic projection for statistical machine translation. *ACM Trans. Asian Low-Resour. Lang. Inf. Process.*, 14(3):13:1–13:23, June.

Kenneth Heafield, Ivan Pouzyrevsky, Jonathan H Clark, and Philipp Koehn. 2013. Scalable modified Kneser-Ney language model estimation. In *ACL (2)*, pages 690–696.

Sho Hoshino, Yusuke Miyao, Katsuhito Sudoh, Katsuhiko Hayashi, and Masaaki Nagata. 2015. Discriminative preordering meets Kendall's τ maximization. In *Proceedings of the 53rd Annual Meeting of the Association for Computational Linguistics and the 7th International Joint Conference on Natural Language Processing (Volume 2: Short Papers)*, pages 139–144, Beijing, China, July. Association for Computational Linguistics.

Hideki Isozaki and Natsume Kouchi. 2015. Dependency analysis of scrambled references for better evaluation of Japanese translation. In *Proceedings of the Tenth Workshop on Statistical Machine Translation*, pages 450–456, Lisbon, Portugal, September. Association for Computational Linguistics.

Hideki Isozaki, Tsutomu Hirao, Kevin Duh, Katsuhito Sudoh, and Hajime Tsukada. 2010a. Automatic evaluation of translation quality for distant language pairs. In *Proceedings of the 2010 Conference on Empirical Methods in Natural Language Processing*, EMNLP '10, pages 944–952, Stroudsburg, PA, USA. Association for Computational Linguistics.

Hideki Isozaki, Katsuhito Sudoh, Hajime Tsukada, and Kevin Duh. 2010b. Head finalization: A simple reordering rule for SOV languages. In *Proceedings of the Joint Fifth Workshop on Statistical Machine Translation and MetricsMATR*, WMT '10, pages 244–251, Stroudsburg, PA, USA. Association for Computational Linguistics.

Marcin Junczys-Dowmunt and Arkadiusz Szal. 2010. SyMGiza++: A tool for parallel computation of symmetrized word alignment models. In *International Multiconference on Computer Science and Information Technology - IMCSIT 2010, Wisla, Poland, 18-20 October 2010, Proceedings*, pages 397–401.

Philipp Koehn, Hieu Hoang, Alexandra Birch, Chris Callison-Burch, Marcello Federico, Nicola Bertoldi, Brooke Cowan, Wade Shen, Christine Moran, Richard Zens, Chris Dyer, Ondřej Bojar, Alexandra Constantin, and Evan Herbst. 2007. Moses: Open source toolkit for statistical machine translation. In *Proceedings of the 45th Annual Meeting of the ACL on Interactive Poster and Demonstration Sessions*, ACL '07, pages 177–180, Stroudsburg, PA, USA. Association for Computational Linguistics.

Philipp Koehn. 2004. Statistical significance tests for machine translation evaluation. In *Proceedings of the 2004 Conference on Empirical Methods in Natural Language Processing , EMNLP 2004, A meeting of SIGDAT, a Special Interest Group of the ACL, held in conjunction with ACL 2004, 25-26 July 2004, Barcelona, Spain*, pages 388–395.

Mamoru Komachi, Yuji Matsumoto, and Masaaki Nagata. 2006. Phrase reordering for statistical machine translation based on predicate-argument structure. In *IWSLT*, pages 77–82. Citeseer.

Heinz-Dirk Luckhardt. 1991. Sublanguages in machine translation. In *EACL 1991, 5th Conference of the European Chapter of the Association for Computational Linguistics, April 9-11, 1991, Congress Hall, Alexanderplatz, Berlin, Germany*, pages 306–308.

Daniel Marcu, Lynn Carlson, and Maki Watanabe. 2000. The automatic translation of discourse structures. In *ANLP*, pages 9–17.

Bart Mellebeek, Karolina Owczarzak, Declan Groves, Josef Van Genabith, and Andy Way. 2006. A syntactic skeleton for statistical machine translation. In *In Proceedings of the 11th Conference of the European Association for Machine Translation*, pages 195–202.

Tetsuji Nakagawa. 2015. Efficient top-down btg parsing for machine translation preordering. In *Proceedings of the 53rd Annual Meeting of the Association for Computational Linguistics and the 7th International Joint Conference on Natural Language Processing (Volume 1: Long Papers)*, pages 208–218, Beijing, China, July. Association for Computational Linguistics.

Kishore Papineni, Salim Roukos, Todd Ward, and Wei-Jing Zhu. 2002. BLEU: A method for automatic evaluation of machine translation. In *Proceedings of the 40th Annual Meeting on Association for Computational Linguistics*, ACL '02, pages 311–318, Stroudsburg, PA, USA. Association for Computational Linguistics.

Masao Utiyama and Hitoshi Isahara. 2007. A Japanese-English patent parallel corpus. In *Proceedings of the Eleventh Machine Translation Summit*, pages 475–482.

Tong Xiao, Jingbo Zhu, and Chunliang Zhang. 2014. A hybrid approach to skeleton-based translation. In *Proceedings of the 52nd Annual Meeting of the Association for Computational Linguistics, ACL 2014, June 22-27, 2014, Baltimore, MD, USA, Volume 2: Short Papers*, pages 563–568.

Kenji Yamada and Kevin Knight. 2001. A syntax-based statistical translation model. In *Proceedings of the 39th Annual Meeting on Association for Computational Linguistics*, pages 523–530. Association for Computational Linguistics.

Neural Reordering Model Considering Phrase Translation and Word Alignment for Phrase-based Translation

Shin Kanouchi [†], Katsuhito Sudoh [‡], and Mamoru Komachi [†]

[†] Tokyo Metropolitan University
{kanouchi-shin at ed., komachi at}tmu.ac.jp
[‡] NTT Communication Science Laboratories, NTT Corporation
sudoh.katsuhito at lab.ntt.co.jp

Abstract

This paper presents an improved lexicalized reordering model for phrase-based statistical machine translation using a deep neural network. Lexicalized reordering suffers from reordering ambiguity, data sparseness and noises in a phrase table. Previous neural reordering model is successful to solve the first and second problems but fails to address the third one. Therefore, we propose new features using phrase translation and word alignment to construct phrase vectors to handle inherently noisy phrase translation pairs. The experimental results show that our proposed method improves the accuracy of phrase reordering. We confirm that the proposed method works well with phrase pairs including NULL alignments.

1 Introduction

Phrase-based statistical machine translation (PBSMT) (Koehn et al., 2003) has been widely used in the last decade. One major problem with PBSMT is word reordering. Since PBSMT models the translation process using a phrase table, it is not easy to incorporate global information during translation. There are many methods to address this problem, such as lexicalized reordering (Tillmann, 2004; Koehn et al., 2007; Galley and Manning, 2008), distance-based reordering (Koehn et al., 2003), pre-ordering (Wu et al., 2011; Hoshino et al., 2015; Nakagawa, 2015), and post-ordering (Sudoh et al., 2011). However, word reordering still faces serious errors, especially when the word order greatly differs in two languages, such as the case between English and Japanese.

In this paper, we focus on the lexicalized reordering model (LRM), which directly constrains reordering of phrases in PBSMT. LRM addresses the problem of a simple distance-based reordering approach in distant language pairs. However, there are some disadvantages: (1) reordering ambiguity, (2) data sparsity and (3) noisy phrases pairs. Li et al. (2014) addressed the problem of reordering ambiguity and data sparsity using a neural reordering model (NRM) that assigns reordering probabilities on the words of both the current and the previous phrase pairs. Also, Cui et al. (2016) tackled the problem of reordering ambiguity by including much longer context information on the source side than other LRMs including NRMs to determine phrase orientations using Long Short-Term Memory (LSTM).

However, there are a large number of noisy phrase pairs in the phrase table. One of the deficiencies of their NRMs is that they generated a phrase vector by simply embedding word vectors of the source and target language phrases and did not consider the adequacy of the translation between the phrase pair and the alignment of words in the phrases. It may be problematic especially when a phrase contains the NULL alignment, such as "," in "日本 で ||| in Japan ,". In addition, it is difficult to integrate the model of Cui et al. (2016) into stack decoding because their model is now conditioned not only on the words of each phrase pair but also on the history of decoded phrases. Furthermore, because they did not compare their model with the original NRM of Li et al. (2014), it is possible that their model is inferior to the previous approach.

Proceedings of the 3rd Workshop on Asian Translation,
pages 94–103, Osaka, Japan, December 11-17 2016.

Therefore, we propose to use phrase translation probability and word alignment features for NRM to address the problem of noisy phrase pairs. Both intrinsic and extrinsic experiments show that our features indeed improve the original NRM. The main contributions of this paper are as follows:

- We propose a new NRM incorporating phrase translation probabilities and word alignment in a phrase pair as features to handle inherently noisy phrase pairs more correctly.

- The experimental results show that our proposed method improves the accuracy of phrase reordering. In particular, the proposed method works well with phrase pairs including NULL alignments.

- We evaluate the proposed method on Japanese-to-English and English-to-Japanese translation using automatic and human evaluation.

2 Lexicalized Reordering Models

Lexicalized reordering models (LRM) maintain a reordering probability distribution for each phrase pair. Given a sequence of source phrases $f = \overline{f}_{a_1}, \ldots, \overline{f}_{a_i}, \ldots, \overline{f}_{a_I}$, we translate and reorder the phrases to generate a sequence of target phrases $e = \overline{e}_1, \ldots, \overline{e}_i, \ldots, \overline{e}_I$. Here $a = a_1, \ldots, a_I$ expresses the alignment between the source phrase $\overline{f}_{a_i}$ and the target phrase $\overline{e}_i$. The alignment a can be used to represent the phrase orientation o. Three orientations with respect to previous phrase (Monotone, Swap, Discontinuous) are typically used in lexicalized reordering models (Galley and Manning, 2008). However, because global phrase reordering appears frequently in Japanese-to-English translation, Nagata et al. (2006) proposed four orientations instead of three by dividing the Discontinous label. In Figure 1, we show four orientations, called Monotone (Mono), Swap, Discontinuous-right (D_{right}) and Discontinuous-left (D_{left}). Using alignments a_i and a_{i-1}, orientation o_i respected to the target phrases $\overline{e}_i$, $\overline{e}_{i-1}$ follows:

$$
o_i = \begin{cases} \text{Mono} & (a_i - a_{i-1} = 1) \\ \text{Swap} & (a_i - a_{i-1} = -1) \\ D_{\text{right}} & (a_i - a_{i-1} > 1) \\ D_{\text{left}} & (a_i - a_{i-1} < -1) \end{cases} \tag{1}
$$

If the reordering probability of every phrase is expressed as $P(o_i|\overline{f}_{a_i}, \overline{e}_i)$, that of the sentence can be approximated as

$$
P(a_1^I|e) = \prod_{i=1}^{I} P(o_i|\overline{f}_{a_i}, \overline{e}_i). \tag{2}
$$

LRM is a simple method to calculate the reordering probability for each phrase pair statistically.

However, the traditional lexicalized reordering model has the following disadvantages:

- **High ambiguity**: The phrase reordering orientation cannot be determined using only a phrase pair $\overline{f}_{a_i}, \overline{e}_i$, because the phrase reordering orientation may not be unique in a limited context.

- **Data sparsity**: The reordering probability is calculated for each phrase pair $\overline{f}_{a_i}, \overline{e}_i$. The phrase pair, which appears only once in training, amounts to 95%[1] of the entire phrase table. The reordering probability of these phrase pairs cannot be easily established.

- **Noisy phrases**: The reordering model does not consider the adequacy of the translation and the word alignments in phrases. For example, almost identical phrase pairs such as "日本 で ||| in Japan" and "日本 で ||| in Japan ," are often found in a phrase table. The difference between them is whether the phrase include "," which corresponds to the NULL alignment. Phrase tables in a distant language pairs like Japanese and English often contain the NULL alignment and mis-aligned words. On the contrary, there are also many phrase pairs that have crossing alignments such as "日本 で ||| in Japan" and "日本 で ||| Japan is." These locally reversed alignments deteriorate reordering accuracy.

---

[1]We experimented in the Kyoto Free Translation Task.

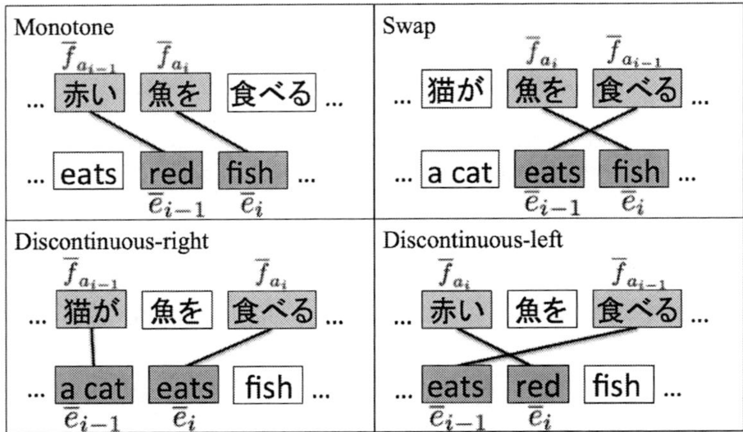

Figure 1: Four orientations, namely Monotone, Swap, Discontinuous-right and Discontinuous-left, are shown. Monotone means that the source phrases $\overline{f}_{a_i}$, $\overline{f}_{a_{i-1}}$ are adjoining and monotonic with respect to the target phrases $\overline{e}_i$, $\overline{e}_{i-1}$. Swap means $\overline{f}_{a_i}$, $\overline{f}_{a_{i-1}}$ are adjoining and swapping. Discontinuous-right means $\overline{f}_{a_i}$, $\overline{f}_{a_{i-1}}$ are separated and monotonic, and Discontinuous-left means $\overline{f}_{a_i}$, $\overline{f}_{a_{i-1}}$ are separated and swapping.

Li et al. (2013) proposed an NRM, which uses a deep neural network to address the problems of high ambiguity and data sparsity. We describe the NRM in the next section and propose our model to improve the NRM to address the problem of noisy phrases in Section 4.

3 Neural Reordering Model

Li et al. (2013) tackled the ambiguity and sparseness problem by distributed representation of phrases. The distributed representation maps *sparse* phrases into a *dense* vector space where elements with similar roles are expected to be located close to each other.

3.1 Distributed Representation of Phrases

Socher et al. (2011) proposed the recursive autoencoder, which recursively compresses a word vector and generates a phrase vector with the same dimension as the word vector. We define a word vector of u dimension $x \in \mathcal{R}^u$, an encoding weight matrix $W_e \in \mathcal{R}^{u \times 2u}$, and a bias term b_e. A phrase vector $p_{1:2}$ is constructed as follows:

$$p_{1:2} = f(W_e[x_1; x_2] + b_e) \tag{3}$$

f is an activation function such as $tanh$, which is used in our experiments.

When a phrase consists of more than two words, we compute a phrase vector $p_{1:n}$ recursively from the phrase vector $p_{1:n-1}$ and the word vector x_n.

$$p_{1:n} = f(W_e[p_{1:n-1}; x_n] + b_e) \tag{4}$$

We learn parameters to minimize the mean squared error between an input vector and the reconstructed vector using the autoencoder.

3.2 Deep Neural Network for Reordering

The NRM consists of an input layer built upon recursive autoencoders and outputs orientation score using a softmax layer (Li et al., 2013). An input is a concatenation of the current and previous phrase vectors in each language $p(\overline{f}_{a_i}), p(\overline{e}_i), p(\overline{f}_{a_{i-1}}), p(\overline{e}_{i-1})$ and an output is the reordering score $P(o_i)$ from the

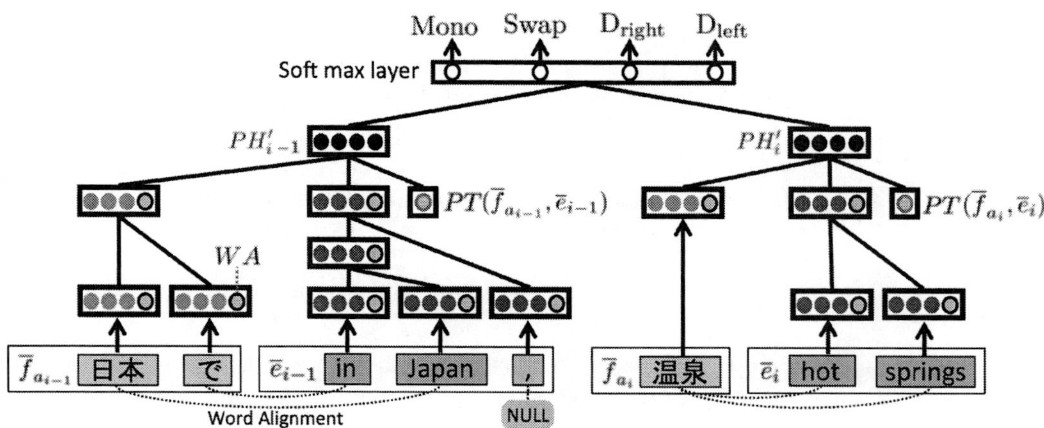

Figure 2: An NRM considering phrase translation and word alignment. PT represents phrase translation shown in Section 4.1 and WA (gray cells) represent the word alignment shown in Section 4.2.

softmax layer. All the phrases in the same language use the same recursive autoencoder.

$$P(o_i) \;=\; \frac{\exp g(o_i)}{\Sigma_{o' \in \{M,S,D_r,D_l\}} \exp g(o')} \tag{5}$$

$$g(o_i) \;=\; f(W_r[PH_i; PH_{i-1}] + b_r) \tag{6}$$

$$PH_i \;=\; [p(\overline{f}_{a_i}); p(\overline{e}_i)] \tag{7}$$

Here, $o \in \{\mathrm{Mono}, \mathrm{Swap}, \mathrm{D_{right}}, \mathrm{D_{left}}\}$ expresses the classes of orientation described in Section 2. $W_r \in \mathcal{R}^{1 \times 4n}$ is a weight matrix; PH_i is a phrase pair vector, which concatenates the phrase vectors $p(\overline{f}_{a_i})$ and $p(\overline{e}_i)$; and b_r is a bias term.

We calculate the error of the NRM $E_{nrm}(\theta)$ in each phrase pair using cross entropy.

$$E_{nrm}(\theta) = -\sum_o d_i(o) \log P(o) \tag{8}$$

where d_i is a correct reordering represented with a four-dimensional probability distribution. Each dimension corresponds to Mono, Swap, $\mathrm{D_{right}}$, and $\mathrm{D_{left}}$.

Finally, we compute the total of error $J(\theta)$, which is the sum of four errors of the recursive autoencoder $E_{rae}(\theta)$ and the error of the NRM $E_{nrm}(\theta)$. α is a hyper parameter controlling the trade-off between the models, and λ is an L_2 regularization coefficient.

$$J(\theta) = \alpha E_{rae}(\theta) + (1 - \alpha)E_{nrm}(\theta) + \lambda ||\theta||^2 \tag{9}$$

4 NRM with Phrase Translation and Word Alignment

The reordering of the phrase pair depends on each $\overline{f}_{a_i}$ and $\overline{e}_i$. However, the NRM generates a phrase vector merely by embedding a word vector, so that it does not take into account the adequacy of the translation between the phrase pair nor the word alignments. Therefore, in this paper, we embed the phrase translation probability and word alignments as features when we constitute a phrase pair. An overview of the model is illustrated in Figure 2.

4.1 Phrase Translation

We represent the translation probabilities between the phrase pair $\overline{f}_{a_i}$ and $\overline{e}_i$ in a four-dimensional vector $PT(\overline{f}_{a_i}, \overline{e}_i)$ to consider the adequacy of the translation between the phrase pair.

$$PT(\overline{f}_{a_i}, \overline{e}_i) = (P(\overline{e}_i|\overline{f}_{a_i}), P(\overline{f}_{a_i}|\overline{e}_i), lex(\overline{e}_i|\overline{f}_{a_i}), lex(\overline{f}_{a_i}|\overline{e}_i)) \tag{10}$$

Dimension	Description	
1	Word translation probability $P(e\|f)$	
2	Word translation probability $P(f\|e)$	
3	Whether the word	to the left of the phrase
4	aligns to a word	to the center of the phrase
5	where its position is	to the right of the phrase
6	Whether the word aligns to the NULL word	

Table 1: Word alignment information WA.

$P(\overline{e}_i|\overline{f}_{a_i})$ and $P(\overline{f}_{a_i}|\overline{e}_i)$ represent the translation probability of the phrase of both directions; $lex(\overline{e}_i|\overline{f}_{a_i})$ and $lex(\overline{f}_{a_i}|\overline{e}_i)$ compute the average of the translation probability of the words in the phrase of both directions.

We then concatenate the phrase pair vector PH_i and the phrase translation vector $PT(\overline{f}_{a_i}, \overline{e}_i)$ to obtain a new phrase pair vector PH'_i by using a weight matrix W_t. Again, b_t is a bias term.

$$PH'_i = f(W_t[PH_i; PT(\overline{f}_{a_i}, \overline{e}_i)] + b_t) \tag{11}$$

4.2 Word Alignment

We define a new word vector x', which incorporates word alignment information "WA" comprising six dimensions to the word vector x to propagate alignment information to the phrase vector.

$$x' = [x; WA] \in \mathcal{R}^{u+6} \tag{12}$$

Word translation probabilities are represented in the first two dimensions, and the location of the word alignment is represented in the following three dimensions. In addition, since some words are not aligned, i.e., "NULL Alignment," we create a special dimension corresponding to the NULL word.

Table 1 explains each dimension of WA. For example, the fourth dimension of WA of the word "日本 (Japan)" in Figure 2 is 1 because the aligned word "Japan" is located at the center of the phrase.

5 Experiment

We conduct two kinds of experiments: intrinsic evaluation of reordering accuracy and extrinsic evaluation of MT quality.

5.1 Setting

We use the Kyoto Free Translation Task[2] (KFTT) for our experiment. It is a task for Japanese-to-English translation that focuses on Wikipedia articles. We use KyTea[3] (ver.0.4.7) for Japanese word segmentation and GIZA++ (Och and Ney, 2003) with grow-diag-final-and for word alignment. We extract 70M phrase bigram pairs and automatically annotate the correct reordering orientation using Moses (Koehn et al., 2007). We filter out phrases that appear only once. We randomly divide the parallel corpus into training, development, and test. We retain 10K instances for development and test and use 1M instances for training.

We experimented 15, 25, 50, and 100-dimensional word vectors; 25-dimensional word vectors are used in all experiments involving our model. Thus, we set the vector size of the recursive auto-encoder to 31, to include the 25-dimensional word embeddings and the 6-dimensional WA. In a preliminary experiment, we compare the performance of randomly initialized word vectors with that of word vectors trained by the word2vec model[4]. Based on the result, we use word vectors trained by the word2vec model because of the performance. The word2vec model is pre-trained on English and Japanese versions of Wikipedia.

---

[2] http://www.phontron.com/kftt/
[3] http://www.phontron.com/kytea/
[4] https://code.google.com/archive/p/word2vec/

		Mono	Swap	D_{right}	D_{left}	Acc.
The ratio of labels [%]		30.39	16.06	31.86	21.69	
Baseline	Lexicalized Reordering Model (LRM)	71.54	36.92	**95.76**	39.33	66.71
	Neural Reordering Model (NRM)	77.06	57.60	70.31	60.63	68.22
Proposed	Phrase Translation (NRM+PT)	76.70	59.78	71.34	60.07	68.53
	Word Alignment (NRM+WA)	76.90	59.84	71.03	**62.38**	69.04
	NRM+PT+WA	**77.53**	**60.83**	72.69	61.78	**69.89**

Table 2: Recall and accuracy of reordering phrases.

Data size	time /epoch	Vocab size		Unknown words		Unknown phrases		Acc.
		ja	en	ja	en	ja	en	
10K	2 min	4,906	4,820	44%	45%	61%	63%	63.50
50K	9 min	10,833	10,880	25%	36%	48%	51%	66.88
200K	35 min	18,239	18,375	13%	22%	36%	39%	68.45
1M	170 min	26,978	27,152	7.3%	13%	24%	28%	**69.89**

Table 3: Data size and the accuracy of reordering. Vocab size reflects the vocabulary in the training data. The numbers of UNK words and UNK phrases are calculated in the test data. A pre-trained word2vec vector was given as the initial value for UNK words. Vocab sizes of test data are en:3,583 and ja:3,470. Phrase sizes of test data are en:8,187 and ja:7,945.

The pre-trained word2vec vector is also used to represent unknown words in the test data. If an unknown word is not included in the word2vec vocabulary, an unknown word vector is used to represent the word. In order to learn the unknown word vector, we randomly choose 1% of the words which appeared only once in the training data. Table 3 shows the size of the vocabulary.

We tune the hyperparameters with the development data up to a maximum of 30 epochs. We use the Adam optimizer with learning rate 0.0001. Our mini-batch size is 25. We drew the hyper parameter α uniformly from 0.05 to 0.3 with the development data and used $\alpha = 0.12$ in our experiments. We also tried dropout but it did not show the improvements in our experiments.

We implemented the basic NRM and our proposed model using Chainer (Tokui et al., 2015) as a deep learning toolkit. When running on a single CPU (Intel Xeon E5-2697 v3@2.6GHz), it took five days to completely train a model.

5.2 Reordering Evaluation

Table 2 shows the accuracy of reordering. The performance of LRM is calculated from the reordering table created during training[5]. The recall of Mono and D_{right} are high because LRM uses only a phrase pair $\overline{f}_{a_i}, \overline{e}_i$ and tends to output major labels. On the other hand, NRMs succeed at estimating minor labels because the score is calculated from the phrase bigram pairs. As a result, only the NRM recall of D_{right} is inferior to LRM, and thus, the overall accuracy improves.

Furthermore, in NRMs, the use of phrase translation and the word alignment improves the accuracy by 0.31 and 0.82 points, respectively. Considering both these features, the accuracy of NRM is improved by 1.67 points.

5.2.1 Data Size

Table 3 shows accuracies according to the size of the training data. The larger the data size, the higher the accuracy, because there are less unknown words and phrases. Note that LRM by Moses cannot calculate phrase orientation score for unknown phrases. Unlike conventional LRM, NRMs can construct a phrase

---

[5]We mix training data in the test data when we calculate the accuracy of LRM because the score can be calculated only for known phrases. Since the NRM can assign a score to unknown phrases, we use only the training data for NRMs.

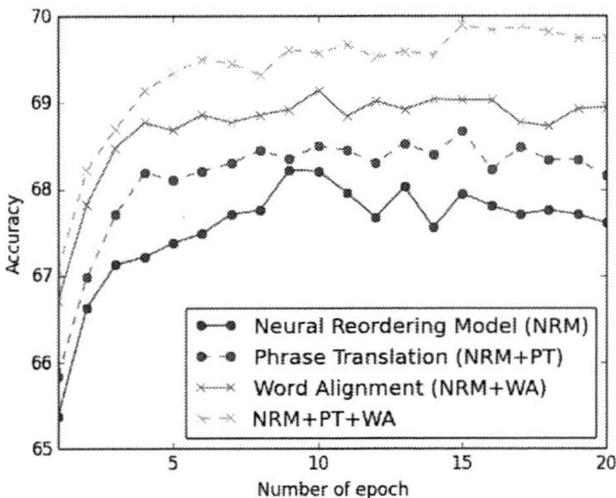

Figure 3: The accuracy of reordering at each epoch.

	Mono	Swap	D_{right}	D_{left}	Acc.
The rate of phrases including NULL Alignment [%]	25.8	45.9	40.8	44.5	
NRM	66.84	57.67	66.79	58.18	62.83
NRM+PT+WA	66.71	62.14	70.56	62.42	66.05

Table 4: Recall and accuracy of reordering phrases that contain NULL alignment.

vector even if the phrase in the test data is not included in the training data. As a result, the accuracy of the trained NRM is superior to that of LRM, only seeing 50K instances.

When we increase the size of the training data, the number of unknown words and unknown phrases decreases and the accuracy is improved further. However, most of the unknown words in the training corpus are named entities such as, "清水寺 (Kiyomizu-dera Temple)," which is a Japanese famous temple, because there are many traditional named entities in the KFTT corpus. Furthermore, it is possible that a new unknown word not in the phrase table appears in decoding. Therefore we expect NRMs to exhibit higher accuracy than LRM owing to their ability to recognize the unknown word.

5.2.2 Number of Epochs

Figure 3 shows the reordering accuracy at each epoch. Our proposed NRM+PT+WA method always achieves better accuracy than the baseline method of NRM. The accuracy is maximized around the 10th epoch in the test data. After that, the accuracy gradually decreases. The test loss shows the same tendency (negatively correlated with accuracy).

5.2.3 Phrase Translation Probabilities

To investigate the relation between the phrase translation feature and accuracy of our proposed method, we bin the test data into each phrase translation probability and evaluate the reordering accuracy.

As a result, the reordering accuracy does not improve in the cases where the translation probability is either too high or too small (e.g., the probability is more than 0.1 or less than 0.001), but overall performance improves a little. In a future study, we investigate as to why the translation probability is helpful for a reordering model.

5.2.4 NULL Alignment

To investigate the relationship between the NULL alignment and the accuracy of our proposed method, we evaluate only the instances when the target side phrases $\overline{e}_i, \overline{e}_{i-1}$ contain the words that have at least one NULL alignment. There are 3,788 such instances in the test data.

Table 4 shows the rate of instances including the NULL alignment for each reordering orientation and the accuracy of the corresponding reordering phrases. Considering each reordering orientation, the proposed method improves the recall over the plain NRM by approximately 4 points in each orientation

Method	ja-en			en-ja		
	BLEU	RIBES	WER	BLEU	RIBES	WER
LRM	18.45	65.64	79.87	21.37	67.01	84.73
NRM	19.16*	66.30	79.15*	**22.69***	68.64*	81.68*
NRM+PT+WA	**19.31***	**66.39**	**78.90***	22.61*	**68.65***	**81.57***

Table 5: Evaluation of translation quality. The symbols of * means statistically significant difference for LRM in bootstrap resampling ($p < 0.01$).

of Swap, D_{right}, and D_{left}, whereas that of Mono is not improved. This result suggests that the instances of Mono are not affected much by the NULL alignment, because they contain less NULL alignment (See the top row in Table 4). Overall, as compared with the NRM, our proposed method using phrase translation and word alignment improves the accuracy by 3.17 points (1.5 points higher than that of all the test data) for instances including the NULL alignment.

5.3 MT Evaluation

We investigate whether our reordering system improves translation accuracy. We use our reordering model for N-best re-ranking and optimize BLEU (Papineni et al., 2002) using minimum error rate training (MERT) (Och, 2003). We output a 1,000-best candidate list of translations that Moses generated for development data and replace the lexical reordering score of Moses with the score of the proposed method. Then, we re-tune the weights of the Moses features using MERT again. BLEU-4, RIBES (Isozaki et al., 2010a) and WER are used as measures for evaluation.

Table 5 shows the BLEU, RIBES and WER scores of the basic system and our proposed system. Bold scores represent the highest accuracies. When we compare the plain NRM and the proposed method with LRM, we confirm significant differences in BLEU, RIBES and WER scores on Japanese-to-English and English-to-Japanese translations using bootstrap resampling. Unfortunately, the proposed method is not able to identify significant differences in comparison with NRM. The reordering accuracy does not necessarily relate to the translation accuracy because we make the training and test data without checking the decoding step. We consider this to be partly of the reason why the BLEU score did not improve.

We conduct ablation tests to investigate which reordering orientation contributes most to BLEU score. The results show that Swap, which contains mostly NULL alignment, accounts for 0.17 points of improvement of the BLEU score in the proposed method. Other labels contribute only 0.01 - 0.05 points. Consequently, we consider that there is little influence on the translation results, because the change in each label of reordering is small, although the reordering accuracy rate of the NRM and the proposed method differ by 1.67 points.

In addition, we conducted human evaluation on Japanese-English translation by randomly choosing 100 sentences from test data. Two evaluators compared the proposed method with NRM fluency and adequacy. As a result, the proposed method improved fluency (NRM:NRM+PT+WA = 17.5:20) but not adequacy (NRM:NRM+PT+WA = 19:14.5). Although the outputs of two methods are similar, the proposed method favored fluent translation and resulted in slight improvements in BLEU and RIBES.

6 Related Work

There are several studies on phrase reordering of statistical machine translation. They are divided into three groups: in-ordering such as distance-based reordering (Koehn et al., 2003) and lexicalized reordering (Tillmann, 2004; Koehn et al., 2007; Galley and Manning, 2008), pre-ordering (Collins et al., 2005; Isozaki et al., 2010b; Wu et al., 2011; Hoshino et al., 2015; Nakagawa, 2015), and post-ordering (Sudoh et al., 2011). In-ordering is performed during decoding, pre-ordering is performed as pre-processing before decoding and post-ordering is executed as post-processing after decoding. In this section, we explain other reordering methods other than lexicalized reordering.

In early studies on PBSMT, a simple distance-based reordering penalty was used (Koehn et al., 2003).

It worked fairly well for some language pairs with similar word order such as English-French but is not appropriate for distant language pairs including Japanese-English. Lexicalized reordering model (LRM) (Tillmann, 2004; Koehn et al., 2007; Galley and Manning, 2008) introduced lexical constraints of the phrase reordering and not just penalizing long-distance reordering.

Pre-ordering methods can be divided into two types: (1) Rule-based preprocessing methods (Collins et al., 2005; Isozaki et al., 2010b) parse source sentences and reorder the words using hand-crafted rules. (2) Discriminative pre-ordering models (Tromble and Eisner, 2009; Wu et al., 2011; Hoshino et al., 2015; Nakagawa, 2015) learn whether children of each node should be reordered using (automatically) aligned parallel corpus. However, pre-ordering models cannot use the target language information in decoding. Therefore, optimizing phrase ordering using target-side features like phrase translation probability and word alignment is not possible, as done in our proposed method.

Post-ordering methods (Sudoh et al., 2011; Goto et al., 2012) are sometimes used in Japanese-to-English translation. They first translate Japanese input into head final English texts, then reorder head final English texts into English word orders. Post-ordering methods have the advantage of being able to use syntactic features at low computational cost, but need an accurate parser on the target side.

7   Conclusion

In this study, we improved a neural reordering model in PBSMT using phrase translation and word alignment. We proposed phrase translation and word alignment features to construct phrase vectors. The experimental results demonstrate that our proposed method improves the accuracy of phrase reordering. In addition, we showed that the proposed method was effective when phrase pairs included the NULL alignment. Evaluation on Japanese-to-English and English-to-Japanese translations indicated that the proposed method does not exhibits significant improvements in BLEU compared with those of the neural reordering model (Li et al., 2014). In the future, we plan to integrate our reordering model into attentional neural machine translations.

Acknowledgments

We thank the anonymous reviewers for their helpful comments on earlier versions. We also thank Yui Suzuki and Aizhan Imankulova for their annotation.

References

Michael Collins, Philipp Koehn, and Ivona Kucerova. 2005. Clause restructuring for statistical machine translation. In *ACL*.

Yiming Cui, Shijin Wang, and Jianfeng Li. 2016. Lstm neural reordering feature for statistical machine translation. In *NAACL*.

Michel Galley and Christopher D Manning. 2008. A simple and effective hierarchical phrase reordering model. In *EMNLP*.

Isao Goto, Masao Utiyama, and Eiichiro Sumita. 2012. Post-ordering by parsing for Japanese-English statistical machine translation. In *ACL*.

Sho Hoshino, Yusuke Miyao, Katsuhito Sudoh, Katsuhiko Hayashi, and Masaaki Nagata. 2015. Discriminative preordering meets Kendall's τ maximization. In *ACL-IJCNLP*.

Hideki Isozaki, Tsutomu Hirao, Kevin Duh, Katsuhito Sudoh, and Hajime Tsukada. 2010a. Automatic evaluation of translation quality for distant language pairs. In *EMNLP*.

Hideki Isozaki, Katsuhito Sudoh, Hajime Tsukada, and Kevin Duh. 2010b. Head finalization: A simple reordering rule for SOV languages. In *WMT*.

Philipp Koehn, Franz Josef Och, and Daniel Marcu. 2003. Statistical phrase-based translation. In *NAACL-HLT*.

Philipp Koehn, Hieu Hoang, Alexandra Birch, Chris Callison-Burch, Marcello Federico, Nicola Bertoldi, Brooke Cowan, Wade Shen, Christine Moran, and Richard Zens. 2007. Moses: Open source toolkit for statistical machine translation. In *ACL (demo)*.

Peng Li, Yang Liu, and Maosong Sun. 2013. Recursive autoencoders for ITG-based translation. In *EMNLP*.

Peng Li, Yang Liu, Maosong Sun, Tatsuya Izuha, and Dakun Zhang. 2014. A neural reordering model for phrase-based translation. In *COLING*.

Masaaki Nagata, Kuniko Saito, Kazuhide Yamamoto, and Kazuteru Ohashi. 2006. A clustered global phrase reordering model for statistical machine translation. In *COLING-ACL*.

Tetsuji Nakagawa. 2015. Efficient top-down BTG parsing for machine translation preordering. In *ACL-IJCNLP*.

Franz Josef Och and Hermann Ney. 2003. A systematic comparison of various statistical alignment models. *Computational Linguistics*, 29(1).

Franz Josef Och. 2003. Minimum error rate training in statistical machine translation. In *ACL*.

Kishore Papineni, Salim Roukos, Todd Ward, and Wei-Jing Zhu. 2002. BLEU: a method for automatic evaluation of machine translation. In *ACL*.

Richard Socher, Jeffrey Pennington, Eric H. Huang, Andrew Y. Ng, and Christopher D. Manning. 2011. Semi-supervised recursive autoencoders for predicting sentiment distributions. In *EMNLP*.

Katsuhito Sudoh, Xianchao Wu, Kevin Duh, Hajime Tsukada, and Masaaki Nagata. 2011. Post-ordering in statistical machine translation. In *MT Summit*.

Christoph Tillmann. 2004. A unigram orientation model for statistical machine translation. In *HLT-NAACL*.

Seiya Tokui, Kenta Oono, and Shohei Hido. 2015. Chainer: a next-generation open source framework for deep learning. In *NIPS Workshop on Machine Learning Systems*.

Roy Tromble and Jason Eisner. 2009. Learning linear ordering problems for better translation. In *EMNLP*.

Xianchao Wu, Katsuhito Sudoh, Kevin Duh, Hajime Tsukada, and Masaaki Nagata. 2011. Extracting pre-ordering rules from predicate-argument structures. In *IJCNLP*.

System Description of bjtu_nlp Neural Machine Translation System

Shaotong Li
Beijing Jiaotong University
15120415@bjtu.edu.cn

JinAn Xu
Beijing Jiaotong University
jaxu@bjtu.edu.cn

Yufeng Chen
Beijing Jiaotong University
chenyf@bjtu.edu.cn

Yujie Zhang
Beijing Jiaotong University
yjzhang@bjtu.edu.cn

Abstract

This paper presents our machine translation system that developed for the WAT2016 evaluation tasks of ja-en, ja-zh, en-ja, zh-ja, JPCja-en, JPCja-zh, JPCen-ja, JPCzh-ja. We build our system based on encoder–decoder framework by integrating recurrent neural network (RNN) and gate recurrent unit (GRU), and we also adopt an attention mechanism for solving the problem of information loss. Additionally, we propose a simple translation-specific approach to resolve the unknown word translation problem. Experimental results show that our system performs better than the baseline statistical machine translation (SMT) systems in each task. Moreover, it shows that our proposed approach of unknown word translation performs effectively improvement of translation results.

1 Introduction

Our system is constructed by using the framework of neural machine translation (NMT). NMT is a recently proposed approach to machine translation. Unlike the traditional SMT, the NMT aims at building a single neural network that can be jointly turned to maximize the translation performance (Kalchbrenner et al., 2013; Sutskever et al., 2014; Luong et al., 2014).

Most of the existing NMT models are built based on Encoder-Decoder framework (Sutskever et al., 2014; Luong et al., 2014). The encoder network encodes the source sentence into a vector, the decoder generates a target sentence. While early models encode the source sentence into a fixed-length vector. For instance, Bahdanau et al. advocate the attention mechanism to dynamically generate a context vector of the whole source sentence (Bahdanau et al., 2014) for improving the performance of the NMT. Recently, a large amount of research works focus on the attention mechanism (Cheng et al., 2015; Firat et al., 2016).

In this paper, we adopt RNN, GRU and attention mechanism to build an Encoder-Decoder network as our machine translation system. Figure 1 shows the framework of our NMT.

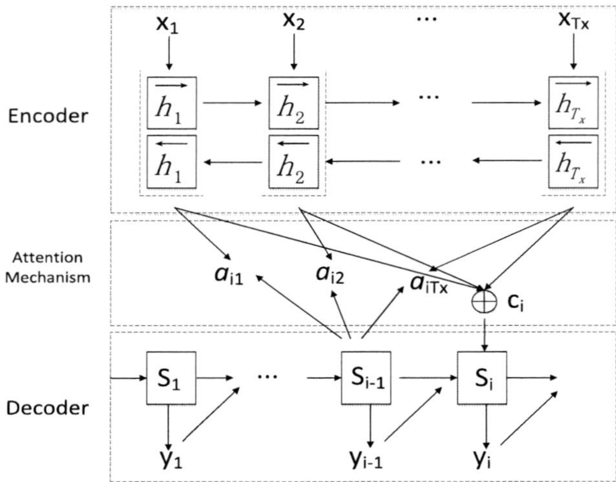

Proceedings of the 3rd Workshop on Asian Translation,
pages 104–110, Osaka, Japan, December 11-17 2016.

Figure 1: The framework of NMT. Where x and y denote embeddings of words in the source vocabulary and target vocabulary respectively, h means the hidden state of Encoder RNN, s is the hidden state of decode RNN, c_i is the context vector, a expresses the attention weight of each position.

Experiment results show that our system achieved significantly higher BLEU scores compared to the traditional SMT system.

2   System overview

Figure 2 shows the structure of our NMT system.

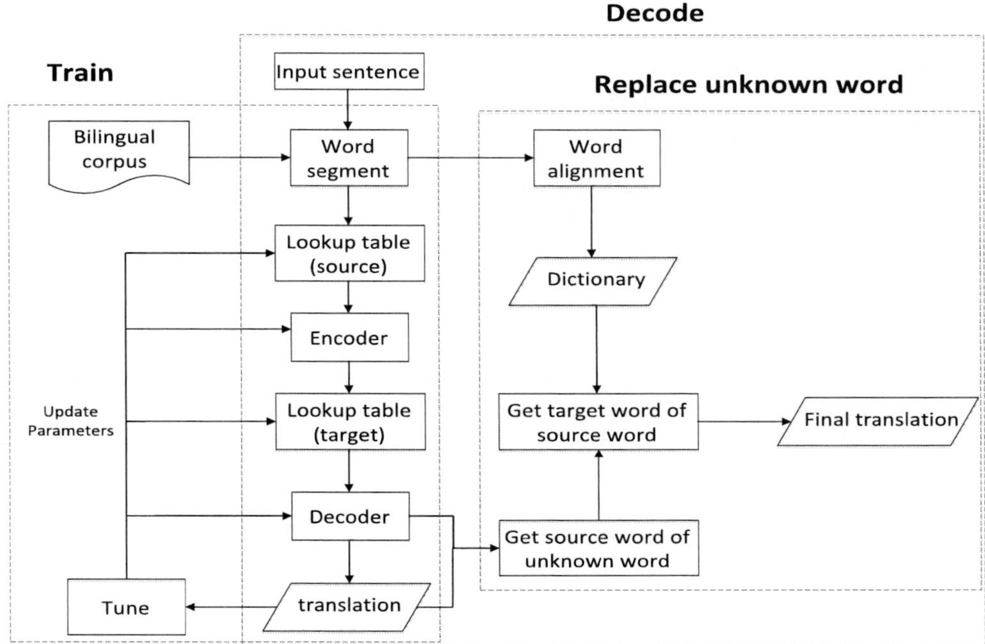

Figure 2: The structure of our system

Our system consists three parts: training part, decode part and the post-processing part of our proposed approach of unknown word processing.

2.1   Word segmentation

We use Stanford POS Tagger[1] and Juman[2] to do Chinese and Japanese segmentation processing, respectively. For English word segmentation, we use Moses tokenizer[3].

All these tools are the same as baseline systems tools.

2.2   Lookup table

For each word of source sentence， we obtain its embedding by using the source vocabulary, and for each target word of being predicted, we obtain its embedding with the target vocabulary. The source vocabulary and target vocabulary were regarded as part of the Encoder-Decoder network and the word embeddings will be tuned together with other parameters.

2.3   Encoder

In the encoder part, in order to make the annotation of each position of the source sequence, it consists two parts, both of the preceding words and the following words. We use a bidirectional RNN (BiRNN)

---

[1] http://nlp.stanford.edu/software/segmenter.shtml

[2] http://nlp.ist.i.kyoto-u.ac.jp/EN/index.php?JUMAN

[3] https://github.com/moses-smt/mosesdecoder/tree/RELEASE-2.1.1

to encode the source sentence (Schuster et al., 1997). We selecting GRU as the update function of hidden states of the BiRNN, which was proposed by Cho et al. (Cho et al., 2014) to make each recurrent unit to adaptively capture dependencies of different time scales.

2.4 Decoder

The decoder is constructed with another RNN, we use this RNN to predict each target word and finally generate an output sequence as the translated result sentence. We also select GRU as the update function of this RNN. We use a context vector which is dynamically generated by the attention mechanism (Bahdanau et al., 2014), as the input of the decode RNN.

2.5 Tune

After generating the output sequence, a softmax function is applied to calculate the cross-entropy as the cost which is used to compute grads of all parameters. We use the method of Adadelta (Zeiler et al., 2012) to tune the parameters.

2.6 Approach of Unknown Words translation problem

As the size of vocabulary of target language is limited owing to decoding complexity, there may be unknown words from the target vocabulary in the translation processing. This is a key point of existing NMTs.

In our system, we adopt a simple translation-specific approach to solve this problem. Firstly, we get a bilingual dictionary using GIZA++[4]. In decoding, each word, including unknown words, in the translation are matched with each word in the source, Secondly, we find the source word corresponding to unknown word with largest score in the decoder attention mechanism. For each unknown word, our approach can automatically select its corresponding word in the source sentence according to its matching scores. Then, we can use the translation of the corresponding source word to replace unknown word.

3 Evaluation

We participated in all tasks related to Chinese and Japanese and English.

3.1 Dataset

We use the given data of Asian Scientific Paper Excerpt Corpus (ASPEC)[5] and JPO Patent Corpus (JPC)[6] as show in table 1.

Corpus	Data Type	Number of sentences
ASPEC-JE	TRAIN	3000000
	DEV	1790
	TEST	1812
ASPEC-JC	TRAIN	672315
	DEV	2090
	TEST	2107
JPC-JE	TRAIN	1000000
	DEV	2000
	TEST	2000
JPC-JC	TRAIN	1000000
	DEV	2000
	TEST	2000

Table 1: Experimental dataset

---

[4] http://code.google.com/p/giza-pp/
[5] http://lotus.kuee.kyoto-u.ac.jp/ASPEC/
[6] http://lotus.kuee.kyoto-u.ac.jp/WAT/patent/index.html

For long sentence, we discarded all of the sentences which length with more than 50 words on both source and target side.

3.2 Training details

We defined hyper-parameters for each task as follows:

On ASPEC-JE corpus, the vocabulary size of English side is 40k while Japanese side is 30k. The number of hidden units is 1000 for both encoder and decoder. And the word embedding dimension is 600 for English side and 500 for Japanese side. For reducing training time and giving full play to the advantages of GPU, we choice 128 sentences as a batch to train together. The dropout rate (Srivastava et al., 2014) in the last layer of the network is set to 0.5 to avoid overfitting. For reducing searching space, we use beam-search algorithm (Tillmann et al., 2003) in the decoder, the beam size is set to 10.

On the other three corpuses, the hyper-parameters are the same, excepting the vocabulary size and word embedding dimension are different. They are set as fallows.

On ASPEC-JC corpus, the vocabulary size of Chinese side is 20k while Japanese side is 20k. And the word embedding dimension is 500 for Chinese side and 500 for Japanese side.

On JPC-JE corpus, the vocabulary size of English side is 30k while Japanese side is 30k. And the word embedding dimension is 500 for English side and 500 for Japanese side.

On JPC-JC corpus, the vocabulary size of Chinese side is 30k while Japanese side is 30k. And the word embedding dimension is 500 for Chinese side and 500 for Japanese side.

3.3 Evaluating results

We evaluated the performance of our two systems, one is the NMT system named as GRUSearch, the other is NMT system named as GRUSearch+UNKreplace, which adopted unknown word solution processing. For comparison, we also conducted evaluation experiments by using the three baseline systems provided by the organizers: Phrase-based SMT, Tree-to-String SMT, Hierarchical Phrase-based SMT.

For automatic evaluation, we use the standard BLEU and RIBES metrics. For human evalution, we use Pairwise Crowdsourcing Evaluation score provided by the organizers. The official evaluation results on ASPEC are shown in table 2, and the evaluation results on JPC are shown in table 3.

Task	System	BLEU	RIBES	HUMAN
en-ja	PB SMT	29.80	0.692	--
	HPB SMT	32.56	0.747	--
	T2S SMT	33.44	0.758	--
	GRUSearch	32.85	0.782	--
	GRUSearch+UNKreplace	**33.47**	**0.787**	**39.50**
Ja-en	PB SMT	18.45	0.645	--
	HPB SMT	18.72	0.651	--
	T2S SMT	**20.36**	0.678	--
	GRUSearch	17.67	0.679	--
	GRUSearch+UNKreplace	18.34	**0.690**	**19.25**
Zh-ja	PB SMT	35.16	0.766	--
	HPB SMT	35.91	0.799	--
	T2S SMT	37.07	0.820	--
	GRUSearch	37.83	0.837	--
	GRUSearch+UNKreplace	**39.25**	**0.846**	**49.00**
Ja-zh	PB SMT	27.96	0.789	--
	HPB SMT	27.71	0.809	--
	T2S SMT	28.65	0.808	--
	GRUSearch	28.21	0.817	--
	GRUSearch+UNKreplace	**30.57**	**0.830**	**46.25**

Table 2: Official automatic evaluation results on ASPEC

Task	System	BLEU	RIBES	HUMAN
JPCen-ja	PB SMT	34.26	0.728	--
	HPB SMT	36.61	0.779	--
	T2S SMT	37.65	0.797	--
	GRUSearch	40.00	0.833	--
	GRUSearch+UNKreplace	**41.16**	**0.840**	**39.50**
JPCja-en	PB SMT	30.80	0.730	--
	HPB SMT	32.23	0.763	--
	T2S SMT	34.40	0.793	--
	GRUSearch	38.13	0.836	--
	GRUSearch+UNKreplace	**41.62**	**0.852**	**41.63**
JPCzh-ja	PB SMT	38.51	0.779	--
	HPB SMT	39.52	0.802	--
	T2S SMT	39.45	0.810	--
	GRUSearch	38.24	0.820	--
	GRUSearch+UNKreplace	**39.72**	**0.831**	**32.25**
JPCja-zh	PB SMT	30.60	0.787	--
	HPB SMT	30.26	0.788	--
	T2S SMT	31.05	0.794	--
	GRUSearch	31.03	0.819	--
	GRUSearch+UNKreplace	**31.49**	**0.823**	**-1.00**

Table 3: Official automatic evaluation results on JPC

We also demonstrate the comparison results on BLEU and on RIBES in Figure 3 and Figure 4, separately.

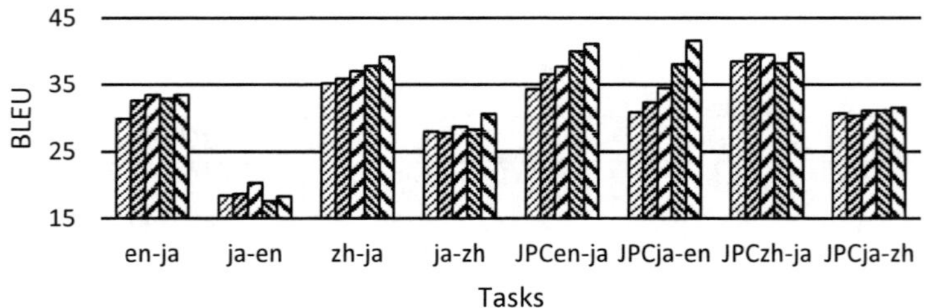

Figure 3: BLEU scores of all systems

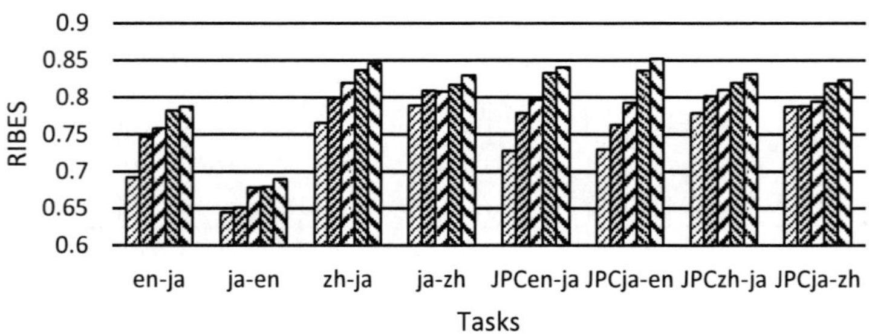

Figure 4: RIBES scores of all systems

As shown in the above tables and figures, our systems, both the GRUSearch+UNKreplace and GRU-Search outperformed the baseline systems in most tasks. In addition, our system with unknown word solution, GRUSearch+UNKreplace performed much better than the system without the unknown word solution, GRUSearch. It is proved that our unknown word translation approach is effective. Therefore, we submitted GRUSearch+UNKreplace to WAT2016 for human evaluation. And all the Pairwise scores of our tasks except JPCja-zh are much bigger than zero, which further proved that GRUSearch+UN-Kreplace performed better than baseline system.

Specifically, in the JPCja-en task, GRUSearch+UNKreplace achieved an improvement of 7.22 of BLEU score, compared with T2S SMT. GRUSearch+UNKreplace also achieved an improvement of 3.49 of BLEU, compared with GRUSearch. It means that the effectiveness of our unknown word reso-lution achieved good performance by the support of a better attention network, and a better dictionary, which obtained from higher quality of training data.

However, our model shows great difference in different tasks, in two tasks, our system performs even worse than the baseline systems. It is considered that we need do more works to find the best hyper-parameters of these tasks. The hyper-parameter optimization will be one of the most important tasks of our future work.

4   Conclusion

In this paper, we described our NMT system which used RNN and GRU, and we adopt the attention mechanism into the encoder–decoder network. We also presented a translation-specific approach to solve the unknown words translation problem. Experiment results show that our system performs good performance in most of the evaluation tasks.

However, there exists some space to improve the performance of our system: The solution for dealing with unknown words is still an open question; Hyper-parameter optimization is one of the most   im-portant tasks in NMT system. We also will try to integrate morphological features such as part-of-speech tags, syntactic dependency labels as input features into NMT systems, to improve model quality, aiming at further improvement of translation results.

Reference

Bahdanau, Dzmitry, Kyunghyun Cho, and Yoshua Bengio. 2014. Neural machine translation by jointly learning to align and translate. Computer Science.

Cheng, Yong, et al. 2015. Agreement-based joint training for bidirectional attention-based neural machine trans-lation. arXiv preprint arXiv:1512.04650.

Cho, Kyunghyun, et al. 2014. Learning phrase representations using RNN encoder-decoder for statistical machine translation. arXiv preprint arXiv:1406.1078.Firat, Orhan, Kyunghyun Cho, and Yoshua Bengio. 2016. Multi-way, multilingual neural machine translation with a shared attention mechanism. arXiv preprint arXiv:1601.01073.

Cho, Kyunghyun, et al. 2014. On the properties of neural machine translation: Encoder-decoder approaches. arXiv preprint arXiv:1409.1259.

Firat, Orhan, Kyunghyun Cho, and Yoshua Bengio. "Multi-way, multilingual neural machine translation with a shared attention mechanism." arXiv preprint arXiv:1601.01073 (2016).

Forcada, Mikel L., and Ramón P. Ñeco. 1997. Recursive hetero-associative memories for translation. In Interna-tional Work-Conference on Artificial Neural Networks (pp. 453-462). Springer Berlin Heidelberg.

Kalchbrenner, Nal, and Phil Blunsom. 2013. Recurrent Continuous Translation Models. In EMNLP (Vol. 3, No. 39, p. 413).

Nakazawa, Toshiaki, et al. 2016. Overview of the 3rd Workshop on Asian Translation. Proceedings of the 3rd Workshop on Asian Translation (WAT2016).

Schuster, Mike, and Kuldip K. Paliwal. 1997. Bidirectional recurrent neural networks. IEEE Transactions on Sig-nal Processing, 45(11), 2673-2681.

Sennrich, Rico, and Barry Haddow. 2016. Linguistic Input Features Improve Neural Machine Translation. arXiv preprint arXiv:1606.02892.

Srivastava, Nitish, et al. 2014. Dropout: a simple way to prevent neural networks from overfitting. Journal of Machine Learning Research, 15(1), 1929-1958.

Sutskever, Ilya, Oriol Vinyals, and Quoc V. Le. 2014. Sequence to sequence learning with neural networks. In Advances in neural information processing systems (pp. 3104-3112).

Tillmann, Christoph, and Hermann Ney. 2003. Word reordering and a dynamic programming beam search algorithm for statistical machine translation. Computational linguistics, 29(1), 97-133.

Toshiaki Nakazawa, Manabu Yaguchi, et al. 2016. ASPEC: Asian Scientific Paper Excerpt Corpus. Proceedings of the 10th Conference on International Language Resources and Evaluation (LREC2016).

Vinyals, Oriol, Suman V. Ravuri, and Daniel Povey. 2012. Revisiting recurrent neural networks for robust ASR. In 2012 IEEE International Conference on Acoustics, Speech and Signal Processing (ICASSP) (pp. 4085-4088). IEEE.

Zeiler, Matthew D. 2012. ADADELTA: an adaptive learning rate method. arXiv preprint arXiv:1212.5701.

Translation systems and experimental results of the EHR group for WAT2016 tasks

Terumasa EHARA
Ehara NLP Research Laboratory
Seijo, Setagaya, Tokyo, JAPAN

eharate @ gmail. com

Abstract

System architecture, experimental settings and experimental results of the EHR group for the WAT2016 tasks are described. We participate in six tasks: en-ja, zh-ja, JPCzh-ja, JPCko-ja, HINDENen-hi and HINDENhi-ja. Although the basic architecture of our systems is PBSMT with reordering, several techniques are conducted. Especially, the system for the HINDENhi-ja task with pivoting by English uses the reordering technique. Because Hindi and Japanese are both OV type languages and English is a VO type language, we can use reordering technique to the pivot language. We can improve BLEU score from 7.47 to 7.66 by the reordering technique for the sentence level pivoting of this task.

1   Introduction

Reasonably sized bilingual corpus is needed for the training of a SMT system. Unfortunately, between most of the Asian language pairs, we do not have such corpora, except a few language pairs like between Japanese, Chinese and Korean. On the other hand, between English and most of the Asian languages, we can obtain a large-sized bilingual corpus. So, we can use pivoting techniques (Utiyama and Isahara, 2007) for the SMT between Asian languages with English as the pivot language. HINDENhi-ja task of WAT2016 is an example. English is the VO type language and several Asian languages are OV type. Hindi and Japanese are both OV type languages. For the SMT between VO type and OV type languages, reordering technique is effective (Xu et al., 2009; Isozaki et al., 2010). We can use this reordering technique for SMT between OV type languages with a VO type pivot language. We apply this method to HINDENhi-ja task.

We participate in en-ja, zh-ja, JPCzh-ja, JPCko-ja, HINDENen-hi and HINDENhi-ja tasks in WAT2016. We will describe overall architecture of our systems and experimental settings in section 2. We will focus on the pivoting technique with reordering in section 3. In section 4, we will show the experimental results. We will conclude our discussion in section 5.

2   System architecture and experimental settings

2.1   Overall system architecture

Our basic system architecture is PBSMT (simply SMT) with reordering. We use Moses v. 3 (Koehn et al., 2003) for SMT tool and MGIZA++ v. 0.7.0 (Och and Ney, 2003; Gao and Vogel, 2008) for the alignment tool. Additional techniques used in our systems are listed in Table 1.

Character-based segmentation (Hyoung-Gyu Lee et al., 2015) for Chinese, Korean and Japanese is used in addition to word-based segmentation for the SMT. RBMT plus SPE (statistical post-editing) technique (Ehara, 2007) is applied to the JPCzh-ja task. Reordering is used for all tasks except for the

Proceedings of the 3rd Workshop on Asian Translation,
pages 111–118, Osaka, Japan, December 11-17 2016.

JPCko-ja task, because of the word order similarity of Korean and Japanese. Pivoting is used for the HINDENhi-ja task.

Task	Word-based PBSMT	Character-based PBSMT	RBMT+SPE	Reordering	Pivoting
en–ja	✔			✔	
zh–ja	✔	✔		✔	
JPCzh–ja	✔	✔	✔	✔	
JPCko–ja	✔	✔			
HINDENen–hi	✔			✔	
HINDENhi–ja	✔			✔	✔

Table 1: Used techniques for the tasks

2.2   en-ja task and HINDENen-hi task

Our English-Hindi or English-Japanese translation system is ordinary word-based SMT with reordering from a VO type language to an OV type language. Our reordering method is rule-based and basically same as (Ehara, 2015) in both tasks. Here, we briefly explain it. English sentences in training corpus are parsed in n-best (n=100) by the Berkeley parser v.1.7 (Petrov et al., 2006)[1] and they are reordered in k-best (k $\leqq$ n)[2] by our rule-based reordering tool. Next, we rerank k-best reordered English sentences by alignment score between English and Hindi or English and Japanese. In the last year's work (Ehara, 2015), we used WER to measure alignment score, however, this year, we use Kendall's tau. Another new thing is that reordering process adopts iterative loop consisting of alignment and reranking. Change of Kendall's tau by this iteration will be shown in section 4.1.

For reordering of dev, devtest and test sentences, we use the LM score calculated by "query" command in Moses to rerank k-best reordered sentences. This LM is trained by the reordered training sentences of the TM training corpus. This reranking method is common to Chinese reordering.

For English sentence reordering, deleting articles ("a", "an" and "the") and adding two case markers (subject and object) (Isozaki et al., 2010) are applied, both in en-ja and HINDENen-hi tasks.

We use Moses' tokenizer for English tokenization, Indic NLP normalizer and tokenizer (Kunchukuttan et al., 2014) for Hindi tokenization and JUMAN (Kurohashi et al., 1994) for Japanese segmentation.

SMT training, tuning, and testing are done by Moses with the default settings. Alignment process in the reordering is done by Moses (MGIZA++) and self-built post processor for GIZA++ outputs. This post processor makes word alignment by heuristics using two GIZA++ outputs (A3.final) and two lexical translation tables (lex.f2e and lex.e2f) obtained by Moses.

Experimental setting is as follows. Training data for SMT and reordering are provided from the organizer. The number of TM training sentence pairs in en-ja task are 1,502,767 shown in Table 2. We extract sentence pairs which have high sentence alignment score ($\geqq 0.08$) from the three training corpora. We also filter out sentence pairs which are too long (> 100 words) or have unbalanced sentence length (ratio of word numbers is > 4 or < 0.25). The latter filtering is common with all tasks.

Task	TM training	LM training
en–ja	1,502,767	3,824,408
zh–ja	667,922	3,680,815
JPCzh–ja	995,385	4,186,284
JPCko–ja	996,339	5,186,284
HINDENen–hi	1,450,896	1,599,708
HINDENhi–ja	149,743	406,766

Table 2: Training corpus size (sentences)
(In HINDENhi-ja task, the corpus size is the case of direct translation without pivoting.)

---

[1] Sentences unparsed by the Berkeley parser are n-best parsed by the Stanford lexicalized parser v.2.0.5 (Klein and Manning, 2003; Levy and Manning, 2003).

[2] Several different parse trees may make same reordered word order. Then k $\leqq$ n.

112

The number of TM training sentence pairs in HINDENen-hi task are 1,450,896. We filter out 21,637 strange sentence pairs such as hi: "à¤¸à¤ à¤ à¥ à¤°à¤¹¹ à¤¸à¥" and en: "Damping :" from the original training corpus.

LM are trained by the tool lmplz in Moses with order 6. This LM training method is common with all tasks. The number of LM training sentences in the en-ja task are 3,824,408. They are extracted from all en-ja training corpora and HINDENhi-ja training corpus. The number of LM training sentences in the HINDENen-hi task are 1,599,708. They are extracted from HINDENen-hi training corpus and HINDENhi-ja training corpus.

The distortion limit for tuning and testing is 6. This DL value is same in all tasks except for JPCko-ja task.

2.3   zh-ja task and JPCzh-ja task

Our Chinese-Japanese translation system is SMT with reordering. Additionally, JPCzh-ja task uses RBMT plus SPE system. In both tasks, our reordering method is basically same as the method described in section 2.2 except for the parsing rules and the reordering rules. For Chinese sentence reordering, deleting case markers of Japanese ("が", "を" ,"は" and "は 、") is done to improve Chinese-Japanese alignment accuracy.

We use Stanford Chinese segmenter (Chang et al., 2008) to segment Chinese. We apply self-built post processor to the output of the Stanford segmenter. This post processor segments alphabetical, numerical and symbolic expressions from Han expressions. It also adjusts several segmentations for Han expressions, for example, "示于表" is segmented to "示 于 表". We use JUMAN for Japanese segmentation. We also add self-built post processor after JUMAN's segmentation that connects forms that have the POS "名詞 サ変名詞" to the forms that have the POS "動詞 * サ変動詞". It also connects forms that have the POS "動詞" to the forms that have the POS "接尾辞 動詞性接尾辞". As the result, "備えて いる" consisting of two morphemes comes to one morpheme. By these post processors, we can balance segmentation granularity between Chinese and Japanese.

For character based SMT, we segment all Han characters only for the Chinese side.

SMT training, tuning, and testing using reordered Chinese and Japanese corpus are done by Moses.

RBMT system and SPE system for JPCzh-ja task are the same as in the previous work (Ehara, 2015).

Two outputs from word based SMT and character based SMT are packed to lattice form using DP matching and the path which has the best LM score is selected as the system output. This method is similar but simpler than the Matusov's method (Matusov et al., 2006). In the case of three outputs from word based SMT, character based SMT and RBMT plus SPE, this packing and selecting procedures are made twice.

Experimental setting is as follows. Training data for SMT and reordering are provided from the organizer and NTCIR-10's PatentMT task EJ subtask site (Goto et al. 2013). The number of TM training sentence pairs in zh-ja task are 667,922. They are extracted from zh-ja task data. The number of TM training sentence pairs in JPCzh-ja task are 995,385. They are extracted from JPCzh-ja task data.

The number of LM training sentences in zh-ja task are 3,680,815. They are extracted from en-ja and zh-ja task data. The number of LM training sentences in JPCzh-ja task are 4,186,284. They are extracted from JPCzh-ja task data and NTCIR-10's PatentMT task EJ subtask's data.

2.4   JPCko-ja task

Korean and Japanese are both OV type language and have a very similar word order structure. So we don't use reordering in this task. We use Mecab-ko[3] for tokenization of Korean and JUMAN for segmentation of Japanese. No Japanese post processor is used for the segmentation for word based SMT in this task. For character based SMT, we segment all characters both for Korean and Japanese.

SMT training, tuning and test using Korean and Japanese corpus is done by Moses.

One problem in JPCko-ja task is an unbalanced usage of parentheses between two languages. As described in (Ehara, 2015), there are mostly parentheses surrounding a number in Korean. On the other hand, there are mostly no parentheses surrounding a number in Japanese. We conduct three methods to

---

[3] https://bitbucket.org/eunjeon/mecab-ko/

address the problem. (1) All parentheses surrounding a number in the Korean side are deleted. (2) Parentheses are added to a number in the Japanese side not surrounded by parentheses and aligned to the number of the Korean side that is surrounded by parentheses. (3) Same as (2) to SMT phase and after decoding parentheses surrounding a number in the translated Japanese are deleted.

Experimental setting is as follows. Training data for SMT and reordering are provided from the organizer and NTCIR-10's PatentMT task EJ subtask site. The number of TM training sentence pairs in JPCko-ja task are 996,339. They are extracted from JPCko-ja task data.

The number of LM training sentence pairs in JPCko-ja task are 5,186,284. They are extracted from JPCko-ja task data, JPCzh-ja task data and NTCIR-10's PatentMT task EJ subtask's data.

The distortion limit for tuning and testing is set to 0, because the word order of Korean is similar to that of Japanese.

2.5 HINDENhi-ja task

Four methods of translation is executed for HINDENhi-ja task. (1) Ordinary PBSMT trained by Hindi-Japanese bilingual corpus. (2) Using Hindi-English and English-Japanese bilingual corpora, pivoting by sentence level without reordering. (3) Same as (2) except for using reordering. (4) Pivoting by table level with reordering.

Pivoting will be described in section 3. Here, we describe other techniques used in this task.

Words in dev and test set not included in the training corpus (train-parallel.hi) is translated by an online free translator and from this translation list, we make a Hindi-Japanese user dictionary, which has 931 entries. This user dictionary is used in the TM training in addition to the training data.

In the TM training of the case (1), we use filtered training data of HINDENhi-ja task. The filtering method is like the method described in section 2.2. For example, the datum hi: "इंटरफ़ेस विकल्प" and ja: "ã ªã   ã ·ã   §ã   ³ > >" is discarded. As the result, we get 148,812 Hindi and Japanese sentence pairs. Adding user dictionary described above, we get 149,743 sentence pairs to train the TM.

Japanese LM is trained not only by the task data but by the TED corpus (Cettolo, 2012)[4]. We extract 260,501 sentences from the <content> part of ted_ja-20160408.xml. Sentences which include sentences in dev or test set are filtered out. As the result, we get 256,891 sentences. Adding Japanese side of the original training data of HINDENhi-ja task, we get 406,766 sentences to train the LM.

SMT training, tuning, testing and pivoting are done by Moses.

3 Pivoting

For the sentence level pivoting, we use the English-Japanese SMT system described in section 2.2. The English side of the TM training data of HINDENen-hi task (1,450,896 sentences) is translated into Japanese by this SMT system, without reordering (case (2)) or with reordering (case (3)). As the result, we get 1,450,896 Hindi and (machine translated) Japanese sentence pairs. Adding TM training corpus of HINDENhi-ja task, we get 1,600,639 sentence pairs to train the TM.

For the table level pivoting, we merge two phrase tables and two reordering tables. They are Hindi-English phrase table and Hindi-English reordering table used in the HINDENen-hi task and English-Japanese phrase table and English-Japanese reordering table used in the en-ja task. Merging two phrase tables, we get Hindi-Japanese pivoted phrase table. Merging two reordering tables, we get Hindi-Japanese pivoted reordering table.

The merging method of the phrase tables is like the "triangulation" (Cohn and Lapata, 2007; Wu and Wang, 2007). Explicitly, four conditional probabilities in the Moses' phrase table are computed as:

$$\emptyset(f|e) = \sum_{p} \emptyset(f|p)\, \emptyset(p|e)$$

$$lex(f|e) = \sum_{p} lex(f|p)\, lex(p|e)$$

$$\emptyset(e|f) = \sum_{p} \emptyset(e|p)\, \emptyset(p|f)$$

$$lex(e|f) = \sum_{p} lex(e|p)\, lex(p|f)$$

---

[4] https://wit3.fbk.eu/ (accessed on 17th August 2016).

where, f, p and e means a source, pivot and target phrases, respectively. We discard data which have a low probability from the pivoted phrase table that is $\emptyset(f|e)\emptyset(e|f) < 0.000001$. We merge this pivoted phrase table and the direct phrase table trained by the Hindi-Japanese parallel corpus (see section 2.5). In the merging, we use token frequencies of f and e obtained from two phrase tables. Considering $\emptyset_p(f|e)$ be the conditional probability in the pivoted phrase table, $\emptyset_d(f|e)$ be the conditional probability in the direct phrase table, $F_p(f)$ be the frequency of f in the pivoted phrase table and $F_d(f)$ be the frequency of f in the direct phrase table, we get the merged conditional probability:

$$\emptyset(f|e) = \frac{\emptyset_p(f|e)\,F_p(f) + \emptyset_d(f|e)\,F_d(f)}{F_p(f) + F_d(f)}.$$

Other probabilities are similarly calculated.

The merging method of the reordering tables is as follows. We assume that the source to target reordering orientations are determined as in Table 3. Here we use the combination of three reordering orientations: monotone (m), swap (s) and discontinuous (d) in the source to pivot reordering table (fp) and pivot to target reordering table (pe).

fp \ pe	m	s	d
m	m	s	d
s	s	m	s
d	d	s	m

Table 3: Source to target reordering orientations

This table is simpler than the orientation table of (Patil et al., 2015), because of the word order similarity of Hindi (source) and Japanese (target). From this table, we can calculate orientation probabilities of source to target reordering table (fe) as:

$$m\,(f \to e) = \sum_p \{m(f \to p)m(p \to e) + s(f \to p)s(p \to e) + d(f \to p)d(p \to e)\}/D$$

$$s(f \to e) = \sum_p \{m(f \to p)s(p \to e) + s(f \to p)m(p \to e) + d(f \to p)s(p \to e) + s(f \to p)d(p \to e)\}/D$$

$$d(f \to e) = \sum_p \{m(f \to p)d(p \to e) + d(f \to p)m(p \to e)\}/D$$

where $m(f \to e)$, $s(f \to e)$ and $d(f \to e)$ are monotone, swap and discontinuous probabilities from source (f) to target (e) and D is a normalizing parameter such that $m(f \to e) + s(f \to e) + d(f \to e) = 1$. Inverse probabilities: $m(e \to f)$, $s(e \to f)$ and $d(e \to f)$ are similarly calculated. We merge this pivoted reordering table and the direct reordering table trained by the Hindi-Japanese parallel corpus (see section 2.5). The merging method is similar to the merging method of the phrase tables described above.

4 Experimental results

4.1 Results of iterative reordering

We conduct iterative reordering consisting of reranking of k-best reordered sentences and alignment loop described in section 2.2 for en-ja, HINDENen-hi, .zh-ja and JPCzh-ja tasks.

Changes of the average of Kendall's tau of the alignment for JPCzh-ja task are shown in Figure 1. Kendall's tau increases by the iteration but an amount of increase is small.

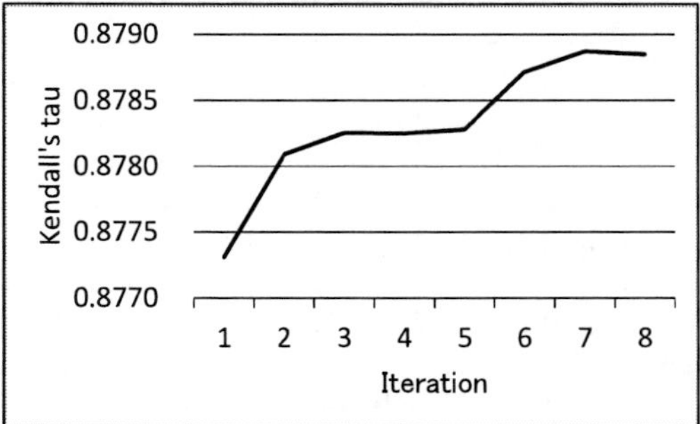

Figure 1: Change of average of Kendall's tau for JPCzh-ja task

For all tasks using the reordering, the number of iterations and average values of Kendall's tau which are obtained by the last iteration are listed in Table 4. The Kendall's tau of en-ja and HINDENeh-hi tasks are rather low than that of zh-ja and JPCzh-ja tasks.

Task	Iteration	Kendall's tau
en-ja	4	0.7655
zh-ja	4	0.9083
JPCzh-ja	8	0.8788
HINDENen-hi	4	0.8398

Table 4: Number of iterations and average values of Kendall's tau for the tasks

4.2 Results of system combination

For JPCzh-ja task, we combine three systems: word based SMT, character based SMT and RBMT plus SPE. We compare translation accuracy using devtest set by BLEU and RIBES. Table 5 shows these scores of several combinations of the systems. We can see our system combination is effective.

No.	System	BLEU	RIBES
1	word based SMT	42.07	82.91
2	char based SMT	41.82	83.03
3	RBMT + SPE	41.61	82.42
4	to combine 1 and 2	42.13	83.13
5	to combine 1, 2 and 3	42.42	83.16

Table 5: Effect of system combination in JPCzh-ja task

4.3 Translation evaluation results

We submitted 12 systems' outputs to the evaluation site. The system descriptions are summarized in Table 6. Official evaluation results of our systems by the organizer (Nakazawa et al., 2016) are listed in Table 7. Evaluation results of the top ranked system are also listed in the table for the comparison.

For JPCzh-ja task, adding RBMT plus SPE increase BLEU score but decrease RIBES, AMFM and HUMAN scores.

For JPCko-ja task, deleting parentheses surrounding a number in Korean side increase three automatic scores. Oppositely, adding parentheses surrounding a number in Japanese side increase HUMAN score.

For HINDENhi-ja task, table level pivoting has higher BLEU and HUMAN score and lower RIBES and AMFM scores than sentence level pivoting. Comparing system 2 and 3 of HINDENhi-ja task, reordering of pivot language (English) is effective with three automatic scores. Pivoting method (system 1, 2 and 3) substantially increases automatic scores compared with the direct method (system 4). However, evaluation scores of this task are largely low compared with the scores of other tasks.

Task	System No.	Word-based PBSMT	Character-based PBSMT	RBMT+SPE	Reordering	Sentence level pivoting	Table level pivoting	Parentheses handling
en-ja	1	✔				✔		
zh-ja	1	✔	✔		✔			
JPCzh-ja	1	✔	✔	✔	✔			
	2	✔	✔		✔			
JPCko-ja	1	✔	✔					del
	2	✔	✔					add & del
	3	✔	✔					add
HINDENen-hi	1	✔				✔		
HINDENhi-ja	1	✔				✔	✔	
	2	✔				✔	✔	
	3	✔					✔	
	4	✔						

Table 6: System descriptions of the tasks

Three systems are evaluated by the JPO adequacy. The system for JPCko-ja task has high JPO adequacy score and systems for HINDENen-hi and HINDENhi-ja tasks have low JPO adequacy score. The former system can translate more than 90% of sentences with 4 or 5 JPO adequacy score, however, the latter systems can only translate 10 or 20% of sentences with 4 or 5 JPO adequacy score (see Figure 2).

Task	System No.	BLEU	RIBES	AMFM	HUMAN	HUMAN (top rank)	JPO adq.	JPO adq. (top rank)
en-ja	1	31.32	0.7599	0.7467	39.000	55.250	---	4.02
zh-ja	1	39.75	0.8437	0.7695	32.500	63.750	---	3.94
JPCzh-ja	1	41.05	0.8270	0.7350	35.500	46.500	---	3.44
	2	40.95	0.8280	0.7451	39.000		---	
JPCko-ja	1	71.51	0.9447	0.8664	-3.000	21.750	---	4.62
	2	68.78	0.9411	0.8517	---		---	
	3	62.33	0.9271	0.8180	21.750		4.56	
HINDENen-hi	1	11.75	0.6719	0.6508	0.000	57.250	2.48	2.55
HINDENhi-ja	1	7.81	0.5793	0.4681	13.750	39.750	2.00	2.13
	2	7.66	0.5860	0.4731	10.000		---	
	3	7.47	0.5823	0.4549	---		---	
	4	2.36	0.4402	0.3628	---		---	

Table 7: Evaluation results (Segmenter for ja is JUMAN)

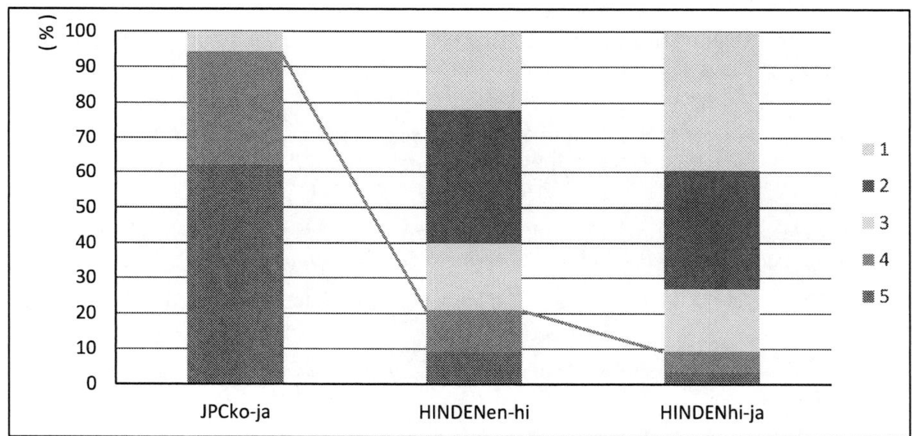

Figure 2: Evaluation results by the JPO adequacy

5   Conclusion

System descriptions, experimental settings and experimental results of EHR group were described. We participate in the 6 tasks and submitted 12 systems' outputs. We can recognize our translation techniques are effective. They are iterative reordering, system combination and pivoting with reordering.

Several remaining issues are as follows. To improve parsing accuracy such that reordering accuracy be higher. To improve English-Hindi and Hindi-Japanese translation accuracy that are largely lower than that of other language pairs. To challenge machine translations for other Asian languages such as Indonesian, Thai, Vietnamese, Mongolian and so on.

Reference

Mauro Cettolo, Christian Girardi, and Marcello Federico. 2012. WIT³: Web Inventory of Transcribed and Translated Talks. *Proceedings of the 16th EAMT Conference*, pages 261-168.

Pi-Chuan Chang, Michel Galley and Chris Manning. 2008. Optimizing Chinese Word Segmentation for Machine Translation Performance. *Proceedings of the Third Workshop on Statistical Machine Translation*, pages 224-232.

Trevor Cohn and Mirella Lapata. 2007. Machine Translation by Triangulation: Making Effective Use of Multi-Parallel Corpora. *Proceedings of the 45th Annual Meeting of the Association of Computational Linguistics*, pages 728–735.

Terumasa Ehara. 2007. Rule Based Machine Translation Combined with Statistical Post Editor for Japanese to English Patent Translation. *Proceedings of Machine Translation Summit XI, Workshop on Patent Translation*, pages 13-18.

Terumasa Ehara. 2015. System Combination of RBMT plus SPE and Preordering plus SMT. *Proceedings of the 2nd Workshop on Asian Translation (WAT2015)*, pages 29–34.

Qin Gao and Stephan Vogel. 2008. Parallel Implementations of Word Alignment Tool. *Software Engineering, Testing, and Quality Assurance for Natural Language Processing*, pages 49–57.

Isao Goto, Ka Po Chow, Bin Lu, Eiichiro Sumita and Benjamin K. Tsou. 2013. Overview of the Patent Machine Translation Task at the NTCIR-10 Workshop. *Proceedings of the 10th NTCIR Conference*, pages 260-286.

Hideki Isozaki, Katsuhito Sudoh, Hajime Tsukada, and Kevin Duh. 2010. Head Finalization: A Simple Reordering Rule for SOV Languages. *Proceedings of the Joint 5th Workshop on Statistical Machine Translation and MetricsMATR*, pages 244–251.

Dan Klein and Christopher D. Manning. 2003. Accurate Unlexicalized Parsing. *Proceedings of the 41st Meeting of the Association for Computational Linguistics*, pages 423-430.

Philipp Koehn, Franz J. Och and Daniel Marcu. 2003. Statistical Phrase-Based Translation. *Proceedings of HLT-NAACL 2003*, pages 48-54.

Anoop Kunchukuttan, Abhijit Mishra, Rajen Chatterjee,Ritesh Shah, and Pushpak Bhattacharyya. 2014. Sata-Anuvadak: Tackling Multiway Translation of Indian Languages. *Proceedings of the Ninth International Conference on Language Resources and Evaluation Conference*.

Sadao Kurohashi, Toshihisa Nakamura, Yuji Matsumoto and Makoto Nagao. 1994. Improvements of Japanese morphological analyzer JUMAN. *Proceedings of The International Workshop on Sharable Natural Language Resources*, pages 22-28.

Hyoung-Gyu Lee, Jaesong Lee, Jun-Seok Kim, and Chang-Ki Lee. 2015. NAVER Machine Translation System for WAT 2015. *Proceedings of the 2nd Workshop on Asian Translation (WAT2015)*, pages 69–73.

Roger Levy and Christopher D. Manning. 2003. Is it harder to parse Chinese, or the Chinese Treebank? *ACL 2003*, pages 439-446.

Evgeny Matusov, Nicola Ueffing and Hermann Ney. 2006. Computing Consensus Translation from Multiple Machine Translation Systems Using Enhanced Hypotheses Alignment. *Proceedings of EACL*, pages 33-40.

Toshiaki Nakazawa, Hideya Mino, Chenchen Ding, Isao Goto, Graham Neubig, Sadao Kurohashi and Eiichiro Sumita. 2016. Overview of the 3rd Workshop on Asian Translation. *Proceedings of the 3rd Workshop on Asian Translation (WAT2016)*.

Franz Josef Och, Hermann Ney. 2003. A Systematic Comparison of Various Statistical Alignment Models. *Computational Linguistics*, volume 29, number 1, pages 19-51.

Deepak Patil, Harshad Chavan and Pushpak Bhattacharyya. 2015. Triangulation of Reordering Tables: An Advancement Over Phrase Table Triangulation in Pivot-Based SMT. *Proceedings of the Twelfth International Conference on Natural Language Processing*.

Slav Petrov, Leon Barrett, Romain Thibaux and Dan Klein. 2006. Learning Accurate, Compact, and Interpretable Tree Annotation. *Proceedings of COLING-ACL 2006*, pages 433-440.

Masao Utiyama and Hitoshi Isahara. 2007. A Comparison of Pivot Methods for Phrase-based Statistical Machine Translation. *Proceedings of NAACL HLT 2007*, pages 484–491.

Hua Wu and Haifeng Wang. 2007. Pivot Language Approach for Phrase-Based Statistical Machine Translation. *Proceedings of the 45th Annual Meeting of the Association of Computational Linguistics*, pages 856–863.

Peng Xu, Jaeho Kang, Michael Ringgaard, and Franz Och. 2009. Using a Dependency Parser to Improve SMT for Subject-Object-Verb Languages. *Human Language Technologies: The 2009 Annual Conference of the North American Chapter of the ACL*, pages 245–253.

Lexicons and Minimum Risk Training for Neural Machine Translation: NAIST-CMU at WAT2016

Graham Neubig[†*]

[†]Nara Institute of Science and Technology, Japan
[*]Carnegie Mellon University, USA
gneubig@cs.cmu.edu

Abstract

This year, the Nara Institute of Science and Technology (NAIST)/Carnegie Mellon University (CMU) submission to the Japanese-English translation track of the 2016 Workshop on Asian Translation was based on attentional neural machine translation (NMT) models. In addition to the standard NMT model, we make a number of improvements, most notably the use of discrete translation lexicons to improve probability estimates, and the use of minimum risk training to optimize the MT system for BLEU score. As a result, our system achieved the highest translation evaluation scores for the task.

1 Introduction

Neural machine translation (NMT; (Kalchbrenner and Blunsom, 2013; Sutskever et al., 2014)), creation of translation models using neural networks, has quickly achieved state-of-the-art results on a number of translation tasks (Luong and Manning, 2015; Sennrich et al., 2016a). In this paper, we describe NMT systems for the Japanese-English scientific paper translation task of the Workshop on Asian Translation (WAT) 2016 (Nakazawa et al., 2016a).

The systems are built using attentional neural networks (Bahdanau et al., 2015; Luong et al., 2015), with a number of improvements (§2). In particular we focus on two. First, we follow the recent work of Arthur et al. (2016) in incorporating discrete translation lexicons to improve the probability estimates of the neural translation model (§3). Second, we incorporate minimum-risk training (Shen et al., 2016) to optimize the parameters of the model to improve translation accuracy (§4).

In experiments (§5), we examine the effect of each of these improvements, and find that they both contribute to overall translation accuracy, leading to state-of-the-art results on the Japanese-English translation task.

2 Baseline Neural Machine Translation Model

Our baseline translation model is the attentional model implemented in the lamtram toolkit (Neubig, 2015), which is a combination of the models of Bahdanau et al. (2015) and Luong et al. (2015) that we found to be effective. We describe the model briefly here for completeness, and refer readers to the previous papers for a more complete description.

2.1 Model Structure

Our model creates a model of target sentence $E = e_1^{|E|}$ given source sentence $F = f_1^{|F|}$. These words belong to the source vocabulary V_f, and the target vocabulary V_e respectively. NMT performs this translation by calculating the conditional probability $p_m(e_i|F, e_1^{i-1})$ of the ith target word e_i based on the source F and the preceding target words e_1^{i-1}. This is done by encoding the context $\langle F, e_1^{i-1}\rangle$ as a fixed-width vector $\boldsymbol{\eta}_i$, and calculating the probability as follows:

$$p_m(e_i|F, e_1^{i-1}) = \text{softmax}(W_s\boldsymbol{\eta}_i + \boldsymbol{b}_s), \tag{1}$$

where W_s and $\boldsymbol{b}_s$ are respectively weight matrix and bias vector parameters. The exact variety of the NMT model depends on how we calculate $\boldsymbol{\eta}_i$ used as input, and as mentioned above, in this case we use an attentional model.

Proceedings of the 3rd Workshop on Asian Translation,
pages 119–125, Osaka, Japan, December 11-17 2016.

First, an *encoder* converts the source sentence F into a matrix R where each column represents a single word in the input sentence as a continuous vector. This representation is generated using a bidirectional encoder

$$\overrightarrow{r}_j = \text{enc}(\text{embed}(f_j), \overrightarrow{r}_{j-1})$$
$$\overleftarrow{r}_j = \text{enc}(\text{embed}(f_j), \overleftarrow{r}_{j+1}).$$

Here the $\text{embed}(\cdot)$ function maps the words into a representation (Bengio et al., 2006), and $\text{enc}(\cdot)$ is long short term memory (LSTM) neural network (Hochreiter and Schmidhuber, 1997) with forget gates set to one minus the value of the input gate (Greff et al., 2015). For the final word in the sentence, we add a sentence-end symbol to the final state of both of these decoders

$$\overrightarrow{r}_{|F|+1} = \text{enc}(\text{embed}(\langle s \rangle), \overrightarrow{r}_{|F|})$$
$$\overleftarrow{r}_{|F|+1} = \text{enc}(\text{embed}(\langle s \rangle), \overleftarrow{r}_1).$$

Finally we concatenate the two vectors $\overrightarrow{r}_j$ and $\overleftarrow{r}_j$ into a bidirectional representation r_j

$$r_j = [\overleftarrow{r}_j; \overrightarrow{r}_j].$$

These vectors are further concatenated into the matrix R where the jth column corresponds to r_j.

Next, we generate the output one word at a time while referencing this encoded input sentence and tracking progress with a *decoder* LSTM. The decoder's hidden state h_i is a fixed-length continuous vector representing the previous target words e_1^{i-1}, initialized as $h_0 = r_{|F|+1}$. This is used to calculate a context vector c_i that is used to summarize the source attentional context used in choosing target word e_i, and initialized as $c_0 = 0$.

First, we update the hidden state to h_i based on the word representation and context vectors from the previous target time step

$$h_i = \text{enc}([\text{embed}(e_{i-1}); c_{i-1}], h_{i-1}). \tag{2}$$

Based on this h_i, we calculate a similarity vector α_i, with each element equal to

$$\alpha_{i,j} = \text{sim}(h_i, r_j). \tag{3}$$

$\text{sim}(\cdot)$ can be an arbitrary similarity function. In our systems, we test two similarity functions, the dot product (Luong et al., 2015)

$$\text{sim}(h_i, r_j) := h_i^\mathsf{T} r_j \tag{4}$$

and the multi-layered perceptron (Bahdanau et al., 2015)

$$\text{sim}(h_i, r_j) := w_{a2}^\mathsf{T} \tanh(W_{a1}[h_i; r_j]), \tag{5}$$

where W_{a1} and w_{a2} are the weight matrix and vector of the first and second layers of the MLP respectively.

We then normalize this into an *attention* vector, which weights the amount of focus that we put on each word in the source sentence

$$a_i = \text{softmax}(\alpha_i). \tag{6}$$

This attention vector is then used to weight the encoded representation R to create a context vector c_i for the current time step

$$c_i = R a_i.$$

Finally, we create η_i by concatenating the previous hidden state with the context vector, and performing an affine transform

$$\eta_i = W_\eta[h_i; c_i] + b_\eta,$$

Once we have this representation of the current state, we can calculate $p_m(e_i | F, e_1^{i-1})$ according to Equation (1). The next word e_i is chosen according to this probability.

2.2 Parameter Optimization

If we define all the parameters in this model as θ, we can then train the model by minimizing the negative log-likelihood of the training data

$$\hat{\theta} = \operatorname*{argmin}_{\theta} \sum_{\langle F, E \rangle} \sum_{i} - \log(p_m(e_i | F, e_1^{i-1}; \theta)).$$

Specifically, we use the ADAM optimizer (Kingma and Ba, 2014), with an initial learning rate of 0.001. Minibatches of 2048 words are created by sorting sentences in descending order of length and grouping sentences sequentially, adding sentences to the minibatch until the next sentence would cause the minibatch size to exceed 2048 words.[1] Gradients are clipped so their norm does not exceed 5.

Training is allowed to run, checking the likelihood of the development set periodically (every 250k sentences processed), and the model that achieves the best likelihood on the development set is saved. Once no improvements on the development set have been observed for 2M training sentences, training is stopped, and re-started using the previously saved model with a halved learning rate 0.0005. Once training converges for a learning rate of 0.0005, the same procedure is performed with a learning rate of 0.00025, resulting in the final model.

2.3 Search

At test time, to find the best-scoring translation, we perform beam search with a beam size of 5. At each step of beam search, the best-scoring hypothesis remaining in the beam that ends with the sentence-end symbol is saved. At the point where the highest-scoring hypothesis in the beam has a probability less than or equal to the best sentence-ending hypothesis, search is terminated and the best sentence-ending hypothesis is output as the translation.

In addition, because NMT models often tend to be biased towards shorter sentences, we add an optional "word penalty" λ, where each hypothesis's probability is multiplied by $e^{\lambda|E'|}$ for comparison with other hypotheses of different lengths. This is equivalent to adding an exponential prior probability on the length of output sentences, and if $\lambda > 0$, then this will encourage the decoder to find longer hypotheses.

3 Incorporating Discrete Lexicons

The first modification that we make to the base model is incorporating discrete lexicons to improve translation probabilities, according to the method of Arthur et al. (2016). The motivation behind this method is twofold:

Handling low-frequency words: Neural machine translation systems tend to have trouble translating low-frequency words (Sutskever et al., 2014), so incorporating translation lexicons with good coverage of content words could improve translation accuracy of these words.

Training speed: Training the alignments needed for discrete lexicons can be done efficiently (Dyer et al., 2013), and by seeding the neural MT system with these efficiently trained alignments it is easier to learn models that achieve good results more quickly.

The model starts with lexical translation probabilities $p_l(e|f)$ for individual words, which have been obtained through traditional word alignment methods. These probabilities must first be converted to a form that can be used together with $p_m(e_i|e_1^{i-1}, F)$. Given input sentence F, we can construct a matrix in which each column corresponds to a word in the input sentence, each row corresponds to a word in the V_E, and the entry corresponds to the appropriate lexical probability:

$$L_F = \begin{bmatrix} p_l(e = 1 | f_1) & \cdots & p_l(e = 1 | f_{|F|}) \\ \vdots & \ddots & \vdots \\ p_l(e = |V_e| | f_1) & \cdots & p_l(e = |V_e| | f_{|F|}) \end{bmatrix}.$$

---

[1] It should be noted that it is more common to create minibatches with a fixed number of sentences. We use words here because the amount of memory used in processing a minibatch is more closely related to the number of words in the minibatch than the number of sentences, and thus fixing the size of the minibatch based on the number of words leads to more stable memory usage between minibatches.

This matrix can be precomputed during the encoding stage because it only requires information about the source sentence F.

Next we convert this matrix into a predictive probability over the next word: $p_l(e_i|F, e_1^{i-1})$. To do so we use the alignment probability a from Equation (6) to weight each column of the L_F matrix:

$$p_l(e_i|F, e_1^{i-1}) = L_F a_i = \begin{bmatrix} p_l(e=1|f_1) & \cdots & p_{lex}(e=1|f_{|F|}) \\ \vdots & \ddots & \vdots \\ p_l(e=V_e|f_1) & \cdots & p_{lex}(e=V_e|f_{|F|}) \end{bmatrix} \begin{bmatrix} a_{i,1} \\ \vdots \\ a_{i,|F|} \end{bmatrix}.$$

This calculation is similar to the way how attentional models calculate the context vector c_i, but over a vector representing the probabilities of the target vocabulary, instead of the distributed representations of the source words.

After calculating the lexicon predictive probability $p_l(e_i|e_1^{i-1}, F)$, next we need to integrate this probability with the NMT model probability $p_m(e_i|e_1^{i-1}, F)$. Specifically, we use $p_l(\cdot)$ to bias the probability distribution calculated by the vanilla NMT model by adding a small constant ϵ to $p_l(\cdot)$, taking the logarithm, and adding this adjusted log probability to the input of the softmax as follows:

$$p_b(e_i|F, e_1^{i-1}) = \text{softmax}(W_s \boldsymbol{\eta}_i + b_s + \log(p_l(e_i|F, e_1^{i-1}) + \epsilon)).$$

We take the logarithm of $p_l(\cdot)$ so that the values will still be in the probability domain after the softmax is calculated, and add the hyper-parameter ϵ to prevent zero probabilities from becoming $-\infty$ after taking the log. We test various values including $\epsilon = \{10^{-4}, 10^{-5}, 10^{-6}\}$ in experiments.

4 Minimum Risk Training

The second improvement that we make to our model is the use of minimum risk training. As mentioned in Section 2.2 our baseline model optimizes the model parameters according to maximize the likelihood of the training data. However, there is a disconnect between the evaluation of our systems using translation accuracy (such as BLEU (Papineni et al., 2002)) and this maximum likelihood objective.

To remove this disconnect, we use the method of Shen et al. (2016) to optimize our systems directly using BLEU score. Specifically, we define the following loss function over the model parameters θ for a single training sentence pair $\langle F, E \rangle$

$$\mathcal{L}_{F,E}(\theta) = \sum_{E'} \text{err}(E, E') P(E'|F; \theta),$$

which is summed over all potential translations E' in the target language. Here $\text{err}(\cdot)$ can be an arbitrary error function, which we define as $1 - \text{SBLEU}(E, E')$, where $\text{SBLEU}(\cdot)$ is the smoothed BLEU score (BLEU+1) proposed by Lin and Och (2004). As the number of target-language translations E' is infinite, the sum above is intractable, so we approximate the sum by randomly sampling a subset of translations S according to $P(E|F; \theta)$, then enumerating over this sample:[2]

$$\mathcal{L}_{F,E}(\theta) = \sum_{E' \in S} \text{err}(E, E') \frac{P(E'|F; \theta)}{\sum_{E'' \in S} P(E''|F; \theta)}.$$

This objective function is then modified by introducing a scaling factor α, which makes it possible to adjust the smoothness of the distribution being optimized, which in turn results in adjusting the strength with which the model will try to push good translations to have high probabilities.

$$\mathcal{L}_{F,E}(\theta) = \sum_{E' \in S} \text{err}(E, E') \frac{P(E'|F; \theta)^\alpha}{\sum_{E'' \in S} P(E''|F; \theta)^\alpha}.$$

In this work, we set $\alpha = 0.005$ following the original paper, and set the number of samples to be 20.

---

[2] The actual procedure for obtaining a sample consists of calculating the probability of the first word $P(e_1|F)$, sampling the first word from this multinomial, and then repeating for each following word until the end of sentence symbol is sampled.

	Attent	Lex (ϵ)	ML (λ=0.0)			ML (λ=0.8)			MR (λ=0.0)		
			B	R	Rat.	B	R	Rat.	B	R	Rat.
(1)	dot	No	22.9	74.4	89.9	24.7	74.3	100.9	25.7	75.4	97.3
(2)	dot	Yes (10^{-4})	23.0	74.6	91.0	24.5	74.2	100.4	25.3	75.3	99.2
(3)	dot	Yes (10^{-5})	23.8	74.6	91.4	25.1	74.2	100.4	25.9	75.5	98.0
(4)	dot	Yes (10^{-6})	23.7	74.4	92.1	25.3	74.3	99.6	26.2	76.0	98.6
(5)	MLP	Yes (10^{-4})	23.7	75.3	88.5	25.5	75.2	97.9	26.9	76.3	98.8
(6)	MLP	Yes (10^{-5})	23.7	75.1	90.5	25.3	74.8	98.6	26.4	75.9	97.7
(7)	MLP	Yes (10^{-6})	23.9	74.6	89.4	25.8	74.6	99.3	26.3	75.7	97.3
(8)	(2)-(7) Ensemble		-			27.3	75.8	99.8	29.3	77.3	97.9

Table 1: Overall BLEU, RIBES, and length ratio for systems with various types of attention (dot product or multi-layer perceptron), lexicon (yes/no and which value of λ), training algorithm (maximum likelihood or minimum risk), and word penalty value.

5   Experiments

5.1   Experimental Setup

To create data to train the model, we use the top 2M sentences of the ASPEC Japanese-English training corpus (Nakazawa et al., 2016b) provided by the task. The Japanese size of the corpus is tokenized using KyTea (Neubig et al., 2011), and the English side is tokenized with the tokenizer provided with the Travatar toolkit (Neubig, 2013). Japanese is further normalized so all full-width roman characters and digits are normalized to half-width. The words are further broken into subword units using joint byte pair encoding (Sennrich et al., 2016b) with 100,000 merge operations.

5.2   Experimental Results

In Figure 1 we show results for various settings regarding attention, the use of lexicons, training criterion, and word penalty. In addition, we calculate the ensemble of 6 models, where the average probability assigned by each of the models is used to determine the probability of the next word at test time.

From the results in the table, we can glean a number of observations.

Use of Lexicons: Comparing (1) with (2-4), we can see that in general, using lexicons tends to provide a benefit, particularly when the ϵ parameter is set to a small value.

Type of Attention: Comparing (2-4) with (5-7) we can see that on average, multi-layer perceptron attention was more effective than using the dot product.

Use of Word Penalties: Comparing the first and second columns of results, there is a large increase in accuracy across the board when using a word penalty, demonstrating that this is an easy way to remedy the length of NMT results.

Minimum Risk Training: Looking at the third column, we can see that there is an additional increase in accuracy from minimum risk training. In addition, we can see that after minimum risk, the model produces hypotheses that are more-or-less appropriate length without using a word penalty, an additional benefit.

Ensemble: As widely reported in previous work, ensembling together multiple models greatly improved performance.

5.3   Manual Evaluation Results

The maximum-likelihood trained ensemble system with a word penalty of 0.8 (the bottom middle system in Table 1) was submitted for manual evaluation. The system was evaluated according to the official

WAT "HUMAN" metric (Nakazawa et al., 2016a), which consists of pairwise comparisons with a baseline phrase-based system, where the evaluated system receives +1 for every win, -1 for every tie, 0 for every loss, these values are averaged over all evaluated sentences, then the value is multiplied by 100. This system achieved a manual evaluation score of 47.50, which was slightly higher than other systems participating in the task. In addition, while the full results of the minimum-risk-based ensemble were not ready in time for the manual evaluation stage, a preliminary system ensembling the minimum-risk-trained versions of the first four systems (1)-(4) in Table 1 was also evaluated (its BLEU/RIBES scores were comparable to the fully ensembled ML-trained system), and received a score of 48.25, the best in the task, albeit by a small margin.

6 Conclusion

In this paper, we described the NAIST-CMU system for the Japanese-English task at WAT, which achieved the most accurate results on this language pair. In particular, incorporating discrete translation lexicons and minimum risk training were found to be useful in achieving these results.

Acknowledgments:

This work was supported by JSPS KAKENHI Grant Number 25730136.

References

Philip Arthur, Graham Neubig, and Satoshi Nakamura. 2016. Incorporating discrete translation lexicons into neural machine translation. In *Proc. EMNLP*.

Dzmitry Bahdanau, Kyunghyun Cho, and Yoshua Bengio. 2015. Neural machine translation by jointly learning to align and translate. In *Proc. ICLR*.

Yoshua Bengio, Holger Schwenk, Jean-Sébastien Senécal, Fréderic Morin, and Jean-Luc Gauvain. 2006. Neural probabilistic language models. In *Innovations in Machine Learning*, volume 194, pages 137–186.

Chris Dyer, Victor Chahuneau, and Noah A. Smith. 2013. A simple, fast, and effective reparameterization of ibm model 2. In *Proc. NAACL*, pages 644–648.

Klaus Greff, Rupesh Kumar Srivastava, Jan Koutník, Bas R. Steunebrink, and Jürgen Schmidhuber. 2015. LSTM: A search space odyssey. *CoRR*, abs/1503.04069.

Sepp Hochreiter and Jürgen Schmidhuber. 1997. Long short-term memory. *Neural computation*, 9(8):1735–1780.

Nal Kalchbrenner and Phil Blunsom. 2013. Recurrent continuous translation models. In *Proc. EMNLP*, pages 1700–1709.

Diederik Kingma and Jimmy Ba. 2014. Adam: A method for stochastic optimization. *arXiv preprint arXiv:1412.6980*.

Chin-Yew Lin and Franz Josef Och. 2004. Orange: a method for evaluating automatic evaluation metrics for machine translation. In *Proc. COLING*, pages 501–507.

Minh-Thang Luong and Christopher D Manning. 2015. Stanford neural machine translation systems for spoken language domains. In *Proc. IWSLT*.

Thang Luong, Hieu Pham, and Christopher D. Manning. 2015. Effective approaches to attention-based neural machine translation. In *Proc. EMNLP*, pages 1412–1421.

Toshiaki Nakazawa, Hideya Mino, Chenchen Ding, Isao Goto, Graham Neubig, Sadao Kurohashi, and Eiichiro Sumita. 2016a. Overview of the 3rd workshop on asian translation. In *Proc. WAT*.

Toshiaki Nakazawa, Manabu Yaguchi, Kiyotaka Uchimoto, Masao Utiyama, Eiichiro Sumita, Sadao Kurohashi, and Hitoshi Isahara. 2016b. ASPEC: Asian scientific paper excerpt corpus.

Graham Neubig, Yosuke Nakata, and Shinsuke Mori. 2011. Pointwise prediction for robust, adaptable Japanese morphological analysis. In *Proc. ACL*, pages 529–533.

Graham Neubig. 2013. Travatar: A forest-to-string machine translation engine based on tree transducers. In *Proc. ACL Demo Track*, pages 91–96.

Graham Neubig. 2015. lamtram: A toolkit for language and translation modeling using neural networks. http://www.github.com/neubig/lamtram.

Kishore Papineni, Salim Roukos, Todd Ward, and Wei-Jing Zhu. 2002. BLEU: a method for automatic evaluation of machine translation. In *Proc. ACL*, pages 311–318.

Rico Sennrich, Barry Haddow, and Alexandra Birch. 2016a. Edinburgh neural machine translation systems for WMT16. In *Proc. WMT*, pages 371–376.

Rico Sennrich, Barry Haddow, and Alexandra Birch. 2016b. Neural machine translation of rare words with subword units. In *Proc. ACL*, pages 1715–1725.

Shiqi Shen, Yong Cheng, Zhongjun He, Wei He, Hua Wu, Maosong Sun, and Yang Liu. 2016. Minimum risk training for neural machine translation. In *Proc. ACL*, pages 1683–1692.

Ilya Sutskever, Oriol Vinyals, and Quoc VV Le. 2014. Sequence to sequence learning with neural networks. In *Proc. NIPS*, pages 3104–3112.

NICT-2 Translation System for WAT2016: Applying Domain Adaptation to Phrase-based Statistical Machine Translation

Kenji Imamura and **Eiichiro Sumita**

National Institute of Information and Communications Technology

3-5 Hikaridai, Seika-cho, Soraku-gun, Kyoto, 619-0289, Japan

{kenji.imamura, eiichiro.sumita}@nict.go.jp

Abstract

This paper describes the NICT-2 translation system for the 3rd Workshop on Asian Translation. The proposed system employs a domain adaptation method based on feature augmentation. We regarded the Japan Patent Office Corpus as a mixture of four domain corpora and improved the translation quality of each domain. In addition, we incorporated language models constructed from Google n-grams as external knowledge. Our domain adaptation method can naturally incorporate such external knowledge that contributes to translation quality.

1 Introduction

In this paper, we describe the NICT-2 translation system for the 3rd Workshop on Asian Translation (WAT2016) (Nakazawa et al., 2016a). The proposed system employs Imamura and Sumita (2016)'s domain adaptation technique, which improves translation quality using other domain data when the target domain data is insufficient. The method employed in this paper assumes multiple domains and improves the quality inside the domains (cf., Section 2).

For WAT2016, the Japan Patent Office (JPO) Corpus can be regarded as multi-domain data because it includes chemistry, electricity, machine, and physics patents with their domain ID, and thus it is suitable for observing the effects of domain adaptation. WAT2016 provides the JPO corpora in Japanese and English (Ja-En), Japanese and Chinese (Ja-Zh), and Japanese and Korean (Ja-Ko) pairs. We used Ja-En and Ja-Zh pairs in order to add Asian Scientific Paper Experts Corpus (ASPEC) (Nakazawa et al., 2016b) as a fifth domain.[1] The relationship between the corpora and domains used in this paper is shown in Table 1.

Corpus	Domain	# of Sentences (Ja-En pair)			# of Sentences (Ja-Zh pair)		
		Training	Development	Test	Training	Development	Test
JPC	Chemistry	250,000	500	500	250,000	500	500
	Electricity	250,000	500	500	250,000	500	500
	Machine	250,000	500	500	250,000	500	500
	Physics	250,000	500	500	250,000	500	500
ASPEC	ASPEC	1,000,000	1,790	1,812	672,315	2,090	2,107

Table 1: Bilingual Corpora and Domains

The remainder of this paper is organized as follows. Section 2 briefly reviews our domain adaptation. Section 3 describes the proposed translation system, including preprocessing, training, and translation. Section 4 explains experimental results focusing on the effects of domain adaptation.

[1]The ASPEC corpus is provided in Ja-En and Ja-Zh pairs.

Proceedings of the 3rd Workshop on Asian Translation,
pages 126–132, Osaka, Japan, December 11-17 2016.

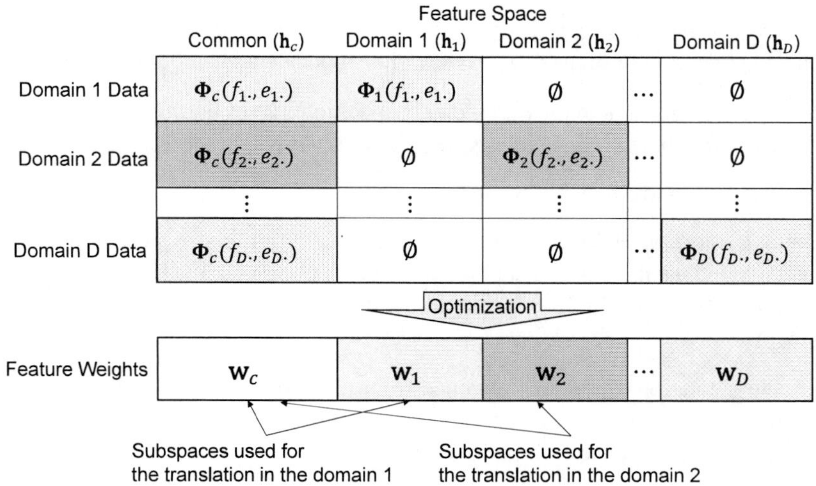

Figure 1: Structure of Augmented Feature Space; $\mathbf{h}_c$ and $\mathbf{h}_i$ denote subvectors of the feature vector $\mathbf{h}(e,f)$. $\mathbf{w}_c$ and $\mathbf{w}_i$ denote subvectors of the weight vector $\mathbf{w}$. $\Phi_c(e,f)$ and $\Phi_i(e,f)$ are feature functions that return feature subvectors (cf., Section 2.2).

2 Domain Adaptation

We used the domain adaptation method proposed by Imamura and Sumita (2016). This method adapts a weight vector by feature augmentation (Daumé, 2007) and a feature vector using a corpus-concatenated model. Since this method only operates in feature space, it can be applied to various translation strategies, such as tree-to-tree translation. In this study, we applied it to phrase-based statistical machine translation (PBSMT) (Koehn et al., 2003; Koehn et al., 2007).

2.1 Adaptation of Weight Vector by Feature Augmentation

Most statistical machine translation employs log-linear models that interpolate feature function values obtained from various submodels, such as phrase tables and language models (LMs). The likelihood of a translation is computed as follows:

$$\log P(e|f) \quad \propto \quad \mathbf{w} \cdot \mathbf{h}(e,f), \tag{1}$$

where $\mathbf{h}(e,f)$ denotes a feature vector and $\mathbf{w}$ denotes its weight vector.

Figure 1 shows a feature space structure of feature augmentation. When we translate texts of D domains, the feature space is segmented into $D+1$ subspaces: common, domain 1, $\cdots$ domain D. A feature vector (subvector) of each subspace is the same as that of a normal translator, i.e., feature function values obtained from phrase tables and language models.

Features of each translation hypothesis are deployed to different spaces depending on the domain of the input data. For example, features obtained from domain 1 data are deployed to the common and domain 1 spaces. Features obtained from domain 2 data are deployed to the common and domain 2 spaces. In other words, features are always deployed to the common spaces.

We obtain the weight vector $\mathbf{w}$ by optimizing a feature matrix of development data acquired by the above process. This weight vector is optimized to each domain. When we translate test data of domain i, only the subspaces of the common and domain i (i.e., subvectors $\mathbf{w}_c$ and $\mathbf{w}_i$) are used.

2.2 Adaptation of Feature Vector using Corpus-Concatenated Model and Single-Domain Models

Our domain adaptation method adapts the feature function $\mathbf{h}(e,f)$ by changing submodels according to the feature spaces.

- For the common space, where all domain features are located, we use a model trained from a concatenated corpus of all domains (i.e., the corpus-concatenated model) to obtain the features.

- For the domain spaces, where only the domain specific features are located, we use models trained from specific domain data (i.e., single-domain models) to obtain the features.

The procedure is summarized as follows.

1. The training corpora of all domains are concatenated. From this corpus, the corpus-concatenated model is trained. This includes all submodels, such as phrase tables, language models, and lexicalized reordering models. Similarly, the single-domain models are trained from the training corpus of each domain.

2. In feature augmentation, the scores obtained from the corpus-concatenated model are deployed to the common space as the feature function values, while those from the single-domain models are deployed to the domain spaces.

   We represent the augmented feature space as follows:

$$\mathbf{h}(f, e) \quad = \quad \langle \mathbf{h}_c, \mathbf{h}_1, \ldots, \mathbf{h}_i, \ldots, \mathbf{h}_D \rangle, \tag{2}$$

   where $\mathbf{h}_c$ denotes a feature vector of the common space, and $\mathbf{h}_i$ denotes a feature vector of the domain i space. The feature vector $\mathbf{\Phi}_c(f, e)$ obtained from the corpus-concatenated model is always located in the common space. The feature vector $\mathbf{\Phi}_i(f, e)$ is located in the domain-specific space i iff the domain of an input sentence is matched to i.

$$\mathbf{h}_c \quad = \quad \mathbf{\Phi}_c(f, e), \tag{3}$$

$$\mathbf{h}_i \quad = \quad \begin{cases} \mathbf{\Phi}_i(f, e) & \text{if domain}(f) = i \\ \emptyset & \text{otherwise.} \end{cases} \tag{4}$$

3. A feature matrix is obtained by translating a development set, and the weight vector $\mathbf{w}$ is acquired by optimizing the feature matrix.

4. For decoding, phrase pairs are first retrieved from both the corpus-concatenated and single-domain phrase tables. Use of the corpus-concatenated phrase table reduces the number of unknown words because phrase pairs appearing in other domains can be used to generate hypotheses.

5. During search of the best hypothesis, the likelihood of each translation hypothesis is computed using only the common space and domain-specific space of the input sentence.

2.3　Implementation Notices

There are some notices for applying the proposed method to phrase-based statistical machine translation.

Empty Value　In the proposed method, several phrases appear in only one of the phrase tables of the corpus-concatenated and single-domain models. The feature functions are expected to return appropriate values for these phrases. We refer to these as empty values.

Even though an empty value is a type of unknown probability and should be computed from the probability distribution of the phrases, we treat it as a hyper-parameter. In other words, an empty value was set experimentally to maximize the BLEU score of a development corpus. Since the BLEU scores were almost stable between -5 and -10 in our preliminary experiments, we used -7 for all settings. If this value is regarded as a probability, it is $\exp(-7) \approx 0.0009$.

Very Large Monolingual Corpora　In machine translation, monolingual corpora are easier to obtain than bilingual corpora. Therefore, language models are sometimes constructed from very large monolingual corpora. They can be regarded as corpus-concatenated models that contain various domains. When we introduce models constructed from external knowledge, they are located in the common space while increasing the dimension. We introduce language models constructed from Google n-grams in Section 4.

		Japanese	English	Chinese
Preprocessing	Character Normalization	NFKC Normalization of Unicode		
	Tokenizer	MeCab	Moses Toolkit	Stanford Segmenter
	TrueCaser	-	Moses Toolkit	-
	PreOrderer	(1) Top-Down BTG		
		(2) Developed by NICT, for Patents (w/ Berkeley Parser)		
Training	Phrase Tables	The same as the baseline system of WAT2016.		
	Lex. Reordering Models	The same as the baseline system of WAT2016.		
	Language Models	(1) 5-gram model built from the target side of the bilingual corpora.		
		(2) Google n-gram	(2) Google n-gram	-
	Optimization	K-Best Batch MIRA		
Translation	Decoder	Clone of Moses Decoder		
	DeTrueCaser	-	Moses Toolkit	-
	DeTokenizer	-	Moses Toolkit	-

Table 2: Summary of Preprocessing, Training, and Translation

Optimization   Imamura and Sumita (2016) proposed joint optimization and independent optimization. We employ independent optimization, which can use existing optimizers.

3   System Description

In this section, we describe the preprocessing, training, and translation components of the proposed system (Table 2).

3.1   Preprocessing

Preprocessing is nearly the same as the baseline system provided by the WAT2016 committee. However, preorderers are added because our system is phrase-based with preordering. We used Nakagawa (2015)'s Top-Down Bracketing Transduction Grammar (TDBTG) trained by the JPO corpus as the preorderer without external knowledge. For the preorderer with external knowledge, we used the one developed in-house (Chapter 4.5 of Goto et al. (2015)),[2] which was tuned for patent translation.

3.2   Training and Optimization

We used the Moses toolkit (Koehn et al., 2007) to train the phrase tables and lexicalized reordering models. We used multi-threaded GIZA++ for word alignment.

For the language models of the corpus-concatenated and single-domain models, we constructed 5-gram models from the target side of the bilingual corpora using KenLM (Heafield et al., 2013). In addition, we included the Google n-gram language models for Japanese and English as the external knowledge. These are back-off models estimated using maximum likelihood. The Japanese model was constructed from Web Japanese N-gram Version 1,[3] and the English model was constructed from Web 1T 5-gram Version 1 (LDC2006T13).

For optimization, we used k-best batch MIRA (Cherry and Foster, 2012).

3.3   Translation

The decoder used here is a clone of the Moses PBSMT decoder. It accepts feature augmentation, i.e., it can use multiple submodels and set an empty value.

---

[2]This preorderer modifies word order based on parse trees output by the Berkeley parser (Petrov et al., 2006; Petrov and Klein, 2007).

[3]http://www.gsk.or.jp/catalog/gsk2007-c/

	JPC			
Method	Ja-En	En-Ja	Ja-Zh	Zh-Ja
Single-Domain Model	34.58	38.06	33.35	39.54
Corpus Concatenation	35.64	38.61	34.27	40.96
Domain Adaptation	**35.68**	**39.03**	**34.64**	**41.09**

Table 3: BLEU Scores on JPO Corpus (official scores)

	JPC			
Method	Ja-En	En-Ja	Ja-Zh	Zh-Ja
Single-Domain Model	35.12(-)	37.40(-)	31.96(-)	38.15(-)
Corpus Concatenation	36.22	38.03(-)	32.92(-)	39.68(-)
Domain Adaptation	**36.29**	**38.48**	**33.36**	**39.85**

Table 4: BLEU Scores on JPO Corpus (MultEval scores)

4 Experimental Results

For evaluation, we used two toolkits based on BLEU (Papineni et al., 2002). One is the official BLEU scores provided by the WAT2016 committee. Because the official tool cannot measure a significance level of two systems, we also used the MultEval tool (Clark et al., 2011), which can measure significance levels based on bootstrap resampling. Since we represent the mean scores of three optimizations, the MultEval scores differ from the official scores.

4.1 JPO Corpus (without External Knowledge)

For JPO corpus experiments, we did not use external knowledge and compared translations of the single-domain model, corpus concatenation, and domain adaptation. The JPO corpus was divided into four domains (chemistry, electricity, machine, and physics). Tables 3 and 4 show the results evaluated by the official scorer and MultEval tools, respectively. The symbol (-) indicates that the score was significantly degraded compared to that of the domain adaptation ($p < 0.05$). Note that test sentences of each domain were translated using the corresponding models, and the BLEU score was computed by concatenating all test sentences as a document.

Results are presented in Table 4. Corpus concatenation corresponds to typical translation quality where only the JPO corpus was used. The single-domain model scores were inferior to the corpus concatenation scores because the corpus sizes were reduced by one-quarter. In contrast, the domain adaptation scores for most language pairs improved significantly and the domain adaptation was successful.

4.2 JPO and ASPEC Corpora (with External Knowledge)

Next, we conducted experiments using five domains with the JPO and ASPEC corpora. In these experiments, we evaluated the effects of external knowledge using the Google n-gram language model. The results are shown in Tables 5 and 6.

We first describe the effects of external knowledge, as shown in Table 6. In Table 6, the upper and lower halves show the BLEU scores before and after adding the Google n-gram language model, respectively. By adding the Google n-gram LMs, 0.27, 0.82, and 0.12 BLEU scores were improved on average in the JPO domains of Ja-En, En-Ja and Zh-Ja pairs, respectively. In the ASPEC domain, -0.03, 0.56, and 0.67 BLEU scores were improved. Except for the Ja-En pair of the ASPEC domain, the Google n-gram language model contributed to translation quality. The Japanese model tends to be suitable for JPO and ASPEC domains compared to the English model.

Next, we focused on the effect of domain adaptation with the Google n-gram LMs. In most cases, domain adaptation worked effectively except for the Ja-En pair of the ASPEC domain because the BLEU scores improved or were maintained the same level compared to those of the single-domain model and

LM	Method	JPC				ASPEC			
		Ja-En	En-Ja	Ja-Zh	Zh-Ja	Ja-En	En-Ja	Ja-Zh	Zh-Ja
w/o GN	Single-Domain Model	33.67	38.75	33.27	40.06	21.54	33.97	**30.12**	39.33
	Corpus Concatenation	35.49	39.18	33.94	41.08	20.90	33.11	29.66	37.84
	Domain Adaptation	35.96	40.14	**34.64**	**41.93**	21.34	34.21	29.97	39.51
w/ GN	Single-Domain Model	33.99	39.63		40.47	**21.64**	34.59		40.01
	Corpus Concatenation	35.73	40.23		41.31	20.80	33.78		38.30
	Domain Adaptation	**36.06**	**40.90**		41.87	21.54	**34.67**		**40.02**

Table 5: BLEU Scores on JPO and ASPEC Corpora (official scores)

LM	Method	JPC				ASPEC			
		Ja-En	En-Ja	Ja-Zh	Zh-Ja	Ja-En	En-Ja	Ja-Zh	Zh-Ja
w/o GN	Single-Domain Model	33.90(-)	38.19(-)	31.78(-)	38.74(-)	22.79	34.80	**29.47**(+)	38.96(-)
	Corpus Concatenation	35.81(-)	38.62(-)	32.76(-)	39.96(-)	22.20(-)	33.94(-)	28.95(-)	37.62(-)
	Domain Adaptation	36.25	39.58	**33.53**	40.76	22.80	34.91	29.28	39.18
w/ GN	Single-Domain Model	34.35(-)	39.04(-)		38.90(-)	**22.87**(+)	**35.42**		39.74(-)
	Corpus Concatenation	36.03(-)	39.48(-)		40.14(-)	22.10(-)	34.55(-)		38.15(-)
	Domain Adaptation	**36.40**	**40.32**		**40.77**	22.74	35.36		**39.87**

Table 6: BLEU Scores on JPO and ASPEC Corpora (MultEval scores)

corpus concatenation. However, we confirmed that the effects of the ASPEC domain were less than those of the JPO domains because the score did not improve significantly. This is because the ASPEC domain uses one million bilingual sentences; thus, domain adaptation could not contribute to the high-resource domains.

5 Conclusions

We have described the NICT-2 translation system. The proposed system employs Imamura and Sumita (2016)'s domain adaptation. In this study, we regarded the JPO corpus as a mixture of four domains and improved the translation quality. Although we added the ASPEC corpus as a fifth domain, the effects were not significant. Our domain adaptation can incorporate external knowledge, such as Google n-gram language models. The proposed domain adaptation can be applied to existing translation systems with little modification.

Acknowledgments

This work was supported by "Promotion of Global Communications Plan — Research and Development and Social Demonstration of Multilingual Speech Translation Technology," a program of the Ministry of Internal Affairs and Communications, Japan.

References

Colin Cherry and George Foster. 2012. Batch tuning strategies for statistical machine translation. In *Proceedings of the 2012 Conference of the North American Chapter of the Association for Computational Linguistics: Human Language Technologies*, pages 427–436, Montréal, Canada, June.

Jonathan H. Clark, Chris Dyer, Alon Lavie, and Noah A. Smith. 2011. Better hypothesis testing for statistical machine translation: Controlling for optimizer instability. In *Proceedings of the 49th Annual Meeting of the Association for Computational Linguistics: Human Language Technologies*, pages 176–181, Portland, Oregon, USA, June.

Hal Daumé, III. 2007. Frustratingly easy domain adaptation. In *Proceedings of the 45th Annual Meeting of the Association of Computational Linguistics*, pages 256–263, Prague, Czech Republic, June.

Isao Goto, Masao Utiyama, Eiichiro Sumita, and Sadao Kurohashi. 2015. Preordering using a target-language parser via cross-language syntactic projection for statistical machine translation. *ACM Trans. Asian Low-Resour. Lang. Inf. Process.*, 14(3):13:1–13:23, June.

Kenneth Heafield, Ivan Pouzyrevsky, Jonathan H. Clark, and Philipp Koehn. 2013. Scalable modified Kneser-Ney language model estimation. In *Proceedings of the 51st Annual Meeting of the Association for Computational Linguistics (Volume 2: Short Papers)*, pages 690–696, Sofia, Bulgaria, August.

Kenji Imamura and Eiichiro Sumita. 2016. Multi-domain adaptation for statistical machine translation based on feature augmentation. In *Proceedings of AMTA 2016: Association for Machine Translation in the Americas*, Austin, Texas, USA, October.

Philipp Koehn, Franz J. Och, and Daniel Marcu. 2003. Statistical phrase-based translation. In *HLT-NAACL 2003: Main Proceedings*, pages 127–133, Edmonton, Alberta, Canada, May 27 - June 1.

Philipp Koehn, Hieu Hoang, Alexandra Birch, Chris Callison-Burch, Marcello Federico, Nicola Bertoldi, Brooke Cowan, Wade Shen, Christine Moran, Richard Zens, Chris Dyer, Ondrej Bojar, Alexandra Constantin, and Evan Herbst. 2007. Moses: Open source toolkit for statistical machine translation. In *Proceedings of the 45th Annual Meeting of the Association for Computational Linguistics Companion Volume Proceedings of the Demo and Poster Sessions*, pages 177–180, Prague, Czech Republic, June.

Tetsuji Nakagawa. 2015. Efficient top-down BTG parsing for machine translation preordering. In *Proceedings of the 53rd Annual Meeting of the Association for Computational Linguistics and the 7th International Joint Conference on Natural Language Processing (ACL-2015) (Volume 1: Long Papers)*, pages 208–218, Beijing, China, July.

Toshiaki Nakazawa, Hideya Mino, Chenchen Ding, Isao Goto, Graham Neubig, Sadao Kurohashi, and Eiichiro Sumita. 2016a. Overview of the 3rd workshop on Asian translation. In *Proceedings of the 3rd Workshop on Asian Translation (WAT2016)*, Osaka, Japan, December.

Toshiaki Nakazawa, Manabu Yaguchi, Kiyotaka Uchimoto, Masao Utiyama, Eiichiro Sumita, Sadao Kurohashi, and Hitoshi Isahara. 2016b. ASPEC: Asian scientific paper excerpt corpus. In *Proceedings of the 10th Conference on International Language Resources and Evaluation (LREC-2016)*, Portoroz, Slovenia, May.

Kishore Papineni, Salim Roukos, Todd Ward, and Wei-Jing Zhu. 2002. Bleu: a method for automatic evaluation of machine translation. In *Proceedings of the 40th Annual Meeting of the Association for Computational Linguistics (ACL)*, pages 311–318, Philadephia, Pennsylvania, USA, July.

Slav Petrov and Dan Klein. 2007. Improved inference for unlexicalized parsing. In *Human Language Technologies 2007: The Conference of the North American Chapter of the Association for Computational Linguistics; Proceedings of the Main Conference*, pages 404–411, Rochester, New York, April. Association for Computational Linguistics.

Slav Petrov, Leon Barrett, Romain Thibaux, and Dan Klein. 2006. Learning accurate, compact, and interpretable tree annotation. In *Proceedings of the 21st International Conference on Computational Linguistics and 44th Annual Meeting of the Association for Computational Linguistics*, pages 433–440, Sydney, Australia, July. Association for Computational Linguistics.

Translation Using JAPIO Patent Corpora: JAPIO at WAT2016

Satoshi Kinoshita   Tadaaki Oshio   Tomoharu Mitsuhashi   Terumasa Ehara[1]
Japan Patent Information Organization
{satoshi_kinoshita, t_oshio, t_mitsuhashi}@ japio.or.jp
eharate@ gmail.com

Abstract

Japan Patent Information Organization (JAPIO) participates in scientific paper subtask (ASPEC-EJ/CJ) and patent subtask (JPC-EJ/CJ/KJ) with phrase-based SMT systems which are trained with its own patent corpora. Using larger corpora than those prepared by the workshop organizer, we achieved higher BLEU scores than most participants in EJ and CJ translations of patent subtask, but in crowdsourcing evaluation, our EJ translation, which is best in all automatic evaluations, received a very poor score. In scientific paper subtask, our translations are given lower scores than most translations that are produced by translation engines trained with the in-domain corpora. But our scores are higher than those of general-purpose RBMTs and online services. Considering the result of crowdsourcing evaluation, it shows a possibility that CJ SMT system trained with a large patent corpus translates non-patent technical documents at a practical level.

1   Introduction

Japan Patent Information Organization (JAPIO) provides a patent information service named GPG-FX[2], which enables users to do cross-lingual information retrieval (CLIR) on patent documents by translating English and Chinese patents into Japanese and storing the translations in a full-text search engine.

For this purpose, we use a rule-based machine translation (RBMT) system and a phrase-based statistical machine translation (SMT) system for English-to-Japanese and Chinese-to-Japanese translation respectively. To improve translation quality, we have been collecting technical terms and building parallel corpora, and the current corpora sizes are 250 million sentence pairs for English-Japanese (EJ) and 100 million for Chinese-Japanese (CJ). We have also built a Korean-Japanese (KJ) corpus which contains about 5 million sentence pairs for adding Korean-to-Japanese translation to enable searching Korean patents as well.

The Japan Patent Office (JPO) and National Institute of Information and Communications Technology (NICT) have also built very large parallel corpora in patent domain. Their EJ, CJ and KJ corpora whose sizes are 350, 130 and 80 million sentence pairs are available at ALAGIN[3] for research purposes. Considering this trend, we think it important to make a research on a methodology to use very large parallel corpora for building a practical SMT system, as well as a research for creating a framework that can provide high automatic evaluation scores using a corpus of small size. This consideration led us to attend the 3rd Workshop on Asian Translation (WAT2016) (Nakazawa et al, 2016) in order to confirm the effectiveness of our own large patent parallel corpora.

---

[1] Guest researcher

[2] http://www.japio.or.jp/service/service05.html

[3] https://alaginrc.nict.go.jp/

Proceedings of the 3rd Workshop on Asian Translation,
pages 133–138, Osaka, Japan, December 11-17 2016.

2 Systems

We used two SMT systems to produce translations for the workshop.

The first one is a phrase-based SMT toolkit licensed by NICT (Utiyama and Sumita, 2014). It includes a pre-ordering module, which changes word order of English and Chinese source sentences into a head-final manner to improve translation into Japanese. We used it for EJ and CJ translation.

The second is Moses (Koehn et al., 2007), which is used for KJ translation. We used no morphological analyser for tokenizing Korean sentences. Instead, we simply decompose them into tokens which consist of only one Hangul character, and add a special token which represents a blank. To tokenize Japanese sentences, we used juman version 7.0 (Kurohashi et al., 1994). Distortion limit is set to 0 when the decoder runs whatever MERT estimates because of linguistic similarity between Korean and Japanese.

In addition, we include the following post-editing functions depending on translation directions and subtasks:

- Changing Japanese punctuation marks "、" to commas, and some patent-specific expressions to what are common in scientific papers (ASPEC-EJ/CJ)
- Recovering lowercased out-of-vocabularies (OOVs) to their original spellings (EJ)
- Balancing unbalanced parentheses (KJ) (Ehara, 2015)

3 Corpora and Training of SMT

Our patent parallel corpora, hereafter JAPIO corpora, are built automatically from pairs of patent specifications called "patent families," which typically consists of an original document in one language and its translations in other languages. Sentence alignment is performed by an alignment tool licensed by NICT (Utiyama and Isahara, 2007).

When we decided to attend WAT2016, we had EJ and CJ SMT systems which were built for research purposes, whose maximum training corpus sizes were 20 and 49 million sentence pairs respectively, and we thought what we had to do was to translate test sets except for KJ patent subtask. However, we found that about 24% and 55% of sentences in the patent subtask test sets were involved in JAPIO corpora for EJ and CJ respectively[4]. Although we built our corpora independently from those of Japan Patent Office corpora (JPC), a similarity to use patent-family documents may have led the situation. In order to make our submission to WAT more meaningful, we determined that we would publish automatic evaluation results of translations by the above SMT systems, but would not ask for human evaluation, and started retraining of SMT systems with corpora which exclude sentences in JPC test sets.

By the deadline of submission, we finished training CJ SMT with 4 million sentence pairs. As for EJ SMT, we finished training with 5 million sentence pairs, and added 1 million sentences of JPC corpus for an extra result.

In the case of KJ patent subtask, JAPIO corpus contains only 0.6% of JPC test set sentences, which are smaller than that of JPC training set[4]. So we used our KJ corpus without removing sentences contained in JPC test set. One thing we'd better to mention here is that 2.6 million sentence pairs out of 5 million, and 2.3 million out of 6 million, were filtered by corpus-cleaning of Moses because of limitation for maximum number of tokens per sentence. This is because we tokenized Korean sentences not by morphological analysis but based on Hangul characters.

As for scientific paper subtask, we did not use ASPEC corpus (Nakazawa et al, 2016), which is provided for this task, but used only our patent corpus. Since ASPEC corpus and our corpus were built from different data sources, our EJ corpus contains no sentence of ASPEC-EJ test set, and CJ corpus contains only 2 sentences of CJ test set. Therefore, we used SMT systems which are trained with our original corpora. For a submission of EJ translations, we chose a result translated by an SMT which was trained with 10 million sentence pairs because its BLEU score was higher than that with 20 million sentence pairs.

Finally, all development sets used in MERT process are from our corpora, whose sizes are about 3,000, 5,000 and 1,900 for EJ, CJ and KJ respectively.

---

[4] JPC training sets contain 1.1%, 2.3% and 1.0% of sentences of EJ, CJ and KJ test sets respectively.

4 Results

Table 1 shows official evaluation results for our submissions[5].

On patent subtask, the result shows that using a larger corpus does not necessarily lead to a higher BLEU score. Translation with our 5 million corpus achieved a lower score than that with 1 million JPC corpus in JPC-KJ subtask although training with our corpora achieved higher BLEU scores than most of the participants in EJ and CJ translations. In addition, those for KJ translations are lower than many of the task participants although our corpus is much larger than JPC corpus. In crowdsourcing evaluation, our EJ result, which received best scores in all automatic evaluations among the results submitted for human evaluation, received a poorer score than we expected.

On scientific paper subtask, we cannot achieve scores which are comparable with scores of translations that are produced by translation engines trained with ASPEC corpora. However, our scores are higher than those of general-purpose RBMTs and online services. Considering the result of crowdsourcing evaluation, this suggests a possibility that a CJ SMT system trained with a large patent corpus translates non-patent technical documents at a practical level even though the used resource is out of domain.

#	Subtask	System	Corpus	Size (million)	BLEU	RIEBS	AMFM	HUMAN
1		JAPIO-a	JAPIO-test	5	45.57	0.851376	0.747910	17.750
2	JPC-EJ	JAPIO-b	JAPIO-test+JPC	6	47.79	0.859139	0.762850	26.750
3		JAPIO-c	JAPIO	5	50.28	0.859957	0.768690	—
4		JAPIO-d	JPC	1	38.59	0.839141	0.733020	—
5		JAPIO-a	JAPIO-test	3	43.87	0.833586	0.748330	43.500
6	JPC-CJ	JAPIO-b	JAPIO-test	4	44.32	0.834959	0.751200	46.250
7		JAPIO-c	JAPIO	49	58.66	0.868027	0.808090	—
8		JAPIO-d	JPC	1	39.29	0.820339	0.733300	—
9		JAPIO-a	JAPIO	5	68.62	0.938474	0.858190	-9.000
10	JPC-KJ	JAPIO-b	JAPIO+JPC	6	70.32	0.942137	0.863660	17.500
11		JAPIO-c	JPC	1	69.10	0.940367	0.859790	—
12		JAPIO-a	JAPIO	10	20.52	0.723467	0.660790	4.250
13	ASPEC-EJ	Online x	—	—	18.28	0.706639	0.677020	49.750
14		RBMT x	—	—	13.18	0.671958	—	—
15		JAPIO-a	JAPIO	49	26.24	0.790553	0.696770	16.500
16	ASPEC-CJ	Online x	—	—	11.56	0.589802	0.659540	-51.250
17		RBMT x	—	—	19.24	0.741665	—	—

Table 1: Official Evaluation Results

5 Discussion

5.1 Error Analysis of Patent Subtask

We analysed errors which are involved in translations of EJ, CJ and KJ patent subtask by comparing our translations with the given references. Analysed translations are the first 200 sentences of each test set, and are from translation #1(EJ), #6(CJ) and #9(KJ) in Table 1.

Table 2 shows the result. Numbers of mistranslation for content words are comparable although that of KJ is less than those of EJ and CJ. This type of error can only be resolved by adding translation examples to a training corpus. Other errors which are critical in EJ and CJ translation are mistranslation

---

[5] Scores of BLEU, RIEBS and AMFM in the table are those calculated with tokens segmented by juman. Evaluation results of an online service and RBMT systems are also listed for the sake of comparison in ASPEC-EJ and CJ subtasks.

of functional words and errors of part of speech (POS) and word order which seem due to errors in pre-ordering. This suggests that improvement of pre-ordering might be more effective to better translation quality than increasing parallel corpora for EJ and CJ translation, which seems compatible with a future work derived from an analysis of crowdsourcing evaluation, which shows a poor correlation between automatic and human evaluations in JPC-EJ, and JPO adequacy evaluation.

Error Type	EJ	CJ	KJ
Insertion	0	0	6
Deletion	4	9	1
OOV	6	9	2
Mistranslation(content word)	44	41	30
Mistranslation(functional word)	21	51	0
Pre-ordering	33	45	0
Other	6	7	2
Total	114	162	41

Table 2: Errors of patent subtask

5.2   Error Analysis of Scientific Paper Subtask

We analysed errors of translations in EJ and CJ scientific paper subtask from a viewpoint of domain adaptation. As described in section 3, what we used to train SMTs for this subtask are not ASPEC corpora but our patent corpora. Therefore, some of the mistranslations must be recognized as domain-specific errors. That is, words and expressions which appear frequently in scientific papers but seldom in patent documents must have tendencies to be mistranslated. Similarly, what appear frequently in patents but seldom in papers and what appear frequently in both domains but are often translated differently might also be mistranslated. We call these types of error as "type A" and "type B" error respectively. Table 3 shows their examples. In example 1, word "paper(academic article)" is mistranslated as "紙(physical paper)," which can be categorized as a type A error. Word "discusses" is mistranslated as "開示されている(disclose)," which can be categorized as a type B error. Example 2 shows another type B error, where word "我们(we)" is mistranslated as "本発明者ら(the inventors)."

Example 1	
Source	This <u>paper</u> <u>discusses</u> the mechanism of the heat return reaction.
Reference	熱戻り反応の機構を議論した
MT	この<u>紙</u>は，熱戻り反応の機構<u>が開示されている</u>。

Example 2	
Source	由此，伴随中国乡镇向城市化发展而增加的环境负荷，<u>我们</u>从大气污染角度着手并利用环境库兹涅茨曲线进行环境分析，再将与他发达国家的城市环境相比较，探讨了降低环境负荷的可能性。
Reference	このような状況から,中国の都市化に伴う環境負荷の増大について大気汚染に着目して環境クズネック曲線を用いて分析し,先進諸国の都市の動向と比較して,その環境負荷低減策の可能性について考察した。
MT	これにより，中国タウン都市化発展に増加した環境負荷を伴って，<u>本発明者ら</u>は，大気汚染の観点から着手し，利用環境库兹涅茨曲線環境分析を行い，さらに，彼と先進国の都市環境と比較して，環境負荷を低減する可能性を検討した。

Table 3: Examples of translation error

Table 4 shows the result. We analysed mistranslated content words from 200 translations of ASPEC-EJ/CJ test sets.

Error Type	EJ	CJ
Type A Error	9 (3.7%)	0
Type B Error	5 (2.1%)	6 (2.7%)
OOV	68 (28.2%)	48 (21.7%)
Others	159 (66.0%)	167 (75.6%)
Total	241	221

Table 4: Errors in translations of scientific paper subtask

As the table shows, domain-specific errors, that is type A and B errors, are only 5.8% in EJ translation and 2.7% in CJ. Rest of errors are related to OOVs or errors which come from the statistical characteristics of training corpora. As in the analysis of 5.1, OOVs can only be resolved by adding translation examples to a training corpus. Some of the other type of errors might, however, be resolved by modifying data in patent corpora. One idea is to remove numbering expressions such as 1 or 1a in "XX system 1" or "YY device 1a." Because usage of numbering in scientific papers is limited compared to that in patent documents, removing uncommon numbering expressions in scientific papers from patent corpora may generate better translation and language models for the domain.

6 Conclusion

In this paper, we described systems and corpora of Team JAPIO for submitting translations to WAT2016. The biggest feature of our experimental settings is that we use larger patent corpora than those prepared by the workshop organizer. We used 3 to 6 million sentence pairs for training SMT systems for patent subtask (JPC-EJ/CJ/KJ) and 10 and 49 million sentence pairs for scientific paper subtask (ASPEC-EJ/CJ). Using the corpora, we achieved higher BLEU scores than most participants in EJ and CJ translations of patent subtask. In crowdsourcing evaluation, however, our EJ translation, which is best in all automatic evaluations, received a very poor score.

In scientific paper subtask, our translations are given lower scores than most translations that are produced by translation engines trained with the in-domain corpora. But our scores are higher than those of general-purpose RBMTs and online services. Considering the result of crowdsourcing evaluation, it shows a possibility that a CJ SMT system trained with a large patent corpus translates non-patent technical documents at a practical level.

References

Terumasa Ehara. 2015. System Combination of RBMT plus SPE and Preordering plus SMT. In *Proceedings of the 2nd Workshop on Asian Translation (WAT2015)*.

Philipp Koehn, Hieu Hoang, Alexandra Birch, Chris Callison-Burch, Marcello Federico, Nicola Bertoldi, Brooke Cowan, Wade Shen, Christine Moran, Richard Zens, Chris Dyer, Ondrej Bojar, Alexandra Constantin, and Evan Herbst. 2007. Moses: Open source toolkit for statistical machine translation. In *Annual Meeting of the Association for Computational Linguistics (ACL)*, demonstration session.

Sadao Kurohashi, Toshihisa Nakamura, Yuji Matsumoto, and Makoto Nagao. 1994. Improvements of Japanese morphological analyzer JUMAN. In *Proceedings of the International Workshop on Sharable Natural Language*, pages 22–28.

Toshiaki Nakazawa, Hideya Mino, Chenchen Ding, Isao Goto, Graham Neubig, Sadao Kurohashi and Eiichiro Sumita. 2016. Overview of the 3rd Workshop on Asian Translation. In *Proceedings of the 3rd Workshop on Asian Translation (WAT2016)*.

Toshiaki Nakazawa, Manabu Yaguchi, Kiyotaka Uchimoto, Masao Utiyama, Eiichiro Sumita, Sadao Kurohashi and Hitoshi Isahara. 2016. ASPEC: Asian Scientific Paper Excerpt Corpus. In *Proceedings of the 10th Conference on International Language Resources and Evaluation (LREC2016)*.

Masao Utiyama and Hiroshi Isahara. 2007. A Japanese-English Patent Parallel Corpus. In *MT summit XI*, pages 475-482.

Masao Utiyama and Eiichiro Sumita. 2014. AAMT Nagao Award Memorial lecture. http://www2.nict.go.jp/astrec-att/member/mutiyama/pdf/AAMT2014.pdf

An Efficient and Effective Online Sentence Segmenter
for Simultaneous Interpretation

Xiaolin Wang   Andrew Finch   Masao Utiyama   Eiichiro Sumita
Advanced Translation Research and Development Promotion Center
National Institute of Information and Communications Technology, Japan
`{xiaolin.wang,andrew.finch,mutiyama,eiichiro.sumita}@nict.go.jp`

Abstract

Simultaneous interpretation is a very challenging application of machine translation in which the input is a stream of words from a speech recognition engine. The key problem is how to segment the stream in an online manner into units suitable for translation. The segmentation process proceeds by calculating a confidence score for each word that indicates the soundness of placing a sentence boundary after it, and then heuristics are employed to determine the position of the boundaries. Multiple variants of the confidence scoring method and segmentation heuristics were studied. Experimental results show that the best performing strategy is not only efficient in terms of average latency per word, but also achieved end-to-end translation quality close to an offline baseline, and close to oracle segmentation.

1 Introduction

Simultaneous interpretation performs spoken language translation in a online manner. A spoken language translation system automatically translates text from an automatic speech recognition (ASR) system into another language. Spoken language translation itself is an important application of machine translation (MT) because it takes one of the most natural forms of human communication – speech – as input (Peitz et al., 2011). Simultaneous interpretation is even more demanding than spoken language translation because the processing must occur online.

Simultaneous interpretation can bridge the language gap in people's daily lives transparently because of its ability to respond immediately to users' speech input. Simultaneous interpretation systems recognize and translate speech at the same time the speakers are speaking, thus the audience can hear the translation and catch the meaning without delay. Potential applications of simultaneous interpretation include interpreting speeches and supporting cross-lingual conversation.

This paper is devoted to online sentence segmentation methods for simultaneous interpretation. Simultaneous interpretation systems are normally comprised of ASR systems and MT systems. The output of ASR systems is typically streams of words, but the input to MT systems is normally sentences. Sentence segmenters bridge this gap by segmenting stream of words into sentences. Figure 1 illustrates this process.

A number of segmentation methods have been proposed to pipeline ASR and MT, yet most of them require a long context of future words that follow sentence boundaries. In addition, they are often computationally expensive. These shortages make them unattractive for use in simultaneous interpretation. To the best of our knowledge, there are no published ready-to-use online sentence segmenters, and this motivated this paper. The proposed method is crafted in a way that requires little computation and minimum future words in order to achieve efficiency. Also the proposed method is directly optimized against the widely used measurement of translation quality – BLEU (Papineni et al., 2002) – in order to achieve effectiveness. We believe that this work can directly contribute to the development of real-world simultaneous interpretation systems.

The main contributions of this paper are,

- proposing a segment boundary confidence score;

Proceedings of the 3rd Workshop on Asian Translation,
pages 139–148, Osaka, Japan, December 11-17 2016.

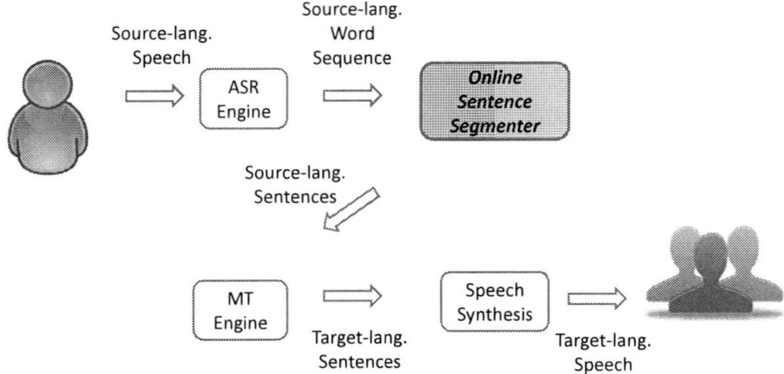

Figure 1: Illustration of Online Sentence Segmenter in Simultaneous Interpretation System

- proposing a hybrid online sentence segmenter;

- an empirical study and analysis of the proposed method on two translation tasks.

The rest of this paper is organized as follows. Section 2 reviews related works on segmentation methods. Section 3 describes our methods. Section 4 presents experiments between English and Japanese. Section 5 concludes this paper with a description of future work.

2 Related Works

A number of methods have been proposed to segment the output of ASR for MT. The works of Stolcke and Shriberg (1996), and Stolcke et al. (1998) are most related to this paper. They treated segmentation boundaries as hidden events occurring between words. They used N-gram language models and Viterbi algorithms to find the most likely sequences of hidden events. We admire them for approaching the problem by language models, which are well-studied techniques that run very fast. For sentence segmentation, they can tackle the task through the insertion of hidden beginning and end of sentence events. However, Stolcke et al. employed off-line Viterbi algorithms that require a long context of words. This will causes long latency for simultaneous interpretation. Therefore, this work has focused on developing lower-latency segmenters that require only one future word. Please note that Stolcke et al.'s methods are implemented using the SRILM toolkit, and it is used as a baseline (denoted *Hidden N-gram*) in our experiments.

Fügen et al. (2007) and Bangalore et al. (2012) proposed using pauses captured by ASR to denote segmentation boundaries. However, studies on human interpreters show that segmenting merely by pauses is insufficient, as human speakers may not pause between sentences. The mean proportion of silence-based chunking by interpreters is 6.6% when the source is English, 10% when it is French, and 17.1% when it is German (Venuti, 2012). Therefore, this paper focuses on using linguistic information. Nevertheless, pauses can be directly integrated into the proposed segment boundary confidence scores to boost performance.

Matusov et al. (2006) proposed a sentence segmentation algorithm which is similar to a conditional random field (CRF) (Lafferty et al., 2001). Lu and Ng (2010) applied CRFs to punctuation prediction which is an almost equivalent task to sentence segmentation. These CRF-based methods achieve high performance as they are able to integrate arbitrary features. However, CRF models take whole sequences as input, thus they cannot be directly applied in an online manner. Online CRFs are beyond the scope of this paper, and we plan to explore this in the future.

Ha et al. (2015) approached sentence segmentation by training a specialized monolingual machine translation system. Kzai et al. (2015) proposed a neural network approach to sentence segmentation. These two methods both require whole sequences as input, and require heavy computation. Therefore, they might not be suitable for online segmentation.

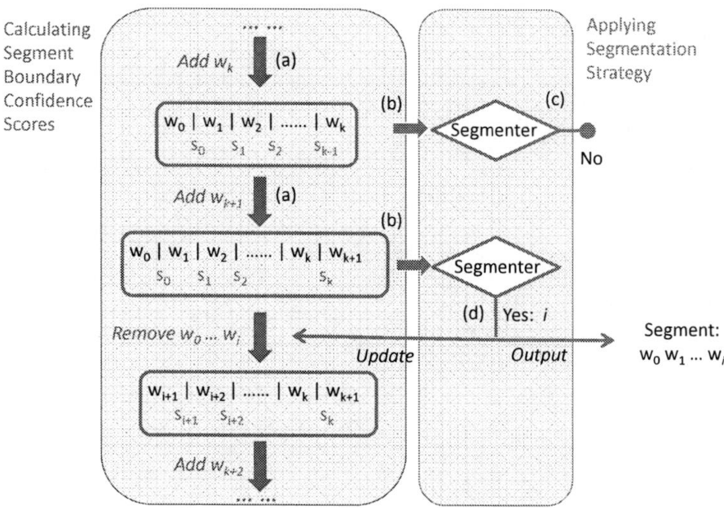

Figure 2: Illustration of Proposed Online Sentence Segmenter

A number of segmentation strategies targeted at splitting an input sentence into smaller pieces for simultaneous interpretation. Yarmohammadi et al. (2013) extracted monotonic phrase alignments from word-aligned sentence pairs and assumed that these phrasal alignments segment the source sentences in an appropriate manner for MT. They used the segmented data to train a binary classifier to predict segmentation boundaries.

Oda et al. (2014) built training data sets for segmentation through a greedy search algorithm, which searches for segmentation boundaries that yield high BLEU score. They trained a linear SVM (Cortes and Vapnik, 1995) to predict these boundaries. To mitigate the effect of noise in the training data sets, they further introduced feature grouping and dynamic programming to the raw greedy search algorithm.

Fujita et al. (2013) used phrase tables and reordering probabilities in phrase-based translation systems to segment an input sentence. Two heuristics were used for segmentation: in the first, if the partial input doesn't exist in phrase tables, segmentation boundaries are generated; in the second, if the right probability of reordering is less than a predefined threshold, segmentation boundaries are generated.

These works aim at outputting shorter segments than sentences, [1] which is capable of further reducing the latency in simultaneous interpretation. However, they assumed that input stream is already segmented into sentences, which is the topic of this paper. As such, our method is orthogonal to these methods, and it would be possible to pipeline our proposed method with them; we plan to explore this in the future. Another shortcoming of these works is that they are tied to specific translation systems, and this narrows their applicability.

3   Methodology

The proposed online sentence segmenters have two components – boundary confidence scoring and segmentation strategies (illustrated in Figure 2 and Algorithm 1). The input is a stream of words, denoted as $w_0, \cdots, w_i, w_{i+1}, \cdots, w_{k+1}$. The boundary confidence score, denoted as s_i, indicates the fitness of breaking after the i-th word. Segment strategies decide whether or not break based on confidence scores, denoted as b_i. The final output is a segmented sentence, e.g. $w_0, \cdots, w_i$.

The proposed segmenters work in an online manner as follows: words are input one by one. The sequence of input words and the derived confidence scores are maintained as states. Once an word is input, its confidence score is calculated and added into the sequence (which is labeled as a in Figure 2). Then a segmentation strategy is applied to the sequence (labeled as (b) in Figure 2). In case that the

---

[1]Fujita et al. (2013)'s method may work on word streams without sentence boundaries; Oda et al. (2014)s' segmentation model uses linear SVMs and local features extracted from just three word lookahead, so it might be adapted.

Algorithm 1 Online Sentence Segmenter

Require: $w_0, w_1, w_2, \ldots,$
1:   $W \leftarrow []; S \leftarrow []$
2:   **for** w_k in stream of words **do**
3:      $W \leftarrow W + [w_k]$ $\triangleright$ assume $W = [w_0, w_1, \ldots, w_{k-1}, w_k]$
4:      $s_{k-1} \leftarrow$ confidence of segmenting before w_k
5:      $S \leftarrow S + [s_{k-1}]$ $\triangleright$ assume $S = [s_0, s_1, \ldots, s_{k-1}]$
6:      $B \leftarrow$ apply segmentation strategy to S $\triangleright$ assume $B = [b_0, b_1, \ldots, b_{k-1}]$
7:      **if** $b_i = 1 \ (0 \leq i \leq k - 1)$ **then**
8:          output $[w_0, w_1, \ldots, w_i]$ as a segment
9:          remove first i elements from W and S
10:     **end if**
11: **end for**

---

segmentation strategy outputs no boundary, no action is taken (represented by (c) in Figure 2). Figure 2, a segment will be output and the inner sequence will be updated accordingly (as in the process represented by (d) in Figure 2).

The following two subsections describe the boundary confidence scores and segmentation strategies in detail, respectively.

3.1   Segment Boundary Confidence Score

This confidence score is based on an N-gram language model. Suppose the language model order is n.

The confidence score represents the plausibility of placing a sentence boundary after the word w_i, that is, converting the stream of words into $\cdots, w_{i-1}, w_i, \langle/s\rangle, \langle s\rangle, w_{i+1}, \cdots$, where $\langle/s\rangle$ and $\langle s\rangle$ are sentence start and end markers. The confidence score is based on the ratio of two probabilities arising from two hypotheses defined below:

Hypothesis I : there is no sentence boundary after word w_i. The corresponding Markov chain is,

$$
\begin{aligned}
P_i^{\langle \mathrm{I} \rangle} &= P_{\text{left}} \cdot P(w_{i+1}^{i+n-1}) \cdot P_{\text{right}} \\
&= P_{\text{left}} \cdot \prod_{k=i+1}^{i+n-1} p(w_k | w_{k-n+1}^{k-1}) \cdot P_{\text{right}}
\end{aligned}
\tag{1}
$$

where p denotes the probability from the language model, P_{left} and P_{right} are the probabilities of the left and right contexts, of the words w_{i+1}^{i+n-1}.

Hypothesis II : there is a sentence boundary after the word w_i. The corresponding Markov chain is,

$$
\begin{aligned}
P_i^{\langle \mathrm{II} \rangle} &= P_{\text{left}} \cdot P(\langle/s\rangle, \langle s\rangle, w_{i+1}^{i+n-1}) \cdot P_{\text{right}} \\
&= P_{\text{left}} \cdot p(\langle/s\rangle | w_{i-n+2}^i) \cdot p(w_{i+1} | \langle s\rangle) \cdot \\
&\quad\quad \prod_{k=i+2}^{i-n+1} p(w_k | w_{i+1}^{k-1}, \langle s\rangle) \cdot P_{\text{right}}
\end{aligned}
\tag{2}
$$

The confidence score is defined as the ratio of the probabilities $P_i^{\langle \mathrm{II} \rangle}$ and $P_i^{\langle \mathrm{I} \rangle}$, that is,

$$
\begin{aligned}
s_i &= \frac{P_i^{\langle \mathrm{II} \rangle}}{P_i^{\langle \mathrm{I} \rangle}} \\
&= p(\langle/s\rangle | w_{i-n+2}^i) \cdot \frac{p(w_{i+1} | \langle s\rangle)}{p(w_{i+1} | w_{i-n-2}^i)} \cdot \prod_{k=i+2}^{i-n+1} \frac{p(w_k | w_{i+1}^{k-1}, \langle s\rangle)}{p(w_k | w_{k-n+1}^{k-1})}
\end{aligned}
\tag{3}
$$

This formula requires a context of $n-1$ future words w_{i+1}^{i+n-1}. This requirement causes a delay of $n-1$ words. If only one future word is used, this delay can be reduced to one word, formulated as,

$$s_i \;\approx\; p(\langle/s\rangle|w_{i-n+2}^i) \cdot \frac{p(w_{i+1}|\langle s\rangle)}{p(w_{i+1}|w_{i-n+2}^i)} \tag{4}$$

Experimental results show that this approximation does not degrade the end-to-end translation quality (see Section 4.3). This might be because, for most languages, the next word w_{i+1} is the most informative to predict whether or not there is a sentence boundary after w_i.

3.2 Segmentation Strategies

In this subsection, two basic segmentation strategies that are based on a threshold heuristic and a latency heuristic, respectively, are first introduced. Then a hybrid strategy that combines these two heuristics is proposed in order to achieve lower delay.

3.2.1 Threshold-based Segmentation Strategy

The threshold-based strategy has a preset threshold parameter denoted: θ_{Th}. The strategy places sentence boundaries where the confidence score exceeds the threshold, formulated as,

$$b_i = \begin{cases} 1 & \text{if } s_i \geqslant \theta_{\text{Th}}, \\ 0 & \text{otherwise.} \end{cases} \tag{5}$$

3.2.2 Latency-based Segmentation Strategy

The latency-based strategy has a maximum latency parameter denoted: θ_{ML}. Once the stream of confidence scores grows to a length of θ_{ML}, the strategy searches for the maximum confidence score in the stream of scores, and places a sentence boundary there, formulated as,

$$b_i = \begin{cases} 1 & \text{if } s_i \geqslant s_j (0 \leqslant j < \theta_{\text{ML}}), \\ 0 & \text{otherwise.} \end{cases} \tag{6}$$

3.2.3 Threshold-latency-based Segmentation Strategy

Both the threshold-based and latency-based segmenters have strengths and weakness with respect to time efficiency. The threshold-based strategy places a sentence boundary immediately when a confidence score exceeds the threshold. In this case, the delay is low. However, continuous sequences of low confidence scores, whose values are all under the threshold, will lead to a long unsegmented stream of words, resulting in high latency.

The latency-based strategy has the opposite behavior. The latency for words ranges from 0 to $\theta_{\text{ML}}-1$. The maximum latency is guaranteed to be $\theta_{\text{ML}}-1$, which is better than threshold-based strategy. But if there are some extremely high confidence scores in the stream, the latency-based strategy will ignore them, leading to unnecessarily long segments.

It is possible to combine to the threshold-based and latency-based strategies to achieve a lower delay. This hybrid threshold-latency-based strategies operates as follows:

- Apply the threshold heuristic to the stream of confidence scores. If a sentence boundary is predicted, then accept the boundary and update the stream.

- If the length of stream grows to θ_{ML}, apply the latency heuristic.

The method is formulated as,

$$b_i = \begin{cases} 1 & \text{if } s_i \geqslant \theta_{\text{Th}}, \\ 1 & \text{if } s_j < \theta_{\text{Th}} \text{ and } s_i \geqslant s_j (0 \leqslant j < \theta_{\text{ML}}), \\ 0 & \text{otherwise.} \end{cases} \tag{7}$$

Corpus	# Sent. Pairs	Japanese		English	
		# Tokens[†]	# Words	# Tokens[†]	# Words
Training	5,134,941	106,044,671	93,672,553	84,371,311	74,733,865
Develop	6,000	150,690	141,036	103,473	95,054
Test	6,000	150,751	141,035	103,638	95,176

Table 1: Experimental Corpora.[†] Including punctuations.

4 Experiments

4.1 Experimental Settings

Experiments were performed on translation between Japanese and English in both directions. The word orders of these two languages are very different, thus long-distance reordering is often obligatory during translation. This makes simultaneous interpretation a very challenging task, and therefore we choose this language pair for experiments.

The experimental corpus was a union of corpora from multiple sources, including shared tasks such as the Basic Travel Expression Corpus (Takezawa et al., 2002), the NTCIR Patent Machine Translation Corpus (Goto et al., 2013), crawled web data and several in-house parallel resources. Table 1 shows the statistics of sentences and words in the training, development and test sets.

The corpora were pre-processed using standard procedures for MT. The Japanese text was segmented into words using Mecab (Kudo, 2005). The English text was tokenized with the tokenization script released with the Europarl corpus (Koehn, 2005) and converted to lowercase.

Two treatments were applied to the development and test sets in order to simulate the output from ASR engines. First, because ASR engines normally do not output punctuation, punctuation was removed. Second, because ASR engines output steams of tokens which are split by long pauses that may contain a few sentences, a random number (from 1 to 10) of sentences were concatenated to form the input.

After segmentation using the proposed methods, punctuation was inserted into the sentences with a hidden N-gram model model (Stolcke et al., 1998; Matusov et al., 2006) prior to translation. In (Anonymous, 2016), this method was shown to be the most effective strategy for the translation of unpunctuated text.

The time efficiency of segmenters were measured by average latency per source word using the definition given in (Finch et al., 2014). The quality of segmenters were measured by the BLEU of end-to-end translation, and because the segmented source sentences did not necessarily agree with the oracle, translations were aligned to reference sentences through edit distance in order to calculate BLEU (Matusov et al., 2005).

The parameters (all of the θ's in the 'Parameters' column in Table 2) were set by grid search to maximize the BLEU score on the development set. 5-gram interpolated modified Kneser-Ney smoothed language models were used to calculate the confidence. These were trained on the training corpus using the SRILM (Stolcke and others, 2002) tools. The machine translation system was an in-house phrase-based system that pre-ordered the input.

4.2 Experimental Results

The performance of the interpretation systems using different sentence segmenters is presented in Table 2. The following observations can be made.

First, the three proposed online sentence segmenters – the threshold-based, latency-based and hybrid ones – work reasonably well. They are much better than the trivial method of fixed-length segmentation, and comparable to the offline method using hidden N-gram models and also to the oracle sentence segmentation.

Second, the proposed threshold-latency-based segmenter consistently outperformed the threshold-based and latency-based segmenters in terms of both end-to-end translation quality and time efficiency.

Third, for Japanese-to-English translation, the threshold-based segmenter outperformed the latency-based segmenter. The reason might be that Japanese language has obvious end of sentence indicators such as "MA SU" and "DE SU", and the segmentation confidence scores immediately following them

Sentence Segmenter	Parameters	Dev. Set		Test Set	
		BLEU	Latency	BLEU	Latency
Japanese-to-English					
Oracle		13.82	NA	13.67	NA
Hidden N-gram [†]	θ_{Bias}=2.6	13.30	NA[‡]	12.97	NA[‡]
Fixed-length	θ_{Len}=36	11.71	16.66	11.55	16.63
Threshold-based	$\theta_{Th}=e^{0.0}$	**13.38**	14.20	13.16	13.68
Latency-based	θ_{ML}=30	13.21	18.04	13.20	18.03
Threshold-latency	$\theta_{Th}=e^{0.0}$, θ_{ML}=38	**13.38**	**12.98**	**13.28**	**12.89**
English-to-Japanese					
Oracle		13.84	NA	14.15	NA
Hidden N-gram[†]	θ_{Bias}=4.2	12.85	NA[‡]	13.10	NA[‡]
Fixed-length	θ_{Len}=18	11.86	8.19	12.15	8.20
Threshold-based	$\theta_{Th}=e^{-0.6}$	12.93	**7.13**	13.19	**7.18**
Latency-based	θ_{ML}=20	**13.18**	12.25	13.38	12.26
Threshold-latency	$\theta_{Th}=e^{0.2}$, θ_{ML}=20	**13.18**	10.01	**13.42**	10.11

Table 2: Performance of interpretation systems that use different sentence segmenters. The confidence scores in threshold-based, latency-based and threshold-latency-based segmenters were calculated using Equation 4. [†] Employed the segment tool from the SRILM toolkit. [‡] The method is not online since it operates on a whole sequence of words, thus the measurement of latency is not applicable.

# Future Words	Parameters	Dev. Set		Test Set	
		BLEU	Latency	BLEU	Latency
Japanese-to-English					
1	$\theta_{Th}=e^{0.0}$, θ_{ML}=38	13.38	12.98	**13.28**	12.89
2	$\theta_{Th}=e^{-0.2}$, θ_{ML}=38	**13.42**	**12.86**	13.21	**12.77**
3	$\theta_{Th}=e^{-0.2}$, θ_{ML}=46	13.40	13.88	13.22	13.80
4	$\theta_{Th}=e^{-0.2}$, θ_{ML}=46	13.38	14.71	13.23	14.65
English-to-Japanese					
1	$\theta_{Th}=e^{0.2}$, θ_{ML}=20	**13.18**	10.01	13.42	10.11
2	$\theta_{Th}=e^{0.2}$, θ_{ML}=18	13.12	**9.92**	**13.44**	**9.99**
3	$\theta_{Th}=e^{0.4}$, θ_{ML}=22	13.14	12.78	13.41	12.78
4	$\theta_{Th}=e^{0.4}$, θ_{ML}=22	13.17	13.65	13.41	13.65

Table 3: Performance of using different numbers of future words to calculate confidence scores.

will be quite high, allowing the threshold-based segmenter to easily identify the corresponding segment boundaries.

4.3 Confidence Scores Using Different Numbers of Future Words

Confidence scores were calculated using a context of up to four future words, as shown in Equation 3. The results are presented in Table 3. Though there is some randomness due to variance on the parameters chosen by grid search, these results show that using more future words does not effectively improve the quality of end-to-end translation, and tends to increase the latency, for the language pair of English and Japanese. Therefore, we found it sufficient to use just one future word.

4.4 Analysis

Table 4 presents an example of the proposed threshold-latency-based sentence segmenter in English-to-Japanese interpretation. The oracle segments of the input in this example are three sentences. The proposed method segments the input into four sentences, two of which are correct. The error is that the third oracle sentence is split into two sentences.

In this example, the proposed segmenter works reasonable accurately, as it recognized two sentences correctly out of three. Here, "i myself think", "but it 's ", "we figured" are typical sentence beginnings in English, which can be recognized by language model. Therefore, the proposed language-model-based segmenters can correctly segment them. The error of splitting "we figured the ultimate test would be …" into two sentences may have arisen from the fact that "we figured" occurs at the end of sentences, or

Input	i myself think that the argument about smoking is a slightly misleading one but it 's not predicted to go as high as once believed we figured the ultimate test would be to ask the dog 's owner to leave
Oracle Segments	<s> i myself think that the argument about smoking is a slightly misleading one </s> <s> but it 's not predicted to go as high as once believed </s> <s> we figured the ultimate test would be to ask the dog 's owner to leave </s>
Oracle Translation	<s> 私自身 が 考える の は 喫煙 について の 議論 は 少し 誤解 を 招く もの だ という こと です </s> <s> しかし 予測 でき ない の は その 高さ が かつて 思わ れ て い た の と 同じ 位 に なる という こと です </s> <s> 我々 が 考え た の は 最終 的 な テスト は 犬 の 所有 者 に 退去 する よう 依頼 する こと です </s>
Predicted Segments	<s> i myself think that the argument about smoking is a slightly misleading one </s> <s> but it 's not predicted to go as high as once believed </s> <s> we figured </s> <s> the ultimate test would be to ask the dog 's owner to leave </s>
Machine Translation	<s> 私 は 自分 の 喫煙 に 関する 議論 が 少し 誤解 を 招く こと と 思い ます </s> <s> しかし 信じ られる よう に 高く なる こと が 予測 さ れ て い ません </s> <s> 私 たち が 予想 し て い た </s> <s> たら 最終 的 な テスト は 犬 の 所有 者 に 出発 する の だ と 考え られ て い ません </s>

Table 4: Example of Threshold-Latency-based Sentence Segmentor.

"the ultimate test would be" occurs as a sentence beginning in the training corpus of the language model. A language model can only capture local patterns, and cannot understand structures of compound sentences. This is a weakness of applying n-gram language modeling techniques to sentence segmentation. As a solution, it may be advantageous to replace the n-gram models with recurrent neural networks that are strong at exploiting long-distant context, and we plan to explore this in the future. It is interesting to note that, the resulting translations of the wrong segmentation "we figured" and "the ultimate test would be ..." are decent, as the origin meaning is delivered. This was an unexpected bonus that we owe to the evaluation framework. The evaluation framework in this paper is end-to-end BLEU, and places no constraints on segmentation positions. This helped to tune the parameters of the proposed methods properly. To sum up, this example illustrates that the proposed methods work reasonably well, and the evaluation framework itself is also making a contributions. However, errors caused by lack of understanding whole sentence structure are inevitable, and these need to be addressed in future work.

5   Conclusion

This paper proposed and studied a segmentation boundary confidence score and a set of online segmentation strategies for simultaneous interpretation. The solution expressed by Equations 4 and 7 was proven empirically to be both effective and efficient.

The choice to use sentence segmentation units was motivated by the desire to handle difficult language pairs that require long-distance intra-sentential word re-ordering (for example the Japanese-English pair studied in this paper). For these cases, using smaller units than sentences will prevent the translation system from being able to correctly re-order the words. For easier language pairs, segments shorter than sentences may be preferable; note that the proposed confidence score can be easily modified to handle sub-sentential segments if necessary. We would like to study this in the context of other language pairs in the future.

The primary motivation for this work was to create an online version of the hidden n-gram approach (Stolcke and Shriberg, 1996; Stolcke et al., 1998), a de facto standard method that is often used for sentence segmentation due to its effectiveness, simplicity and speed. However, it has a latency issue that prevents it from being used in simultaneous interpretation. The proposed method alleviates this latency issue while preserving all its merits, and we show empirically that the new method maintains the effectiveness of the hidden n-gram method even when the future context is reduced as far as a single word. We believe that the proposed method will not only lead to workable systems, but also establish

146

a meaningful baseline for related research. In the long term, we plan to incorporate the findings in this paper into an industrial simultaneous interpretation system.

References

Anonymous. 2016. A study of punctuation handling for speech-to-speech translation. In *22nd Annual Meeting on Natural Language Processing*, page to appear.

Srinivas Bangalore, Vivek Kumar Rangarajan Sridhar, Prakash Kolan, Ladan Golipour, and Aura Jimenez. 2012. Real-time incremental speech-to-speech translation of dialogs. In *Proceedings of the 2012 Conference of the North American Chapter of the Association for Computational Linguistics: Human Language Technologies*, pages 437–445. Association for Computational Linguistics.

Corinna Cortes and Vladimir Vapnik. 1995. Support-vector networks. *Machine learning*, 20(3):273–297.

Andrew Finch, Xiaolin Wang, and Eiichiro Sumita. 2014. An Exploration of Segmentation Strategies in Stream Decoding. In *IWSLT*.

Christian Fügen, Alex Waibel, and Muntsin Kolss. 2007. Simultaneous translation of lectures and speeches. *Machine Translation*, 21(4):209–252.

Tomoki Fujita, Graham Neubig, Sakriani Sakti, Tomoki Toda, and Satoshi Nakamura. 2013. Simple, lexicalized choice of translation timing for simultaneous speech translation. In *INTERSPEECH*, pages 3487–3491.

Isao Goto, Ka Po Chow, Bin Lu, Eiichiro Sumita, and Benjamin K Tsou. 2013. Overview of the patent machine translation task at the ntcir-10 workshop. In *Proceedings of the 10th NTCIR Workshop Meeting on Evaluation of Information Access Technologies: Information Retrieval, Question Answering and Cross-Lingual Information Access, NTCIR-10*.

Thanh-Le Ha, Jan Niehues, Eunah Cho, Mohammed Mediani, and Alex Waibel. 2015. The KIT Translation Systems for IWSLT 2015. In *Proceedings of the twelveth International Workshop on Spoken Language Translation (IWSLT), Da Nang, Veitnam*, pages 62–69.

Philipp Koehn. 2005. Europarl: A parallel corpus for statistical machine translation. In *Proceedings of MT Summit*, volume 5, pages 79–86.

Taku Kudo. 2005. Mecab: Yet another part-of-speech and morphological analyzer. *http://mecab. sourceforge. net/*.

Michaeel Kzai, Brian Thompson, Elizabeth Salesky, Timothy Anderson, Grant Erdmann, Eric Hansen, Brian Ore, Katherine Young, Jeremy Gwinnup, Michael Hutt, and Christina May. 2015. The MITLL-AFRL IWSLT 2015 Systems. In *Proceedings of the twelveth International Workshop on Spoken Language Translation (IWSLT), Da Nang, Veitnam*, pages 23–30.

John Lafferty, Andrew McCallum, and Fernando Pereira. 2001. Conditional random fields: Probabilistic models for segmenting and labeling sequence data. In *Proceedings of the eighteenth international conference on machine learning, ICML*, volume 1, pages 282–289.

Wei Lu and Hwee Tou Ng. 2010. Better punctuation prediction with dynamic conditional random fields. In *Proceedings of the 2010 conference on empirical methods in natural language processing*, pages 177–186. Association for Computational Linguistics.

Evgeny Matusov, Gregor Leusch, Oliver Bender, Hermann Ney, et al. 2005. Evaluating machine translation output with automatic sentence segmentation. In *IWSLT*, pages 138–144. Citeseer.

Evgeny Matusov, Arne Mauser, and Hermann Ney. 2006. Automatic sentence segmentation and punctuation prediction for spoken language translation. In *IWSLT*, pages 158–165.

Yusuke Oda, Graham Neubig, Sakriani Sakti, Tomoki Toda, and Satoshi Nakamura. 2014. Optimizing segmentation strategies for simultaneous speech translation. In *ACL (2)*, pages 551–556.

Kishore Papineni, Salim Roukos, Todd Ward, and Wei-Jing Zhu. 2002. BLEU: a method for automatic evaluation of machine translation. In *Proceedings of the 40th Annual Meeting on Association for Computational Linguistics*, pages 311–318. Association for Computational Linguistics.

Stephan Peitz, Markus Freitag, Arne Mauser, and Hermann Ney. 2011. Modeling punctuation prediction as machine translation. In *IWSLT*, pages 238–245.

Andreas Stolcke et al. 2002. Srilm-an extensible language modeling toolkit. In *INTERSPEECH*.

Andreas Stolcke and Elizabeth Shriberg. 1996. Automatic linguistic segmentation of conversational speech. In *Spoken Language, 1996. ICSLP 96. Proceedings., Fourth International Conference on*, volume 2, pages 1005–1008. IEEE.

Andreas Stolcke, Elizabeth Shriberg, Rebecca A Bates, Mari Ostendorf, Dilek Hakkani, Madelaine Plauche, Gökhan Tür, and Yu Lu. 1998. Automatic detection of sentence boundaries and disfluencies based on recognized words. In *ICSLP*, pages 2247–2250.

Toshiyuki Takezawa, Eiichiro Sumita, Fumiaki Sugaya, Hirofumi Yamamoto, and Seiichi Yamamoto. 2002. Toward a broad-coverage bilingual corpus for speech translation of travel conversations in the real world. In *LREC*, pages 147–152.

Lawrence Venuti. 2012. *The translation studies reader*. Routledge.

Mahsa Yarmohammadi, Vivek Kumar Rangarajan Sridhar, Srinivas Bangalore, and Baskaran Sankaran. 2013. Incremental segmentation and decoding strategies for simultaneous translation. In *IJCNLP*, pages 1032–1036.

Similar Southeast Asian Languages:
Corpus-Based Case Study on Thai-Laotian and Malay-Indonesian

Chenchen Ding, Masao Utiyama, Eiichiro Sumita
Advanced Translation Technology Laboratory, ASTREC
National Institute of Information and Communications Technology
3-5 Hikaridai, Seikacho, Sorakugun, Kyoto, 619-0289, Japan
`{chenchen.ding, mutiyama, eiichiro.sumita}@nict.go.jp`

Abstract

This paper illustrates the similarity between Thai and Laotian, and between Malay and Indonesian, based on an investigation on raw parallel data from Asian Language Treebank. The cross-lingual similarity is investigated and demonstrated on metrics of correspondence and order of tokens, based on several standard statistical machine translation techniques. The similarity shown in this study suggests a possibility on harmonious annotation and processing of the language pairs in future development.

1 Introduction

Research and technique development of natural languages processing (NLP) on many understudied and low-resource Southeast Asian languages are launched in recent years. Some attempts on transferring available techniques on a well-developed language to an understudied language have been proved efficient (Ding et al., 2014). However, such a research direction must be established on an *a priori* observation on the similarity between languages. Generally, linguistically oriented issues, i.e., etymology, vocabulary, or syntactic structure, are discussed when two (or more) languages are referred to as "similar to each other". In engineering practice, however, statistical metrics, i.e., word alignment precision, or word order differences, are more addressed in NLP applications.

In this study, we focus on two Southeast Asian languages pairs, Thai-Laotian and Malay-Indonesian. Both language pairs have mutual intelligibility to a certain extend in spoken form. We conducted a data-driven investigation of the language pairs, trying to figure out the similarity from an engineering viewpoint, which can provide a basis of further NLP techniques development on these languages. The Asian Language Treebank (ALT)[1] (Utiyama and Sumita, 2015; Riza et al., 2016), containing approximately $20,000$ parallel sentence pairs on several Asian languages, facilitates statistical approaches. Specifically, we conducted word aligning on the two language pairs to find out the accordance on token-level, and translation experiments to find out the accordance on sentence-level. The experimental results reveal that the similarity on Thai-Laotian pair is nearly as same as that of Japanese-Korean, i.e., an extremely similar East Asian language pair; for the case of Malay-Indonesian, they are extremely similar to each other that basically they can be considered as two registers of one language. Based on the observation, we think the Thai-Laotian and Malay-Indonesian pairs can be handled simultaneously and harmoniously in further research, including corpus annotation, technique development, and NLP applications.

The remaining of the paper is arranged as following. In section 2, we introduce the background of the languages discussed in this paper. In section 3, we describe the experiment settings used and discuss the numerical results obtained. Section 4 concludes the paper and provides our future work.

2 Background

Specific approaches to process similar languages is an interesting topic in NLP (Vilar et al., 2007; Ding et al., 2015). In this research direction, *a priori* knowledge of the languages is required and specific approaches can thus be designed by taking advantage of the similarities to outperform a general approach. Here we provide outlines of linguistic features of the four languages mentioned in this paper.

---

[1] `http://www2.nict.go.jp/astrec-att/member/mutiyama/ALT/index.html`

Proceedings of the 3rd Workshop on Asian Translation,
pages 149–156, Osaka, Japan, December 11-17 2016.

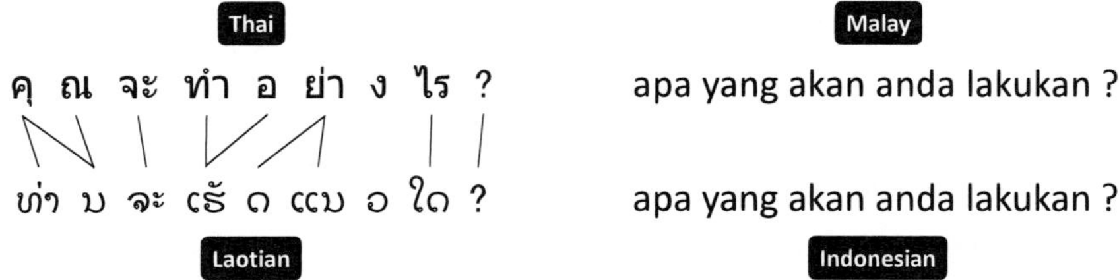

Figure 1: Parallel translations on different languages from SNT.82657.8332-1 in ALT data. The original English is *"What would you do about it?"*

Thai and Laotian are both tonal languages from the Tai-Kadai language family. Spoken Thai and Laotian are mutually intelligible. The two languages share a large amount of etymologically related words and have similar head-initial syntactic structures. Both the languages are written with abugida scripts, slightly different from each other but linguistically similar. A Thai-Laotian example is shown in the left part of Fig. 1. The alignment of tokens is generated by the approach mentioned in the next section. It can be observed the similarity in the shape of certain tokens.

Malay and Indonesian are both from the Austronesian languages family, applying Latin alphabet in their writing systems. Actually, Indonesian can be considered as a standardized register of Malay. The two languages are also mutually intelligible, with several difference in orthography, pronunciation, and vocabulary. The right part in Fig. 1 is an example on the Malay-Indonesian pair, where the expressions are actually identical.

3   Investigation

3.1   Data

We used the parallel raw sentences of corresponding languages from the ALT data. There are $20,106$ sentences in total, which is not a huge size, but a valuable parallel data set. As the Malay and Indonesian use Latin alphabet in their writing systems, the pre-processing of them is relatively simple, we applied naïve tokenization to detach the punctuation marks and lowercasing all the letters. The abugida writing systems of Thai and Laotian are more problematic. As we did not have available tokenization tools for the two languages, we segmented the sentences of the two languages into *unbreakable writing units* for experiments. Specifically, standalone consonant letters with dependent diacritics[2] attached to them are segmented and taken as tokens. The western name entities in sentences were also lowercased.

For the following alignment-based analysis, all the $20,106$ sentences were used as training data for unsupervised word aligning. For the statistical machine translation experiments, the last $2,000$ to $1,000$ sentences were left out as the development set and the last $1,000$ sentences were reserved for test. As the corpus is not large, the aim of the translation experiments is not a pursuit of high performance, but to provide evidence for the similarity of the languages. Statistics of the data we used is list in Table 1.

3.2   Alignment-Based Analysis

We used **GIZA++**[3] (Brown et al., 1993; Och and Ney, 2003) to align all the $20,106$ tokenized sentences for the two language pairs. Based on the aligned results, we investigate (1) token orders by *Kendall's τ* and (2) varieties in token accordance by entropies.

The Kendall's τ was calculated according to several previous work (Isozaki et al., 2012), which mainly focused on the difficulties in word reordering in SMT. The distribution of Kendall's τ is illustrated in Figs. 2 and 3 on the two languages pairs. The Thai-Laotian pair shows a relative similar order with an average

---

[2]Both post-positioned and pre-positioned
[3]http://www.statmt.org/moses/giza/GIZA++.html

τ around 0.71, and the Malay-Indonesian pair shows an extremely identical order that the average τ is as high as 0.98. These evidences demonstrated the similarity in token orders on the two language pairs.

The statistics on token-level entropy are shown from Fig. 4 to Fig. 9, where Figs. 6 and 7 are based on the patent data from WAT2015's Japanese-Korean task (Nakazawa et al., 2015), shown here for comparison. The entropies were calculated by the lexical translation probabilities from *grow-diag-final-and* symmetrized word alignment (Och and Ney, 2003). Tokens of punctuation marks and numbers are not included in these figures. Generally, the entropies observed in Thai-Laotian and Malay-Indonesian are not large, which suggests the varieties are not large in token corresponding.[4] The scatter plots on Japanese and Korean seem more similar to Thai and Laotian rather than Malay and Indonesian, because the statistics of Japanese and Korean are based on characters, which are smaller units than words as the units used of Thai and Laotian. From the Thai-Laotian pairs, a relative clear tendency can be observed that tokens with very high and very low probabilities have lower entropies in translation. This phenomena is reasonable, because a large portion of vocabulary of the two languages are etymologically related, as well as their syntactic structures. So, common tokens may be aligned well by the similarity in syntax and rare tokens may be aligned well by the similarity in vocabulary. The tendency on Malay-Indonesian is not as obvious as that on Thai-Laotian. A reason is that the vocabulary size is much larger on the Malay-Indonesian pair than the number of unbreakable unit types on the Thai-Laotian pair, which may decrease the precision of alignment on the small training set.

3.3   Translation-Based Analysis

We used the phrase-based (PB) SMT in **MOSES**[5] (Koehn et al., 2007) for the translation experiments. Default setting were applied except for the Thai-Laotian pair the maximum phrase length was set to nine due to the tokens are over-segmented. **SRILM**[6] was use to train a 5-gram language model (LM) for the Malay-Indonesian pair and a 9-gram LM for the Thai-Laotian pair. Modified Kneser-Ney interpolation (Chen and Goodman, 1996) was applied for the LMs. We tested different distortion-limit (DL) in experiments to check the requirement of reordering process in translation. The test set BLEU (Papineni et al., 2002) and RIBES (Isozaki et al., 2010) are listed in Table 2.

From the evaluation, it can be observed the absolute BLEU scores are not quite high, i.e., between 30 and 40, compared with the performance on Japanese-Korean task in WAT2015, which achieved over 70 in terms of BLEU. Generally, the data we used for the experiment is quite limited for statistical model training. Furthermore, as the sentences in different languages are translated from original English articles, the quality between specific language pairs may affected. On the other hand, we observed two phenomena from the translation evaluation. One is the RIBES meets the Kendall'd τ quite well, to show that reordering is not a serious problem in the translation. A further evidence is that the distortion limit did not affect the performance much. This feature is quite like those observed in Japanese-Korean pair. Based on the observation, we consider the Thai-Laotian and Malay-Indonesian have considerable similarities, even from the observation on the relatively small data set.

4   Conclude and Future Work

This paper illustrates the similarity between Thai and Laotian, and between Malay and Indonesian, based on the ALT data. The similarity shown in this study suggests a possibility on harmonious annotation and processing of the language pairs in our further annotated corpus construction based on the ALT data.

References

Peter F. Brown, Vincent J. Della Pietra, Stephen A. Della Pietra, and Robert L. Mercer. 1993. The mathematics of statistical machine translation: Parameter estimation. *Computational linguistics*, 19(2):263–311.

Stanley F. Chen and Joshua Goodman. 1996. An empirical study of smoothing techniques for language modeling. In *Proc. of ACL*, pages 310–318.

---

[4]The logarithm used in this paper is based on 10.

[5]`http://www.statmt.org/moses/`

[6]`http://www.speech.sri.com/projects/srilm/`

	Thai (th)	**Laotian** (lo)	**Malay** (ms)	**Indonesian** (id)
training	$1,291,784$	$1,245,748$	$435,705$	$432,456$
development	$65,387$	$64,538$	$23,143$	$22,978$
test	65.014	$64,420$	$23,880$	$23,392$
total	$1,422,185$	$1,374,706$	$482,728$	$478,826$

Table 1: Number of tokens in the data used in experiment.

DL.	th-lo	lo-th	ms-id	id-ms
0	32.2 / .745	37.0 / .753	31.5 / .867	31.0 / .869
3	32.2 / .743	36.8 / .753	31.3 / .867	31.2 / .869
6	31.4 / .737	37.1 / .754	31.4 / .866	31.2 / .869
9	32.2 / .744	37.0 / .753	31.3 / .866	31.1 / .869

Table 2: BLEU / RIBES for source-target language pairs.

Chenchen Ding, Ye Kyaw Thu, Masao Utiyama, Andrew Finch, and Eiichiro Sumita. 2014. Empirical dependency-based head finalization for statistical chinese-, english-, and french-to-myanmar (burmese) machine translation. In *Proc. of IWSLT*, pages 184–191.

Chenchen Ding, Masao Utiyama, and Eiichiro Sumita. 2015. NICT at WAT 2015. In *Proc. of WAT*, pages 42–47.

Hideki Isozaki, Tsutomu Hirao, Kevin Duh, Katsuhito Sudoh, and Hajime Tsukada. 2010. Automatic evaluation of translation quality for distant language pairs. In *Proc. of EMNLP*, pages 944–952.

Hideki Isozaki, Katsuhito Sudoh, Hajime Tsukada, and Kevin Duh. 2012. Hpsg-based preprocessing for english-to-japanese translation. *ACM TALIP*, 11(3):8.

Philipp Koehn, Hieu Hoang, Alexandra Birch, Chris Callison-Burch, Marcello Federico, Nicola Bertoldi, Brooke Cowan, Wade Shen, Christine Moran, Richard Zens, Chris Dyer, Ondřej Bojar, Alexandra Constantin, and Evan Herbst. 2007. Moses: Open source toolkit for statistical machine translation. In *Proc. of ACL (Demo and Poster Sessions)*, pages 177–180.

Toshiaki Nakazawa, Hideya Mino, Isao Goto, Graham Neubig, Sadao Kurohashi, and Eiichiro Sumita. 2015. Overview of the 2nd Workshop on Asian Translation. In *Proc. of WAT2015*, pages 1–28.

Franz Josef Och and Hermann Ney. 2003. A systematic comparison of various statistical alignment models. *Computational linguistics*, 29(1):19–51.

Kishore Papineni, Salim Roukos, Todd Ward, and Wei-Jing Zhu. 2002. BLEU: a method for automatic evaluation of machine translation. In *Proc. of ACL*, pages 311–318.

Hammam Riza, Michael Purwoadi, Gunarso, Teduh Uliniansyah, Aw Ai Ti, Sharifah Mahani Aljunied, Luong Chi Mai, Vu Tat Thang, Nguyen Phuong Thai, Vichet Chea, Rapid Sun, Sethserey Sam, Sopheap Seng, Khin Mar Soe, Khin Thandar Nwet, Masao Utiyama, and Chenchen Ding. 2016. Introduction of the asian language treebank. In *Proc. of Oriental COCOSDA (to apprear)*.

Masao Utiyama and Eiichiro Sumita. 2015. Open collaboration for developing and using asian language treebank (ALT). ASEAN IVO Forum.

David Vilar, Jan-T Peter, and Hermann Ney. 2007. Can we translate letters? In *Proc. of WMT*, pages 33–39.

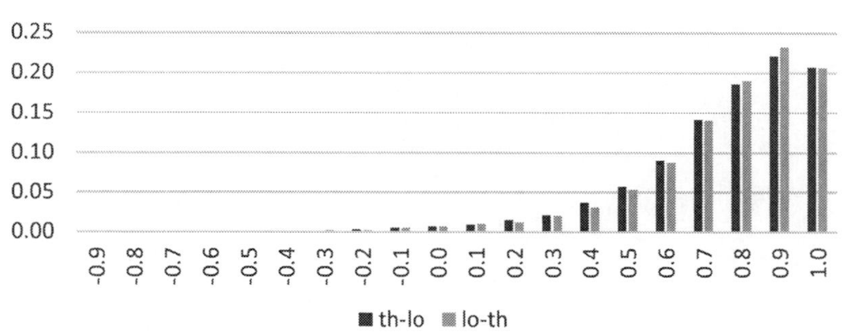

Figure 2: Distribution of Kendall's τ on Thai-to-Laotian (th-lo) and Laotian-to-Thai (lo-th).

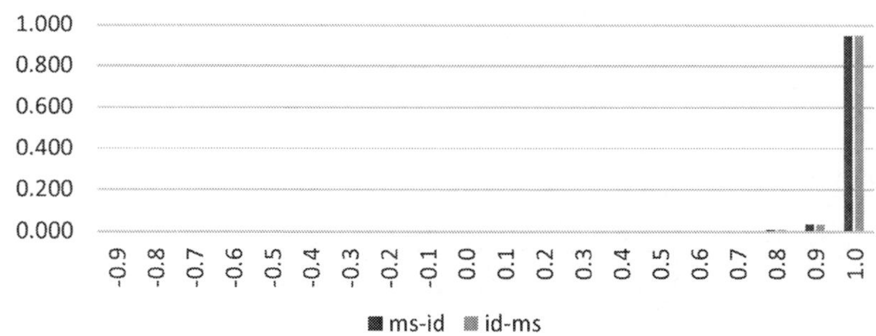

Figure 3: Distribution of Kendall's τ on Malay-to-Indonesian (ms-id) and Indonesian-to-Malay (id-ms).

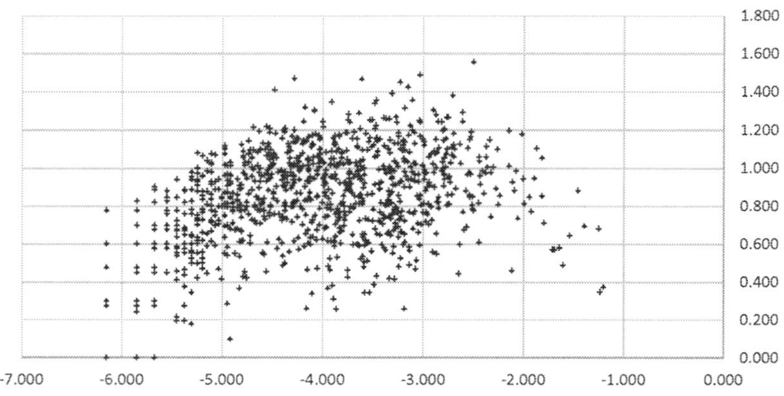

Figure 4: Scatter plot of Thai tokens. *X*-axis is the logarithmic probability of tokens; *Y*-axis is the entropy on corresponding Laotian tokens.

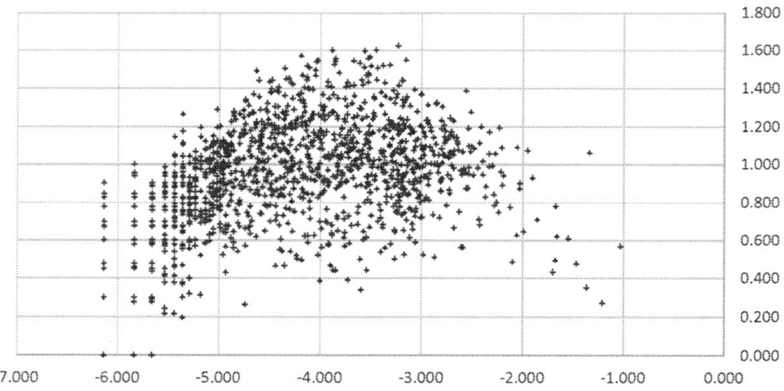

Figure 5: Scatter plot of Laotian tokens. *X*-axis is the logarithmic probability of tokens; *Y*-axis is the entropy on corresponding Thai tokens.

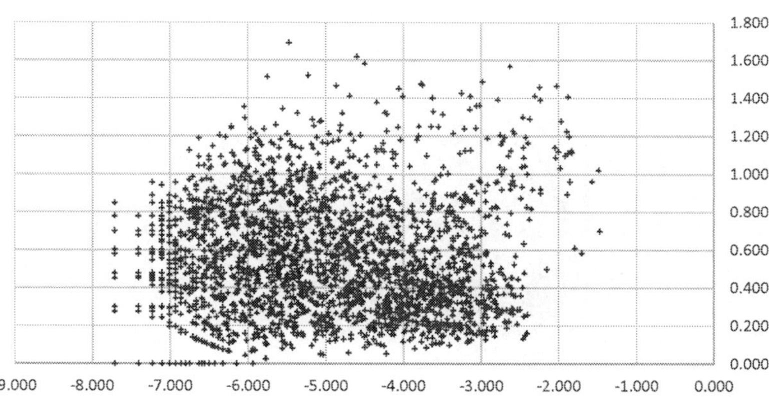

Figure 6: Scatter plot of Japanese tokens. *X*-axis is the logarithmic probability of tokens; *Y*-axis is the entropy on corresponding Korean tokens.

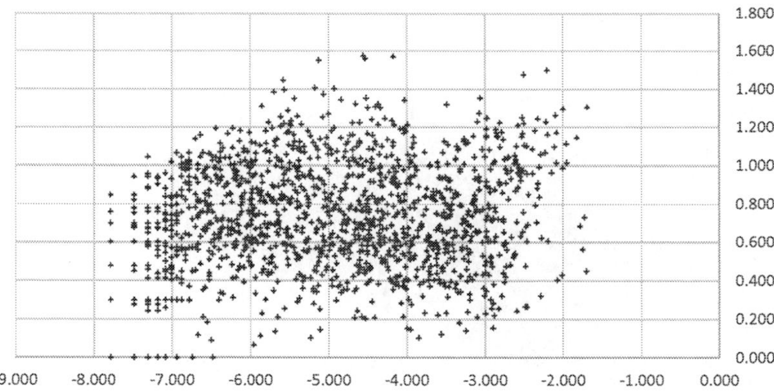

Figure 7: Scatter plot of Korean tokens. *X*-axis is the logarithmic probability of tokens; *Y*-axis is the entropy on corresponding Japanese tokens.

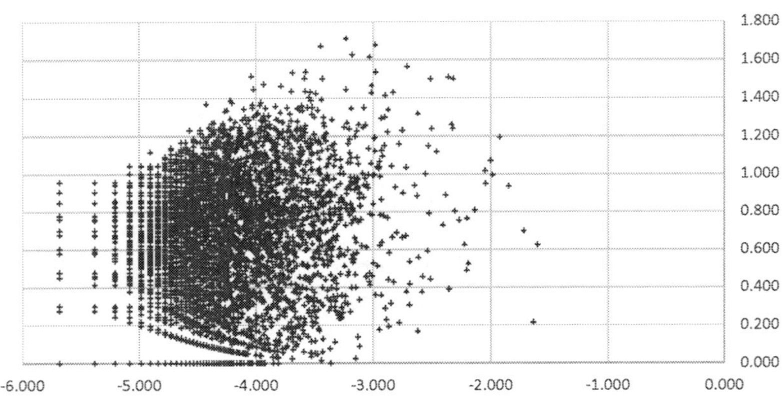

Figure 8: Scatter plot of Malay tokens. *X*-axis is the logarithmic probability of tokens; *Y*-axis is the entropy on corresponding Indonesian tokens.

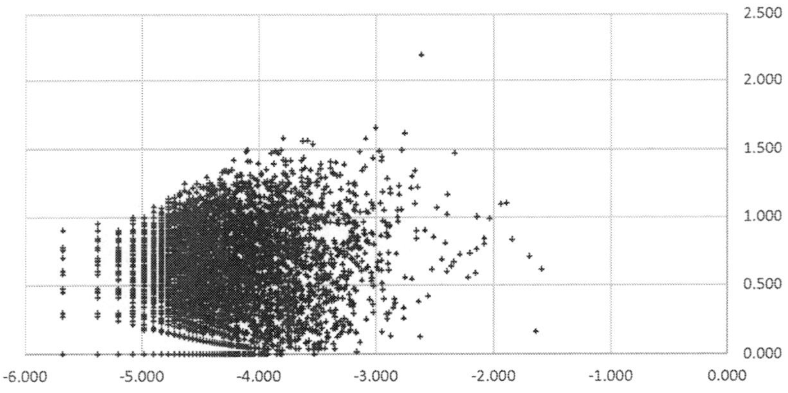

Figure 9: Scatter plot of Indonesian tokens. *X*-axis is the logarithmic probability of tokens; *Y*-axis is the entropy on corresponding Malay tokens.

Integrating empty category detection into Preordering Machine Translation

Shunsuke Takeno[†] Masaaki Nagata[‡], Kazuhide Yamamoto[†]
[†]Nagaoka University of Technology,
1603-1 Kamitomioka, Nagaoka, Niigata, 940-2188 Japan
{takeno, yamamoto}@jnlp.org
[‡]NTT Communication Science Laboratories, NTT Corporation,
2-4 Hikaridai, Seika-cho, Soraku-gun, Kyoto, 619-0237 Japan
nagata.masaaki@labs.ntt.co.jp

Abstract

We propose a method for integrating Japanese empty category detection into the preordering process of Japanese-to-English statistical machine translation. First, we apply machine-learning-based empty category detection to estimate the position and the type of empty categories in the constituent tree of the source sentence. Then, we apply discriminative preordering to the augmented constituent tree in which empty categories are treated as if they are normal lexical symbols. We find that it is effective to filter empty categories based on the confidence of estimation. Our experiments show that, for the IWSLT dataset consisting of short travel conversations, the insertion of empty categories alone improves the BLEU score from 33.2 to 34.3 and the RIBES score from 76.3 to 78.7, which imply that reordering has improved For the KFTT dataset consisting of Wikipedia sentences, the proposed preordering method considering empty categories improves the BLEU score from 19.9 to 20.2 and the RIBES score from 66.2 to 66.3, which shows both translation and reordering have improved slightly.

1   Introduction

Empty categories are phonetically null elements that are used for representing dropped pronouns ("pro" or "small pro"), controlled elements ("PRO" or "big pro") and traces of movement ("T" or "trace"). Dropped pronouns are one of the major problems caused on machine translation from the pro-drop language such as Japanese to the non-pro-drop language such as English because it is difficult to produce the correct pronouns on the target side when the pronoun is missing on the source side.

The effects of empty categories in machine translation have previously been examined (Chung and Gildea, 2010; Taira et al., 2012; Xiang et al., 2013; Kudo et al., 2014; Wang et al., 2016). In this paper, we address two new problems that were not fully discussed in previous work. The first problem is that, even if empty categories are correctly recovered, it is difficult to automatically obtain the correct word alignment for languages with a completely different word order such as Japanese and English. The second problem is that it is not only difficult to translate non-existent pronouns but also relative clauses because relative pronouns do not exist in Japanese. In theory, we can safely ignore PRO in control structures for translation because they are absent from both Japanese and English.

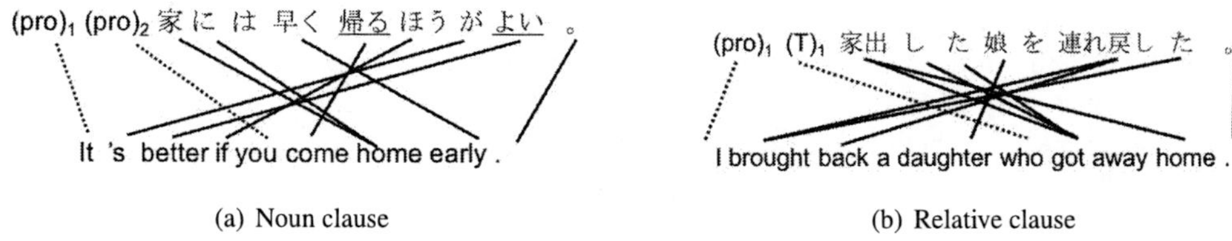

(a) Noun clause   (b) Relative clause

Figure 1: Recovering empty categories makes word alignment more difficult

Fig. 1 shows examples for which there are two empty categories in the source Japanese sentence, which results in complicated word alignments. In Fig. 1(a), the first *pro* should be aligned to "it"

Proceedings of the 3rd Workshop on Asian Translation,
pages 157–165, Osaka, Japan, December 11-17 2016.

because it is the subject of a matrix clause of which the verb is "よい (good)", whereas the second *pro* should be aligned to "you" because is it the subject of a noun clause of which the verb is "帰 る (come home)". In Fig. 1(b), the first *pro* should be aligned to "I" because it is the subject of matrix clause whose verb is "連れ戻す (bring back)", while the second *T* could arguably be aligned to the relative pronoun "who" because it is the subject of the relative clause of which the verb is "家出した (ran away from home)".

This means that inserting empty categories into source sentences could worsen automatic word alignment and result in less accurate machine translation outputs. We solve this problem by integrating empty category detection into preordering-based statistical machine translation. We first insert empty categories into the source sentence, and then reorder them such that the word order is similar to that of the target sentence. We find it is effective to filter out unreliable empty category candidates to improve the accuracy of machine translation. In the following sections, we first briefly describe related works. We then describe empty category detection method (Takeno et al., 2015) and discriminative preordering method (Hoshino et al., 2015) used in the proposed method. We then report experiment results of Japanese-to-English translation on both spoken (IWSLT dataset) and written (KFTT dataset) languages.

2   Related works

Conventional approaches to recover zero pronouns in Japanese are to frame it as zero anaphora resolution, which is a sub-problem of predicate argument structure analysis (Nakaiwa and Ikehara, 1995; Iida et al., 2007; Hangyo et al., 2013). Zero anaphora resolution consists of two procedures: zero pronoun detection and anaphora resolution.

It is difficult to integrate zero anaphora resolution (or predicate-argument structure analysis) into SMT for two reasons. The first is that anaphora resolution requires context analysis, which complicates the translation method. The second is that predicate argument structure analysis provides semantic relations, not syntactic structure. This makes it difficult to use the information of recovered zero pronouns in SMT, because there is no position information for the zero pronouns in the word sequence (for phrase-based translation) or syntactic tree (for tree-based translation).

Only a few studies on the recovery of zero pronouns for Japanese-to-English statistical machine translation have been reported. Taira et al.(2012) reported that recovering zero pronouns in source Japanese sentence, both by human and by simple rule-based methods, improved the accuracy of generating correct personal pronouns in target English sentence. However, they also reported that the BLEU scores remained unchanged in both cases. Kudo et al. (2014) showed that generating zero subjects in Japanese improved the BLEU score in preordering-based translation by about 0.5 points. They designed a specific probabilistic model for dependency-based preordering to generate the subject when it was omitted from the source Japanese sentence.

Chinese also has zero pronoun problems. Based on Chinese Penn Treebank, recovering zero pronouns in Chinese is framed as a sub-problem of empty category detection, and some previous work on applying empty category detection in Chinese-to-English statistical machine translation has been published.

Chung and Gildea (2010) reported that the automatic insertion of empty categories improved the accuracy of phrased-based machine translation. Xiang et al. (2013) proposed a log-linear model for the empty category detection as a post-processor of the constituent parser, and combined it with Hiero and a tree-to-string system. Wang et al. (2016) proposed NN-based unsupervised empty category detection and its integration into phrase-based SMT. Their method succeeded in dialogue corpus in which the difference in the word-order problems between Chinese and English are alleviated compared to written language corpus because both Chinese and English have an SVO grammatical structure in shorter sentence.

Our approach is very close to the Xiang et al., (2013)'s method. We used an empty category detector (Takeno et al., 2015) implemented as a post-processor of a Japanese constituent parser, and combined it with preordering-based translation system (Hoshino et al., 2015). Yet, there are some differences between our work and theirs. We used preordering as a way to improve the word alignment accuracy after empty categories are recovered. We examined the effect of recovering *T* (trace) for the translation of a relative clause.

3 Preordering with empty categories

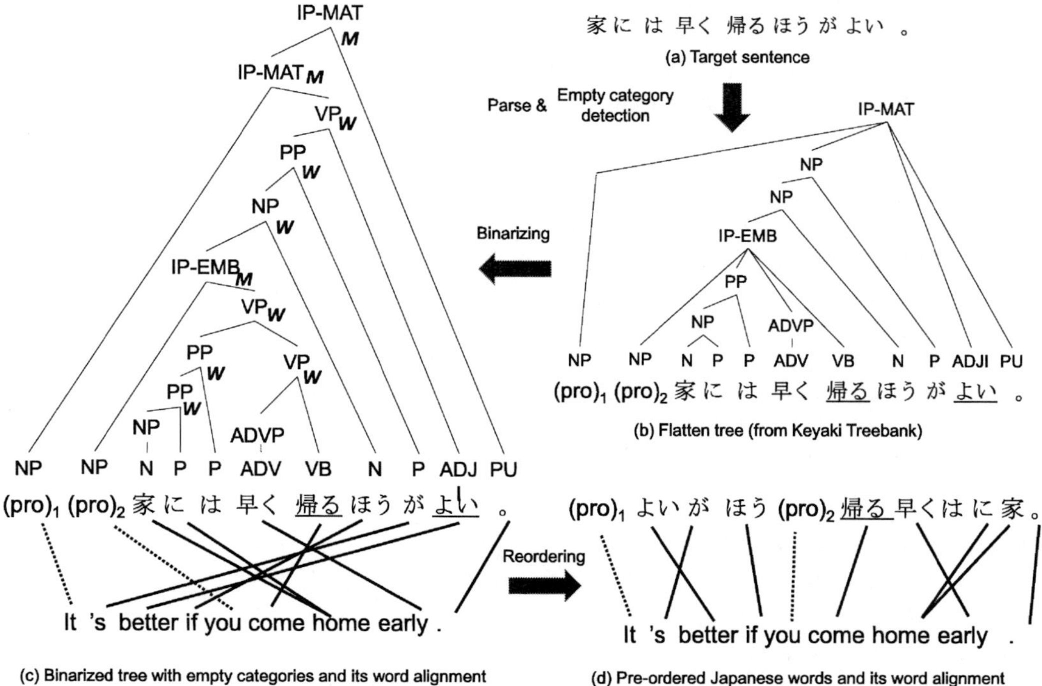

Figure 2: Progress to integrate empty category detection into machine translation. In Fig.2(b), we annotate reordering mark.W indicates that branches are to be swapped M indicates monotone

Fig. 2 shows the process of preordering with empty category detection for Japanese-to-English translation. We first parse the source Japanese sentence to obtain a constituent parse tree and apply empty category detection to recover empty categories. We then binarize the augmented tree and apply the discriminative preordering model to the binary tree to decide whether the children of each node should be swapped (W=swap) or not (M=monotone). We then obtain reordered Japanese sentence as the yield of the reordered tree. We provide details of each step as follows.

The remainder of this section contains further details of each step.

Japanese constituent parsing and empty category detection

We used a spinal tree-based shift-reduce parser (Hayashi et al., 2016) to obtain a constituent parse tree for the source Japanese sentence. It is trained on the Keyaki Treebank and outputs flat phrase structure as shown in Fig. 2(b). As this parser ignores empty categories, we used a log-linear model-based empty category detector (Takeno et al., 2015) to recover empty categories. The parser can detect two empty category types: dropped pronouns *pro* and the trace of the movement of the noun phrase (NP) *T*. Although the original Keyaki Treebank has sub-categories of *pro*, such as *speaker* and *hearer*, we unified them into *pro* as was done in our previous work of Takeno et al., (2015).

We used a rule-based tree binarization tool [1] provided with the Keyaki Treebank to convert a flat tree as shown in Fig. 2(b) to a binary tree as shown in Fig. 2(c).

Building preordering model with empty categories

We extended Hoshino et al., (2015)'s preordering method to process empty categories in the source Japanese sentence. According to Hoshino et al., (2015), they build a classifier for each node in the

---

[1] http://www.compling.jp/haruniwa/#create_stripped

source tree to decide whether its children need to be swapped. The oracle is decided to maximize the Kendall's τ between the reordered source sentence and the target sentences based on the word alignment between the source and target sentences.

We used two methods to process empty categories in Hoshino et al., (2015)'s preordering method, namely REORDERING(H) and REORDERING(C). The former of these methods trains the preordering model using sentences with a manually constructed word alignment. As the currently available manual word alignment examples do not have alignment information on empty categories, the trained preordering model is agnostic with regard to empty categories. If the input parse tree has an empty category, it is treated as an NP with an unknown lexical symbol.

The latter of these two methods trains the preordering model using sentences with automatic word alignment, which is obtained by using unsupervised word alignment tool GIZA++ (Och, 2007) for the source Japanese sentences with empty categories recovered and the target sentences. If the input parse tree has an empty category, it is treated as a noun phrases with a known lexical symbol.

It is noteworthy that the preordering procedure involves training the translation model on the reordered source sentence as shown in Fig. 2(d). We can expect the word alignment for empty categories is improved by this preordering. This is different from previous approaches such as Xiang et al., (2013), where word alignment is automatically obtained from original source sentences with empty categories recovered.

Filtering out unreliable empty categories

As we report with the experiment, the accuracy of Japanese empty category detection is relatively low, even if we were to use the state-of-the-art Takeno et al., (2015)'s method. Therefore, we modified this method to filter out unreliable empty categories.

Let $T = t_1 t_2 \cdots t_n$ be the sequence of nodes produced by the post-order traversal of the parse tree from its root node, and e_i be the empty category tag associated with t_i. In Takeno et al., (2015), the empty category tag for each node is decided by the following log-linear model:

$$\hat{e}_i = \arg\max_{e \in \mathcal{E}} P(e|e_1^{i-1}, T) = \arg\max_{e \in \mathcal{E}} \frac{\exp(\boldsymbol{\theta} \cdot \boldsymbol{\phi}(e, e_1^{i-1}, T))}{Z(e_1^i, T)}$$

where $\mathcal{E}$ represents the set of all empty category types to be detected including NULL label (in our case, either *pro*, *T*, or NULL).

The above equation means that an empty category is inserted if its probability is larger than that of the NULL label. We modified the decision function so that, for a given threshold θ, we remove empty categories if its probability is less than θ:

$$\hat{e}_i = \begin{cases} NULL & if \;\; \arg\max_{e \in \mathcal{E}} P(e|e_1^{i-1}, T) < \theta \\ \arg\max_{e \in \mathcal{E}} P(e|e_1^{i-1}, T) & otherwise \end{cases}$$

The threshold θ is decided using development set on experiment.

4 Experiments

4.1 Empty category detection (before filtering)

We trained and evaluated the empty category detection model, following Takeno et al., (2015) settings.

We used the Keyaki Treebank as of November 15, 2015, which included 30,872 annotated sentences. We used 1,000 sentences as the development set, and 1,003 sentences as the test set. These sentences were taken from the files blog_KNB.psd (blog), spoken_CIAIR.psd (transcript), newswire_MAINICHI-1995.psd (newswire) to balance the domain. The remaining 20,646 sentences were used for training. We used GloVe as word embedding, and Wikipedia articles in Japanese as of January 18, 2015, were used for training, which amounted to 660 million words and 23.4 million sentences. We used the development set to decide the dimension of word embedding and the window size for co-occurrence counts as 200 and 10, respectively.

We performed the tests under two conditions: gold parse and system parse. Under the gold parse condition, we used trees from Keyaki Treebank without empty categories as input to the systems. Under the system parse condition, we used the output of the spinal tree-based shift-reduce parser (Hayashi et al., 2016).

We evaluated these conditions using the word-position-level identification metrics described in Xiang et al.,(2013). This approach projects the predicted empty category tags to the surface level. An empty node is regarded as correctly predicted surface position in the sentence if and only if type (*T* or *pro*) and function (SBJ, OB1 and so on) matches with the reference.

The results are presented in Table 1. For *pro* and *T*, the detector achieved 74.9%, 91.9% in F scores, respectively, under the gold parse condition. However, the performance of detector is reduced considerably under the system parse condition. In particular, the decline in the accuracy of *T* is remarkable. These tendencies are the same as described in Takeno et al., (2015).

types	INPUT	P	R	F
pro	GOLDEN	74.3	75.6	74.9
T	GOLDEN	89.0	95.0	91.9
pro	SYSTEM	60.9	66.2	63.4
T	SYSTEM	50.0	42.2	45.8

Table 1: Empty category detection results[%]

4.2 Effects of empty categories on Machine Translation

Datasets and Tools

We tested the proposed method on two Japanese-to-English translation tasks; one of which involved the IWSLT dataset, which was provided during the International Workshop on Spoken Language Translation in 2005 (Eck and Hori, 2005). The dataset contains 19,972 sentences for training, 500 sentences for tuning, and 1,000 sentences for testing. Although this dataset is small, it is appropriate for evaluating the effectiveness of the proposed method since a spoken language corpus generally has many empty categories. In particular, *pro* appears very often. The other dataset is the Kyoto Free Translation Task corpus, the so called KFTT (Neubig, 2011). The KFTT is made from the "Japanese-English Bilingual Corpus of Wikipedia's Kyoto Articles", which is created by manually translating Japanese Wikipedia articles related to Kyoto City into English. The dataset consists of 440,000, 1,235, and 1,160 sentences for training, tuning, and testing, respectively.

We built the preordering model by applying the empty category detection method to source Japanese sentences to obtain syntactic trees with empty categories, as described in the previous section. We achieved this by first tokenizing Japanese sentences by using a CRF-based tokenizing and chunking software (Uchimoto and Den, 2008) to obtain the long unit words required by the Japanese parser (Hayashi et al., 2016). We then achieved word alignment by using short unit words in Japanese obtained by using the MeCab morphological analyzer with the UniDic dictionary[2].

For the Japanese-to-English translation experiment, we used a phrase-based translation model (Koehn et al., 2007). For all systems we compared, the language model is a 5-gram KenLM (Heafield, 2011), which uses modified Kneser-Ney smoothing and tuning is performed to maximize the BLEU score using minimum error rate training (Och, 2007). Other configurable setting of all tool use default values unless otherwise stated.

We compared three translation methods, each with and without empty category detection. BASELINE is a phrase-based machine translation system (Moses) (Koehn et al., 2007) which consists of training data comprising a bilingual dataset without preordering. REORDERING(H) and REORDERING(C) are described in the previous section. For REORDERING(H), 5,319 sentences with manual word alignment

---

[2] http://taku910.github.io/mecab/unidic

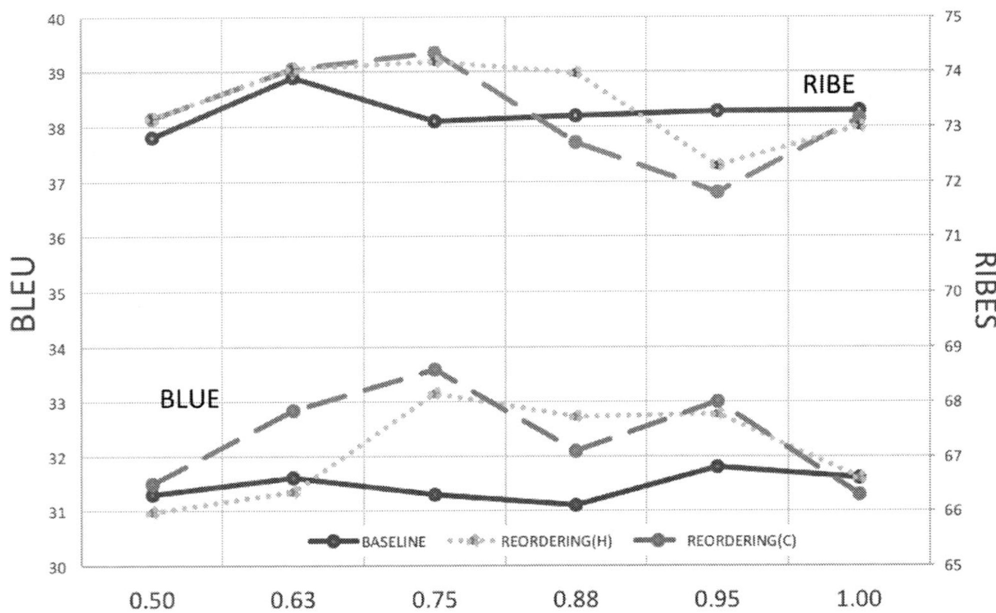

Figure 3: Characteristic of machine translation evaluation scores to empty categories filtered for development set of the IWSLT dataset

is used. These systems are equivalent to Hoshino et al., (2015)'s method. They are taken from both the spoken language (CSJ) and written (KTC) language corpus.

As for evaluation measures, we use the standard BLEU (Papineni et al., 2002) as well as RIBES (Isozaki et al., 2010), which is a rank correlation based metric that has been shown to be highly correlated with human evaluations of machine translation systems between languages with a very different word order such as Japanese and English.

Result of filtering empty categories

In this experiment, we search for the best threshold value to filter out empty categories in Sec 3. Changing the threshold values θ from 0.50 to 1.0, we measure both BLEU and RIBES, where $\theta = 1.0$ corresponds to the result produces by machine translation systems trained from a dataset without empty categories. When decoding the text into English, we set the distortion limit to 20 in all systems.

The result of the IWSLT dataset is shown in Fig. 3. It indicates that the threshold that are used to filter out empty categories affect the result of machine translation accuracy and that setting the threshold appropriately improves the result. For REORDERING(C), we achieved 33.6 in BLEU and 74.4 in RIBES for a threshold value of $\theta = 0.75$.

Fig. 3 shows that the BLEU score generally decreases as the threshold value is lowered. In particular for REORDERING(H), the BLEU score drops dramatically for lower threshold value. A decrease in the threshold value signifies an increase in the number of empty categories inserted into source languages and REORDERING(H) does not consider empty categories explicitly on reordering. Therefore, we suspect that REORDERING(H) tends to locate empty categories in unfavorable places.

The tendency displayed by BLEU and RIBES are differs for lower threshold values; BLEU decreases dramatically, whereas RIBES is reduced moderately. We consider the difference to be caused by their definitions: BLEU is sensitive to the word choice while RIBES is sensitive to the word order.

Inserting an element in the source sentence could result in inserting some words in the target sentence. The change directly could affect word-sensitive metrics such as BLEU, but it does not necessarily affect order-sensitive metrics such as RIBES, since RIBES changes only when the same word appears in both the decoded sentence and the reference sentence.

Result of machine translation of empty categories

METHODS	IWSLT-2005 JE dataset				KFTT JE dataset			
	BLEU		RIBES		BLEU		RIBES	
	dl=6	dl=20	dl=6	dl=20	dl=6	dl=20	dl=6	dl=20
BASELINE w/o EC	29.6	33.1	73.6	74.2	17.9	18.5	62.4	66.4
BASELINE w/ EC	29.2	33.6	74.1	75.7	18.1	18.6	62.5	65.4
REORDERING(C) w/o EC	29.4	33.2	74.6	76.3	19.2	19.3	64.8	65.7
REORDERING(C) w/ EC	29.6	**34.3**	**75.8**	**78.8**	19.4	19.8	65.2	66.0
REORDERING(H) w/o EC	**29.7**	33.8	74.1	76.8	19.3	19.9	65.2	66.2
REORDERING(H) w/ EC	29.3	34.1	75.6	78.6	**19.5**	**20.2**	**65.5**	**66.3**

Table 2: machine translation results with empty categories. *dl* means the distortion limit. EC indicates empty categories are detected in dataset

We compared the machine translation accuracies between the baseline systems and the proposed systems integrated with empty category detection. In all experiments, we set the threshold value to 0.75 to remove unreliable empty categories by filtering. Table 2 shows the results for IWSLT dataset and KFTT datasets.

In the result for the IWSLT dataset, we find that empty category detection improves both of the metrics RIBES and BLEU in each system when the distortion limit is set to 20. Empty category detection increases the BLEU score by +0.5, +1.1, and +0.3 points for BASELINE, REORDERING(C) (empty categories are preordered as known words) and REORDERING(H) (empty categories are preordered as unknown words), respectively. As for the RIBES metrics, it increases +1.5 points, +2.5 points and +1.8 points respectively. The best result we achieved was 34.3 in the BLUE score and 78.8 for the RIBES score when REORDERING(C) with empty categories was used.

The result for the KFTT dataset showed that integration of empty category detection into the preordering model slightly improves both of the metrics RIBES and BLEU in each system when the distortion limit is set to 6. Empty category detection has slightly bad effect on the BLEU score when the distortion limit is set to lower value. The differences are +0.1 point, +0.2 point and 0.2 point for BASELINE, REORDERING(C) and REORDERING(H) respectively. The RIBES metrics increase by +0.1 point, +0.4 point and +0.3 point respectively. The best result we achieved was 20.2 in BLEU score and 66.3 for the RIBES score when REORDERING(H) with empty categories was used.

Empty category detection considerably improves the IWSLT dataset, which is a spoken language corpus, whereas it moderately improves the KFTT dataset, which is a written language corpus. Although the improvement resulting from inserting empty categories into REORDERING(H), of which the empty categories are regarded as unknown words, is +0.3 points in BLEU and 1.8 points in RIBES for the IWSLT dataset, the improvement of inserting empty categories in REORDERING(C) is +0.5 points in BLEU and +0.3 point RIBES. This shows that a preordering method which considers empty categories has a slightly better.

Finally, we include several translation samples in Table 3 to illustrate the translation errors caused by empty categories. The insertion of empty categories enables us to improve the translation if there are missing elements on the source side. The first and second sample showed that we can obtain additional grammatical output by making null elements explicit.

Some problems remain to be solved on the translation of empty categories. One of them is the excessive insertion of empty categories as we mentioned in our experiment. Filtering unreliable empty category candidates enables us to alleviate the problem. However, we expect to improve the translation accuracy by using both source and target contexts for filtering. Another major problem is the inference of the attribute of empty categories such as the person, gender, and number. The last example in Table 3 necessity of inferring the person information of *pro*.

Success translation	
Reference	i 'm in a hurry .
Source(EC)	*pro* 急い で いる ん です 。
NO EC	are in a hurry .
ECs	i 'm in a hurry .
Reference	how much to rent it for three days ?
Source	*pro* 三 日間 借りる と いくら に なります か 。
Reordered Source	*pro* いくら に ます なり と 借りる 三 日間 か 。
NO ECs	i have a three days and how much will it be ?
ECs	i have a three days and how much will it be ?
Pre-ordered w/o EC	what would you like to hire and three days .
Pre-ordered w/ EC	how much will it cost to three days ?
Failed translation	
Reference	do you have any fruits or plants ?
Source	*pro* 果物 や 植物 を 持っ て います か 。
Reordered Source	*pro* いて 持っ ます 果物 や 植物 を か 。
NO ECs	i have a carrying any plants and fruits ?
ECs	i have fruit or plant ?
Pre-ordered w/o EC	do you have some fruit or plants ?
Pre-ordered w/ EC	i have a carrying any plants and fruits ?

Table 3: Translation Examples

5 Conclusion

In this paper, we propose a method to integrate empty category detection into preordering-based machine translation system.

We examined the effect of empty category detection on both the IWSLT and KFTT datasets. We showed by experiments that empty category detection results in an improvement in machine translation, in particular for the IWSLT dataset, which is a spoken language corpus. We also showed that, by using preordering with empty categories, we were able to achieve consistent improvement in translation accuracy for the KFTT dataset.

In future, we would like to improve the filtering strategy for empty categories. The integration of empty categories into machine translation is problematic in that empty categories are inserted excessively. There are some empty categories that are not aligned to any words in the target language. In this work, we simply filtered these empty categories based on the probability to alleviate the problem. However, for addressing this problem more appropriately, we should consider both source language context and target language context. We expect the corpus-based approach such as Wang et al., (2016) address this problem.

References

Tagyoung Chung and Daniel Gildea. 2010. Effects of Empty Categories on Machine Translation. In *Proceedings of the EMNLP2010*, pages 636–645.

Matthias Eck and Chiori Hori. 2005. Overview of the iwslt 2005 evaluation campaign. In *Proceedings of the IWSLT2005*, pages 1–22.

Masatugu Hangyo, Daisuke Kawahara, and Sadao Kurohashi. 2013. Japanese Zero Reference Resolution Considering Zero Exophora and Author/Reader Mentions. In *Proceedings of the EMNLP2013*, pages 924–934.

Katsuhiko Hayashi, Jun Suzuki, and Masaaki Nagata. 2016. Shift-reduce spinal tag parsing with dynamic programming. *Transactions of the Japanese Society for Artificial Intelligence*, 31(2):1–8.

Kenneth Heafield. 2011. Kenlm: Faster and smaller language model queries. In *Proceedings of the Sixth Workshop on Statistical Machine Translation*, pages 187–197.

Sho Hoshino, Yusuke Miyao, Katsuhito Sudoh, Katsuhiko Hayashi, and Masaaki Nagata. 2015. Discriminative preordering meets kendall ' s tau maximization. In *Proceedings of the ACL-IJCNLP2015*, pages 139–144.

Ryu Iida, Kentaro Inui, and Yuji Matsumoto. 2007. Zero-anaphora resolution by learning rich syntactic pattern features. *ACM Transactions on Asian Language Information Processing*, 6(4):1–22.

Hideki Isozaki, Tsutomu Hirao, Kevin Duh, Katsuhito Sudoh, and Hajime Tsukada. 2010. Automatic evaluation of translation quality for distant language pairs. In *Proceedings of the EMNLP2010*, pages 944–952.

Philipp Koehn, Hieu Hoang, Alexandra Birch, Chris Callison-Burch, Marcello Federico, Nicola Bertoldi, Brooke Cowan, Wade Shen, Christine Moran, Richard Zens, et al. 2007. Moses: Open source toolkit for statistical machine translation. In *Proceedings of the ACL2007*, pages 177–180.

Taku Kudo, Hiroshi Ichikawa, and Hideto Kazawa. 2014. A joint inference of deep case analysis and zero subject generation for Japanese-to-English statistical machine translation. In *Proceedings of the ACL2014*, pages 557–562.

Hiromi Nakaiwa and Satoru Ikehara. 1995. Intrasentential Resolution of Japanese Zero Pronouns using Pragmatic and Semantic Constraints. In *Proceeedings of the International Conference on Theoretical and Methodological Issues in Machine Translation*, pages 96–105.

Graham Neubig. 2011. The Kyoto free translation task. http://www.phontron.com/kftt.

Franz Josef Och. 2007. Minimum error rate training in statistical machine translation. In *Proceedings of the ACL2007*, pages 160–167.

Kishore Papineni, Salim Roukos, Todd Ward, and Wei-Jing Zhu. 2002. Bleu: a method for automatic evaluation of machine translation. In *Proceedings of the ACL2002*, pages 311–318.

Hirotoshi Taira, Katsuhito Sudoh, and Masaaki Nagata. 2012. Zero pronoun resolution can improve the quality of je translation. In *Proceedings of the Sixth Workshop on Syntax, Semantics and Structure in Statistical Translation*, pages 111–118.

Shunsuke Takeno, Nagata Masaaki, and Kazuhide Yamamoto. 2015. Empty Category Detection using Path Features and Distributed Case Frames. In *Proceedings of the EMNLP2015*, pages 1335–1340.

Kiyotaka Uchimoto and Yasuharu Den. 2008. Word-level dependency-structure annotation to corpus of spontaneous japanese and its application. In *Proceedings of the LREC2008*, pages 3118–3122.

Longyue Wang, Zhaopeng Tu, Xiaojun Zhang, Hang Li, Andy Way, and Qun Liu. 2016. A Novel Approach to Dropped Pronoun Translation. In *Proceedings of the NAACL-HLT2016*, pages 983–993.

Bing Xiang, Xiaoqiang Luo, and Bowen Zhou. 2013. Enlisting the ghost: Modeling empty categories for machine translation. In *Proceedings of the ACL2013*, pages 822–831.

Kyoto University Participation to WAT 2016

Fabien Cromieres and **Chenhui Chu** and **Toshiaki Nakazawa**
Japan Science and Technology Agency
5-3, Yonbancho, Chiyoda-ku, Tokyo, 102-8666, Japan
{fabien, chu, nakazawa}@pa.jst.jp

Sadao Kurohashi
Kyoto University
Yoshida-honmachi, Sakyo-ku, Kyoto, 606-8501, Japan
kuro@i.kyoto-u.ac.jp

Abstract

We describe here our approaches and results on the WAT 2016 shared translation tasks. We tried to use both an example-based machine translation (MT) system and a neural MT system. We report very good translation results, especially when using neural MT for Chinese-to-Japanese translation. Overall, we could obtain best or close-to-best results in this shared task.

1 Introduction

This paper describes the experiments we did for the WAT 2016 (Nakazawa et al., 2016a) shared translation task. We used two different machine translation (MT) approaches. On one hand, we used an incremental improvement to an example-based MT (EBMT) system: the KyotoEBMT system we used for WAT 2015. On the other hand, we implemented a neural MT (NMT) system that makes use of the recent results obtained by researchers in the field. We found that the NMT approach works very well on the ASPEC (Nakazawa et al., 2016b) data, especially for the Chinese-to-Japanese direction. Overall, we could obtain the best results reported for several language directions.

This paper is decomposed as such: in Section 2, we describe the incremental improvements to our EBMT system compared with the WAT 2015 workshop. We then describe our NMT implementation and the settings we used for our experiments in Section 3. Finally, we discuss the results obtained in the shared task.

2 EBMT

The EBMT results that we submitted this year are essentially based on our KyotoEBMT system of last year (Richardson et al., 2015), but with some improvements for the data preprocessing step.

2.1 Overview of KyotoEBMT

Figure 1 shows the basic structure of the KyotoEBMT translation pipeline. The training process begins with parsing and aligning parallel sentences from the training corpus. The alignments are then used to build an example database ('translation memory') containing 'examples' or 'treelets' that form the hypotheses to be combined during decoding. Translation is performed by first parsing an input sentence then searching for treelets matching entries in the example database. The retrieved treelets are combined by a lattice-based decoder that optimizes a log linear model score. Finally, we use a reranker to select the optimal translation from the n-best list provided by the decoder using additional non-local features.[1]

2.2 Improved Data Preprocessing

English spelling correction. The English data of the ASPEC-JE task contains a lot of spelling errors. For example, the word "dielectric" is misspelled as "dieletcric" in many sentences. To address this, we apply a lattice-based correction method. We first collect correction candidates for misspelled words using the GNU Aspell toolkit.[2] In the case of "dieletcric," Aspell gives five correction candidates of "dielectric," "dielectrics," "dielectric's," "electric," and "dialectic." To select the correct correction for the misspelled

---

[1]Note that the results we submitted this year did not perform this reranking step.
[2]http://aspell.net

Proceedings of the 3rd Workshop on Asian Translation,
pages 166–174, Osaka, Japan, December 11-17 2016.

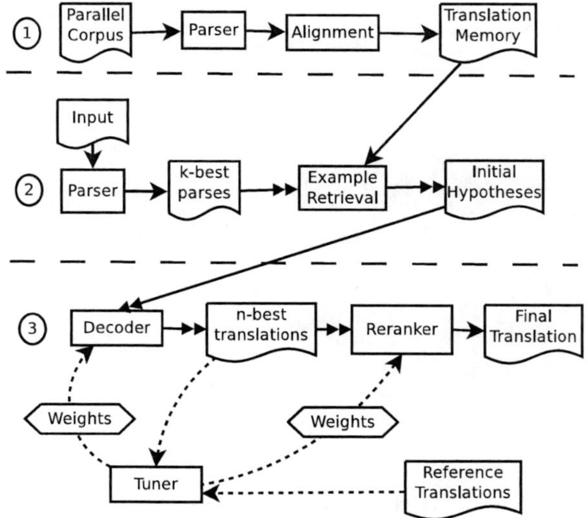

Figure 1: Overview of KyotoEBMT. The translation pipeline can be roughly divided in 3 steps. Step 1 is the creation of the example database, trained from a parallel corpus. Step 2 is the parsing of an input sentence and the generation of sets of initial hypotheses. Step 3 consists in decoding and reranking. The tuning of the weights for decoding and reranking is done by a modified version of step 3.

word, we use all the candidates given by Aspell, and compose a lattice for the sentence that contains this misspelled word. Finally, we select the best candidate based on the KyotoEBMT decoder with hand-crafted weights for three features of the edit distance between the misspelled word, the language model score, and the sentence length penalty. We verified that the correction precision of this method is about 95%. However, although over 1/3 of sentences in the training data of the ASPEC-JE task were changed after applying the spelling correction, only slight MT performance improvement was observed (about 0.1 BLEU).

Chinese short unit segmentation. For the Chinese data of the ASPEC-JC task, we applied a new segmentation standard. This standard is based on character-level POS patterns (Shen et al., 2016), which can circumvent inconsistency and address data sparsity of conventional segmentation standards. As this standard tends to segment words shorter than the conventional standards, we call it short unit segmentation. Applying short unit segmentation improves the MT performance by 0.3 BLEU on the Chinese-to-Japanese translation direction of the ASPEC-JC task.

Because of time limitation, we were not able to apply the above improved data preprocessing for our NMT system before the submission due for pairwise crowdsourcing evaluation. After the submission due, we conducted experiments using Chinese short unit segmentation on the Chinese-to-Japanese translation direction of the ASPEC-JC task, and further updated the state-of-the-art result (46.04 → 46.36 BLEU).

3 NMT

NMT is a new approach to MT that, although recently proposed, has quickly achieved state-of-the-art results (Bojar et al., 2016). We implemented our own version of the sequence-to-sequence with attention mechanism model, first proposed in (Bahdanau et al., 2015). Our implementation was done using the Chainer[3] toolkit (Tokui et al., 2015). We make this implementation available under a GPL license.[4]

---

[3] http://chainer.org/
[4] https://github.com/fabiencro/knmt . See also (Cromieres, 2016)

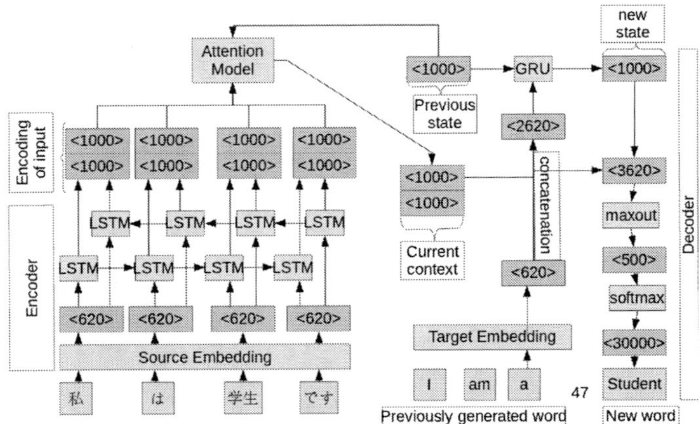

Figure 2: The structure of a NMT system with attention, as described in (Bahdanau et al., 2015) (but with LSTMs instead of GRUs). The notation "<1000>" means a vector of size 1000. The vector sizes shown here are the ones suggested in the original paper.

3.1 Overview of NMT

We describe here briefly the (Bahdanau et al., 2015) model. As shown in Figure 2, an input sentence is first converted into a sequence of vector through an embedding layer; these vectors are then fed to two LSTM layers (one going forward, the other going backward) to give a new sequence of vectors that encode the input sentence. On the decoding part of the model, a target-side sentence is generated with what is conceptually a recurrent neural network language model: an LSTM is sequentially fed the embedding of the previously generated word, and its output is sent through a deep softmax layer to produce the probability of the next word. This decoding LSTM is also fed a context vector, which is a weighted sum of the vectors encoding the input sentence, provided by the attention mechanism.

3.2 Network Settings

For all experiments, we have used the following basic settings, which are mostly the same as in the original (Bahdanau et al., 2015) paper:

- Source and target-side embeddings of size 620

- Source and target-side hidden states of size 1000

- Attention mechanism hidden states of size 1000

- Deep softmax output with a 2-maxout layer of size 500

For the recurrent cells of the encoder and the decoder, we first used GRUs (Chung et al., 2014), but then switched to LSTMs (Hochreiter and Schmidhuber, 1997), as they seemed to give slightly better results. We also considered stacking several LSTMs for both the encoder and the decoder. We considered stacks of two and three LSTMs. Most of the results we provide are with stacks of two LSTMs. Although in theory we would have expected 3-layer LSTMs to performe better, we did not get better results in the few experiments we used them. One explanation is that 3-layer LSTMS are typically more difficult to train. In addition, due to time constraints, we did not take as much time as in the 2-layer setting for finding good hyperparameters for 3-layer LSTMs and training them sufficiently. In case of stacked LSTMs, we used some inter-layer dropout regularization (Srivastava et al., 2014), as first suggested by (Zaremba et al., 2014).

In addition, we have considered various vocabulary sizes. It is usually necessary to restrict the vocabulary size when using NMT systems. Especially for the target language, as the output layer will become proportionally slower to compute (and use more memory) as vocabulary size increases. We considered restricting vocabulary to 30k words and 200k words for source language. And we considered 30k and 50k words for the target languages. This means that we just keep the most frequent words, and replace less frequent words by an UNK tag.

Because of this, the network can also sometime generate UNK tags when translating an input sentence. To alleviate this issue, we use an idea first proposed in (Luong et al., 2015), which consists in replacing the generated UNK tag by a dictionary-based translation of the corresponding source word. Finding the corresponding source word is, however, not trivial. The scheme used in (Luong et al., 2015) for finding the source word does not seem like a good fit in our case, because it considers implicitly that source and target languages have similar word orders. This can be the case for English and French, but not for English and Japanese or Japanese and Chinese, as in the tasks of WAT. Therefore, we find the corresponding source word by using the attention mechanism: the word is the one on which the maximum of attention was focused on when the UNK tag was generated. The problem here is that the attention is not always focused on the correct word. This quite often leads to errors such as translating twice an input word. Still, even with this approximate unknown word replacement method, we typically get around +1~1.5 BLEU after replacement.

3.3 Training Settings

We used ADAM (Kingma and Ba, 2014) as the learning algorithm. We found it works better than ADADELTA (Zeiler, 2012) and a simple stochastic gradient descent without fine-tuning hyper-parameters. We used a dropout rate of 20% for the inter-layer dropout. We also found that using L2 regularization through weight decay was quite useful. We found that a weight decay coefficient of 1e-6 was giving optimal results for our settings. Using 1e-7 was not as effective, and using 1e-5 lead to under fitting of the model.

The training sentences were randomized, and then processed by minibatches of size 64. As processing time tends to be proportional to the length of the largest sentence in the minibatch, we used an often-used technique to make sentences in a given minibatch have similar sizes: we extract 20 x 64 sentences, sort them by size, and then create 20 minibatches from these sorted sentences. Due to memory and performance issues, it can also be necessary to limit the maximum size of training sentences. We discarded training sentences whose source or target side was larger than a given length L. Depending on the network settings, we chose L to be 80, 90 or 120.

We also used an early stopping scheme: every 200 training iterations, we computed the perplexity of the development part of the ASPEC data. We also computed a BLEU score by translating this development data with a "greedy search."[5] We kept track of the parameters that gave the best development BLEU and the best development perplexity so far. Empirically, we found that the parameter with best "greedy search" BLEU score was consistently beating the parameter with best perplexity when using beam-search. However, we could obtain even better results by ensembling these two parameters, as described in section 3.6.

3.4 Adding Noise to the Target Embeddings

We found it quite efficient to add noise to the output of the target embedding layer during training. Our rationale for doing this was that, when translating a new input, there is a risk of cascading errors: if we predict an incorrect word at time t, the embedding of this incorrect word is fed at time $t + 1$ to predict the next word, increasing the likelihood that this next word is itself incorrect. We felt that, by adding noise to the target embedding during training, we force the rest of the network to trust this input less, and therefore to be more robust to prediction errors at previous steps. The noised embeddings are created by multiplying the original embeddings with a random vector generated from a gaussian distribution with both mean and variance equal to 1.

This did appear to significantly help in our preliminary experiments, with gains ranging from +1 to +2 BLEU. However, it might be that these improvements only come from the regularization created by

---

[5]i.e., we did not use the beam search procedure described in section 3.5, but simply translated with the most likely word at each step. Using a beam search is to slow when we need to do frequent BLEU evaluations.

the noise, and is not directly linked to an increased robustness to prediction errors. We should do further experiments to verify if there is a marked difference in results between adding noise the way we do, and simply adding a dropout layer to any part of the network.

3.5 Beam Search

The naive way to translate using an NMT system such as the one we described is, after feeding the input sentence, to produce the target words with the highest probability at each step. This is however sub-optimal, as a better translation might include a sub-sequence that is locally less likely than another. Hence, the idea is to use a form of beam-search to keep track of several translation hypotheses at once.

There are a few differences in the way we handle beam search, compared with other NMT implementations such as the one originally provided by the LISA lab of Université de Montréal.[6] We came to this method after a few iterative trials. We detail our beam search procedure in Algorithm 1.

Given an input sentence i of length L_i, we first estimate the maximum length of the translation L_{mt}. L_{mt} is estimated by $L_{mt} = r \cdot L_i$, where r is a language dependent ratio. We empirically found the following values to work well : $r = 1.2$ for Japanese-to-English, $r = 2$ for English-to-Japanese, and $r = 1.5$ for Japanese-to-Chinese and Chinese-to-Japanese.

At the end, we found it beneficial to rank the generated translations by their log-probability divided by their length, instead of simply using the log-probability. This helps to counter-balance the fact that the model will otherwise tend to be biased towards shorter translations. One could fear that doing this will actually bias the model towards longer translations, but we did not observe such a thing; maybe in part due to the fact that our algorithm caps the maximum length of a translation through the language-dependent length ratio.

Although we have seen some claims that large beam width was not very helpful for NMT decoding, we actually verified empirically that using a beam-width of 100 could give significantly better results than a beam-width of 30 or less (of course, at the cost of a serious slow-down in the translation speed). We used a beam-width of 100 in all our submitted results.

Algorithm 1 Beam Search

1: Input: decoder dec conditionalized on input sentence i, beam width B
2: $L_{mt} \leftarrow r \cdot |i|$ ▷ L_{mt}: Maximum translation length, r: Language-dependent length ratio
3: $finished \leftarrow []$ ▷ list of finished translations (log-prob, translation)
4: $beam \leftarrow$ array of L_{mt} $item$ lists   ▷ an $item$: (log-probability, decoder state, partial translation)
5: $beam[0] \leftarrow [(0, st_i, ")]$ ▷ st_i: initial decoder state
6: **for** $n \leftarrow 1$ to L_{mt} **do**
7:      **for** $(lp, st, t) \in beam[n-1]$ **do**
8:          $prob, st' \leftarrow dec(st, t[-1])$ ▷ dec return the probability of next words, and the next state
9:          **for** $w, p_w \in top_B(prob)$ **do**   ▷ top_B return the B words with highest probability
10:             **if** $w = EOS$ **then**
11:                add $(lp + log(p_w), t)$ to $finished$
12:             **else**
13:                add $(lp + log(p_w), st', t + w)$ to $beam[n]$
14:             **end if**
15:          **end for**
16:      **end for**
17:      prune $beam[n]$
18: **end for**
19: Sort $(lp, t) \in finished$ according to $lp/|t|$
20: **return** t s.t. $lp/|t|$ is maximum

---

[6]https://github.com/lisa-groundhog/

3.6 Ensembling

Ensembling has previously been found to widely increase translation quality of NMT systems. Ensembling essentially means that, at each translation step, we predict the next word using several NMT models instead of one. The two "classic" ways of combining the prediction of different systems are to either take the geometric average or the arithmetic average of their predicted probabilities. Interestingly, although it seems other researchers have reported that using the arithmetic average works better (Luong et al., 2016), we actually found that geometric average was giving better results for us.

Ensembling usually works best with independently trained parameters. We actually found that even using parameters from a single run could improve results. This had also been previously observed by (Sennrich et al., 2016). Therefore, for the cases when we could only run one training session, we ensembled the three parameters corresponding to the best development loss, the best development BLEU, and the final parameters (obtained after continuing training for some time after the best development BLEU was found). We refer to this as "self-ensembling" in the result section. When we could do n independent training, we kept these three parameters for each of the independent run and ensembled the $3 \cdot n$ parameters.

3.7 Preprocessing

The preprocessing steps were essentially the same as for KyotoEBMT. We lowercased the English sentences, and segmented automatically the Japanese and Chinese sentences. We used JUMAN to segment the Japanese and SKP to segment the Chinese. We also tried to apply BPE segmentation (Sennrich et al., 2015) in some cases.[7]

4 Results

We submitted the translation results of both EBMT and NMT systems, however, the automatic evaluation results of NMT seemed to be quite superior to those of EBMT. Therefore, we selected NMT results for the human evaluations for almost all the subtasks.

4.1 Specifics NMT Settings for Each Language Pair

The NMT training is quite slow. On an Nvidia Titan X (Maxwell), we typically needed 4~7 days of training for ASPEC-CJ, and more than 2 weeks for ASPEC-EJ. Therefore, it took us a lot of time to experiment with different variations of settings, and we did not have the time to fully re-run experiments with the best settings. We describe here the settings of the results we submitted for human evaluation.

Ja → En Submission 1 corresponds to only one trained model, with self-ensembing (see Section 3.6). In this case, source vocabulary was reduced to 200k words. For target vocabulary, we reduced the vocabulary to 52k using BPE. We used a double-layer LSTM.

Submission 2 is an ensemble of four independently trained models, two of which were using GRUs, and two of which were using LSTM. Source and target vocabularies were restricted to 30k words. For each model, we actually used three sets of parameters (best development BLEU, best development perplexity, final), as described in Section 3.6. Therefore, ensembling was actually using 12 different models.

En → Ja Submission 1 also corresponds to only one trained model. BPE was applied to both source and target sides to reduce vocabulary to 52k. We used a double-layer LSTM and self-ensembling.

Ja → Zh Submission 1 corresponds to one trained model with self-ensembling, with double-layer LSTM and 30k words for both source and target vocabularies.

Zh → Ja Submission 1 corresponds to ensembling two independently trained models using double-layer LSTM with 30k source and target vocabularies. In addition, a model was trained on reversed Japanese sentences and was used to rescore the translations.

Submission 2 corresponds to one independently trained model, using self-ensembling and using 200k words for source vocabulary and 50k words for target vocabulary.

---

[7]using the BPE segmentation code at https://github.com/rsennrich/subword-nmt

| Subtask | Ja $\rightarrow$ En | | | En $\rightarrow$ Ja | | Ja $\rightarrow$ Zh | | Zh $\rightarrow$ Ja | | |
| Model | EBMT | NMT | | EBMT | NMT | EBMT | NMT | EBMT | NMT | |
Human Evaluation		1	2		1		1		1	2
BLEU	21.22	24.71	26.22	31.03	36.19	30.27	31.98	36.63	46.04	44.29
RIBES	70.57	75.08	75.66	77.12	81.98	81.31	83.76	82.03	87.65	86.94
AM-FM	59.52	56.27	55.85	74.75	73.87	76.42	76.33	76.71	78.59	78.44
Pairwise	-	47.00	44.25	-	55.25	30.75	58.75	-	63.75	56.00
Rank	-	3/9	4/9	-	1/10	3/5	1/5	-	1/9	2/9
JPO adequacy	-	3.89	-	-	4.02	-	3.88	-	3.94	-
Rank	-	1/3	-	-	1/4	-	1/3	-	1/3	-

Table 1: Official automatic and human evaluation results of our EBMT and NMT systems for the ASPEC subtasks.

Source	本フローセンサーの型式と基本構成，規格を 図示，紹介。
Reference	Shown here are type and basic configuration and standards of this flow **with some diagrams**.
EBMT	This flow sensor type and the basic composition, standard **is illustrated**, and introduced.
NMT	This paper introduces the type, basic configuration, and standards of this flow sensor.

Table 2: A Japanese-to-English translation example by our EBMT and NMT systems.

4.2 Official Evaluation Results

Table 1 shows the official automatic and human evaluation results of the ASPEC subtasks that we participated in. "Rank" shows the ranking of our submissions among all the submissions for each subtask.

In view of the pairwise evaluation, our system achieved the best translation quality for all the subtasks except for Ja $\rightarrow$ En. The difference of the pairwise scores between the best system and our system for Ja $\rightarrow$ En is 1.25, which is *not* statistically significant. For all the other subtasks, the differences between our system and others are statistically significant ($p < 0.01$).

As for the JPO adequacy evaluation, our system achieved the best translation quality for all the subtasks. The differences of the score between our system and the 2nd graded systems are 0.058, 0.305, 0.245 and 0.300 for Ja $\rightarrow$ En, En $\rightarrow$ Ja, Ja $\rightarrow$ Zh and Zh $\rightarrow$ Ja respectively.

4.3 Error Analysis

We analyzed the translation results of both our EBMT and NMT systems. We found that the biggest problem of EBMT is word order errors, which affects the fluency and meaning of the translations. This is due to the reason that the word order of the translations in EBMT depends on the parse trees of the input sentences, but the parsing accuracy is not perfect especially for Chinese. NMT tends to produce fluent translations, however it lacks of adequacy sometimes.

The most common problem of NMT is that it could produce under or over translated translations, due to the lack of a way for the attention mechanism to memorize the source words that have been translated during decoding. We plan to address this problem with the coverage model proposed in (Tu et al., 2016). The UNK words are also a big problem. Although we deal with them using the UNK replacement method (Luong et al., 2015), it could simply fail because of errors for finding the corresponding source words using attention.

We show a Japanese-to-English translation example by our EBMT and NMT systems in Table 2 to illustrate some of the above problems. The translation produced by the EBMT system has a word order problem that changes the meaning, making "the basic composition, standard" independent from "this flow sensor." It also has an agreement violation problem between the argument and the predicate that "is illustrated" should be "are illustrated". The translation produced by the NMT system is more fluent, but it does not translate the source word "図示 (be illustrated)". In addition, it adds the additional information "this paper" to the translation.

It is interesting to note that the performance gap between NMT and EBMT is largest for Zh $\rightarrow$ Ja, when Chinese is also the language most difficult to parse. The gap is smaller when Japanese, the easiest language to parse, is the source language. We can infer that the EBMT system is somehow quite handicapped by source sentence parsing issues, as we had noted in our previous results.

5 Conclusion

We have described our experiments for WAT 2016 using both an EBMT system and a NMT system. We could obtain the best or close-to-best results in each translation task. The NMT approach proved to be quite successful, which is in line with other recent MT evaluation results (Bojar et al., 2016). In the future, we will probably continue to explore the NMT approach, if possible merging in some elements of our EBMT system. We could then hope to solve the weaknesses of the two systems that we identified in our error analysis.

References

Dzmitry Bahdanau, Kyunghyun Cho, and Yoshua Bengio. 2015. Neural machine translation by jointly learning to align and translate. In *ICLR 2015*.

Ondrej Bojar, Rajen Chatterjee, Christian Federmann, Yvette Graham, Barry Haddow, Matthias Huck, Antonio Jimeno Yepes, Philipp Koehn, Varvara Logacheva, Christof Monz, et al. 2016. Findings of the 2016 conference on machine translation (wmt16). In *Proceedings of WMT 2016*.

Junyoung Chung, Caglar Gulcehre, KyungHyun Cho, and Yoshua Bengio. 2014. Empirical evaluation of gated recurrent neural networks on sequence modeling. *arXiv preprint arXiv:1412.3555*.

Fabien Cromieres. 2016. Kyoto-NMT: a neural machine translation implementation in Chainer. In *Coling 2016 System Demonstration*.

Sepp Hochreiter and Jürgen Schmidhuber. 1997. Long short-term memory. *Neural computation*, 9(8):1735–1780.

Diederik Kingma and Jimmy Ba. 2014. Adam: A method for stochastic optimization. *arXiv preprint arXiv:1412.6980*.

Minh-Thang Luong, Ilya Sutskever, Quoc V Le, Oriol Vinyals, and Wojciech Zaremba. 2015. Addressing the rare word problem in neural machine translation. In *Proceedings of ACL 2015*.

Thang Luong, Kyunghyun Cho, and Christopher D. Manning. 2016. Neural machine translation (ACL tutorial). *https://sites.google.com/site/acl16nmt/*.

Toshiaki Nakazawa, Hideya Mino, Chenchen Ding, Isao Goto, Graham Neubig, Sadao Kurohashi, and Eiichiro Sumita. 2016a. Overview of the 3rd workshop on asian translation. In *Proceedings of the 3rd Workshop on Asian Translation (WAT2016)*, Osaka, Japan, October.

Toshiaki Nakazawa, Manabu Yaguchi, Kiyotaka Uchimoto, Masao Utiyama, Eiichiro Sumita, Sadao Kurohashi, and Hitoshi Isahara. 2016b. Aspec: Asian scientific paper excerpt corpus. In *Proceedings of the 10th Conference on International Language Resources and Evaluation (LREC2016)*, Portoroz, Slovenia, 5.

John Richardson, Raj Dabre, Chenhui Chu, Fabien Cromières, Toshiaki Nakazawa, and Sadao Kurohashi. 2015. KyotoEBMT System Description for the 2nd Workshop on Asian Translation. In *Proceedings of the 2nd Workshop on Asian Translation (WAT2015)*, pages 54–60, Kyoto, Japan, October.

Rico Sennrich, Barry Haddow, and Alexandra Birch. 2015. Neural machine translation of rare words with subword units. *arXiv preprint arXiv:1508.07909*.

Rico Sennrich, Barry Haddow, and Alexandra Birch. 2016. Edinburgh neural machine translation systems for wmt 16. In *Proceedings of the first Conference on Machine Translation (WMT2016)*.

Mo Shen, Li Wingmui, HyunJeong Choe, Chenhui Chu, Daisuke Kawahara, and Sadao Kurohashi. 2016. Consistent word segmentation, part-of-speech tagging and dependency labelling annotation for chinese language. In *Proceedings of the 26th International Conference on Computational Linguistics*, Osaka, Japan, December. Association for Computational Linguistics.

Nitish Srivastava, Geoffrey E Hinton, Alex Krizhevsky, Ilya Sutskever, and Ruslan Salakhutdinov. 2014. Dropout: a simple way to prevent neural networks from overfitting. *Journal of Machine Learning Research*, 15(1):1929–1958.

Seiya Tokui, Kenta Oono, Shohei Hido, and Justin Clayton. 2015. Chainer: a next-generation open source framework for deep learning. In *Proceedings of Workshop on Machine Learning Systems (LearningSys) in The Twenty-ninth Annual Conference on Neural Information Processing Systems (NIPS)*.

Zhaopeng Tu, Zhengdong Lu, Yang Liu, Xiaohua Liu, and Hang Li. 2016. Modeling coverage for neural machine translation. In *Proceedings of the 54th Annual Meeting of the Association for Computational Linguistics (Volume 1: Long Papers)*, pages 76–85, Berlin, Germany, August. Association for Computational Linguistics.

Wojciech Zaremba, Ilya Sutskever, and Oriol Vinyals. 2014. Recurrent neural network regularization. *arXiv preprint arXiv:1409.2329*.

Matthew D Zeiler. 2012. Adadelta: an adaptive learning rate method. *arXiv preprint arXiv:1212.5701*.

Character-based Decoding in
Tree-to-Sequence Attention-based Neural Machine Translation

Akiko Eriguchi, Kazuma Hashimoto, and **Yoshimasa Tsuruoka**
The University of Tokyo, 7-3-1 Hongo, Bunkyo-ku, Tokyo, Japan
`{eriguchi, hassy, tsuruoka}@logos.t.u-tokyo.ac.jp`

Abstract

This paper reports our systems (UT-AKY) submitted in the 3rd Workshop of Asian Translation 2016 (WAT'16) and their results in the English-to-Japanese translation task. Our model is
based on the tree-to-sequence Attention-based NMT (ANMT) model proposed by Eriguchi et al.
(2016). We submitted two ANMT systems: one with a word-based decoder and the other with
a character-based decoder. Experimenting on the English-to-Japanese translation task, we have
confirmed that the character-based decoder can cover almost the full vocabulary in the target
language and generate translations much faster than the word-based model.

1 Introduction

End-to-end Neural Machine Translation (NMT) models have recently achieved state-of-the-art results
in several translation tasks (Luong et al., 2015a; Luong et al., 2015b). Those NMT models are based
on the idea of sequence-to-sequence learning (Sutskever et al., 2014), where both of the source and the
target sentences are considered as a sequence of symbols (e.g. words or characters) and they are directly
converted via a vector space. The sequence of symbols on the source side is input into a vector space,
and the sequence of symbols on the target side is output from the vector space. In the end-to-end NMT
models, the above architectures are embodied by a single neural network.

The optimal unit for NMT is an important research question discussed in the community. Early NMT
models employ a word as a unit of the sequence (Cho et al., 2014b; Sutskever et al., 2014). Sennrich et
al. (2016) have used a Byte-Pair Encoding (BPE) method to create a sub-word level vocabulary according to the frequencies of sub-word appearance in the corpus. They successfully replaced a large word
vocabulary in German and Russian with a much smaller sub-word vocabulary. They have also shown
that their sub-word-based NMT model gives better translations than the word-based NMT models.

The smallest unit of a sequence of text data is a character. The character-based approach has attracted
much attention in the field of NMT, because it enables an NMT model to handle all of the tokens in the
corpus (Costa-jussà and Fonollosa, 2016; Chung et al., 2016). A hybrid model of the word-based and the
character-based model has also been proposed by Luong and Manning (2016). These studies reported
the success and effectiveness in translating the out-of-vocabulary words.

In this paper, we apply character-based decoding to a tree-based NMT model (Eriguchi et al., 2016).
The existing character-based models focus only on the sequence-based NMT models. The objective of
this paper is to analyze the results of the character-based decoding in the tree-based NMT model. We
also enrich the tree-based encoder with syntactic features. Figure 1 shows an overview of our system. We
conducted the English-to-Japanese translation task on the WAT'16 dataset. The results of our character-
based decoder model show that its translation accuracy is lower than that of the word-based decoder
model by 1.34 BLEU scores, but the character-based decoder model needed much less time to generate
a sentence.

2 Neural Machine Translation

End-to-end NMT models have recently outperformed phrase-based statistical machine translation (SMT)
models in several languages (Luong et al., 2015a; Eriguchi et al., 2016). Those NMT models are ba-

175

Proceedings of the 3rd Workshop on Asian Translation,
pages 175–183, Osaka, Japan, December 11-17 2016.

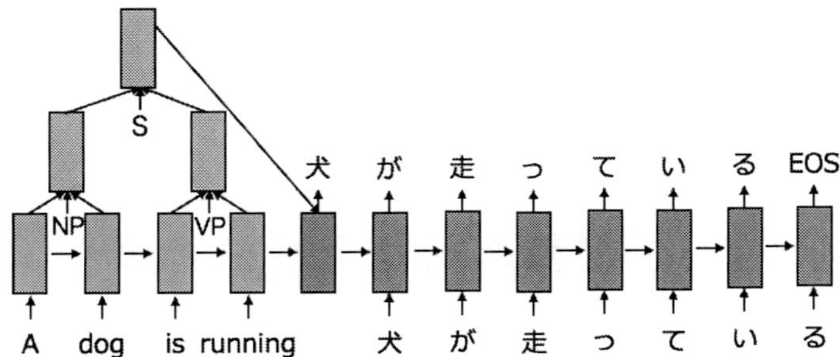

Figure 1: WAT'16 Our system: tree-to-character Neural Machine Translation model.

sically composed of two processes called an *encoder* and a *decoder*. We feed a sequence of words $x = (x_1, x_2, \cdots, x_n)$ in the source language into the encoder, and the encoder converts the input data into a vector space until the last n-th word in the sentence is input. Recurrent Neural Networks (RNNs) are used to obtain the vectors of the sequence of data in the recent NMT models. The i-th hidden state $h_i \in \mathbb{R}^{d \times 1}$ in the RNN holds a vector computed by the current input x_i and the previous hidden state $h_{i-1} \in \mathbb{R}^{d \times 1}$:

$$h_i = RNN_{encoder}(Embed(x_i), h_{i-1}), \tag{1}$$

where $Embed(x_i)$ is the word embedding vector of the i-th source word x_i. h_0 is set to $\mathbf{0}$.

Another RNN is used as the decoder to obtain the vectors for predicting the words on the target side. The j-th hidden state $s_j \in \mathbb{R}^{d \times 1}$ of the RNN is computed from the previous hidden state $s_{j-1} \in \mathbb{R}^{d \times 1}$ and the previous output word y_{j-1} as follows:

$$s_j = RNN_{decoder}(Embed(y_{j-1}), s_{j-1}), \tag{2}$$

where $Embed(y_{j-1})$ is the word embedding vector of the $(j-1)$-th target word y_{j-1}. The first decoder s_1 is initialized with the last hidden state of the encoder h_n.

The NMT models that simply connect the above two types of RNNs cannot capture strong relations between the encoder units and the decoder unit, and they often fail to translate a long sentence. An attention mechanism has been introduced to solve the problem by creating an attention path so that the hidden states of the decoder can access each hidden state of the encoder (Bahdanau et al., 2015). Luong et al. (2015a) have refined the calculation of the attention mechanism. In the decoder process, the attention score $\alpha_j(i)$ is computed by the j-th hidden state of the decoder s_j and each hidden state of the encoder h_i as follows:

$$\alpha_j(i) = \frac{\exp(h_i \cdot s_j)}{\sum_{k=1}^{n} \exp(h_k \cdot s_j)}, \tag{3}$$

where $\cdot$ represents the inner product, and its value of $h_i \cdot s_j$ is the similarity score between h_i and s_j. The j-th context vector $d_j \in \mathbb{R}^{d \times 1}$ are computed as the summation of the hidden states:

$$d_j = \sum_{i=1}^{n} \alpha_j(i) h_i, \tag{4}$$

where each of the hidden states is weighted by $\alpha_j(i)$. We compute the j-th final decoder $\tilde{s}_j \in \mathbb{R}^{d \times 1}$ as follows:

$$\tilde{s}_j = \tanh(W_d[s_j; d_j] + b_d), \tag{5}$$

where $[s_j; d_j] \in \mathbb{R}^{2d \times 1}$ denotes the concatenation of s_j and d_j. $W_d \in \mathbb{R}^{d \times 2d}$ is a weight matrix. $b_d \in \mathbb{R}^{d \times 1}$ is a bias vector. The conditional probability of predicting an output is defined as follows:

$$p(y_j | x, y_{<j}) = \text{softmax}(W_s \tilde{s}_j + b_s), \tag{6}$$

where $\boldsymbol{W}_s \in \mathbb{R}^{d \times d}$ is a matrix and $\boldsymbol{b}_s \in \mathbb{R}^{d \times 1}$ is a bias.

The objective function to train the NMT models is defined as the sum of the log-likelihoods of the translation pairs in the training data:

$$J(\boldsymbol{\theta}) \;=\; \frac{1}{|\mathcal{D}|} \sum_{(\boldsymbol{x},\boldsymbol{y}) \in \mathcal{D}} \log p(\boldsymbol{y}|\boldsymbol{x}), \tag{7}$$

where $\mathcal{D}$ denotes the set of parallel sentence pairs. When training the model, the parameters $\boldsymbol{\theta}$ are updated by Stochastic Gradient Descent (SGD).

3   Our systems: tree-to-character attention-based NMT model

Our system is mostly based on the tree-to-sequence Attention-based NMT (ANMT) model described in Eriguchi et al. (2016) which has a tree-based encoder and a sequence-based decoder. They employed Long Short-Term Memory (LSTM) as the units of RNNs (Hochreiter and Schmidhuber, 1997; Gers et al., 2000). In their proposed tree-based encoder, the phrase vectors are computed from their child states by using Tree-LSTM units (Tai et al., 2015), following the phrase structure of a sentence. We incorporate syntactic features into the tree-based encoder, and the k-th phrase vector $\boldsymbol{h}_k^{(p)} \in \mathbb{R}^{d \times 1}$ in our system is computed as follows:

$$
\begin{aligned}
\boldsymbol{i}_k &= \sigma(\boldsymbol{U}_l^{(i)} \boldsymbol{h}_k^l + \boldsymbol{U}_r^{(i)} \boldsymbol{h}_k^r + \boldsymbol{W}^{(i)} \boldsymbol{z}_k + \boldsymbol{b}^{(i)}), &
\boldsymbol{f}_k^l &= \sigma(\boldsymbol{U}_l^{(f_l)} \boldsymbol{h}_k^l + \boldsymbol{U}_r^{(f_l)} \boldsymbol{h}_k^r + \boldsymbol{W}^{(f_l)} \boldsymbol{z}_k + \boldsymbol{b}^{(f_l)}), \\
\boldsymbol{f}_k^r &= \sigma(\boldsymbol{U}_l^{(f_r)} \boldsymbol{h}_k^l + \boldsymbol{U}_r^{(f_r)} \boldsymbol{h}_k^r + \boldsymbol{W}^{(f_r)} \boldsymbol{z}_k + \boldsymbol{b}^{(f_r)}), &
\boldsymbol{o}_k &= \sigma(\boldsymbol{U}_l^{(o)} \boldsymbol{h}_k^l + \boldsymbol{U}_r^{(o)} \boldsymbol{h}_k^r + \boldsymbol{W}^{(o)} \boldsymbol{z}_k + \boldsymbol{b}^{(o)}), \\
\tilde{\boldsymbol{c}}_k &= \tanh(\boldsymbol{U}_l^{(\tilde{c})} \boldsymbol{h}_k^l + \boldsymbol{U}_r^{(\tilde{c})} \boldsymbol{h}_k^r + \boldsymbol{W}^{(o)} \boldsymbol{z}_k + \boldsymbol{b}^{(\tilde{c})}), &
\boldsymbol{c}_k &= \boldsymbol{i}_k \odot \tilde{\boldsymbol{c}}_k + \boldsymbol{f}_k^l \odot \boldsymbol{c}_k^l + \boldsymbol{f}_k^r \odot \boldsymbol{c}_k^r, \\
\boldsymbol{h}_k^{(p)} &= \boldsymbol{o}_k \odot \tanh(\boldsymbol{c}_k),
\end{aligned}
\tag{8}
$$

where each of $\boldsymbol{i}_k$, $\boldsymbol{o}_k$, $\tilde{\boldsymbol{c}}_k$, $\boldsymbol{c}_k$, $\boldsymbol{c}_k^l$, $\boldsymbol{c}_k^r$, $\boldsymbol{f}_k^l$, and $\boldsymbol{f}_k^r \in \mathbb{R}^{d \times 1}$ denotes an input gate, an output gate, a state for updating the memory cell, a memory cell, the memory cells of the left child node and the right child node, the forget gates for the left child and for the right child, respectively. $\boldsymbol{W}^{(\cdot)} \in \mathbb{R}^{d \times d}$ and $\boldsymbol{U}^{(\cdot)} \in \mathbb{R}^{d \times m}$ are weight matrices, and $\boldsymbol{b}^{(\cdot)} \in \mathbb{R}^{d \times 1}$ is a bias vector. $\boldsymbol{z}_k \in \mathbb{R}^{m \times 1}$ is an embedding vector of the phrase category label of the k-th node. $\sigma(\cdot)$ denotes the logistic function. The operator $\odot$ is element-wise multiplication.

The decoder in our system outputs characters one by one. Note that the number of characters in a language is far smaller than the vocabulary size of the words in the language. The character-based approaches thus enable us to significantly speed up the softmax computation for generating a symbol, and we can train the NMT model and generate translations much faster. Moreover, all of the raw text data are directly covered by the character units, and therefore the decoder in our system requires few preprocessing steps such as segmentation and tokenization.

We also use the *input-feeding* technique (Luong et al., 2015a) to improve translation accuracy. The j-th hidden state of the decoder is computed in our systems as follows:

$$\boldsymbol{s}_j = RNN_{decoder}(Embed(y_{j-1}), [\boldsymbol{s}_{j-1}; \tilde{\boldsymbol{s}}_{j-1}]), \tag{9}$$

where $[\boldsymbol{s}_{j-1}; \tilde{\boldsymbol{s}}_{j-1}] \in \mathbb{R}^{2d \times 1}$ denotes the concatenation of $\boldsymbol{s}_{j-1}$ and $\tilde{\boldsymbol{s}}_{j-1}$.

4   Experiment in WAT'16 task

4.1   Experimental Setting

We conducted experiments for our system using the 3rd Workshop of Asian Translation 2016 (WAT'16)[1] English-to-Japanese translation task (Nakazawa et al., 2016a). The data set is the Asian Scientific Paper Excerpt Corpus (ASPEC) (Nakazawa et al., 2016b). The data setting followed the ones in Zhu (2015) and Eriguchi et al. (2016). We collected 1.5 million pairs of training sentences from *train-1.txt* and the first

---

[1] http://lotus.kuee.kyoto-u.ac.jp/WAT/

	Sentences	Parsed sentences
Train dataset	1,346,946	1,346,946
Dev. dataset	1,790	1,789
Test dataset	1,812	1,811

Table 1: The details of dataset in the ASPEC corpus.

	Vocabulary size
$|V_{word}|$ in English	87,796
$|V_{word}|$ in Japanese	65,680
$|V_{character}|$ in Japanese	3,004

Table 2: Vocabulary sizes in the training models.

half of *train-2.txt*. We removed the sentences whose lengths are greater than 50 words. In the tree-based encoder, binary trees of the source sentences were obtained by Enju (Miyao and Tsujii, 2008), which is a probabilistic HPSG parser. We used phrase category labels as the syntactic features in the proposed tree-based encoder. There are 19 types of phrase category labels given by Enju. In the word-based decoder model, we employed KyTea (Neubig et al., 2011) as the segmentation tool for the Japanese sentences. We performed the preprocessing steps of the data as recommended in WAT'16.[2] Table 1 and Table 2 show the details of the final dataset and the vocabulary sizes in our experiments. Each vocabulary includes the words and the characters whose frequencies exceed five or two in the training data, respectively. The out-of-vocabulary words are mapped into a special token i.e. "UNK". As a result, the vocabulary size of the characters in Japanese is about 22 times smaller than that of the words.

NMT models are often trained on a limited vocabulary, because the high computational cost of the softmax layer for target word generation is usually the bottleneck when training an NMT model. In the word-based models, we use the BlackOut sampling method (Ji et al., 2016) to approximately compute the softmax layer. The parameter setting of BlackOut follows Eriguchi et al. (2016). In the character-based models, we use the original softmax in the softmax layer. All of the models are trained on CPUs.[3] We employed multi-threading programming to update the parameters in a mini-batch in parallel. The training times of the single word-based model and the single character-based model were about 11 days and 7 days, respectively.

We set the dimension size of the hidden states to 512 in both of the LSTMs and the Tree LSTMs. The dimension size of embedding vectors is set to 512 for the words and to 256 for the characters. In our proposed tree-based encoder, we use 64 and 128 for the dimension size of the phrase label embedding. The model parameters are uniformly initialized in $[-0.1, 0.1]$, except that the forget biases are filled with 1.0 as recommended in Józefowicz et al. (2015). Biases, softmax weights and BlackOut weights are filled with 0. We shuffle the training data randomly per each epoch. All of the parameters are updated by the plain SGD algorithm with a mini-batch size of 128. The learning rate of SGD is set to 1.0, and we halve it when the perplexity of development data becomes worse. The value of gradient norm clipping (Pascanu et al., 2012) is set to 3.0.

We use a beam search in order to obtain a proper translation sentence with the size of 20 and 5 in the word-based decoder and the character-based decoder, respectively. The maximum length of a generated sentence is set to 100 in the word-based decoder and to 300 in the character-based decoder. Cho et al. (2014a) reported that an RNN-based decoder generates a shorter sentence when using the original beam search. We used the beam search method proposed in Eriguchi et al. (2016) in order to output longer translations. We evaluated the models by the BLEU score (Papineni et al., 2002) and the RIBES score (Isozaki et al., 2010) employed as the official evaluation metrics in WAT'16.

4.2 Experimental Results

Table 3 shows the experimental results of the character-based models, the word-based models and the baseline SMT systems. BP denotes the brevity penalty in the BLEU score. First, we can see small improvements in the RIBES score of the single tree-to-sequence ANMT models with the character-based decoder using syntactic features, compared to our proposed baseline system. System 1 is one of our submitted systems. The translations are output by the ensemble of the three models, and we used a simple

---

[2]http://lotus.kuee.kyoto-u.ac.jp/WAT/baseline/dataPreparationJE.html
[3]16 threads on Intel(R) Xeon(R) CPU E5-2667 v3 @ 3.20GHz

Model	BLEU (BP)	RIBES
Character-based decoder		
Our proposed baseline: tree-to-seq ANMT model	31.52 (0.96)	79.39
+ phrase label input ($m = 64$)	31.49 (0.95)	79.51
+ phrase label input ($m = 128$)	31.46 (0.95)	79.48
System1: Ensemble of the above three models w/ the original beam search	33.21 (0.86)	81.45
Word-based decoder		
seq-to-seq ANMT model (Luong et al., 2015a)	34.64 (0.93)	81.60
tree-to-seq ANMT model ($d = 512$)	34.91 (0.92)	81.66
System2: Ensemble of the tree-to-seq ANMT models (Eriguchi et al., 2016)	36.95 (0.92)	82.45
Baseline system		
Baseline 1: Phrase-based SMT	29.80 (——)	69.19
Baseline 2: Hierarchical Phrase-based SMT	32.56 (——)	74.70
Baseline 3: Tree-to-string SMT	33.44 (——)	75.80

Table 3: The results of our systems and the baseline systems.

beam search to confirm how much it effects the BLEU scores in the character-based models. We showed the results of our proposed character-based decoder models by using the beam search method proposed in Eriguchi et al. (2016). We collects the statistics of the relation between the source sentence length (L_s) and the target sentence length (L_t) from training dataset and adds its log probability ($\log p(L_t|L_s)$) as the penalty of the beam score when the model predicts "EOS". The BLEU score is sensitive to the value of BP, and we observe the same trend in that the character-based approaches generate a shorter sentence by the original beam search. As a result, each of the character-based models can generate longer translation by +0.09 BP scores at least than System 1 using the original beam search.

The word-based tree-to-sequece decoder model shows slightly better performance than the word-based sequence-to-sequence ANMT model (Luong et al., 2015a) in both of the scores. The results of the baseline systems are the ones reported in Nakazawa et al. (2015). Compared to these SMT baselines, each of the character-based models clearly outperforms the phrase-based system in both of the BLEU and RIBES scores. Although the hierarchical phrase-based SMT system and the tree-to-string SMT system outperforms the single character-based model without phrase label inputs by +1.04 and by +1.92 BLEU scores, respectively, our best ensemble of character-based models shows better performance (+5.65 RIBES scores) than the tree-to-string SMT system.

All the submitted systems are evaluated by pairwise cloudsourcing. System 1 is ranked as the 9th out of the 10 submitted models, and System 2 is ranked as the 6th.

5 Discussion

Table 4 shows a comparison of the speeds to predict the next word between the word-based decoder and the character-based decoder when generating a sentence by a beam size of 1. The character-based decoder is about 41 times faster than the word-based decoder. It is because the time to output a word by using a softmax layer is roughly proportional to the vocabulary sizes of the decoders. In addition to the low cost of predicting the outputs in the character-based model, the character-based decoder requires the smaller size of beam search than the word-based model. The word-based decoder requires a beam size of 20 when decoding, but a beam size of 5 is enough for the character-based decoder. It requires smaller beam size for the character-based decoder to find the best hypothesis. We therefore conclude that the character-based model works more efficiently as a translation model than the word-based model in terms of the cost of the outputs.

Some translation examples of our systems are shown in Table 5. There are two types of source sen-

	Time (msec / sentence)
Word-based decoder	363.7
Character-based decoder	8.8

Table 4: Comparison of the times when outputting a sentence.

Source sentence A	The electric power generation was the 380 micro watt.
Ground truth A	発電量は３８０マイクロワットであった。
Word-based	発電は３８０ UNKW であった。
Character-based	発電は３８０マイクロワットであった。
+ label input ($m = 64$)	電力発電は３８０マイクロワットであった。
Source sentence B	This paper describes development outline of low-loss forsterite porcelain.
Ground truth B	低損失フォルステライト磁器の開発概要などをのべた 。
Word-based	ここでは，UNK UNK の開発概要を述べた。
Character-based	低損失フォルステライト磁器の開発概要を述べた。
+ label input ($m = 64$)	低損失フォルステライト磁器の開発概要を述べた。

Table 5: Translation examples of test data.

tences, the ground truth target sentences, and the translated sentences by the word-based model, by the character-based model, and the character-based model using the syntactic features embedded with a dimension size of 64. The words in the same color semantically correspond to each other.

In sentence A, we can see that the character-based models correctly translated the source word "micro" with the characters "マイクロ", while the word-based decoder requires the unknown replacement (Luong et al., 2015b; Jean et al., 2015). When the word-based model outputs the target word "UNK", the source phrase "micro watt" has the highest attention score ($\alpha = 0.78$) and the source word "micro" has the second highest attention score ($\alpha = 0.16$). The word-based decoder model is successful in outputting the original number ("３８０") in the source side to the target side, and both of the character-based decoder model has also succeeded in predicting a correct sequence of characters "３", "８", and "０" one by one. The training dataset includes the translation of the word "380" into the characters "３８０", so the character-based model can be trained without copy mechanism (Ling et al., 2016) in this case.

In sentence B, the character-based models successfully translate "low-loss forsterite porcelain" into " 低損失フォルステライト磁器". The word-based decoder model generates two "UNK"s. The source word "forsterite" ("フォルステライト" in Japanese) has the highest attention score ($\alpha = 0.23$) to the first "UNK", and the phrase "forsterite porcelain" has the second highest attention score ($\alpha = 0.21$). The second "UNK" is softly alined to the source word "porcelain" ("磁器" in Japanese) with the highest attention score ($\alpha = 0.26$) and to the source phrase "forsterite porcelain" with the second highest attention score ($\alpha = 0.16$).

6 Related Work

There are many NMT architectures: a convolutional network-based encoder (Kalchbrenner and Blunsom, 2013), sequence-to-sequence models (Cho et al., 2014b; Sutskever et al., 2014) and a tree-based encoder (Eriguchi et al., 2016). The objective of these research efforts focused on how to encode the data in a language into a vector space and to decode the data in another language from the vector space. Sennrich and Haddow (2016) improved the vector space of NMT models by adding linguistic features. The text data is basically considered as the sequence of words.

The word-based NMT models cannot usually cover the whole vocabulary in the corpus. Rare words are mapped into "unknown" words when the NMT models are trained. Luong et al. (2015b) proposed an ex post facto replacement technique for such unknown words, and Jean et al. (2015) replace the unknown word with the source word which has the highest attention score to the unknown word. Sennrich et al. (2016) adopted a sub-word as a unit of the vocabulary for the NMT models and created the sub-word-based vocabulary by the BPE method. The vocabulary based on the sub-words can cover much more words in German and Russian, compared to the vocabulary based on the words. The NMT models trained with the sub-word-based vocabulary performed better than the ones trained on the word-based vocabulary.

Since the smallest units of text data are characters, character-based approaches have been introduced into the fields of NMT. Costa-jussà and Fonollosa (2016) have shown that the character-based encoding by using convolutional networks and the highway network as shown in Kim et al. (2016). Chung et al. (2016) applied the character-based decoding to the NMT models, whose encoder is based on the BPE units. Luong and Manning (2016) have proposed a hybrid NMT model flexibly switching from the word-based to the character-based model. Each character-based NMT model shows better performance than the word-based NMT models. All of theses models are, however, applied to sequence-based NMT models, and there are no results of the character-based decoding applied to tree-based NMT models yet.

7 Conclusion

In this paper, we reported our systems (UT-AKY) submitted to the English-to-Japanese translation task in WAT'16. Both of our systems are based on tree-to-sequence ANMT models, and one is a word-based decoder model and the other is a character-based decoder model. We incorporated phrase category labels into the tree-based ANMT model. The experimental results on English-to-Japanese translation shows that the character-based decoder does not outperform the word-based decoder but exhibits two promising properties: 1) It takes much less time to compute the softmax layer; and 2) It can translate any word in a sentence.

Acknowledgements

This work was supported by CREST, JST, and JSPS KAKENHI Grant Number 15J12597.

References

Dzmitry Bahdanau, Kyunghyun Cho, and Yoshua Bengio. 2015. Neural Machine Translation by Jointly Learning to Align and Translate. In *Proceedings of the 3rd International Conference on Learning Representations*.

KyungHyun Cho, Bart van Merrienboer, Dzmitry Bahdanau, and Yoshua Bengio. 2014a. On the Properties of Neural Machine Translation: Encoder-Decoder Approaches. In *Proceedings of Eighth Workshop on Syntax, Semantics and Structure in Statistical Translation (SSST-8)*.

Kyunghyun Cho, Bart van Merrienboer, Caglar Gulcehre, Dzmitry Bahdanau, Fethi Bougares, Holger Schwenk, and Yoshua Bengio. 2014b. Learning Phrase Representations using RNN Encoder–Decoder for Statistical Machine Translation. In *Proceedings of the 2014 Conference on Empirical Methods in Natural Language Processing*, pages 1724–1734.

Junyoung Chung, Kyunghyun Cho, and Yoshua Bengio. 2016. A character-level decoder without explicit segmentation for neural machine translation. In *Proceedings of the 54th Annual Meeting of the Association for Computational Linguistics*, pages 1693–1703.

R. Marta Costa-jussà and R. José A. Fonollosa. 2016. Character-based neural machine translation. In *Proceedings of the 54th Annual Meeting of the Association for Computational Linguistics*, pages 357–361.

Akiko Eriguchi, Kazuma Hashimoto, and Yoshimasa Tsuruoka. 2016. Tree-to-sequence attentional neural machine translation. In *Proceedings of the 54th Annual Meeting of the Association for Computational Linguistics*, pages 823–833.

Felix A. Gers, Jürgen Schmidhuber, and Fred A. Cummins. 2000. Learning to Forget: Continual Prediction with LSTM. *Neural Computation*, 12(10):2451–2471.

Sepp Hochreiter and Jürgen Schmidhuber. 1997. Long Short-Term Memory. *Neural Computation*, 9(8):1735–1780.

Hideki Isozaki, Tsutomu Hirao, Kevin Duh, Katsuhito Sudoh, and Hajime Tsukada. 2010. Automatic Evaluation of Translation Quality for Distant Language Pairs. In *Proceedings of the 2010 Conference on Empirical Methods in Natural Language Processing*, pages 944–952.

Sébastien Jean, Kyunghyun Cho, Roland Memisevic, and Yoshua Bengio. 2015. On Using Very Large Target Vocabulary for Neural Machine Translation. In *Proceedings of the 53rd Annual Meeting of the Association for Computational Linguistics and the 7th International Joint Conference on Natural Language Processing (Volume 1: Long Papers)*, pages 1–10.

Shihao Ji, S. V. N. Vishwanathan, Nadathur Satish, Michael J. Anderson, and Pradeep Dubey. 2016. BlackOut: Speeding up Recurrent Neural Network Language Models With Very Large Vocabularies. In *Proceedings of the 4th International Conference on Learning Representations*.

Rafal Józefowicz, Wojciech Zaremba, and Ilya Sutskever. 2015. An Empirical Exploration of Recurrent Network Architectures. In *Proceedings of the 32nd International Conference on Machine Learning*, volume 37, pages 2342–2350.

Nal Kalchbrenner and Phil Blunsom. 2013. Recurrent continuous translation models. In *Proceedings of the 2013 Conference on Empirical Methods in Natural Language Processing*, pages 1700–1709.

Yoon Kim, Yacine Jernite, David Sontag, and Alexander M. Rush. 2016. Character-aware neural language models. In *The Thirtieth AAAI Conference on Artificial Intelligence, AAAI 2016*.

Wang Ling, Phil Blunsom, Edward Grefenstette, Moritz Karl Hermann, Tomáš Kočiský, Fumin Wang, and Andrew Senior. 2016. Latent predictor networks for code generation. In *Proceedings of the 54th Annual Meeting of the Association for Computational Linguistics (Volume 1: Long Papers)*, pages 599–609. Association for Computational Linguistics.

Minh-Thang Luong and D. Christopher Manning. 2016. Achieving open vocabulary neural machine translation with hybrid word-character models. In *Proceedings of the 54th Annual Meeting of the Association for Computational Linguistics*, pages 1054–1063.

Thang Luong, Hieu Pham, and Christopher D. Manning. 2015a. Effective Approaches to Attention-based Neural Machine Translation. In *Proceedings of the 2015 Conference on Empirical Methods in Natural Language Processing*, pages 1412–1421.

Thang Luong, Ilya Sutskever, Quoc Le, Oriol Vinyals, and Wojciech Zaremba. 2015b. Addressing the Rare Word Problem in Neural Machine Translation. In *Proceedings of the 53rd Annual Meeting of the Association for Computational Linguistics and the 7th International Joint Conference on Natural Language Processing (Volume 1: Long Papers)*, pages 11–19.

Yusuke Miyao and Jun'ichi Tsujii. 2008. Feature Forest Models for Probabilistic HPSG Parsing. *Computational Linguistics*, 34(1):35–80.

Toshiaki Nakazawa, Hideya Mino, Isao Goto, Graham Neubig, Sadao Kurohashi, and Eiichiro Sumita. 2015. Overview of the 2nd Workshop on Asian Translation. In *Proceedings of the 2nd Workshop on Asian Translation (WAT2015)*, pages 1–28.

Toshiaki Nakazawa, Hideya Mino, Chenchen Ding, Isao Goto, Graham Neubig, Sadao Kurohashi, and Eiichiro Sumita. 2016a. Overview of the 3rd workshop on asian translation. In *Proceedings of the 3rd Workshop on Asian Translation (WAT2016)*, Osaka, Japan, December.

Toshiaki Nakazawa, Manabu Yaguchi, Kiyotaka Uchimoto, Masao Utiyama, Eiichiro Sumita, Sadao Kurohashi, and Hitoshi Isahara. 2016b. Aspec: Asian scientific paper excerpt corpus. In *Proceedings of the 10th Conference on International Language Resources and Evaluation (LREC2016)*, Portoroz, Slovenia, 5.

Graham Neubig, Yosuke Nakata, and Shinsuke Mori. 2011. Pointwise Prediction for Robust, Adaptable Japanese Morphological Analysis. In *Proceedings of the 49th Annual Meeting of the Association for Computational Linguistics: Human Language Technologies*, pages 529–533.

Kishore Papineni, Salim Roukos, Todd Ward, and Wei-Jing Zhu. 2002. BLEU: A Method for Automatic Evaluation of Machine Translation. In *Proceedings of the 40th Annual Meeting on Association for Computational Linguistics*, pages 311–318.

Razvan Pascanu, Tomas Mikolov, and Yoshua Bengio. 2012. Understanding the exploding gradient problem. *arXiv: 1211.5063*.

Rico Sennrich and Barry Haddow. 2016. Linguistic input features improve neural machine translation. In *Proceedings of the First Conference on Machine Translation*, pages 83–91.

Rico Sennrich, Barry Haddow, and Alexandra Birch. 2016. Neural machine translation of rare words with subword units. In *Proceedings of the 54th Annual Meeting of the Association for Computational Linguistics*, pages 1715–1725.

Ilya Sutskever, Oriol Vinyals, and Quoc V. Le. 2014. Sequence to Sequence Learning with Neural Networks. In *Advances in Neural Information Processing Systems 27*, pages 3104–3112.

Kai Sheng Tai, Richard Socher, and Christopher D. Manning. 2015. Improved Semantic Representations From Tree-Structured Long Short-Term Memory Networks. In *Proceedings of the 53rd Annual Meeting of the Association for Computational Linguistics and the 7th International Joint Conference on Natural Language Processing*, pages 1556–1566.

Zhongyuan Zhu. 2015. Evaluating Neural Machine Translation in English-Japanese Task. In *Proceedings of the 2nd Workshop on Asian Translation (WAT2015)*, pages 61–68.

Faster and Lighter Phrase-based Machine Translation Baseline

Liling Tan, Jon Dehdari and Josef van Genabith
Universität des Saarlandes, Germany
liling.tan@uni-saarland.de, jon.dehdari@dfki.de,
josef.van_genabith@dfki.de

Abstract

This paper describes the SENSE machine translation system participation in the Third Workshop for Asian Translation (WAT2016). We share our best practices to build a fast and light phrase-based machine translation (PBMT) models that have comparable results to the baseline systems provided by the organizers. As Neural Machine Translation (NMT) overtakes PBMT as the state-of-the-art, deep learning and new MT practitioners might not be familiar with the PBMT paradigm and we hope that this paper will help them build a PBMT baseline system quickly and easily.

1   Introduction

With the advent of Neural Machine Translation (NMT), the Phrased-Based Machine Translation (PBMT) paradigm casts towards the sunset (Neubig et al., 2015; Sennrich et al., 2016; Bentivogli et al., 2016; Wu et al., 2016; Crego et al., 2016). As the NMT era dawns, we hope to document the best practices in building a fast and light phrase-based machine translation baseline. In this paper, we briefly describe the PBMT components, list the tools available for PBMT systems prior to the neural tsunami, and present our procedures to build fast and light PBMT models with our system's results in the WAT2016 (Nakazawa et al., 2016).

1.1   Phrase-Based Machine Translation

The objective of the machine translation system is to find the best translation $\hat{t}$ that maximizes the translation probability $p(t|s)$ given a source sentence s; mathematically:

$$\hat{t} = \underset{t}{argmax}\ p(t|s) \tag{1}$$

Applying the Bayes' rule, we can factorized the $p(t|s)$ into three parts:

$$p(t|s) = \frac{p(t)}{p(s)} p(s|t) \tag{2}$$

Substituting our $p(t|s)$ back into our search for the best translation $\hat{t}$ using *argmax*:

$$\begin{aligned}
\hat{t} &= \underset{t}{argmax}\ p(t|s) \\
&= \underset{t}{argmax}\ \frac{p(t)}{p(s)} p(s|t) \\
&= \underset{t}{argmax}\ p(t)p(s|t)
\end{aligned} \tag{3}$$

We note that the denominator $p(s)$ can be dropped because for all translations the probability of the source sentence remains the same and the *argmax* objective optimizes the probability relative to the set of possible translations given a single source sentence. The $p(t|s)$ variable can be viewed as the bilingual dictionary with probabilities attached to each entry to the dictionary (*aka* **phrase table**). The $p(t)$ variable

Proceedings of the 3rd Workshop on Asian Translation,
pages 184–193, Osaka, Japan, December 11-17 2016.

governs the grammaticality of the translation and we model it using an ***n*-gram language model** under the PBMT paradigm.

Machine Translation developed rapidly with the introduction of IBM **word alignment** models (Brown et al., 1990; Brown et al., 1993) and *word-based* MT systems performed word-for-word decoding word alignments and n-gram language model.

The word-based systems eventually developed into the phrase-based systems (Och and Ney, 2002; Marcu and Wong, 2002; Zens et al., 2002; Koehn et al., 2003) which relies on the word alignment to generate phrases. The phrase-based models translate contiguous sequences of words from the source sentence to contiguous words in the target language. In this case, the term *phrase* does not refer to the linguistic notion of syntactic constituent but the notion of n-grams. Knight (1999) defined the word/phrase-based model as a search problem that grows exponentially to the sentence length. The phrase-based models significantly improve on the word-based models, especially for closely-related languages. This mainly due to the modeling of local reordering and the assumption that most orderings of contiguous n-grams are monotonic. However, that is not the case of translation between language pairs with different syntactic constructions; e.g. when translating between SVO-SOV languages.

Tillmann (2004) and Al-Onaizan and Papineni (2006) proposed several **lexicalized reordering** and distortion models to surmount most long-distance reordering issues. Alternatively, to overcome reordering issues with simple distortion penalty, Zollmann et al. (2008) memorized a larger phrase n-grams sequence from a huge training data and allow larger distortion limits; it achieves similar results to more sophisticated reordering techniques with lesser training data. In practice, reordering is set to a small window and Birch et al. (2010) has shown that phrase-based models perform poorly even with short and medium range reordering.

Och and Ney (2002) simplified the integration of additional model components using the *log-linear model*. The model defines feature functions *h(x)* with weights λ in the following form:

$$P(x) = \frac{exp(\sum_{i=1}^{n} \lambda_i h_i(x))}{Z} \tag{4}$$

where the normalization constant Z turns the numerator into a probability distribution.

In the case of a simple model in Equation (3), it contains the two primary features, we define the components as such:

$$\begin{aligned} h_1(x) &= logp(t) \\ h_2(x) &= logp(s|t) \end{aligned} \tag{5}$$

where the $h(x_1)$ and $h(x_2)$ are associated with the λ_1 and λ_2 respectively.

The flexibility of the log-linear model allows for additional translation feature components to be added to the model easily, e.g. the lexicalized reordering is modeled as additional feature(s) *h(x_i)* in PBMT. Additionally, the weights λ associated with the ***n*** components can be tuned to optimize the translation quality over the parallel sentences, ***D*** (often known as the development set):

$$\lambda_1^n = \underset{\lambda_1^n}{argmax} \sum_{d=1}^{D} \log P_{\lambda_1^n}(t_d|s_d) \tag{6}$$

Minimum Error Rate Training (MERT), a co-ordinate descent learning algorithm, is one of the commonly used algorithms used for tuning the the the λ weights.

The resulting PBMT system is generally made up of the following (i) n-gram language model(s), (ii) probabilistic phrase table (optionally with additional feature(s)), (iii) probabilistic lexicalized reordering table and (iv) a set of λ weights for their respective *h(x)*.

The hierarchical phrase-based machine translation (aka *hiero*) extends the phrase-based models notion of phrase from naive contiguous words to a sequence of words and sub-phrases (Chiang, 2005). Within the hiero model, translation rules make use of the standard phrases and the reordering of the subphrases. Such reordering can be expressed as a lexicalized *gappy* hierarchical rule using X_1 and X_2 as placeholders for the subphrases.

At the onset of SMT, the importance of linguistic information to translation was recognized by Brown et al. (1993):

> *But it is not our intention to ignore linguistics, neither to replace it. Rather, we hope to enfold it in the embrace of a secure probabilistic framework so that the two together may draw strength from one another and guide us to better natural language processing systems in general and to better machine translation systems in particular.*

Factored SMT embarked on the task of effectively incorporating linguistics information from taggers, parses and morphological analyzers into the machine translation pipeline. It is motivated by fact that (i) linguistics information provides a layer of disambiguation to the ambiguity of natural language, (ii) generalized translation of out-of-vocabulary (OOV) words to overcome sparsity of training data and (iii) replace arbitrary limits with linguistics constraints put in place in the decoding process too keep the search space tractable (Hoang and Lopez, 2009; Koehn et al., 2010; Hoang, 2011).

Among the numerous Machine Translation tools, the Moses Statistical Machine Translation system is the de facto tool for building various machine translation models (vanilla, hierarchical or factored PBMT). The Pharaoh system is its predecessor (Koehn, 2004). Other than the Moses system, the Joshua[1] (Weese et al., 2011), Jane[2] (Vilar et al., 2010), Phrasal[3] (Cer et al., 2010) and `cdec`[4] (Dyer et al., 2010) systems are viable alternatives to build statistical MT models.

2 Fast and Light PBMT Setup

We used the phrase-based SMT implemented in the Moses toolkit (Koehn et al., 2003; Koehn et al., 2007) with the following vanilla Moses experimental settings:

i. Language modeling is trained using KenLM using 5-grams, with modified Kneser-Ney smoothing (Heafield, 2011; Kneser and Ney, 1995; Chen and Goodman, 1998). The language model is quantized to reduce filesize and improve querying speed (Whittaker and Raj, 2001; Heafield et al., 2013)

ii. Clustercat word clusters (Dehdari et al., 2016b) with `MGIZA++` implementation of IBM word alignment model 4 with grow-diagonal-final-and heuristics for word alignment and phrase-extraction (Koehn et al., 2003; Och and Ney, 2003; Gao and Vogel, 2008)

iii. Bi-directional lexicalized reordering model that considers monotone, swap and discontinuous orientations (Koehn, 2005; Galley and Manning, 2008)

iv. To minimize the computing load on the translation model, we compressed the phrase-table and lexical reordering model using Phrase Rank Encoding (Junczys-Dowmunt, 2012)

v. Minimum Error Rate Training (MERT) (Och, 2003) to tune the decoding parameters

Differing from the baseline systems proposed by the WAT2016 organizers, we have used (a) trie language model with quantization in *Step i* (b) Clustercat with multi-threaded word aligments (`MGIZA++`) instead of `mkcls` (Och, 1995) with `GIZA++` in *Step ii* and (c) phrase table compression in *Step iv*.

Although MT practitioners can use Moses' *Experiment Management System* (Koehn, 2010) to build a PBMT baseline, the models might not be easily modifiable due to the pre-coded configurations. The configuration constraints could become particularly frustrating when the model becomes prohibitively huge with limited read-only and random access memory.

---

[1] joshua.incubator.apache.org
[2] http://www-i6.informatik.rwth-aachen.de/jane/
[3] http://nlp.stanford.edu/phrasal/
[4] https://github.com/redpony/cdec

2.1 Quantization and Binarization of Language Models

Heafield et al. (2013) compared KenLM's trie data structure against other n-gram language model toolkit. He empirically showed that it uses less memory than the smallest model produced by other tools that creates lossless models and it was faster than SRILM (Stolcke, 2002) that also uses a trie data structure.

The floating point non-positive log probabilities of the n-gram and its backoff penalty can be stored in the trie exactly using 31 and 32 bits[5] respectively. These floating point values can be quantized using q bits per probability and r bit per backoff to save memory at the expense of decreased accuracy. KenLM uses the binning method to sort floats, divides them into equal size bins and averages the value within each bin. As such floats under the same bin shares the same value.

While quantization is lossy, we can use point compression (Whittaker and Raj, 2001) to remove the leading bits of the pointers and implicitly store the table of offsets into the array. Although point compression reduces the memory size of the language model, retrieving the offsets takes additional time.

The trie is produced by using the KenLM's `build_binary` tool. The quantization and trie binarization is performed using the last command below:

```
LM_ARPA=`pwd`/${TRAINING_DIR}/lm/lm.${LANG_E}.arpa.gz
LM_FILE=`pwd`/${TRAINING_DIR}/lm/lm.${LANG_E}.kenlm

${MOSES_BIN_DIR}/lmplz --order ${LM_ORDER} -S 80% -T /tmp \
< ${CORPUS_LM}.${LANG_E} | gzip > ${LM_ARPA}

${MOSES_BIN_DIR}/build_binary trie -a 22 -b 8 -q 8 ${LM_ARPA} ${LM_FILE}
```

The `-a` option sets the maximum number of leading bits that the point compression removes. The `-q` and `-b` options sets the number of bits to store the n-gram log probability and backoff respectively[6]. We can stack the point compression with quantization as shown above, the `-a 22 -b 8 -q 8` will set the maximum leading bits removal to 22 and stores the floating points for log probabilities and backoff penalties using 8 bits.

2.2 `MGIZA++` and Clustercat

Gao and Vogel (2008) implemented two parallelized versions of the original `GIZA++` tool, `PGIZA++` that uses multiple aligning processes where when the processes are finished, the master process collects the normalized counts and updates the model and child processes are restarted in the next iteration and `MGIZA++` that uses multi-threading on shared memory with locking mechanism to synchronize memory access.

Given a computing cluster (i.e. multiple machines), using `PGIZA++` would be appropriate whereas `MGIZA++` is suited for a single machine with multiple cores. An up-to-date fork of `MGIZA++` is maintained by the Moses community at `https://github.com/moses-smt/mgiza`.

While one might face issues with creating the `MGIZA++` binaries from source compilation[7], the Moses community provides pre-built binaries[8] on `http://www.statmt.org/moses/?n=moses.releases`. These can be easily downloaded and saved to a directory (e.g. `/path/to/moses-training-tools`) on the terminal as such:

```
wget -r -nH -nd -np -R index.html* \
http://www.statmt.org/moses/RELEASE-3.0/binaries/linux-64bit/training-tools/ \
-P /path/to/moses-training-tools
```

And the `EXT_BIN_DIR` variable in the training script can be set and be used in the translation model training process as such:

---

[5] Backoff penalty may sometimes be positive

[6] Note that unigram probabilities are never quantized

[7] Following the instructions on http://www.statmt.org/moses/?n=Moses.ExternalTools#ntoc3

[8] E.g. the direct link for the Linux OS can be found on http://www.statmt.org/moses/RELEASE-3.0/binaries/linux-64bit/training-tools/

```
EXT_BIN_DIR=/path/to/moses-training-tools/

${MOSES_SCRIPT}/training/train-model-10c.perl \
  --root-dir `pwd`/${TRAINING_DIR} \
  --model-dir `pwd`/${MODEL_DIR} \
  --corpus ${CORPUS} \
  --external-bin-dir ${EXT_BIN_DIR} \
  --mgiza -mgiza-cpus 10 \
  --f ${LANG_F} \
  --e ${LANG_E} \
  --parallel \
  --alignment grow-diag-final-and \
  --reordering msd-bidirectional-fe \
  --score-options "--GoodTuring" \
  --lm 0:${LM_ORDER}:${LM_FILE}:8 \
  --cores ${JOBS} \
  --sort-buffer-size 10G \
  --parallel \
  >& ${TRAINING_DIR}/training_TM.log
```

The `--mgiza` option activates the `MGIZA++` binary and `-mgiza-cpus 10` specifies the training
to be done with 10 CPU threads. The default option is to use IBM model 4 where the probability for each
word is conditioned on both the previously aligned word and on the word classes of its context words[9].

To generate the word classes, `MGIZA++` uses a single-threaded version of an old exchange clustering
algorithm implementation, `mkcls`, which can be rather slow when the training corpus is sufficiently
huge. Instead, we suggest the use of `Clustercat`[10], another exchange clustering algorithm that has a
wrapper to emulate `mkcls` command-line interface and outputs. `Clustercat` is an implementation of
the Bidirectional, Interpolated, Refining, and Alternating (BIRA) predictive exchange algorithm; notably,
`ClusterCat` clusters a 1 billion token English News Crawl corpus in 1.5 hours while `mkcls` might
take 3 days on the same machine (Dehdari et al., 2016a). To use `Clustercat` with `MGIZA++`, simply
create a symbolic link the `mkcls` wrapper from `Clustercat` to the `moses-training-tools`
directory, e.g.:

```
EXT_BIN_DIR=/path/to/moses-training-tools/
mv ${EXT_BIN_DIR}/mkcls mkcls-original
ln -s /path/to/clustercat/bin/mkcls ${EXT_BIN_DIR}/mkcls
```


2.3 Phrase Table and Lexicalized Reordering Table Compression

Extending the classic dictionary-based compression methods, Junczys-Dowmunt (2012) proposed the
phrasal rank encoding compression algorithm where repeated sub-phrases are replaced by pointers in the
phrase dictionary which results in a reduction in phrase table size. At decompression, the sub-phrases
are looked up and re-inserted based on the pointers.

Strangely, Moses implementation of MERT releases the phrase table and lexicalized reordering tables
after every cycle and reload it when attempting to decode the development data with the updated feature
parameters. A reduced phrase table size would not only speed up the table loading in decoding time but
more importantly, it speeds up the table loading at every MERT epoch.

The table compression tools are found in the Moses binary directory and can be activated while filtering the phrase table and lexicalized reordering table using `-Binarizer` option as shown below:

```
${MOSES_SCRIPT}/training/filter-model-given-input.pl \
  ${MODEL_DIR}.filtered/dev \
  ${MODEL_DIR}/moses.ini \
  ${DEV_F} \
  -Binarizer ${MOSES_BIN_DIR}/processPhraseTableMin ${MOSES_BIN_DIR}/processLexicalTableMin \
  -threads ${JOBS}
```

---

[9]`--giza-option` allows users to use train with other word alignment models
[10]https://github.com/jonsafari/clustercat

3 Results

Team	Other Resources	System	BLEU	HUMAN
JAPIO	JAPIO corpus	PBMT with pre-ordering	**58.66**	46.25
NTT	-	NMT with bidi-LSTM	44.99	**46.50**
NTT	-	PBMT with pre-ordering	40.75	39.25
SENSE	-	Vanilla PBMT (clustercat)	38.90	-
SENSE	-	Vanilla PBMT (mkcls)	38.75	-
ORGANIZER	-	Baseline PBMT	38.34	0

Table 1: Top Systems and Our Submissions to WAT2016 Patent Task (Chinese-Japanese)

Team	Other Resources	System	BLEU	HUMAN
NICT-2	ASPEC	PBMT with Preordering + Domain Adaptation	**34.64**	**14.00**
NICT-2	-	PBMT with Preordering + Domain Adaptation	34.64	-11.00
BJTU_NLP	-	NMT using RNN Encoder-Decoder with attention	32.79	-1.00
SENSE	-	Vanilla PBMT (clustercat)	32.11	-
ORGANIZER	-	Baseline PBMT	32.03	0
SENSE	-	Vanilla PBMT (mkcls)	31.84	-

Table 2: Top Systems and Our Submissions to WAT2016 Patent Task (Japanese-Chinese)

Using the fast and light PBMT system described in the previous section, we submitted the system outputs to the WAT 2016 shared task (Nakazawa et al., 2016) for Japanese to Chinese patent translation task and the Indonesian to English news domain task[11].

The Japan Patent Office (JPO) Patent corpus is the official resource provided for the Japanese-Chinese-Korean-English shared task. The training dataset is made up of 1 million sentences (250k each from the chemistry, electricity, mechanical engineering and physics domains). The Badan Pengkajian dan Penerapan Teknologi (BPPT) corpus is the official resource provided for the English-Indonesian shared task. The training dataset is made up of 1 million 50,000 training sentences from the general news domain.

Table 1 and 2 present our submission to the Japanese-Chinese Patent Task in WAT2016. Due to time constraint, we were not able to make the submission in time for the manual evaluation. Looking at the BLEU scores, we achieved relatively close BLEU scores for both translation directions as compared to the organizers' PBMT baseline.

From Table 1, we see that the NMT system achieved the best HUMAN score given a lower BLEU[12], this reinforced the rise of NMT era. More importantly, we see a huge difference in JAPIO's PBMT BLEU score (58.66) and NTT's NMT BLEU score (58.66) but both system achieved similar HUMAN scores. The same disparity in BLEU and HUMAN scores is evident from Table 2 where both NICT-2 PBMT systems (one trained with additional ASPEC corpus and the other without) scored 34.64 BLEU but the HUMAN score disparity ranges from -11.00 to +14.00. Such disparity reiterated the disparity between n-gram based metric and human evaluation in Tan et al. (2015a).

---

[11]In previous editions of WAT (Nakazawa et al., 2014; Nakazawa et al., 2015), we had participated using similar PBMT system in the English-Japanese-Chinese scientific text translation task using the ASPEC corpus, our results had been presented in Tan and Bond (2014) and Tan et al. (2015b) and in the Korean-English patent translation task using the JPO corpus (Tan et al., 2015a)

[12]Reported BLEU scores on JUMAN tokenizer

Team	System	BLEU	HUMAN
SENSE	Vanilla PBMT (clustercat)	**25.31**	1.250
SENSE	Vanilla PBMT (mkcls)	25.16	-2.750
ORGRANIZER	Online A	24.20	**35.75**
ORGRANIZER	Baseline PBMT	23.95	0
IITB	Bilingual Neural LM	22.35	-9.250
ORGRANIZER	Online B	18.09	10.50

Table 3: Results of WAT2016 English-Indonesian News Domain Task

Team	System	BLEU	HUMAN
ORGANIZER	Online A	**28.11**	**49.25**
SENSE	Vanilla PBMT (clustercat)	25.97	-8.25
SENSE	Vanilla PBMT (mkcls)	25.62	-5.00
ORGANIZER	Baseline PBMT	24.57	0
IITB	Bilingual Neural LM	22.58	-
ORGANIZER	Online B	19.69	34.50

Table 4: Results of WAT2016 Indonesian-English News Domain Task

Table 3 and 4 presents the results for the Indonesian-English News Domain Task. From Table 3, we achieve the highest BLEU scores in the English-Indonesia direction with a difference of >1.0+ BLEU score with respect to the baseline PBMT provided by the organizers. However, our HUMAN scores show that the quality of our system output is only marginally better than the baseline. Comparatively, the online system A has similar BLEU scores to the organizer's baseline but achieved stellar HUMAN scores of +35.75. Table 4 shows the results for the English-Indonesian task, the online system A and B achieved the best HUMAN scores. In both directions, we see the same automatic *vs* manual evaluation disparity from System B's low BLEU and high HUMAN scores and from our system's high BLEU and low/marginal HUMAN scores.

4   Conclusion

We motivate and describe the steps to build a fast and light phrase-based machine translation model that achieved comparable results to the WAT2016 baseline. We hope that our baseline system helps new MT practitioners that are not familiar with the Moses ecology[13] to build PBMT models. The full training script is available on `https://github.com/alvations/vanilla-moses/blob/master/train-vanilla-model.sh`.

Acknowledgements

The research leading to these results has received funding from the People Programme (Marie Curie Actions) of the European Union's Seventh Framework Programme FP7/2007-2013/ under REA grant agreement no. 317471.

References

Yaser Al-Onaizan and Kishore Papineni. 2006. Distortion models for statistical machine translation. In *Proceedings of the 21st International Conference on Computational Linguistics and the 44th annual meeting of the Association for Computational Linguistics*, pages 529–536.

Luisa Bentivogli, Arianna Bisazza, Mauro Cettolo, and Marcello Federico. 2016. Neural versus Phrase-Based Machine Translation Quality: a Case Study. *ArXiv e-prints*, August.

Alexandra Birch, Miles Osborne, and Phil Blunsom. 2010. Metrics for mt evaluation: evaluating reordering. *Machine Translation*, 24(1):15–26.

---

[13]Our Vanilla PBMT system is complimentary to the steps described in http://www.statmt.org/moses/?n=Moses.Tutorial

Peter F Brown, John Cocke, Stephen A Della Pietra, Vincent J Della Pietra, Fredrick Jelinek, John D Lafferty, Robert L Mercer, and Paul S Roossin. 1990. A statistical approach to machine translation. *Computational linguistics*, 16(2):79–85.

Peter F Brown, Vincent J Della Pietra, Stephen A Della Pietra, and Robert L Mercer. 1993. The mathematics of statistical machine translation: Parameter estimation. *Computational linguistics*, 19(2):263–311.

Daniel Cer, Michel Galley, Daniel Jurafsky, and Christopher D Manning. 2010. Phrasal: a toolkit for statistical machine translation with facilities for extraction and incorporation of arbitrary model features. In *Proceedings of the NAACL HLT 2010 Demonstration Session*, pages 9–12.

Stanley Chen and Joshua T. Goodman. 1998. An empirical study of smoothing techniques for language modeling. Technical Report 10-98, Harvard University.

David Chiang. 2005. A hierarchical phrase-based model for statistical machine translation. In *Proceedings of the 43rd Annual Meeting on Association for Computational Linguistics*, pages 263–270. Association for Computational Linguistics.

Josep Crego, Jungi Kim, Guillaume Klein, Anabel Rebollo, Kathy Yang, Jean Senellart, Egor Akhanov, Patrice Brunelle, Aurelien Coquard, Yongchao Deng, Satoshi Enoue, Chiyo Geiss, Joshua Johanson, Ardas Khalsa, Raoum Khiari, Byeongil Ko, Catherine Kobus, Jean Lorieux, Leidiana Martins, Dang-Chuan Nguyen, Alexandra Priori, Thomas Riccardi, Natalia Segal, Christophe Servan, Cyril Tiquet, Bo Wang, Jin Yang, Dakun Zhang, Jing Zhou, and Peter Zoldan. 2016. SYSTRAN's Pure Neural Machine Translation Systems. *ArXiv e-prints*, October.

Jon Dehdari, Liling Tan, and Josef van Genabith. 2016a. Bira: Improved predictive exchange word clustering. In *Proceedings of the 2016 Conference of the North American Chapter of the Association for Computational Linguistics: Human Language Technologies*, pages 1169–1174, San Diego, California, June. Association for Computational Linguistics.

Jon Dehdari, Liling Tan, and Josef van Genabith. 2016b. Scaling up word clustering. In *Proceedings of the 2016 Conference of the North American Chapter of the Association for Computational Linguistics: Demonstrations*, pages 42–46, San Diego, California, June. Association for Computational Linguistics.

Chris Dyer, Adam Lopez, Juri Ganitkevitch, Johnathan Weese, Ferhan Ture, Phil Blunsom, Hendra Setiawan, Vladimir Eidelman, and Philip Resnik. 2010. cdec: A decoder, alignment, and learning framework for finite-state and context-free translation models. In *Proceedings of the Association for Computational Linguistics (ACL)*.

Michel Galley and Christopher D Manning. 2008. A simple and effective hierarchical phrase reordering model. In *Proceedings of the Conference on Empirical Methods in Natural Language Processing*, pages 848–856.

Qin Gao and Stephan Vogel. 2008. Parallel implementations of word alignment tool. In *Software Engineering, Testing, and Quality Assurance for Natural Language Processing*, pages 49–57.

Kenneth Heafield, Ivan Pouzyrevsky, Jonathan H. Clark, and Philipp Koehn. 2013. Scalable modified Kneser-Ney language model estimation. In *Proceedings of the 51st Annual Meeting of the Association for Computational Linguistics (Volume 2: Short Papers)*, pages 690–696, Sofia, Bulgaria.

Kenneth Heafield. 2011. KenLM: Faster and smaller language model queries. In *Proceedings of the EMNLP 2011 Sixth Workshop on Statistical Machine Translation*, pages 187–197, Edinburgh, Scotland, United Kingdom.

Hieu Hoang and Adam Lopez. 2009. A unified framework for phrase-based, hierarchical, and syntax-based statistical machine translation. In *In Proceedings of the International Workshop on Spoken Language Translation (IWSLT*, pages 152–159.

Hieu Hoang. 2011. *Improving statistical machine translation with linguistic information*. The University of Edinburgh.

Marcin Junczys-Dowmunt. 2012. Phrasal rank-encoding: Exploiting phrase redundancy and translational relations for phrase table compression. *The Prague Bulletin of Mathematical Linguistics*, 98:63–74.

Reinhard Kneser and Hermann Ney. 1995. Improved backing-off for m-gram language modeling. In *Acoustics, Speech, and Signal Processing, 1995. ICASSP-95., 1995 International Conference on*, volume 1, pages 181–184. IEEE.

Kevin Knight. 1999. Decoding complexity in word-replacement translation models. *Computational Linguistics*, 25(4):607–615.

Philipp Koehn, Franz Josef Och, and Daniel Marcu. 2003. Statistical phrase-based translation. In *Proceedings of the 2003 Conference of the North American Chapter of the Association for Computational Linguistics on Human Language Technology-Volume 1*, pages 48–54.

Philipp Koehn, Hieu Hoang, Alexandra Birch, Chris Callison-Burch, Marcello Federico, Nicola Bertoldi, Brooke Cowan, Wade Shen, Christine Moran, Richard Zens, Chris Dyer, Ondřej Bojar, Alexandra Constantin, and Evan Herbst. 2007. Moses: Open source toolkit for statistical machine translation. In *Proceedings of the 45th Annual Meeting of the ACL on Interactive Poster and Demonstration Sessions*, pages 177–180.

Philipp Koehn, Barry Haddow, Philip Williams, and Hieu Hoang. 2010. More linguistic annotation for statistical machine translation. In *Proceedings of the Joint Fifth Workshop on Statistical Machine Translation and MetricsMATR*, WMT '10, pages 115–120, Stroudsburg, PA, USA. Association for Computational Linguistics.

Philipp Koehn. 2004. Pharaoh: a beam search decoder for phrase-based statistical machine translation models. In *Machine translation: From real users to research*, pages 115–124. Springer.

Philipp Koehn. 2005. Europarl: A parallel corpus for statistical machine translation. In *Proceedings of MT Summit*, volume 5, pages 79–86.

Philipp Koehn. 2010. An experimental management system. *The Prague Bulletin of Mathematical Linguistics*, 94:87–96.

Daniel Marcu and William Wong. 2002. A phrase-based, joint probability model for statistical machine translation. In *Proceedings of the ACL-02 conference on Empirical methods in natural language processing-Volume 10*, pages 133–139. Association for Computational Linguistics.

Toshiaki Nakazawa, Hideya Mino, Isao Goto, Sadao Kurohashi, and Eiichiro Sumita. 2014. Overview of the first workshop on Asian translation. In *Proceedings of the First Workshop on Asian1 Translation (WAT2014)*, Tokyo, Japan.

Toshiaki Nakazawa, Hideya Mino, Isao Goto, Graham Neubig, Sadao Kurohashi, and Eiichiro Sumita. 2015. Overview of the 2nd workshop on Asian translation. In *Proceedings of the 2nd Workshop on Asian Translation (WAT2015)*, Kyoto, Japan.

Toshiaki Nakazawa, Hideya Mino, Isao Goto, Graham Neubig, Sadao Kurohashi, and Eiichiro Sumita. 2016. Overview of the 3rd workshop on Asian translation. In *Proceedings of the 3rd Workshop on Asian Translation (WAT2016)*, Kyoto, Japan.

Graham Neubig, Makoto Morishita, and Satoshi Nakamura. 2015. Neural Reranking Improves Subjective Quality of Machine Translation: NAIST at WAT2015. In *Proceedings of the 2nd Workshop on Asian Translation (WAT2015)*, pages 35–41, Kyoto, Japan, October.

Franz Josef Och and Hermann Ney. 2002. Discriminative training and maximum entropy models for statistical machine translation. In *Proceedings of the 40th Annual Meeting of the Association for Computational Linguistics, July 6-12, 2002, Philadelphia, PA, USA.*, pages 295–302.

Franz Josef Och and Hermann Ney. 2003. A systematic comparison of various statistical alignment models. *Computational linguistics*, 29(1):19–51.

Franz Och. 1995. Maximum-Likelihood-Schätzung von Wortkategorien mit Verfahren der kombinatorischen Optimierung. Bachelor's thesis (Studienarbeit), Universität Erlangen-Nürnburg.

Franz Josef Och. 2003. Minimum error rate training in statistical machine translation. In *Proceedings of the 41st Annual Meeting on Association for Computational Linguistics-Volume 1*, pages 160–167.

Rico Sennrich, Barry Haddow, and Alexandra Birch. 2016. Edinburgh neural machine translation systems for wmt 16. In *Proceedings of the First Conference on Machine Translation*, pages 371–376, Berlin, Germany, August. Association for Computational Linguistics.

Andreas Stolcke. 2002. Srilm-an extensible language modeling toolkit. In *Seventh International Conference on Spoken Language Processing*, pages 901–904.

Liling Tan and Francis Bond. 2014. Manipulating input data in machine translation. In *Proceedings of the 1st Workshop on Asian Translation (WAT2014)*.

Liling Tan, Jon Dehdari, and Josef van Genabith. 2015a. An Awkward Disparity between BLEU / RIBES Scores and Human Judgements in Machine Translation. In *Proceedings of the 2nd Workshop on Asian Translation (WAT2015)*, pages 74–81, Kyoto, Japan, October.

Liling Tan, Josef van Genabith, and Francis Bond. 2015b. Passive and pervasive use of bilingual dictionary in statistical machine translation. In *Proceedings of the Fourth Workshop on Hybrid Approaches to Translation (HyTra)*, pages 30–34, Beijing.

Christoph Tillmann. 2004. A unigram orientation model for statistical machine translation. In *Proceedings of HLT-NAACL 2004: Short Papers*, pages 101–104.

David Vilar, Daniel Stein, Matthias Huck, and Hermann Ney. 2010. Jane: Open source hierarchical translation, extended with reordering and lexicon models. In *Proceedings of the Joint Fifth Workshop on Statistical Machine Translation and MetricsMATR*, pages 262–270.

Jonathan Weese, Juri Ganitkevitch, Chris Callison-Burch, Matt Post, and Adam Lopez. 2011. Joshua 3.0: Syntax-based machine translation with the thrax grammar extractor. In *Proceedings of the Sixth Workshop on Statistical Machine Translation*, pages 478–484.

Edward W. D. Whittaker and Bhiksha Raj. 2001. Quantization-based language model compression. In *Proceedings of INTER-SPEECH*, pages 33–36.

Yonghui Wu, Mike Schuster, Zhifeng Chen, Quoc V. Le, Mohammad Norouzi, Wolfgang Macherey, Maxim Krikun, Yuan Cao, Qin Gao, Klaus Macherey, Jeff Klingner, Apurva Shah, Melvin Johnson, Xiaobing Liu, ukasz Kaiser, Stephan Gouws, Yoshikiyo Kato, Taku Kudo, Hideto Kazawa, Keith Stevens, George Kurian, Nishant Patil, Wei Wang, Cliff Young, Jason Smith, Jason Riesa, Alex Rudnick, Oriol Vinyals, Greg Corrado, Macduff Hughes, and Jeffrey Dean. 2016. Google's Neural Machine Translation System: Bridging the Gap between Human and Machine Translation. *ArXiv e-prints*, September.

Richard Zens, Franz Josef Och, and Hermann Ney. 2002. Phrase-based statistical machine translation. In *KI 2002: Advances in Artificial Intelligence*, pages 18–32. Springer.

Andreas Zollmann, Ashish Venugopal, Franz Och, and Jay Ponte. 2008. A systematic comparison of phrase-based, hierarchical and syntax-augmented statistical mt. In *Proceedings of the 22nd International Conference on Computational Linguistics-Volume 1*, pages 1145–1152.

Improving Patent Translation using Bilingual Term Extraction and Re-tokenization for Chinese–Japanese

Wei Yang
IPS, Waseda University
2-7 Hibikino, Wakamatsu Kitakyushu
Fukuoka,, Japan
`kevinyoogi@akene.waseda.jp`

Yves Lepage
IPS, Waseda University
2-7 Hibikino, Wakamatsu Kitakyushu
Fukuoka,, Japan
`yves.lepage@waseda.jp`

Abstract

Unlike European languages, many Asian languages like Chinese and Japanese do not have typographic boundaries in written system. Word segmentation (tokenization) that break sentences down into individual words (tokens) is normally treated as the first step for machine translation (MT). For Chinese and Japanese, different rules and segmentation tools lead different segmentation results in different level of granularity between Chinese and Japanese. To improve the translation accuracy, we adjust and balance the granularity of segmentation results around terms for Chinese–Japanese patent corpus for training translation model. In this paper, we describe a statistical machine translation (SMT) system which is built on re-tokenized Chinese–Japanese patent training corpus using extracted bilingual multi-word terms.

1 Introduction

China and Japan are producing a large amount of patents in their respective languages. Making Chinese patents available in Japanese, and Japanese patents in Chinese is an important task for increasing economical development in Asia and international world. The translation of patents is a key issue that should be helped by the use of SMT.

Word segmentation is normally treated as the first step for SMT between Chinese and Japanese. Patents contain large amounts of domain-specific terms in words or multi-word expressions. This brings up the question of word segmentation: we may not want to tokenize terms in specific domains in patents. But we cannot control the tokenization of the multi-word terms: a large number of multi-word terms are always segmented into several single-word terms in one language but may not be segmented in another language, or some of the multi-word terms in two languages have different levels of granularity in segmentation because of different conventions of segmentation in different languages.

The related work by Chang et al. (2008) shows that segmentation granularity of Chinese word segmentation affects the translation accuracy and that it is very important for MT. In (Chu et al., 2013), for improving the translation accuracy of scientific papers, they make use of a constructed mapping table for adjusting Chinese segmentation results according to Japanese segmentation based on characters shared between Chinese and Japanese. In our work, we focus on terms and patent segmentation and translation. To improve SMT translation accuracy, we change and adjust the segmentation for terms using extracted bilingual multi-word terms for both languages (not only for Chinese or Japanese).

Frantzi et al. (2000) describes a combination of linguistic and statistical methods (C-value/NC-value) for the automatic extraction of multi-word terms from English corpora. In (Mima and Ananiadou, 2001), it is showed that the C-/NC-value method is an efficient domain-independent multi-word term recognition not only in English but in Japanese as well. In this paper, we adopt the C-value method to extract monolingual multi-word terms in Chinese and Japanese, and combine it with the sampling-based alignment method (Lardilleux and Lepage, 2009) and kanji-hanzi conversion method for bilingual multi-word term extraction. We build SMT systems based on re-tokenized Chinese–Japanese patent training corpus using the extracted bilingual multi-word terms.

Place licence statement here for the camera-ready version, see Section ?? of the instructions for preparing a manuscript.

Proceedings of the 3rd Workshop on Asian Translation,
pages 194–202, Osaka, Japan, December 11-17 2016.

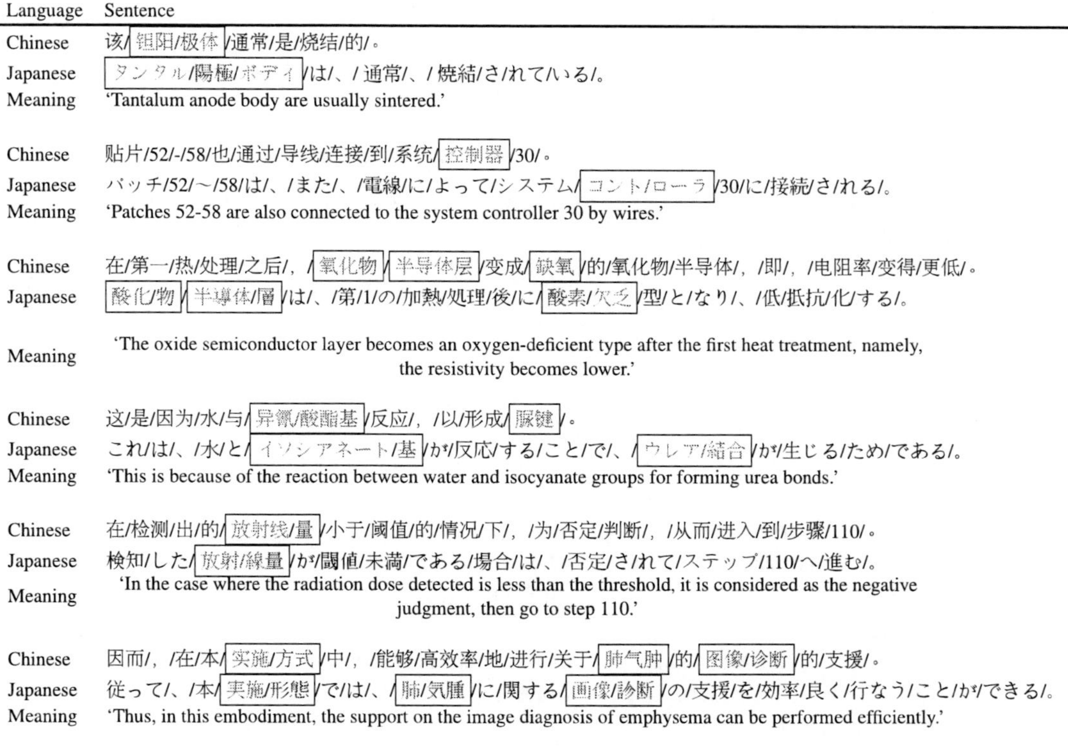

Figure 1: Examples of Chinese–Japanese patent segmentation. Terms in different languages are tokenized at different levels of granularity. Segmentation tools used are Stanford for Chinese and Juman for Japanese. The words given in the box are the multi-word terms or single-word terms in Chinese or Japanese. The words in the same color have corresponding translation relations between two languages.

2   Word Segmentation for Chinese–Japanese Patent Corpus

Figure 1 gives the examples for Chinese–Japanese patent sentences which are tokenized at different levels of granularity based on different segmentation tools. For instance, the multi-word term 钽阳/极体 ('tantalum anode body') in Chinese has a translation relation with the multi-word タンタル/陽極/ボディ in Japanese, but actually, they do not have any correspondence in word-to-word alignments. Similar examples are given as 异氰/酸酯基 ('isocyanate group') in Chinese and イソシアネート/基 in Japanese, 放射线/量 ('radiation dose') in Chinese and 放射/線量 in Japanese. Another case is that some terms are multi-word terms in one language but single-word terms in another language. For instance, the single-word term 肺气肿 ('emphysema') in Chinese and the multi-word term 肺/气腫 in Japanese. For keeping the direct and exact translations between Chinese and Japanese terms, we intend to re-tokenize Chinese–Japanese parallel sentences center around bilingual multi-word terms. As such, correspondence and meaning of terms come into focus when adjusting word tokenization granularity.

To do this, we extract bilingual multi-word terms from an existing Chinese–Japanese training corpus, then we build SMT systems based on the re-tokenized training corpus using these extracted bilingual multi-word terms by enforcing them to be considered as one token.

3   Chinese–Japanese Bilingual Multi-word Term Extraction

In this section, we describe a bilingual multi-word term extraction method used in our work. We combine using C-value for monolingual multi-word extraction with the sampling-based alignment method and kanji-hanzi conversion method for bilingual multi-word term extraction.

3.1 Monolingual Multi-word Term Extraction

The C-value is an automatic domain-independent method, commonly used for multi-word term extraction. This method has two main parts: linguistic part and statistical part. The linguistic part gives the type of multi-word terms extracted relying on part-of-speech tagging, linguistic filters, stop list, etc. The statistical part measure a termhood to a candidate string, and output a list of candidate terms with decreasing order of C-value. In our experiments, we extract multi-word terms which contain a sequence of nouns or adjectives followed by a noun in both Chinese and Japanese. This linguistic pattern[1] can be written as follows using a regular expression: $(Adjective|Noun)^+ Noun$. The segmenter and part-of-speech tagger that we use are the Stanford parser[2] for Chinese and Juman[3] for Japanese.

The statistical part, the measure of termhood, called the C-value, is given by the following formula:

$$\text{C–value}(a) = \begin{cases} \log_2 |a| \cdot f(a) & \text{if } a \text{ is not nested,} \\ \log_2 |a| \big(f(a) - \dfrac{1}{P(T_a)} \sum_{b \in T_a} f(b) \big) & \text{otherwise} \end{cases} \tag{1}$$

where a is the candidate string, f(.) is its frequency of occurrence in the corpus, T_a is the set of extracted candidate terms that contain a, $P(T_a)$ is the number of these candidate terms.

In our experiments, we follow the basic steps of the C-value approach to extract Chinese and Japanese monolingual multi-word terms respectively from the existing Chinese–Japanese training corpus. We firstly tag each word in the Chinese and the Japanese corpus respectively; we then extract multi-word terms based on the linguistic pattern and the formula given above for each language. The stop list is used to avoid extracting infelicitous sequences of words consists of 240 function words (including numbers, letters and punctuations etc.). Examples of term candidates in Chinese and Japanese extracted are shown in Table 1. We then re-tokenize such candidate terms in the Chinese–Japanese training corpus by enforcing them to be considered as one token. Each candidate multi-word term is aligned with markers.

3.2 Bilingual Multi-word Term Extraction

We extract bilingual multi-word terms based on re-tokenized Chinese–Japanese training corpus (with extracted monolingual muti-word terms) with two methods: one is using the sampling-based alignment method, another one is taking kanji-hanzi conversion into consideration.

3.2.1 Using Sampling-based Method

To extract bilingual aligned multi-word terms, we use the open source implementation of the sampling-based alignment method, Anymalign (Lardilleux and Lepage, 2009), to perform word-to-word alignment (token-to-token alignment)[4] from the above monolingual terms based re-tokenized Chinese–Japanese training corpus. We recognize the multi-word term to multi-word term alignments between Chinese and Japanese by using the markers. We then filter these aligned multi-word candidate terms by setting some threshold P for the translation probabilities in both directions.

Table 2 shows some bilingual multi-word terms that we extracted by setting a threshold P with 0.6. It is possible that some incorrect alignments are extracted. Such examples appear on the alignments with $*$. To improve the precision (good match) of the results, we further filter these extracted bilingual multi-word terms (obtained by setting threshold P) by computing the ratio of the lengths in words between the Chinese (Japanese) part and its corresponding Japanese (Chinese) part.

We set the ratio of the length in words between two languages with 1.0, 1.5, 2.0 and 2.5. The precision of the kept bilingual multi-word terms in each ratio is assessed by sampling 100 bilingual multi-word terms. On the bilingual multi-word term extraction results obtained by setting P=0.6, the precisions

---

[1] Pattern for Chinese: $(JJ|NN)^+ NN$, pattern for Japanese: (形容詞 | 名詞)$^+$ 名詞. 'JJ' and '形容詞' are codes for adjectives, 'NN' and '名詞' are codes for nouns in the Chinese and the Japanese taggers that we use.

[2] http://nlp.stanford.edu/software/segmenter.shtml

[3] http://nlp.ist.i.kyoto-u.ac.jp/index.php?JUMAN

[4] This is done by the option -N 1 on the command line. Experiments were also done with GIZA++, the sampling-based alignment method is more efficient than GIZA++.

Chinese or Japanese sentences	Extracted monolingual terms
Chinese: 在/P 糖尿病/NN ，/PU 更/AD 具体/VA 地/DEV 1/CD 型/NN 或/CC 2/CD 型/NN 糖尿病/NN 患者/NN 的/DEC 情况/NN 中/LC ，/PU 本/DT 发明/NN 的/DEC 药物/NN 容许/VV 血液/NN 葡萄糖/NN 浓度/NN 更/AD 有效/VA 地/DEV 适应/VV 于/P 血糖/NN 正常/JJ 水平/NN 。/PU **Japanese:** 本/接頭辞 発明/名詞 の/助詞 薬剤/名詞 は/助詞 、/特殊 糖尿/名詞 病/名詞 、/特殊 より/副詞 詳細に/形容詞 は/助詞 1/特殊 型/接尾辞 又は/助詞 2/特殊 型/接尾辞 糖尿/名詞 病/名詞 の/助詞 患者/名詞 の/助詞 場合/名詞 に/助詞 血/名詞 中/接尾辞 グルコース/名詞 濃度/名詞 を/助詞 正常/形容詞 血糖/名詞 レベル/名詞 まで/助詞 より/助詞 効果/名詞 的に/接尾辞 適合/名詞 さ/動詞 せる/接尾辞 こと/名詞 を/助詞 可能に/形容詞 する/接尾辞 。/特殊 English meaning: 'In diabetes, more particularly, type 1 or 2 diabetes cases, the drug of the present invention allows the blood glucose concentration more effectively adapt to normal blood glucose levels.'	型 糖尿病 'the type of diabetes' 葡萄糖 浓度 'glucose concentration' 血糖 正常 水平 'normal blood glucose level' 糖尿 病 'diabetes' グルコース 濃度 'glucose concentration' 正常 血糖 レベル 'normal blood glucose level'
Chinese: 在/P 该/DT 方法/NN 中/LC ，/PU 能够/VV 得到/VV 从/P 心脏/NN 周期/NN 内/LC 的/DEG 心收缩/NN 期/NN 到/VV 心/NN 舒张/VV 期/NN 之间/LC 的/DEG 血液/NN 移动/VV 的/DEC 1/CD 个/M 以上/LC 的/DEG 图像/NN 。/PU **Japanese:** この/連体詞 方法/名詞 に/助詞 おいて/動詞 は/助詞 、/特殊 心臓/名詞 周期/名詞 内/接尾辞 の/助詞 心/名詞 収縮/名詞 期/名詞 から/助詞 心/名詞 拡張/名詞 期/名詞 まで/助詞 の/助詞 間/名詞 の/助詞 血液/名詞 移動/名詞 の/助詞 1/名詞 枚/接尾辞 以上/接尾辞 の/助詞 画像/名詞 が/助詞 得/動詞 られる/接尾辞 。/特殊 English meaning: 'In this method, we can obtain more than one images of blood moving from systole of cardiac cycle to diastole.'	心脏 周期 'cardiac cycle' 心收缩 期 'systole' 心臓 周期 'cardiac cycle' 心 収縮 期 'systole' 心 拡張 期 'diastole' 血液 移動 'blood moving'

Table 1: Examples of multi-word term extracted using C-value, based on the linguistic pattern: $(Adjective|Noun)^{+} Noun$.

for each ratio are 94%, 92%, 90% and 80%. It is obvious that the precision of the extracted bilingual multi-word terms decreases rapidly when the ratio tends to 2.5, thus we set the ratio of the lengths in both directions to a maximum value of 2.0 to keep precision and recall high at the same time. Another filtering constraint is to filter out alignments of the Japanese part which contains hiragana. This constraint results from an investigation of the distribution of the components in Japanese by which we found that multi-word terms made up of "kanji + hiragana" or "kanji + hiragana + katakana" have lower chance to be aligned with Chinese multi-word terms (see Table 3).

3.2.2 Using Kanji-hanzi Conversion Method

Table 2 leads to the observation that some correctly aligned bilingual terms cannot be extracted by using the methods we described in Section 3.2.1. Such examples of terms are given in Table 2 with ×. Such examples are the multi-word terms on one side (Chinese or Japanese) are not multi-word terms in another side (Japanese or Chinese), or filtered by setting a threshold on translation probabilities. Kanji-hanzi

Extract or not	Correct or not	Chinese	Japanese	Meaning	$P(t|s)$	$P(s|t)$
○	√	葡萄糖_浓度	グルコース_濃度	'glucose concentration'	0.962121	0.891228
○	√	血糖_正常_水平	正常_血糖_レベル	'normal blood glucose level'	1.000000	1.000000
○	√	心脏_周期	心臓_周期	'cardiac cycle'	1.000000	1.000000
○	√	心收缩_期	心_収縮_期	'systole'	1.000000	0.833333
○	√	脂肪_酸酯	脂肪_酸_エステル	'fatty acid ester'	1.000000	0.983333
○	*	糖尿病_小鼠_中肾_小管_上皮_细胞	上皮_細胞	-	1.000000	1.000000
○	*	上述_液体状	前記_アルカリ_活性_結合_材	-	1.000000	1.000000
○	*	上述靶_蛋白	種々の_上記	-	1.000000	1.000000
×	√	糖尿病	糖尿_病	'diabetes'	1.000000	0.666667
×	√	肺癌	肺_癌	'lung cancer'	1.000000	1.000000
×	√	杀生_物剂	殺生_物_剤	'biocide'	0.600000	0.107143
×	√	官能_基	官能_基	'functional group'	0.250000	0.009231
×	√	废_热	廃_熱	'waste heat'	0.844444	0.240506

Table 2: Extraction of Chinese–Japanese bilingual multi-word terms by setting a threshold P with 0.6 for both directions. ○ and × show the bilingual multi-word term alignment that are kept or excluded. √ and * show the extracted multi-word terms are correct or incorrect alignments by human assessment.

197

Components for multi-word terms in Japanese	Sample	♯ of these terms
all kanji	心_収縮_期	28,978 (55%)
kanji/katakana + katakana	正常_血糖_レベル ホスト_システム	19,913 (37.7%)
kanji + hiragana	様々な_分野	3,377 (6.3%)
kanji + hiragana + katakana	好適な_重力_ミキサー	517 (1%)

Table 3: Distribution of the components for multi-word terms in Japanese (52,785 bilingual multi-word terms obtained by setting threshold P with 0).

conversion method can be used to extract this kind of bilingual multi-word terms.

We keep the alignments where either one side is a multi-word term; we convert Japanese words only made up of Japanese kanji into simplified Chinese characters through kanji-hanzi conversion. By doing so, we generate a Zh–Ja–Converted-Ja file automatically where each line consists in the Chinese term, the original Japanese term and the converted Japanese term (simplified Chinese term). We compare Converted-Ja with the Zh, if a converted Japanese term is equal to its corresponding Chinese term in each character, we keep this pair of bilingual term. In this way, we can extract more reliable Chinese–Japanese bilingual aligned multi-word terms.

We combined three different freely available sources of data to maximize our conversion results. The first source of data we used is the Unihan database[5]. In particular we used the correspondence relation SimplifiedVariant in the Unihan Mapping Data of the Unihan database. The second source of data we used is the Langconv Traditional-Simplified Conversion[6] data. It contains a database for traditional-simplified character. The third source of data we used concerns the case where the characters in Japanese are proper to Japanese. For this case, we used a hanzi-kanji mapping table, provided in the resource 簡体字と日本漢字対照表[7] which consists of simplified hanzi and kanji pairs. Table 4 shows the results of extracted bilingual multi-word terms by kanji-hanzi conversion using these three sources of data.

	Zh	Ja	Converted-Ja	Meaning	Human assessment
Without any Conversion	官能_基	官能_基	官能_基	'functional group'	√
	肺癌	肺_癌	肺_癌	'lung cancer'	√
	免疫原	免疫_原	免疫_原	'immunogen'	√
By Traditional-Simplified Conversion	脉管	脈_管	脉_管	'vessel'	√
	高温_杀菌	高温_殺菌	高温_杀菌	'high temperature sterilization'	√
	放射线_源	放射_線_源	放射_线_源	'radiation source'	√
By hanzi-kanji Mapping Table	心收缩_期	心_収縮_期	心_收缩_期	'systole'	√
	废热_回收	廃_熱_回収	废_热_回收	'waste heat recovery'	√
	肺气肿	肺_気腫	肺_气肿	'pulmonary emphysema'	√
	添加剂	添加_剤	添加_剂	'additive'	√
	肝脏_再生_作用	肝臓_再生_作用	肝脏_再生_作用	'liver regeneration action'	√

Table 4: Extraction of bilingual Chinese–Japanese multi-word terms using kanji-hanzi conversion.

3.3 Bilingual Multi-word Terms Used in SMT

We re-tokenize the Chinese–Japanese training parallel corpus with the further filtered bilingual multi-word terms (by ratio of the lengths in words and components of the terms) combine with the extraction results by kanji-hanzi conversion. Each pair of bilingual multi-word terms are re-tokenized as one token and aligned with markers. In the procedure for building SMT systems, we training the Chinese–Japanese translation models on the re-tokenized training corpus. A language model is trained with the Japanese corpus without re-tokenizing annotation. We then remove the markers from the phrase tables before perform tuning and decoding in SMT experiments.

---

[5] http://www.unicode.org/Public/UNIDATA/
[6] http://code.google.com/p/advanced-langconv/source/browse/trunk/langconv/?r=7
[7] http://www.kishugiken.co.jp/cn/code10d.html

4 Experiments and Results

4.1 Chinese–Japanese Experimental Data Used

The Chinese–Japanese parallel sentences used in our experiments are randomly extracted from the Chinese–Japanese JPO Patent Corpus (JPC)[8]. JPC consists of about 1 million parallel sentences with four sections (Chemistry, Electricity, Mechanical engineering, and Physics). It is already divided into training, tuning and test sets: 1 million sentences, 4,000 sentences and 2,000 sentences respectively. For our experiments, we randomly extract 100,000 parallel sentences from the training part, 1,000 parallel sentences from the tuning part, and 1,000 from the test part. Table 5 shows basic statistics on our data sets.

	Baseline	Chinese	Japanese
	sentences (lines)	100,000	100,000
train	words	2,314,922	2,975,479
	mean $\pm$ std.dev.	23.29 $\pm$ 11.69	29.93 $\pm$ 13.94
	sentences (lines)	1,000	1,000
tune	words	28,203	35,452
	mean $\pm$ std.dev.	28.31 $\pm$ 17.52	35.61 $\pm$ 20.78
	sentences (lines)	1,000	1,000
test	words	27,267	34,292
	mean $\pm$ std.dev.	27.34 $\pm$ 15.59	34.38 $\pm$ 18.78

Table 5: Statistics on our experimental data sets (after tokenizing and lowercasing). Here 'mean $\pm$ std.dev' gives the average length of the sentences in words.

4.2 Monolingual and Bilingual Multi-word Term Extraction

We extract 81,618 monolingual multi-word terms for Chinese and 93,105 for Japanese respectively based on the 100,000 lines of training corpus as indicated in Table 5. The precision was 95% in both languages. For keeping the balance between monolingual term used for re-tokenization in both languages, we re-tokenize the training corpus in each language with the same number of Chinese and Japanese monolingual multi-word terms. They are the first 80,000 monolingual multi-word terms with higher C-value in both languages.

Table 6 gives the number of bilingual multi-word terms obtained for different thresholds P (translation probabilities) from the re-tokenized (with extracted monolingual multi-word terms) 100,000 lines of training corpus (given in column (a)). Table 6 also gives the results of filtering with the constraints on the ratio of lengths in words between Chinese and Japanese terms and filtering out Japanese terms containing hiragana (given in column (a + b)). We extracted 4,591 bilingual multi-word terms (100% good match) from 309,406 phrase alignments obtained by word-to-word alignment from Chinese–Japanese training corpus using kanji-hanzi conversion. The number of the extracted multi-word terms using kanji-hanzi conversion combined with further filtering by constraints are given in Table 6 (column (a + b + c)).

5 Translation Accuracy in BLEU and Result Analysis

We build several SMT systems with Chinese–Japanese training corpora re-tokenized using:

- several thresholds P for filtering (Table 6 (a))

- further filtering with several thresholds combined with kanji-hanzi conversion results (Table 6 (a +b + c))

We train several Chinese-to-Japanese SMT systems using the standard GIZA++/MOSES pipeline (Koehn et al., 2007). The Japanese corpus without re-tokenizing is used to train a language model using KenLM (Heafield, 2011). After removing markers from the phrase table, we tune and test.

---

[8]http://lotus.kuee.kyoto-u.ac.jp/WAT/patent/index.html

Thresholds P	Filtering by thresholds P (a)			Filtering by thresholds P (a) + the ratio of lengths + the components (b) + kanji-hanzi conversion (c)			
	♯ of bilingual multi-word terms (a)	BLEU	p-value	♯ of bilingual multi-word terms (a + b)	♯ of bilingual multi-word terms (a + b + c)	BLEU	p-value
≥ 0.0	52,785 (35%)	32.63	> 0.05	48,239 (63%)	49,474 (70%)	33.15	< 0.01
≥ 0.1	31,795 (52%)	32.76	> 0.05	29,050 (68%)	30,516 (78%)	33.10	< 0.01
≥ 0.2	27,916 (58%)	32.57	> 0.05	25,562 (75%)	27,146 (83%)	33.05	< 0.01
Baseline	-	32.38	-	-	-	32.38	-
≥ 0.3	25,404 (63%)	33.07	< 0.01	23,321 (78%)	25,006 (83%)	33.21	< 0.01
≥ 0.4	23,515 (72%)	32.92	< 0.01	21,644 (80%)	23,424 (84%)	33.29	< 0.01
≥ 0.5	21,846 (76%)	33.05	< 0.01	20,134 (85%)	22,000 (88%)	33.38	< 0.01
≥ 0.6	**20,248 (78%)**	**33.61**	< 0.01	18,691 (88%)	**20,679 (89%)**	**33.93**	< 0.01
≥ 0.7	18,759 (79%)	32.92	< 0.01	17,340 (88%)	19,460 (90%)	33.43	< 0.01
≥ 0.8	17,311 (79%)	33.34	< 0.01	16,001 (89%)	18,265 (90%)	33.41	< 0.01
≥ 0.9	15,464 (80%)	33.47	< 0.01	14,284 (92%)	16,814 (93%)	33.52	< 0.01

Table 6: Evaluation results in BLEU for Chinese to Japanese translation based on re-tokenized training corpus using different thresholds (a); based on combination of the ratio of lengths + the components (b) with kanji-hanzi conversion (c).

In all experiments, the same data sets are used, the only difference being whether the training data is re-tokenized or not with bilingual multi-word terms. Table 6 shows the evaluation of the results of Chinese-to-Japanese translation in BLEU scores (Papineni et al., 2002). Compared with the baseline system, for the training corpus re-tokenized with further filtering combined with kanji-hanzi conversion results (a +b + c), we obtain significant improvements in all thresholds. We obtain 1.55 BLEU point (threshold of 0.6) improvements compare with the baseline system. In this case, 20,679 re-tokenized terms are used. It is also improve 0.3 BLEU point comparing with the case of the bilingual terms are filtered only by thresholds (a). We then test 2,000 sentences based on this best SMT system and the baseline system. We obtain a significant BLEU score with 33.61 compare with the baseline system 32.29 (p-value < 0.01).

Figure 2 gives an example of improvement in Chinese-to-Japanese translation. Thanks to our method, re-tokenizing the training corpus with bilingual multi-word terms gave a better translation accuracy (BLEU=15.92) of the test sentence given in this example. Re-tokenizing and grouping the bilingual multi-word term together increased the probability of multi-word term to multi-word term translation, i.e., "免疫　測定　方法" to "免疫　測定　方法" ('immunoassay') in this example. This prevents the separated 1-to-1 or 2-to-2 gram translation of isolated source words in inappropriate order or position, like "免疫" to "免疫" ('immunity') and "測定　方法" to "測定　方法" ('measuring method'). In this example, re-tokenization of the training corpus with extracted bilingual multi-word terms induced a direct and exact translation.

Test sentence (Chinese):	作为(0) 测定(1) 被(2) 检液(3) 中(4) 的(5) 特定(6) 成分(7) 的(8) 方法(9) ，(10) 存在(11) 许多(12) 利用(13) 了(14) 抗原(15) 抗体(16) 反应(17) 的(18) 免疫(19) 测定(20) 方法(21) 。(22)
Baseline (BLEU=15.92):	測定 |1-1| は |2-2| 、 |10-11| 多く の |12-12| 方法 |9-9| として |0-0| は |13-13| 、 |14-14| 抗原 抗体 |15-16| 反応 の |17-18| 免疫 |19-19| 検液 |3-3| 内 の |4-5| 特定 の |6-6| 成分 |7-7| の |8-8| 測定 |20-20| 方法 |21-21| 。 |22-22|
Re-tokenizing training corpus with bilingual multi-word terms (**BLEU=25.54**):	測定 |1-1| が |2-2| 液 |3-3| 内 の |4-5| 特定 の |6-6| 成分 の |7-8| 方法 |9-9| として |0-0| 、 |10-11| 抗原 抗体 反応 さ せ |15-17| の |18-18| 免疫 測定 方法 |19-21| に ついて は 多数 の |12-12| 利用 |13-13| されている |14-14| 。 |22-22|
Reference (Japanese):	被 検 液 中 の 特定 成分 を 測定 する 方法 として 、 抗原 抗体 反応 を 利用 した 免疫 測定 方法 が 数多く 存在 する 。

Figure 2: Example of Chinese-to-Japanese translation improvement. The numbers in the parentheses show the position of the word in the test sentence. The numbers in the vertical lines show for the translation result (Japanese), the position of the n-gram used in the test sentence (Chinese).

6 Conclusion and Future Work

In this paper, we described a Chinese–Japanese SMT system for the translation of patents built on a training corpus re-tokenized using automatically extracted bilingual multi-word terms.

We extracted monolingual multi-word terms from each part of the Chinese–Japanese training corpus by using the C-value method. For extraction of bilingual multi-word terms, we firstly re-tokenized the training corpus with these extracted monolingual multi-word terms for each language. We then used the sampling-based alignment method to align the re-tokenized parallel corpus and only kept the aligned bilingual multi-word terms by setting different thresholds on translation probabilities in both directions. We also used kanji-hanzi conversion to extract bilingual multi-word terms which could not be extracted using thresholds or only one side is multi-word terms. We did not use any other additional corpus or lexicon in our work.

Re-tokenizing the parallel training corpus with the results of the combination of the extracted bilingual multi-word terms led to statistically significant improvements in BLEU scores for each threshold. We then test 2,000 sentences based on the SMT system with the highest BLEU score (threshold of 0.6). We also obtained a significant improvement in BLEU score compare with the baseline system.

In this work, we limited ourselves to the cases where multi-word terms could be found in both languages at the same time, e.g., 血糖__正常__水平 (Chinese) 正常__血糖__レヘル (Japanese) ('normal blood glucose level'), and the case where multi-word terms made up of hanzi/kanji are recognized in one of the languages, but not in the other language. e.g. 癌细胞 (Chinese) 癌__細胞 (Japanese) ('cancer cell') or 低__压 (Chinese) 低圧 (Japanese) ('low tension').

Manual inspection of the data allowed us to identify a third case. It is the case where only one side is recognized as multi-word term, but the Japanese part is made up of katakana or a combination of kanji and katakana, or the Japanese part is made up of kanji but they do not share the same characters with Chinese after kanji-hanzi conversion. Such a case is, e.g., 碳纳米管 (Chinese) カーボン__ナノチューブ (Japanese) ('carbon nano tube') and 控制器 (Chinese) コント__ローラ (Japanese) ('controller'), or 逆变__器 (Chinese) インバータ (Japanese) ('inverter') or still 乙酸乙酯 (Chinese) 酢酸__エチル (Japanese) ('ethyl acetate') and 尿键 (Chinese) ウレア__結合 (Japanese) ('urea bond') , or 氧化物 (Chinese) 酸化__物 (Japanese) ('oxide') and 缺氧 (Chinese) 酸素__欠乏 (Japanese) ('oxygen deficit'). In a future work, we intend to address this third case and expect further improvements in translation results.

Acknowledgements

References

Pi-Chuan Chang, Michel Galley, and Christopher D Manning. 2008. Optimizing Chinese word segmentation for machine translation performance. In *Proceedings of the third workshop on statistical machine translation*, pages 224–232. Association for Computational Linguistics.

Chenhui Chu, Toshiaki Nakazawa, Daisuke Kawahara, and Sadao Kurohashi. 2013. Chinese-Japanese machine translation exploiting Chinese characters. *ACM Transactions on Asian Language Information Processing (TALIP)*, 12(4):16.

Katerina Frantzi, Sophia Ananiadou, and Hideki Mima. 2000. Automatic recognition of multi-word terms: the C-value/NC-value method. *International Journal on Digital Libraries*, 3(2):115–130.

Kenneth Heafield. 2011. Kenlm: Faster and smaller language model queries. In *Proceedings of the Sixth Workshop on Statistical Machine Translation*, pages 187–197. Association for Computational Linguistics.

Philipp Koehn, Hieu Hoang, Alexandra Birch, Chris Callison-Burch, Marcello Federico, Nicola Bertoldi, Brooke Cowan, Wade Shen, Christine Moran, Richard Zens, and et al. 2007. Moses: Open source toolkit for statistical machine translation. In *Proceedings of the 45th Annual Meeting of the ACL on Interactive Poster and Demonstration Sessions (ACL 2007)*, pages 177–180. Association for Computational Linguistics.

Adrien Lardilleux and Yves Lepage. 2009. Sampling-based multilingual alignment. In *Recent Advances in Natural Language Processing*, pages 214–218.

Hideki Mima and Sophia Ananiadou. 2001. An application and evaluation of the C/NC-value approach for the automatic term recognition of multi-word units in Japanese. *Terminology*, 6(2):175–194.

Kishore Papineni, Salim Roukos, Todd Ward, and Wei-Jing Zhu. 2002. BLEU: a method for automatic evaluation of machine translation. In *ACL 2002*, pages 311–318.

Controlling the Voice of a Sentence in Japanese-to-English Neural Machine Translation

Hayahide Yamagishi, Shin Kanouchi, Takayuki Sato, and Mamoru Komachi

Tokyo Metropolitan University
{yamagishi-hayahide, kanouchi-shin, sato-takayuki} at ed.tmu.ac.jp,
komachi at tmu.ac.jp

Abstract

In machine translation, we must consider the difference in expression between languages. For example, the active/passive voice may change in Japanese-English translation. The same verb in Japanese may be translated into different voices at each translation because the voice of a generated sentence cannot be determined using only the information of the Japanese sentence. Machine translation systems should consider the information structure to improve the coherence of the output by using several topicalization techniques such as passivization.

Therefore, this paper reports on our attempt to control the voice of the sentence generated by an encoder-decoder model. To control the voice of the generated sentence, we added the voice information of the target sentence to the source sentence during the training. We then generated sentences with a specified voice by appending the voice information to the source sentence. We observed experimentally whether the voice could be controlled. The results showed that, we could control the voice of the generated sentence with 85.0% accuracy on average. In the evaluation of Japanese-English translation, we obtained a 0.73-point improvement in BLEU score by using gold voice labels.

1 Introduction

In a distant language pair such as Japanese-English, verbs between the source language and the target language are often used differently. In particular, the voices of the source and target sentences are sometimes different in a fluent translation when considering the discourse structure of the target side because Japanese is a pro-drop language and does not the use passive voice for object topicalization.

In Table 1, we show the number of occurrences of each voice in high-frequency verbs in Asian Scientific Paper Expert Corpus (ASPEC; Nakazawa et al. (2016b)). In the top seven high frequency verbs, "show" tended to be used in active voice, whereas "examine," "find," and "observe" tended to be used in the passive voice. However, "describe," "explain," and "introduce" tended not to be used in any particular voice. For example, the voice of the verb "introduce" could not be determined uniquely, because it was sometimes used in phrases like "This paper introduces ..." and, sometimes, "... are introduced." Therefore, it is possible that the translation model failed to learn the correspondence between Japanese and English.

Recently, recurrent neural networks (RNNs) such as encoder-decoder models have gained considerable attention in machine translation because of their ability to generate fluent sentences. However, compared to traditional statistical machine translation, it is not straightforward to interpret and control the output of the encoder-decoder models. Several attempts have been made to control the output of the encoder-decoder models. First, Kikuchi et al. (2016) proposed a new Long Short-Term Memory (LSTM) network to control the length of the sentence generated by an encoder-decoder model in a text summarization task. In their experiment, they controlled the sentence length while maintaining the performance compared to the results of previous works. Second, Sennrich et al. (2016) attempted to control the honorific in English-German neural machine translation (NMT). They trained an attentional encoder-decoder model using English (source) data to which the honorific information of a German (target) sentence was added. They restricted the honorific on the German side at the test phase.

Proceedings of the 3rd Workshop on Asian Translation,
pages 203–210, Osaka, Japan, December 11-17 2016.

Verb	# Active	# Passive		# Total
show	21,703	10,441	(32.5%)	32,144
describe	12,300	17,474	(58.7%)	29,774
explain	7,210	13,073	(64.5%)	20,283
introduce	6,030	9,167	(60.3%)	15,197
examine	3,795	11,100	(74.5%)	14,895
find	2,367	12,507	(84.1%)	14,874
observe	1,000	12,626	(92.7%)	13,626
All verbs	383,052	444,451	(53.7%)	827,503

Table 1: Number of occurrences of each voice in high-frequency verbs.

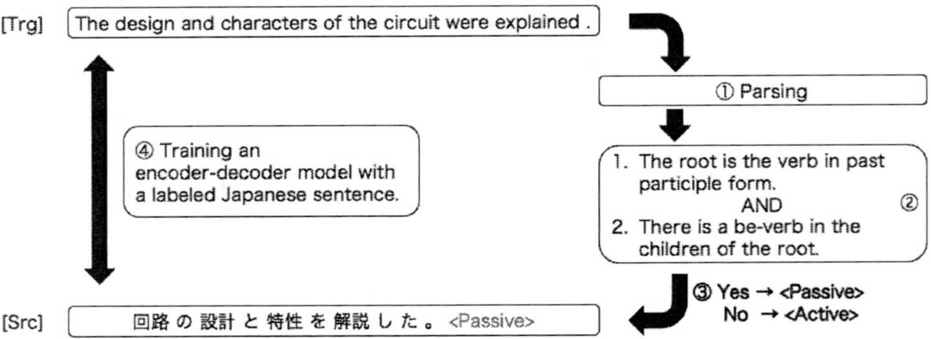

Figure 1: Flow of the automatic annotation for training an NMT.

Similar to Sennrich et al. (2016), this paper reports on our attempt to control the voice of a sentence generated by an encoder-decoder model. At the preprocessing phase, we determined the voice of the root phrase in the target side by parsing and added it to the end of the source sentence as a voice label. At the training phase, we trained an attentional encoder-decoder model by using the preprocessed source data. Lastly, we controlled the voice of the generated sentence by adding a voice label to the source sentence at the test phase. We tested several configurations: (1) controlling all sentences to active/passive voices, (2) controlling each sentence to the same voice as the reference sentence, and (3) predicting the voice using only the source sentence. The result showed that we were able to control the voice of the generated sentence with 85.0% accuracy on average. In the evaluation of the Japanese-English translation, we obtained a 0.73-point improvement in BLEU score compared to the NMT baseline, in the case of using the voice information of the references.

2 Controlling Voice in Neural Machine Translation

2.1 The Control Framework

In Japanese-English translation, the voices of the source and target sentences sometimes differ because the use of the verbs between the source and the target languages is different. In particular, English uses the passive voice to change the word order of a sentence for object topicalization to encode the information structure. Thus, it is beneficial to control the syntactic structure of the English sentences for discourse-aware machine translation. Moreover, if the voice of the generated sentence fluctuates at each sentence, it is difficult to train a translation model consistently.

In this paper, we attempt to add a ability of voice control to an encoder-decoder model, based on Sennrich et al. (2016), which controls the honorifics in English-German neural machine translation. They restricted the honorifics of the generated sentence by adding the honorific information to the source side. Instead of the honorific information, we extracted the voice information of the target sentence as a gold standard label to annotate the source sentence. At the test phase, we specified the voice of the generated

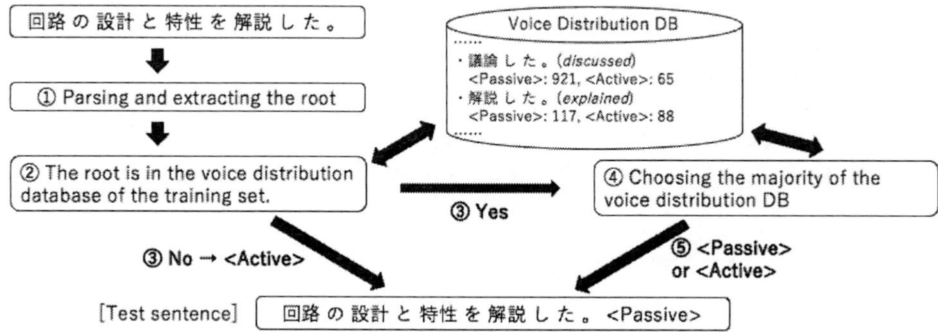

Figure 2: Flow of the voice prediction for testing an NMT.

sentence, and instructed the model to translate along with it.

In the following experiment, we used the attentional encoder-decoder model by Bahdanau et al. (2015). It is the same model that Sennrich et al. (2016) used. This model uses a bi-directional RNN as an encoder with attention structure. The proposed method can be adapted to any sequence-to-sequence model because it does not depend on the network structure.

2.2 Automatic Labeling of the Voice for Training

The performance of this method depends on the annotation performance of the voice at the training phase. Figure 1 shows the flow of the automatic annotation for training the attentional encoder-decoder model. We recognized the voice of the target (English) sentence by parsing. Then, the result of the parsing was checked to determine whether the root was a verb in the past participle form or not and whether it had a be-verb in the children or not. If both conditions were satisfied, the target sentence was recognized as being in the passive voice; otherwise, it was in the active voice[1]. For the voice controlling, we added a special token, <Active> or <Passive>, as a word to the end of the sentence, which became the input to the encoder. The special token, <Active> or <Passive>, encoded the voice of the root of the target sentence. The decoder considered only these tokens to determine the voice of the target sentence. For simplicity, we annotated only one voice for each sentence. In other words, if the sentence was a complex sentence, we selected the root verb for annotation. How the non-root verb must be treated in order to obtain the consistency of the document expression will be studied in a future work.

2.3 Voice Prediction for Testing

This study assumed that the voice label was determined in advance, but it was sometimes difficult to determine which label was suitable just from the source sentence alone. Even in this case, we had to add a voice label to the end of the source sentence to generate a target sentence because the proposed method necessarily uses a voice label.

Thus, we attempted to predict the voice for each sentence. Figure 2 shows the flow of the voice prediction. We investigated the voice distribution of the English verb in each root phrase of the Japanese side in the training data to predict the voice of the generated sentence.

At the test phase, we also obtained the root phrase of the Japanese sentence. If the root phrase was included in the training data, we added the majority label of the voice distribution in the training data as a predicted label. If the root phrase was not in the training data, the voice label was <Active>.

3 Experiments

We conducted two types of evaluations: evaluation of the controlling accuracy and evaluation of the machine translation quality. We tested the following four patterns of labeling the voice features to evaluate

---

[1]Strictly speaking, we checked whether the target sentence was in the passive voice or not, but we did not distinguish "not in passive voice" from "active voice."

	# Active	# Passive	# Error	Accuracy	BLEU
Reference	100	100	0	—	—
Baseline (No labels)	74	117	9	(72.0)	20.53
ALL_ACTIVE	151	36	13	75.5	19.93
ALL_PASSIVE	17	175	8	87.5	19.63
REFERENCE	97	94	9	89.5	**21.26**
PREDICT	72	121	7	87.5	20.42

Table 2: Accuracy of voice controlling and BLEU score of the translation.

the extent to which the voice of the generated sentence was controlled correctly.

ALL_ACTIVE. Controlling all target sentences to the active voice.

ALL_PASSIVE. Controlling all target sentences to the passive voice.

REFERENCE. Controlling each target sentence to the same voice as that of the reference sentence.

PREDICT. Controlling each target sentence to the predicted voice.

There were two reasons for testing ALL_ACTIVE and ALL_PASSIVE: to evaluate how correctly we counld control the voice, and to discuss the source of errors. In REFERENCE, the generated sentences tended to be natural. However, in ALL_ACTIVE and ALL_PASSIVE, the generated sentences were sometimes unnatural in terms of the voice. We identified these sentences to investigate the reasons why these errors occurred.

We checked the voice of the generated sentence and calculated the accuracy manually because the performance of voice labeling depends on the performance of the parser. We used the Stanford Parser (ver. 3.5.2) to parse the English sentence. The labelling performance was 95% in this experiment. We used CaboCha (ver. 0.68; Kudo and Matsumoto (2002)) to obtain the root phrase of the Japanese sentence in PREDICT. If the sentence was a complex sentence, we checked the voice of the root verb[2].

The test data of ASPEC consisted of 1,812 sentences in total. The evaluation data for the voice controlling consisted of 100 passive sentences and 100 active sentences chosen from the top of the test data. We did not consider subject and object alternation because this evaluation only focused on the voice of the sentence. Only one evaluator performed an annotation. In this experiment, the accuracy was calculated as the agreement between the label and the voice of the generated sentence. "Error sentence" means the root verb of the generated sentence could not be distinguished manually, or it did not include a verb, and so on. The baseline was an attentional encoder-decoder by Bahdanau et al. (2015), which does not control the voice. In the evaluation of the Japanese-English translation, we calculated the BLEU (Papineni et al., 2002) score with the test data of all 1,812 sentences.

At the training phase, we used 827,503 sentences, obtained by eliminating sentences with more than 40 words in the first 1 million sentences of the ASPEC. Word2Vec[3] (Mikolov et al., 2013) was trained with all 3 million sentences of ASPEC. The vocabulary size was 30,000[4]. The dimension of the embeddings and hidden units was 512. The batch size was 128. The optimizer was Adagrad, and the learning rate was 0.01. We used Chainer 1.12 (Tokui et al., 2015) to implementing the neural network.

4 Result and Discussion

4.1 Experiments with a Gold Voice Label

Table 2 shows the accuracy of the voice control and the BLEU score of the translation[5]. In the baseline, our system tended to generate a passive sentence compared to the voice distribution of the reference

---

[2]Even if the root phrase of the Japanese sentence was semantically different from the root of the English sentence, we still checked the voice of the root of the English sentence without considering the meanings.

[3]https://radimrehurek.com/gensim/models/word2vec.html

[4]We did not perform any processing of unknown words because we focused on the control of the voice.

[5]In this experiment, the BLEU score was calculated before the detokenization because we focused on the voice controlling. We submitted our system for the crowdsourcing evaluation after the detokenization.

because the number of passive sentences was greater than that of the active sentences in the training data. The accuracy of the baseline was calculated as the agreement between the voice of the generated sentence and that of the reference.

ALL_ACTIVE and ALL_PASSIVE demonstrated that the voice could be controlled with high performance. The BLEU score became lower than the baseline because some sentences were transformed into different voices regardless of the contexts and voice distribution. In other words, active sentences in the test data included sentences whose root verb of the reference was an intransitive verb. Even in that case, we forced the voice of the generated sentence to become passive in ALL_PASSIVE. As a result, the voice of some sentences did not become passive, compared to other sentences that were controlled to become passive sentences if not natural.

REFERENCE achieved the highest accuracy, and its voice distribution was close to that of the references. As mentioned earlier, the voice of REFERENCE was more natural than that of ALL_ACTIVE or ALL_PASSIVE. We obtained a 0.73-point improvement in the BLEU score compared to the baseline[6]. Therefore, we found that there is room for improvement if we can correctly predict the voice of the reference.

PREDICT used the labels predicted from the voice distribution. It tended to generate a passive sentence compared to the baseline. The controlling accuracy was 87.5% because the voice distributions were skewed in many verbs. However, the agreement rate between the predicted and the reference voices was 63.7%. Therefore, PREDICT failed to predict the voice of the reference, especially with high-frequency verbs, resulting in decrease in the BLEU score. We leave the prediction of the voice of references as a future work.

We show the output examples in Table 3. Examples 1, 2, and 3 are the success cases, whereas Examples 4 and 5 are the failure cases.

Examples 1 and 2 showed that the voice of the generated sentence was correctly controlled. When a passive sentence was changed into an active sentence, a subject was needed. Both examples generated adequate subjects depending on the context. In Example 3, although the voice was controlled, the subject and object were not exchanged. Besides this example, there were many sentences that persisted the "be-verb + verb in past participle form" structure when adding the <Passive> label was added. For example, the "... can be done ..." structure was changed into the "... is able to be done ..." structure. In this experiment, we did not evaluate whether the subject and object were exchanged, but it may be necessary to distinguish these patterns for the purpose of improving the coherence of the discourse structure.

In Example 4, it was impossible to make a passive sentence because the root verb in the target sentence should be an intransitive verb. Most of the active sentences in ALL_PASSIVE should stay active sentences that used intransitive verbs. Like Example 3, there were many sentences that were successfully controlled by using the "be found to be ..." structure when an intransitive verb was included as a root verb. Example 5 showed the case wherein the voice could not be controlled despite the attempt to control it to the active voice. The frequency of the voice of the verb "detect" in the training data consisted of 468 active-voice sentences and 2,858 passive sentences. When we forced the voice of the generated sentence to become active, the result of generation tended to fail sometimes if we input the verb that had few examples of active sentences in the training data. The subject should be generated if we forced the voice of the generated sentence to become active. However, the encoder-decoder model did not know what to generate as a subject if the training data had only a few examples of an active sentence for that verb. On the other hand, when we forced the voice of the generated sentence to become passive, we failed to find any tendencies of this type of the failure. We would like to do some additional investigation on the tendency of this result.

4.2 Experiments with Predicated Voice: TMU at WAT 2016

Table 4 shows the results of two methods submitted for the shared task at WAT 2016 (Nakazawa et al., 2016a). The BLEU, RIBES (Isozaki et al., 2010), and AMFM (Banchs et al., 2015) were calculated

---

[6] We were not able to submit REFERENCE for the human evaluation because we were not allowed to look at the references in WAT 2016.

Example 1	Source	熱戻り反応の機構を議論した。
	Reference	This paper discusses the mechanism of the heat return reaction.
	Controlling to Active	We discuss the mechanism of the thermal return reaction.
	Controlling to Passive	The mechanism of the thermal return reaction is discussed.
Example 2	Source	リサイクルに関する最近の話題を紹介した。
	Reference	Recent topics on recycling are introduced.
	Controlling to Active	This paper introduces recent topics on recycling.
	Controlling to Passive	Recent topics on recycling are introduced.
Example 3	Source	自己組織化構造に分子の形と分子間相互作用が大きく影響する。
	Reference	Molecular shape and intermolecular interaction influence self-assembled structures greatly.
	Controlling to Active	The molecular structure and molecular interaction greatly affect the self-organization structure.
	Controlling to Passive	The molecular structure and molecular interaction are greatly affected by the self-organization structure.
Example 4	Source	テロメラーゼ活性は生殖細胞と癌細胞で高い。
	Reference	Telomerase activity is high in reproductive cells and cancer cells.
	Controlling to Active	The telomerase activity is high in the reproductive cell and cancer cells.
	Controlling to Passive	The telomerase activity is high in the reproductive cell and cancer cells.
Example 5	Source	その結果, thz 波は stj でのトンネリング電流信号として検出できる。
	Reference	Consequently, the thz waves can be detected as tunneling current signals at stj.
	Controlling to Active	As a result, the thz wave can be detected as a current current signal in the <unk>.
	Controlling to Passive	As a result, the thz wave can be detected as a current current signal in the <unk>.

Table 3: Examples of the generated sentences

System	BLEU	RIBES	AMFM	HUMAN
NMT Baseline	16.89	0.700849	0.546038	—
6 ensemble	**18.45**	**0.711452**	0.546880	**+25.000**
PREDICT	18.29	0.710613	**0.565270**	+16.000

Table 4: Evaluation scores of WAT 2016.

automatically, and HUMAN was evaluated by the pairwise crowdsourcing. Note that the NMT baseline is different from the baseline of the voice controlling experiment reported in the previous section.

6 ensemble: We performed an ensemble learning of the NMT baseline. Because of the lack of time, we trained the baseline NMT only twice. Thus, we chose three models that showed the three highest BLEU scores from all epochs of the development set for each NMT baseline, resulting in 6 ensemble. As a result, BLEU score achieves 18.45. It improves 1.56 point compared with the result of the single NMT Baseline.

PREDICT (2016 our proposed method to control output voice):   We submitted our system in the configuration of PREDICT for pairwise crowdsourcing evaluation. It improved by 1.40 points in the BLEU score compared to the NMT baseline. Since we did not perform an ensemble learning for PREDICT, we expected a similar improvement in the BLEU score if we combined multiple models of PREDICT using an ensemble technique.

5   Related Work

An NMT framework consists of two recurrent neural networks (RNNs), called the RNN encoder-decoder, proposed by Cho et al. (2014) and Sutskever et al. (2014). The accuracy of NMT improves by using the attention structure (Bahdanau et al., 2015; Luong et al., 2015). However, the optimization of an RNN using log-likelihood does not always yield a satisfactory performance depending on the tasks at hand. For example, one may prefer a polite expression for generating conversation in a dialog system. Thus, several methods have been proposed several methods to control the output of encoder-decoder models.

First, Kikuchi et al. (2016) tried to control the length of the sentence generated by an encoder-decoder model in a text summarization task. They proposed four methods for restricting the length in the text summarization task and compared them. In their result, they obtained a learning-based decoder for controlling the sentence length without compromising on the quality of the generated sentence.

Second, Sennrich et al. (2016) tried to control the honorifics in the task of English-German NMT. They trained an attentional encoder-decoder model by modifying the English data to include the honorific information of the German side. The result showed that the accuracy of enforcing the honorifics to the sentence was 86%, and that of constraining the sentence to not have the honorifics was 92%. They obtained an improvement of 3.2 points in the BLEU score when the sentence was limited to the gold honorifics as the reference sentence.

6 Conclusion

This paper reported on our attempt to control the voice of the sentence generated by in an encoder-decoder model. At the preprocess phase, we determined the voice of the root verb of the target language by parsing, and added a voice label to the end of the source sentence as a special token. At the training phase, we trained an attentional encoder-decoder model by using a preprocessed parallel corpus. At the test phase, we restricted the target sentence to have a particular voice by specifying a voice label in the encoder. The result showed that we were able to control the voice of the generated sentence with 85.0% accuracy on average. In the evaluation of the Japanese-English translation, we obtained a 0.73-point improvement in the BLEU score by using gold voice labels compared to the baseline.

Our future work includes making a supervised classifier for predicting the voice, controlling another stylistic expression, and implementing the control function into the network structure such as a gate in an LSTM.

References

Dzmitry Bahdanau, Kyunghyun Cho, and Yoshua Bengio. 2015. Neural machine translation by jointly learning to align and translate. In *Proceedings of the International Conference on Learning Representations (ICLR)*.

Rafael E. Banchs, Luis F. D'Haro, and Hizhou Li. 2015. Adequacy-fluency metrics: Evaluating MT in the continuous space model framework. *IEEE/ACM Transactions on Audio, Speech, and Language Processing*, 23(3):472–482.

Kyunghyun Cho, Bart van Merrienboer, Caglar Gulcehre, Dzmitry Bahdanau, Fethi Bougares, Holger Schwenk, and Yoshua Bengio. 2014. Learning phrase representations using RNN encoder–decoder for statistical machine translation. In *Proceedings of the 2014 Conference on Empirical Methods in Natural Language Processing (EMNLP)*, pages 1724–1734.

Hideki Isozaki, Tsutomu Hirao, Kevin Duh, Katsuhito Sudoh, and Hajime Tsukada. 2010. Automatic evaluation of translation quality for distant language pairs. In *Proceedings of the 2010 Conference on Empirical Methods in Natural Language Processing*, pages 944–952.

Yuta Kikuchi, Graham Neubig, Ryohei Sasano, Hiroya Takamura, and Manabu Okumura. 2016. Controlling output length in neural encoder-decoders. In *Proceedings of the 2016 Conference on Empirical Methods in Natural Language Processing (EMNLP)*, pages 1328–1338.

Taku Kudo and Yuji Matsumoto. 2002. Japanese dependency analysis using cascaded chunking. In *CoNLL 2002: Proceedings of the 6th Conference on Natural Language Learning 2002 (COLING 2002 Post-Conference Workshops)*, pages 63–69.

Thang Luong, Hieu Pham, and Christopher D. Manning. 2015. Effective approaches to attention-based neural machine translation. In *Proceedings of the 2015 Conference on Empirical Methods in Natural Language Processing (EMNLP)*, pages 1412–1421.

Tomas Mikolov, Ilya Sutskever, Kai Chen, Greg S Corrado, and Jeff Dean. 2013. Distributed representations of words and phrases and their compositionality. In *Advances in Neural Information Processing Systems 26*, pages 3111–3119.

Toshiaki Nakazawa, Hideya Mino, Chenchen Ding, Isao Goto, Graham Neubig, Sadao Kurohashi, and Eiichiro Sumita. 2016a. Overview of the 3rd workshop on Asian translation. In *Proceedings of the 3rd Workshop on Asian Translation (WAT2016)*, Osaka, Japan, October.

Toshiaki Nakazawa, Manabu Yaguchi, Kiyotaka Uchimoto, Masao Utiyama, Eiichiro Sumita, Sadao Kurohashi, and Hitoshi Isahara. 2016b. ASPEC: Asian scientific paper excerpt corpus. In *Proceedings of the Ninth International Conference on Language Resources and Evaluation (LREC 2016)*, pages 2204–2208.

Kishore Papineni, Salim Roukos, Todd Ward, and Wei-Jing Zhu. 2002. BLEU: a method for automatic evaluation of machine translation. In *Proceedings of the 40th annual meeting on Association for Computational Linguistics (ACL)*, pages 311–318.

Rico Sennrich, Barry Haddow, and Alexandra Birch. 2016. Controlling politeness in neural machine translation via side constraints. In *Proceedings of the 2016 Conference of the North American Chapter of the Association for Computational Linguistics: Human Language Technologies (NAACL-HLT)*, pages 35–40.

Ilya Sutskever, Oriol Vinyals, and Quoc V Le. 2014. Sequence to sequence learning with neural networks. In *Advances in Neural Information Processing Systems 27*, pages 3104–3112.

Seiya Tokui, Kenta Oono, Shohei Hido, and Justin Clayton. 2015. Chainer: a next-generation open source framework for deep learning. In *Proceedings of Workshop on Machine Learning Systems (LearningSys) in the 2015 Conference on Neural Information Processing Systems (NIPS)*.

Chinese-to-Japanese Patent Machine Translation based on Syntactic Pre-ordering for WAT 2016

Katsuhito Sudoh and **Masaaki Nagata**
Communication Science Laboratories, NTT Corporation
2-4 Hikaridai, Seika-cho, Soraku-gun, Kyoto 619-0237, Japan
sudoh.katsuhito@lab.ntt.co.jp

Abstract

This paper presents our Chinese-to-Japanese patent machine translation system for WAT 2016 (Group ID: ntt) that uses syntactic pre-ordering over Chinese dependency structures. Chinese words are reordered by a learning-to-rank model based on pairwise classification to obtain word order close to Japanese. In this year's system, two different machine translation methods are compared: traditional phrase-based statistical machine translation and recent sequence-to-sequence neural machine translation with an attention mechanism. Our pre-ordering showed a significant improvement over the phrase-based baseline, but, in contrast, it degraded the neural machine translation baseline.

1 Introduction

Patent documents, which are well-structured written texts that describe the technical details of inventions, are expected to have almost no semantic ambiguities caused by indirect or rhetorical expressions. Therefore, they are good candidates for literal translation, which most machine translation (MT) approaches aim to do.

One technical challenge for patent machine translation is the complex syntactic structure of patent documents, which typically have long sentences that complicate MT reordering, especially for word order in distant languages. Chinese and Japanese have similar word order in noun modifiers but different subject-verb-object order, requiring long distance reordering in translation. In the WAT 2016 evaluation campaign (Nakazawa et al., 2016), we participated in a Chinese-to-Japanese patent translation task and tackled long distance reordering by syntactic pre-ordering based on Chinese dependency structures, as in our last year's system (Sudoh and Nagata, 2015). We also use a recent neural MT as the following MT implementation for comparison with a traditional phrase-based statistical MT.

Our system basically consists of three components: Chinese syntactic analysis (word segmentation, part-of-speech (POS) tagging, and dependency parsing) adapted to patent documents; dependency-based syntactic pre-ordering with hand-written rules or a learning-to-rank model; and the following MT component (phrase-based MT or neural MT). This paper describes our system's details and discusses our evaluation results.

2 System Overview

Figure 1 shows a brief workflow of our Chinese-to-Japanese MT system. Its basic architecture is standard with syntactic pre-ordering. Input sentences are first applied to word segmentation and POS tagging, parsed into dependency trees, reordered using pre-ordering rules or a pre-ordering model, and finally translated into Japanese by MT.

3 Chinese Syntactic Analysis: Word Segmentation, Part-of-Speech Tagging, and Dependency Parsing

Word segmentation and POS tagging are solved jointly (Suzuki et al., 2012) for better Chinese word segmentation based on POS tag sequences. The dependency parser produces *untyped* dependency trees. The

Proceedings of the 3rd Workshop on Asian Translation,
pages 211–215, Osaka, Japan, December 11-17 2016.

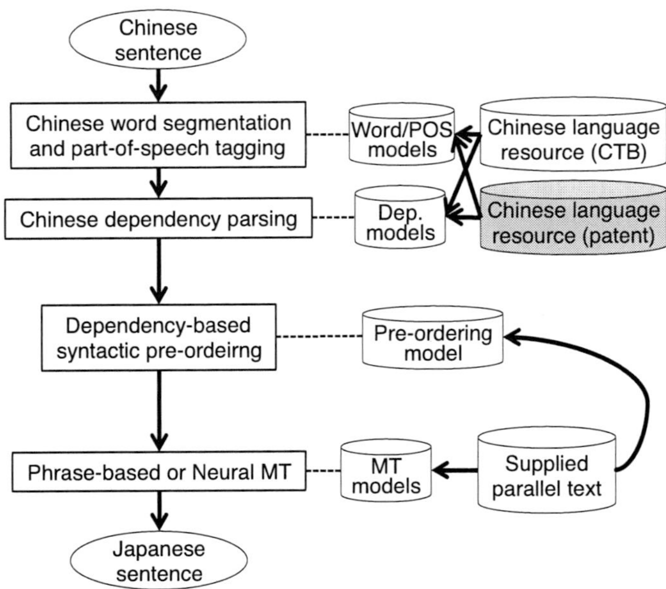

Figure 1: Brief workflow of our MT system. Gray-colored resource is an in-house one.

Chinese analysis models were trained using an in-house Chinese treebank of about 35,000 sentences in the patent domain (Sudoh et al., 2014) as well as the standard Penn Chinese Treebank dataset. The training also utilized unlabeled Chinese patent documents (about 100 G bytes) for semi-supervised training (Suzuki et al., 2009; Sudoh et al., 2014).

4   Syntactic Pre-ordering

Data-driven pre-ordering obtains the most probable reordering of a source language sentence that is *monotone* with the target language counterpart. It learns rules or models using reordering oracles over word-aligned bilingual corpora.

We used a pairwise-classification-based model for pre-ordering (Jehl et al., 2014), instead of Ranking SVMs (Yang et al., 2012) that we used the last year. An advantage of pairwise classification is that we can use features defined on every node pair, while we can only use node-wise features with Ranking SVMs. We found that the pairwise-based method gave slightly better pre-ordering performance than the Ranking SVMs in our pilot test, as did Jehl et al. (2014).

We also renewed the features for this year's system. We used span-based features (word and part-of-speech sequences over dependency sub-structures) like Hoshino et al. (2015), word and part-of-speech n-grams (n=2,3,4) including head word annotations, and those described in Jehl et al. (2014). Since these features are very sparse, we chose those appearing more than twice in the training parallel data. The reordering oracles were determined to maximize Kendall's τ over automatic word alignment in a similar manner to Hoshino et al. (2015). We used the intersection of bidirectional automatic word alignment (Nakagawa, 2015). The pairwise formulation enables a simple solution to determine the oracles for which we choose a binary decision, obtaining higher Kendall's τ with and without swapping every node pair.

5   Evaluation

5.1   Pre-ordering Setup

The pre-ordering model for the data-driven method was trained over the MGIZA++ word alignment used for the phrase tables described later. We trained a logistic-regression-based binary classification model using the reordering oracles over training data with LIBLINEAR (version 2.1). Hyperparameter c was set to 0.01, chosen by the binary classification accuracy on the development set.

5.2 Phrase-based MT Setup

The phrase-based MT used in our system was a standard Moses-based one. We trained a word n-gram language model and phrase-based translation models with and without pre-ordering. We used all of the supplied Chinese-Japanese bilingual training corpora of one million sentence pairs (except for long sentences over 64 words) for the MT models: phrase tables, lexicalized reordering tables, and word 5-gram language models using standard Moses and KenLM training parameters. We applied modified Kneser-Ney phrase table smoothing with an additional phrase scoring option: `--KneserNey`. The model weights were optimized by standard Minimum Error Rate Training (MERT), but we compared five independent MERT runs and chose the best weights for the development test set. The distortion limit was 9 for both the baseline and pre-ordering conditions, chosen from 0, 3, 6, and 9 by comparing the results of the MERT runs.

5.3 Neural MT Setup

We also tried a recent neural MT for comparison with a phrase-based MT. We used a sequence-to-sequence attentional neural MT (Luong et al., 2015) implemented by the Harvard NLP group[1] with a vocabulary size of 50,000 and a 2-layer bidirectional LSTM with 500 hidden units on both the encoder/decoder[2]. The neural MT, which was word-based with the same tokenizer used in the phrase-based MT setting, did not employ recent subword-based or character-based methods. The training time of the neural MT was about two days (13 epochs with 3.5 hours/epoch) with a NVIDIA Tesla K80 GPU. The decoding employed a beam search with a beam size of five and dictionary-based unknown word mapping with the IBM-4 lexical translation table obtained by MGIZA++.

5.4 Official Results

Table 1 shows the official evaluation results by the organizers in the JPO Adequacy, the Pairwise Crowdsourcing Evaluation scores (Human), BLEU, RIBES, and AMFM. This year's data-driven pre-ordering gave competitive performance with last year's rule-based pre-ordering with a refined model and features, but the difference was not significant. The neural MT gave very surprising results; its baseline achieved 45% in BLEU and 85% in RIBES, both of which were much higher than our PBMT results and other good-scored phrase-based MT systems. The syntactic pre-ordering negatively affected the neural MT, resulting in about 1% lower BLEU and RIBES (less severe in AMFM). But the pre-ordering-based neural MT results was still the best in human evaluation.

We chose pre-ordering-based systems with PBMT and NMT for the official human evaluation. With respect to the human evaluation results, our neural MT was very competitive with the best-scored phrase-based MT system using external resources. Surprisingly, an un-tuned neural MT (even a state-of-the-art one) showed competitive performance with a highly tuned statistical pre-ordering MT. However, we have to keep in mind that the crowdsourcing evaluation was just based on win/lose counts against the organizers' baseline system and did not reflect all aspects of the translation quality.

5.5 Discussion

Syntactic pre-ordering achieved consistent improvements in phrase-based MT in many language pairs with large word order differences. Our results this year also suggest an advantage of pre-ordering in Chinese-to-Japanese phrase-based MT tasks. We expected that pre-ordering would also help a neural attentional MT because the attention mechanism would also be affected by word order problems. However, pre-ordering significantly decreased the evaluation scores. We do not have a solid answer yet, but one possible reason may be the consistency in the source language; pre-ordering reconstructs a source language sentence close to the target language word order for the effective phrase-based MT, but it may also introduce noise on source language structures that hurts neural MT. We actually found that pre-ordering

---

[1] `https://github.com/harvardnlp/seq2seq-attn` (We used the version of 08/12/2016.)
[2] They are the default network settings of the toolkit, except for bidirectionality.

System	JPO Adequacy	Pairwise	BLEU	RIBES	AMFM
PBMT w/o pre-ordering	n/a	n/a	0.3903	0.8057	0.7203
PBMT w/pre-ordering	n/a	39.250	**0.4075**	**0.8260**	**0.7302**
PBMT w/pre-ordering (2015/rule-based)	n/a	n/a	0.4060	0.8234	n/a
PBMT w/pre-ordering (2015/data-driven)	n/a	n/a	0.3977	0.8163	n/a
NMT w/o pre-ordering	n/a	n/a	**0.4499**	**0.8530**	**0.7522**
NMT w/pre-ordering	**3.44**	46.500	0.4347	0.8453	0.7493
JAPIO PBMT w/pre-ordering†	3.24	46.250	0.4432	0.8350	0.7512
NICT PBMT w/pre-ordering†	3.23	43.250	0.4187	0.8296	0.7399
NICT PBMT w/pre-ordering	n/a	36.750	0.4109	0.8270	0.7330

Table 1: Official evaluation results in JPO Adequacy, Pairwise Crowdsourcing Evaluation scores (Pairwise), BLEU, RIBES, and AMFM. Automatic evaluation scores are based on JUMAN Japanese word segmentation. Scores in **bold** are best in the same group. †: Systems used external resources.

Language	ppl. (dev)	ppl. (devtest)	ppl. (test)
Chinese	185.573	211.370	220.821
Pre-ordered Chinese	203.639	231.218	240.533

Table 2: Source-side test set perplexities on dev, devtest, and test sets by word 5-gram language models of Chinese and pre-ordered Chinese. The vocabulary size is 172,108.

increased the test set perplexity in the source language (Chinese) by about 10% (Table 2). Since this time we do not have human evaluation results of the baseline neural MT, we cannot evaluate the actual influence of pre-ordering in the neural MT for human understanding. This issue needs further analysis and investigation.

6   Conclusion

This paper presented our pre-ordering-based system for a Chinese-to-Japanese patent MT for the WAT 2016 evaluation campaign. Our results showed that pre-ordering worked effectively with a phrase-based MT but not with a neural MT. The neural MT surprisingly improved the translation performance without any careful tuning. Its result was competitive with a highly tuned phrase-based MT system.

Acknowledgments

We greatly appreciate the workshop organizers for this valuable evaluation campaign. We also thank the Japan Patent Office for providing its patent translation dataset.

References

Sho Hoshino, Yusuke Miyao, Katsuhito Sudoh, Katsuhiko Hayashi, and Masaaki Nagata. 2015. Discriminative Preordering Meets Kendall's τ Maximization. In *Proceedings of the 53rd Annual Meeting of the Association for Computational Linguistics and the 7th International Joint Conference on Natural Language Processing (Volume 2: Short Papers)*, pages 139–144.

Laura Jehl, Adrià de Gispert, Mark Hopkins, and Bill Byrne. 2014. Source-side Preordering for Translation using Logistic Regression and Depth-first Branch-and-Bound Search. In *Proceedings of the 14th Conference of the European Chapter of the Association for Computational Linguistics*, pages 239–248.

Thang Luong, Hieu Pham, and Christopher D. Manning. 2015. Effective approaches to attention-based neural machine translation. In *Proceedings of the 2015 Conference on Empirical Methods in Natural Language Processing*, pages 1412–1421, Lisbon, Portugal, September. Association for Computational Linguistics.

Tetsuji Nakagawa. 2015. Efficient top-down btg parsing for machine translation preordering. In *Proceedings of the 53rd Annual Meeting of the Association for Computational Linguistics and the 7th International Joint*

Conference on Natural Language Processing (Volume 1: Long Papers), pages 208–218, Beijing, China, July. Association for Computational Linguistics.

Toshiaki Nakazawa, Hideya Mino, Chenchen Ding, Isao Goto, Graham Neubig, Sadao Kurohashi, and Eiichiro Sumita. 2016. Overview of the 3rd Workshop on Asian Translation. In *Proceeding of the 3rd Workshop on Asian Translation (WAT2016)*, Osaka, Japan, December.

Katsuhito Sudoh and Masaaki Nagata. 2015. Chinese-to-Japanese Patent Machine Translation based on Syntactic Pre-ordering for WAT 2015. In *Proceedings of the 2nd Workshop on Asian Translation (WAT2015)*, pages 95–98.

Katsuhito Sudoh, Jun Suzuki, Yasuhiro Akiba, Hajime Tsukada, and Masaaki Nagata. 2014. An English/Chinese/Korean-to-Japanese Statistical Machine Translation System for Patent Documents. In *Proceedings of the 20th Annual Meeting of the Association for Natural Language Processing*, pages 606–609. (in Japanese; 須藤, 鈴木, 秋葉, 塚田, 永田: 英中韓から日本語への特許文向け統計翻訳システム).

Jun Suzuki, Hideki Isozaki, Xavier Carreras, and Michael Collins. 2009. An Empirical Study of Semi-supervised Structured Conditional Models for Dependency Parsing. In *Proceedings of the 2009 Conference on Empirical Methods in Natural Language Processing*, pages 551–560.

Jun Suzuki, Kevin Duh, and Masaaki Nagata. 2012. Joint Natural Language Analysis using Augmented Lagrangian. In *Proceedings of the 18th Annual Meeting of the Association for Natural Language Processing*, pages 1284–1287. (in Japanese; 鈴木, Duh, 永田: 拡張ラグランジュ緩和を用いた同時自然言語解析法).

Nan Yang, Mu Li, Dongdong Zhang, and Nenghai Yu. 2012. A Ranking-based Approach to Word Reordering for Statistical Machine Translation. In *Proceedings of the 50th Annual Meeting of the Association for Computational Linguistics (Volume 1: Long Papers)*, pages 912–920.

IITP English-Hindi Machine Translation System at WAT 2016

Sukanta Sen, Debajyoty Banik, Asif Ekbal, Pushpak Bhattacharyya
Department of Computer Science and Engineering
Indian Institute of Technology Patna
Bihar, India
{sukanta.pcs15,debajyoty.pcs13,asif,pb}@iitp.ac.in

Abstract

In this paper we describe the system that we develop as part of our participation in WAT 2016. We develop a system based on hierarchical phrase-based SMT for English to Hindi language pair. We perform reordering and augment bilingual dictionary to improve the performance. As a baseline we use a phrase-based SMT model. The MT models are fine-tuned on the development set, and the best configurations are used to report the evaluation on the test set. Experiments show the BLEU of 13.71 on the benchmark test data. This is better compared to the official baseline BLEU score of 10.79.

1 Introduction

In this paper, we describe the system that we develop as part of our participation in the Workshop on Asian Translation (WAT) 2016 (Nakazawa et al., 2016) for English-Hindi language pair. This year English-Hindi language pair is adopted for translation task for the first time in WAT. Apart from that, the said language pair was introduced in WMT 14 (Bojar et al., 2014). Our system is based on Statistical Machine Translation (SMT) approach. The shared task organizers provide English-Hindi parallel corpus for training and tuning and monolingual corpus for building language model. Literature shows that there exists many SMT based appraoches for differnt language pairs and domains. Linguistic-knowledge independent techniques such as phrase-based SMT (Koehn et al., 2003) and hierarchical phrase-based SMT (Chiang, 2005; Chiang, 2007) manage to perform efficiently as long as sufficient parallel text are available. Our submitted system is based on hierarchical SMT, performance of which is improved by performing reordering in the source side and augmenting English-Hindi bilingual dictionary.

The rest of the paper is organized as follows. Section 2 describes the various methods that we use. Section 3 presents the details of datasets, experimental setup, results and analysis. Finally, Section 4 concludes the paper.

2 Method

For WAT-2016, we have submitted two systems for English to Hindi (En-Hi) translation, *viz.* one without adding any external data to the training corpus and the other by augmenting bilingual dictionary in training. Both systems are reordered in the source side. As a baseline model we develop a phrase-based SMT model using Moses (Koehn et al., 2007). We perform several experiments with the hierarchical SMT in order to study the effectiveness of reordering and bilingual dictionary augmentation. These were done to improve syntactic order and alignment with linguistic knowledge.

2.1 Phrase-based Machine Translation

Phrase-based statistical machine translation (PBSMT) (Koehn et al., 2003) is the most popular approach among all other approaches to machine translation and it has became benchmark for machine translation systems in academia as well as in industry. A phrase-based SMT consists

Proceedings of the 3rd Workshop on Asian Translation,
pages 216–222, Osaka, Japan, December 11-17 2016.

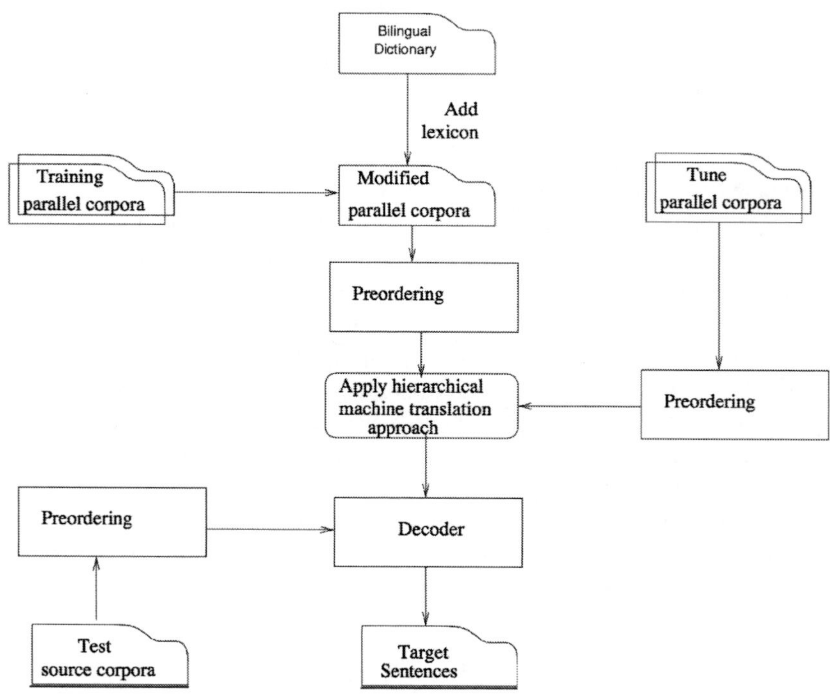

Figure 1: Hierarchical approach with reordering and dictionary augmentation.

of a language model, a translation model and a distortion model. Mathematically, it can be expressed as:

$$e_{best} = argmax_e P(e|f) = argmax_e [P(f|e)P_{LM}(e)] \qquad (1)$$

where, e_{best} is the best translation, f is the source sentence, e is target sentence, $P(f|e)$ and $P_{LM}(e)$ are translation model and language model respectively. $P(f|e)$ (translation model) is further decomposed in phrase based SMT as,

$$P(\bar{f}_1^{\,I}|\bar{e}_1^{\,I}) = \prod_{i=1}^{I} \phi(\bar{f}_i|\bar{e}_i)d(start_i - end_{i-1} - 1)$$

where, $\phi(\bar{f}_i|\bar{e}_i)$ is, the probability that the phrase $\bar{f}_i$ is the translation of the phrase $\bar{e}_i$, known as phrase translation probability which is learned from parallel corpus and $d(start_i - end_{i-1} - 1)$ is distortion probability which imposes an exponential cost on number of input words the decoder skips to generate next output phrase. Decoding process works by segmenting the input sentence f into sequence of I phrases $\bar{f}_1^{\,I}$ distributed uniformly over all possible segmentations. Finally, it uses beam search to find the best translation.

2.2 Hierarchical Phrase based model

Phrase-based model treats phrases as atomic units, where a phrase, unlike a linguistic phrase, is a sequence of tokens. These phrases are translated and reordered using a reordering model to produce an output sentence. This method can robustly translate the phrases that commonly occur in the training corpus. But authors (Koehn et al., 2003) have found that phrases longer than three words do not improve the performance much because data may be too sparse for learning longer phrases. Also, though the phrase-based approach is good at reordering of words but it fails at long distance phrase reordering using reordering model. To over come this, (Chiang, 2005) came up with Hierarchical PBSMT model which does not interfere with the strengths of the PBSMT instead capitalizes on them. Unlike the phrase-based SMT, it uses

hierarchical phrases that contain sub-phrases. A weighted synchronous context-free grammar is
induced from the parallel corpus and the weight of a rule tells the decoder how probable the rule
is. Decoder implements a parsing algorithm which is inspired by monolingual syntactic chart
parsing along with a beam search to find the best target sentence.

2.3   Reordering

One of the major difficulties of machine translation lies in handling the structural differences
between the language pair. Translation from one language to another becomes more challenging
when the language pair follows different word order. For example, English language follows
subject-verb-object (SVO) whereas Hindi follows subject-object-verb (SOV) order. Research
(Collins et al., 2005; Ramanathan et al., 2008) has shown that syntactic reordering of the source-
side to conform the syntax of the target-side alleviates the structural divergence and improves
the translation quality significantly. Though the PBSMT has an independent reordering model
which reorders the phrases but it has limited potential to model the word-order differences
between different languages (Collins et al., 2005).

We perform syntactic reordering of the source sentences in the preprocessing phase in which
every English sentence is modified in such a way that its word order is almost similar to the
word order of the Hindi sentence.
For example,

English: The president of America visited India in June.

Reordered: America of the president June in India visited.

Hindi: अमेरिका के राष्ट्रपति ने जून में भारत की यात्रा की।
(amerikA ke rAShTrapati ne jUna meM bhArata kI yAtrA kI .)

For source-side reordering we use the rule-based preordering tool[1] , which takes parsed English
sentence as input and generates sentence whose word order is similar to that of Hindi. This
reordering is based on the approach developed by (Patel et al., 2013) which is an extension of an
earlier work reported in (Ramanathan et al., 2008). For parsing source side English sentences,
we use Stanford parser[2].

2.4   Augmenting Bilingual Dictionary

Bilingual dictionaries are always useful in SMT as it improves the word-alignment which is the
heart of every SMT. In addition to reordering the source corpus, we add a English-Hindi bilingual
dictionary to improve our MT system. We show our proposed model in Figure 1. We use Moses
(Koehn et al., 2007), an open source toolkit for training different systems. We start training with
Phrase-based SMT as a baseline system. Then, augment bilingual dictionary to the training
corpus and perform reordering in the source side to improve syntactic order. Thereafter, we train
a hierarchical phrase-based SMT model. For preparing bilingual dictionary, we use English-
Hindi bilingual mapping[3] which contains many Hindi translations for each English word. We
preprocess it and add it to the parallel corpus. After preprocessing, it contains 157975 English-
Hindi word translation pairs.

2.5   Data Set

For English-Hindi task, we use IIT Bombay English-Hindi Corpus[4] which contains training set,
test set, development set and as well as a monolingual Hindi corpus. The training set was
collected from the various existing sources. However, development set and test set are the same

---

[1]http://www.cfilt.iitb.ac.in/ moses/download/cfilt_preorder
[2]http://nlp.stanford.edu/software/lex-parser.html
[3]http://www.cfilt.iitb.ac.in/ sudha/bilingual_mapping.tar.gz
[4]http://www.cfilt.iitb.ac.in/iitb_parallel/

newswire test and development set of WMT 14. The corpus belongs to miscellaneous domain. Train set consists of 1,492,827 parallel sentences, whereas test set and development set contain 2,507 and 520 parallel sentences, respectively. Monolingual Hindi corpus comprises 45,075,279 sentences. Table 1 shows the details of the corpus.

Set	#Sentences	#Tokens	
		En	Hi
Train	1,492,827	20,666,365	22164816
Test	2507	49,394	57,037
Development	520	10,656	10174
Monolingual Hindi corpus	45,075,279	844,925,569	

Table 1: Statistics of data set

2.6 Preprocessing

We begin with a preprocessing of raw data, which includes tokenization, true-casting, removing long sentences as well as sentences with a length mismatch exceeding certain ratio. Training and development sets were already tokenized. For tokenizing English sentences we use tokenizer.perl[5] script and for Hindi sentences we use indic_NLP_Library[6].

2.7 Training

For all the systems we train, we build n-gram (n=4) language model with modified Kneser-Ney smoothing (Kneser and Ney, 1995) using KenLM (Heafield, 2011). We build two separate language models, one using the monolingual Hindi corpus and another merging the Hindi training set with the monolingual corpus. In our experiment, as we find language model built using only monolingual Hindi corpus produces better results in terms of BLEU (Papineni et al., 2002) score therefore, we decide to use the former language model. For learning the word alignments from the parallel training corpus, we used GIZA++ (Och and Ney, 2003) with grow-diag-final-and heuristics.

We build several MT systems using Moses based on two models, namely phrase-based SMT and hierarchical phrase-based SMT. For building phrase-based systems, we use msd-bidirectional-fe as reordering model, set distortion limit to 6. For other parameters of Moses, default values were used. For building hierarchical phrase-based systems we use default values of the parameters of Moses. Finally, the trained system was tuned with Minimum Error Rate Training (MERT) (Och, 2003) to learn the weights of different parameters of the model.

3 Results and Analysis

We build the following systems using Moses[7].

1. Phrase-based model (Phr)

2. Phrase-based model after reordering the source side (PhrRe)

3. Hierarchical phrase-based model (Hie)

4. Hierarchical phrase-based model after reordering the source side. We build two variations of this model: one (HieRe) without adding any external resources to the train set and another (HieReDict) with adding bilingual dictionary to the train set.

---

[5]https://github.com/moses-smt/mosesdecoder/blob/RELEASE-3.0/scripts/tokenizer/tokenizer.perl
[6]https://bitbucket.org/anoopk/indic_nlp_library
[7]https://github.com/moses-smt/mosesdecoder

We evaluate each system using BLEU metric on WMT 14 test set. The official baseline model reports the BLEU of 10.79 for En-Hi translation task. Our baseline, phrase-based model using 4-gram language model achieves the BLEU score of 11.79. In our hierarchical phrase-based model we obtain the BLEU score of 13.18. After reordering the source (i.e. English corpus), we obtain the BLEU score of 13.56 in the hierarchical phrase based SMT. The performance is further improved to 13.71 when we augment English-Hindi bilingual dictionary with the training set. We summarize the BLEU scores of the different systems in Table 2.

Approach	BLEU Score
Baseline (official)	10.79
Phr	11.79
Hie	13.18
HieRe	13.57
HieReDict	13.71

Table 2: Results of different models

We study the the output sentences of the final system and classify the error according to the linguistic error categories as given in (Vilar et al., 2006) and find that the following are the the most common errors.

1.The translated word is not according to the context.

Source: <u>cat</u> is a brand that has been offering strong, durable, beautiful and high quality products for the past one hundred years .
Reference: कैट एक ऐसा ब्राड है जो पिछले सौ साल से मजबूत, टिकाऊ, सुंदर और बेहतरीन उत्पाद पेश कर रहा है।
(kaiTa eka aisA brADa hai jo piChale sau sAla se majabUta, TikAU, suMdara aura behatarIna utpAda pesha kara rahA hai.)
Output: बिल्ली एक ब्रांड है कि पिछले सौ वर्षों के लिए मजबूत, टिकाऊ, सुन्दर और उच्च गुणवत्ता वाले उत्पादों की पेशकश की गई है।
(billI eka brAMDa hai ki piChale sau varShoM ke lie majabUta, TikAU, sundara aura uchcha guNavattA vAle utpAdoM kI peshakasha kI gaI hai.)

Here, the word "cat" is translated as बिल्ली (billI) which is a wrong translation in the context of the source sentence.

2. Word order error.

Source: all the guests will join the Lakshmi Puja for the birthday party on Friday.
Reference: शुक्रवार को सभी मेहमान यहां जन्मदिन पर लक्ष्मी पूजा के लिए जुटेंगे।
(shukravAra ko sabhI mehamAna yahAM janmadina para lakShmI pUjA ke lie juTeMge.)
Output: सभी अतिथियों का जन्मदिन शुक्रवार को लक्ष्मी पूजन में शामिल होंगे।
(sabhI atithiyoM kA janmadina shukravAra ko lakShmI pUjana meM shAmila hoMge.)

Here, words in the output are not properly ordered, the correct word ordering is the following: शुक्रवार को सभी अतिथियों जन्मदिन का लक्ष्मी पूजन में शामिल होंगे। (shukravAra ko sabhI atithiyoM janmadina kA lakShmI pUjana meM shAmila hoMge.).

We also find that test set contains longer sentences compared to the training set. Average sentence lengths of training sentences are approximately 14 and 15 for English and Hindi, respectively, whereas for test set, average sentence lengths are approximately 20 and 23, respectively. Now we give some examples where reordering and dictionary augmentation improve translation outputs.

1. Example 1

Source: the rain and cold wind on Wednesday night made people feel cold.

Hie: बुधवार रात को बरसात और ठंडी हवा ने लोगों को ठंड लग रही थी।

(budhavAra rAta ko barasAta aura ThaMDI havA ne logoM ko ThaMDa laga rahI thI.)

HieRe: बुधवार की रात को बरसात और ठंडी हवा से ठंडक महसूस हुई।

(budhavAra kI rAta ko barasAta aura ThaMDI havA se ThaMDaka mahasUsa huI.)

HieReDict: बुधवार रात बारिश और ठंडी हवा से लोगों को ठंड लगने लगा।

(budhavAra rAta bArisha aura ThaMDI havA se logoM ko ThaMDa lagane lagA.)

In the above example, **Hie** approach generates wrong postposition ने (ne), whereas **HieRe** outputs correct postposition से (se). So reordering helps here but it drops the word लोगों (logoM), which is brought back by **HieReDict** approach.

2. Example 2

Source: he demanded the complete abolition of house tax in Panchkula.

Hie: वे को पंचकूला में हाउस टैक्स को समाप्त करने की मांग की।

(ve ko paMchakUlA meM hAusa Taiksa ko samApta karane kI mAMga kI.)

HieRe: वह पंचकूला में हाउस टैक्स से पूरी तरह दूर करने की मांग की।

(vaha paMchakulA meM hAusa Taiksa se pUrI taraha dUra karane kI mAMga kI.)

HieReDict: पंचकूला में हाउस टैक्स की पूरी तरह समाप्ति की मांग की।

(paMchakUlA meM hAusa Taiksa kI pUrI taraha samApti kI mAMga kI.)

Here, **Hie** approach generates wrong output वे को (ve ko) for source word 'he' but reordering helps by translating it as वह (vaha). Also, we can see when we add dictionary, it generates better Hindi translation समाप्ति (samApti) for source word 'abolition'.

It is not that reordering and augmenting dictionary always helps. There are some source sentences for which these approaches deteriorate the translation quality but these two approaches improve the overall system.

4   Conclusion

In this paper we describe the system that we develop as part of our participation in the shared task of WAT 2016. We have submitted models for English-Hindi language pair. We have developed various models based on phrase-based as well as hierarchical MT models. Empirical analysis shows that we achieve the best performance with a hierarchical SMT based approach. We also show that hierarchical SMT model, when augmented with bilingual dictionary along with syntactic reordering of English sentences produces better translation score.

5   Acknowledgments

We acknowledge Salam Amitra Devi *(lexicographer, IIT Patna)* for contributing in qualitative error analysis.

References

Ondrej Bojar, Christian Buck, Christian Federmann, Barry Haddow, Philipp Koehn, Johannes Leveling, Christof Monz, Pavel Pecina, Matt Post, Herve Saint-Amand, Radu Soricut, Lucia Specia, and Aleš Tamchyna. 2014. Findings of the 2014 workshop on statistical machine translation. In *Proceedings of the Ninth Workshop on Statistical Machine Translation*, pages 12–58, Baltimore, Maryland, USA, June. Association for Computational Linguistics.

David Chiang. 2005. A hierarchical phrase-based model for statistical machine translation. In *Proceedings of the 43rd Annual Meeting on Association for Computational Linguistics*, pages 263–270. Association for Computational Linguistics.

David Chiang. 2007. Hierarchical phrase-based translation. *computational linguistics*, 33(2):201–228.

Michael Collins, Philipp Koehn, and Ivona Kučerová. 2005. Clause restructuring for statistical machine translation. In *Proceedings of the 43rd annual meeting on association for computational linguistics*, pages 531–540. Association for Computational Linguistics.

Kenneth Heafield. 2011. Kenlm: Faster and smaller language model queries. In *Proceedings of the Sixth Workshop on Statistical Machine Translation*, pages 187–197. Association for Computational Linguistics.

Reinhard Kneser and Hermann Ney. 1995. Improved backing-off for m-gram language modeling. In *Acoustics, Speech, and Signal Processing, 1995. ICASSP-95., 1995 International Conference on*, volume 1, pages 181–184. IEEE.

Philipp Koehn, Franz Josef Och, and Daniel Marcu. 2003. Statistical phrase-based translation. In *Proceedings of the 2003 Conference of the North American Chapter of the Association for Computational Linguistics on Human Language Technology-Volume 1*, pages 48–54. Association for Computational Linguistics.

Philipp Koehn, Hieu Hoang, Alexandra Birch, Chris Callison-Burch, Marcello Federico, Nicola Bertoldi, Brooke Cowan, Wade Shen, Christine Moran, Richard Zens, et al. 2007. Moses: Open source toolkit for statistical machine translation. In *Proceedings of the 45th annual meeting of the ACL on interactive poster and demonstration sessions*, pages 177–180. Association for Computational Linguistics.

Toshiaki Nakazawa, Hideya Mino, Chenchen Ding, Isao Goto, Graham Neubig, Sadao Kurohashi, and Eiichiro Sumita. 2016. Overview of the 3rd workshop on asian translation. In *Proceedings of the 3rd Workshop on Asian Translation (WAT2016)*, Osaka, Japan, December.

Franz Josef Och and Hermann Ney. 2003. A systematic comparison of various statistical alignment models. *Computational linguistics*, 29(1):19–51.

Franz Josef Och. 2003. Minimum error rate training in statistical machine translation. In *Proceedings of the 41st Annual Meeting on Association for Computational Linguistics-Volume 1*, pages 160–167. Association for Computational Linguistics.

Kishore Papineni, Salim Roukos, Todd Ward, and Wei-Jing Zhu. 2002. Bleu: a method for automatic evaluation of machine translation. In *Proceedings of the 40th annual meeting on association for computational linguistics*, pages 311–318. Association for Computational Linguistics.

Raj Nath Patel, Rohit Gupta, Prakash B Pimpale, and Sasikumar M. 2013. Reordering rules for english-hindi smt. In *Proceedings of the Second Workshop on Hybrid Approaches to Translation*, pages 34–41. Association for Computational Linguistics.

Ananthakrishnan Ramanathan, Jayprasad Hegde, Ritesh M Shah, Pushpak Bhattacharyya, and M Sasikumar. 2008. Simple syntactic and morphological processing can help english-hindi statistical machine translation. In *IJCNLP*, pages 513–520.

David Vilar, Jia Xu, Luis Fernando d'Haro, and Hermann Ney. 2006. Error analysis of statistical machine translation output. In *Proceedings of LREC*, pages 697–702.

Residual Stacking of RNNs for Neural Machine Translation

Raphael Shu
The University of Tokyo
shu@nlab.ci.i.u-tokyo.ac.jp

Akiva Miura
Nara Institute of Science and Technology
miura.akiba.lr9@is.naist.jp

Abstract

To enhance Neural Machine Translation models, several obvious ways such as enlarging the hidden size of recurrent layers and stacking multiple layers of RNN can be considered. Surprisingly, we observe that using naively stacked RNNs in the decoder slows down the training and leads to degradation in performance. In this paper, We demonstrate that applying residual connections in the depth of stacked RNNs can help the optimization, which is referred to as residual stacking. In empirical evaluation, residual stacking of decoder RNNs gives superior results compared to other methods of enhancing the model with a fixed parameter budget. Our submitted systems in WAT2016 are based on a NMT model ensemble with residual stacking in the decoder. To further improve the performance, we also attempt various methods of system combination in our experiments.

1 Introduction

Recently, the performance of machine translation is greatly improved by applying neural networks partially in a Statistical Machine Translation (SMT) pipeline (Zou et al., 2013) or training a end-to-end neural network based machine translation model (Sutskever et al., 2014). The latter approach, or Neural Machine Translation (NMT), possess several advantages compared to conventional SMT approaches. Firstly, as the translation process is done with a single network, the pipeline of NMT training is simpler. This advantage also indicates a much lower implementation cost. Developing a SMT decoder will cost one to three months for a graduate student, while training a NMT model requires merely a script that contains the network definition. Secondly, the memory consumption is vastly reduced when translating with a NMT model. While a conventional phrase-based model trained on a large bilingual corpus can easily consumes over 100GB memory space, a trained NMT model typically requires less than 1GB GPU on-board memory in test time.

The most significant difference of NMT approach in contrast with SMT is that the information for producing the translation is held in continuous space but not discrete values. While this characteristics of neural network introduces huge difficulties in debugging, this allows the model to learn translation knowledge beyond the conventional hand-crafted MT framework. Recently, even the word embeddings obtained from NMT training demonstrates advantages over specific tasks (Hill et al., 2014).

The network architectures of NMT models are simple but effective. It produces a sentence representation with the encoder, then the decoder generates the translation from the vector of sentence representation. Generally the encoder is composed of a single recurrent neural network (RNN). The decoder reads the vector representations created by the encoder and produce a series of output vectors. A linear transformation is applied to each vector in order to create a large softmax layer in size of the whole vocabulary. Soft attention mechanism introduced in (Bahdanau et al., 2014) further boosted the performance by increasing the computational complexity.

With the advance of deep learning, deeper network architectures are favored as the models become more expressive with more layers. An absolute way to deepening NMT models is to stack multiple layers of RNN in either encoder or decoder side. However, our experiments show that stacking RNNs naively in the decoder will cause significant slowdown in training and results in degraded performance.

Proceedings of the 3rd Workshop on Asian Translation,
pages 223–229, Osaka, Japan, December 11-17 2016.

In this paper, we explores the effects of applying residual connection (He et al., 2015) between stacked RNNs in the decoder. We found the residual connection successfully helps the deepened NMT model, which leads to a performance gain of evaluation scores.

In our submitted systems for English-Japanese translation task in WAT2016 (Nakazawa et al., 2016a), we also attempts to combination the advantages of Tree-to-String (T2S) SMT systems and NMT models. Specifically, we experimented combination methods with both simple heuristics and Minimum Bayesian Risk (MBR) based approach (Duh et al., 2011).

2 Background

2.1 Neural Machine Translation

In this paper, we adapt the same network architecture of (Bahdanau et al., 2014), in which a bi-directional RNN is used as the encoder. Let $e_1, ..., e_N$ be the word embeddings of input words. Note these embeddings are initialized randomly and optimized simultaneously with other parameters. The hidden states of the bi-directional RNN are computed as:

$$\overrightarrow{h}_i = f(e_i, \overrightarrow{h}_{i-1}; \theta_r) \tag{1}$$

$$\overleftarrow{h}_i = f(e_i, \overleftarrow{h}_{i+1}; \theta_l) \tag{2}$$

$$\bar{h}_i = concat[\overrightarrow{h}_i; \overleftarrow{h}_i] \tag{3}$$

Where f is the RNN computation, $\overrightarrow{h}_i$ and $\overleftarrow{h}_i$ are the hidden states of the RNNs in two directions in time step t. The two RNNs possess different parameters: θ_r and θ_l. The final output of the encoder in each time step is a concatenated vector of the hidden states in two networks.

The decoder firstly computes attention weights for each $\bar{h}_i$ in each time step t as:

$$a_t(i) = \frac{\text{score}(\bar{h}_i, h_{t-1})}{\sum_j \text{score}(\bar{h}_j, h_{t-1})} \tag{4}$$

$$\text{score}(\bar{h}_i, h_{t-1}) = v_a^\top \tanh(W_a concat[\bar{h}_i; h_{t-1}]) \tag{5}$$

Where the attentional weight $a_t(i)$ is determined by a score function, which receives one encoder state $\bar{h}_i$ and the previous decoder state h_t as input. Several possible implementation of this score function is discussed in (Luong et al., 2015) in detail. In this paper, the score function in the original paper of (Bahdanau et al., 2014) is adopted, which has two parameters: v_a and W_a. In the decoder part, a context vector, which is a weighted summarization of encoder states is calculated as:

$$c_t = \sum_i a_t(i)\bar{h}_i \tag{6}$$

The computation of each hidden state h_t of the decoder RNN is shown as follows:

$$h_t = f(c_t, e_{t-1}, h_{t-1}; \theta_d) \tag{7}$$

$$o_t = W_o h_t + b_o \tag{8}$$

Where e_{t-1} is the word embedding of the previous generated word. A large softmax layer o_t is then computed based on the decoder state h_t, which is used to compute the cross-entropy cost. Notably, although e_{t-1} shall be the embedding of previous generated word, this word is directly drawn from the target translation during training time. This aims to speed up the training but also introduces exposure bias, which is further discussed in a recent paper (Shen et al., 2015).

2.2 Generalized Minimum Bayes Risk System Combination

In this section, we briefly introduce Generalized Minimum Bayes Risk (GMBR) system combination (Duh et al., 2011), which is used in our evaluations, more details can be found in the original paper.

The objective of the system combination is to find a decision rule $\delta(f) \rightarrow e'$, which takes f as input and generates a e' as output. MBR system combination search for an optimized decision with:

$$\arg\min_{\delta(f)} \sum_e L\left(\delta\left(f\right)|e\right) p\left(e|f\right) \tag{9}$$

$$\approx \arg\min_{e' \in N(f)} \sum_{e \in N(f)} L\left(e'|e\right) p\left(e|f\right) \tag{10}$$

Where L is a loss function for scoring $\delta(f)$ given a reference e. $p(e|f)$ is a posterior for e to be translated from f. In Equation 10, the true set of translation is approximated by N-best list. GMBR method does not directly take the scores of candidate systems to compute the loss as they are not comparable. Instead, it substitutes $L(e'|e)$ with $L(e'|e; \theta)$, where θ is a parameter. In (Duh et al., 2011), the loss function is computed based on several features including n-gram precision and brevity penalty. The parameters are trained on a development dataset.

3 Residual Stacking of decoder RNNs

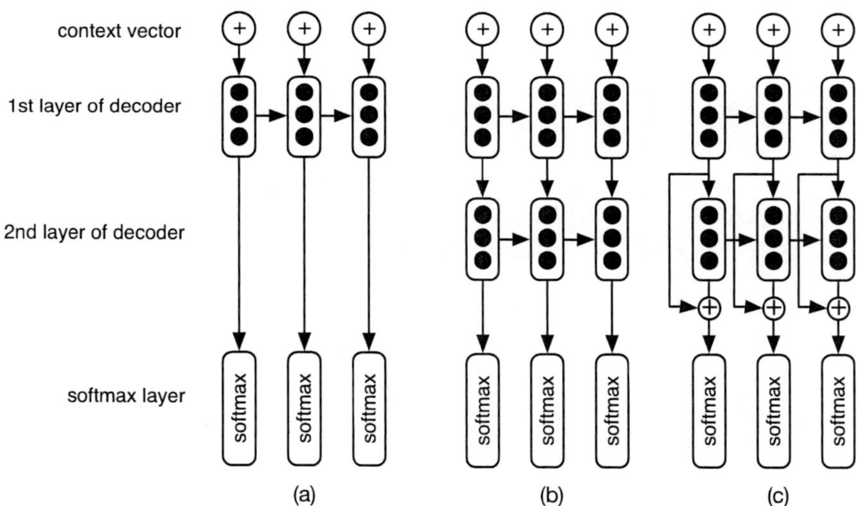

Figure 1: A comparison of three kinds of decoders. (a) A single-layer RNN (b) A stacked two-layer RNN (c) A two-layer residual stacking of RNNs

In this sections, we consider several possible ways to enhance the decoder of NMT models. Two obvious approaches is to enlarge the hidden size of the decoder RNN and to stack more RNNs. Unfortunately, in our experiments we found deepening the decoder slows down the training and finally degrades the final performance. In Figure 1, a decoder with stacked multi-layer RNNs is shown in (b), in comparison with the normal decoder shown in (a).

Recently, several techniques are proposed mainly in computer vision to help the training of very deep networks, such as Highway Networks (Srivastava et al., 2015) and Residual Learning (He et al., 2015). In this paper, we examine the effect of applying Residual Learning to RNN in sequence-to-sequence learning task, where we refer to as residual stacking of RNNs. The implementation of residual stacking is simple and does not involve extra parameters compared to stacked RNNs. The computation of a decoder with Residual RNN is shown as follows:

$$h_t = f(c_t, e_{t-1}, h_{t-1}; \theta_d) \tag{11}$$

$$h'_t = f(h_t, h'_{t-1}; \theta_{d'}) \tag{12}$$

$$o_t = W_o(h_t + h'_t) + b_o \tag{13}$$

As demonstrated in Figure 1(c), another RNN is stacked upon the original decoder RNN, whose hidden states are computed based on the original decoder states. In Equation 13, similar to Residual Learning, instead directly compute the softmax layer based on the outputs of the second RNN, a summation of the states in two RNNs is used. This simple technique is expected to shorten the back-propagation path of the deepened NMT model, which eventually helps the optimization algorithms to train the network.

4 Experiments of residual decoder RNNs

4.1 Settings

In our experimental evaluations, we adopt the fore-mentioned architecture of NMT models described in (Bahdanau et al., 2014). The baseline model contains a single RNN for the decoder. We use LSTM instead of GRU in our experiments. All RNNs have 1000 hidden units for recurrent computation. We then make three model variations and test them in our experiments:

1. Enlarged decoder RNN: the decoder RNN has 1400 hidden units

2. Stacked decoder RNN: the decoder has two-layer RNN stacked, corresponding to Figure 1(b)

3. Residual decoder RNN: the decoder is a two-layer residual stacking of RNNs, corresponding to Figure 1(c)

We design these three model variations in purpose to keep the same number of overall parameters. However, training speed may be vary due to the difference of implementations.

All experiments are performed on ASPEC English-Japanese translation dataset(Nakazawa et al., 2016b). The pre-processing procedure for English-Japanese task contains three steps. Firstly, we tokenize English-side corpus, while Japanese sentences are separated in *character level*. We filter out all sentences that contain more than 50 tokens in either side. Secondly, we make vocabulary sets for both languages. The vocabulary size for English is limited to 200k, no limitation is applied to Japanese data. Out-of-vocabulary tokens are converted to "UNK". Finally, The sentences are sorted according to their lengths. We group them to mini-batches, each batch is composed of 64 bilingual sentences. The order of mini-batches is further randomly shuffled before use.

We adopt Adam optimizer (Kingma and Ba, 2014) to train our end-to-end models with an initial learning rate of 0.0001. Then training ends at the end of 6th epoch, and the learning rate halves at the beginning of last 3 epochs. We keep track of the cross-entropy loss of both training and validation data. Trained models are then evaluated with automatic evaluation metrics.

4.2 Evaluation Results

In Table 1, we show the empirical evaluation results of the fore-mentioned models. Enlarging the single-layer decoder RNN to 1400 hidden units boosted BLEU by 0.92%. Surprisingly, stacking another layer of decoder RNN degraded the performance in automatic evaluation. This is also confirmed by a significant slowdown of the decreasing of the validation loss. With the residual stacking, we get the best performance in all four model variations.

5 Submitted systems and results in WAT2016

5.1 Submitted systems

Our submitted systems for WAT2016 are based an ensemble of two same NMT models with different weight initialization. The decoder of the NMT models are composed by two-layer residual RNNs, which

Model	RIBES(%)	BLEU(%)
Baseline model	79.49	29.32
Enlarged decoder RNN	79.60	30.24
Stacked decoder RNN	79.25	29.07
Residual decoder RNN	**79.88**	**30.75**

Table 1: Automatic evaluation results in English-Japanese translation task on ASPEC corpus. Both baseline model and enlarged decoder RNN has a single-layer RNN with 1000 and 1400 hidden units respectively in decoder. Stacked decoder RNN and residual decoder RNN are both composed of two-layer RNNs with 1000 hidden units each.

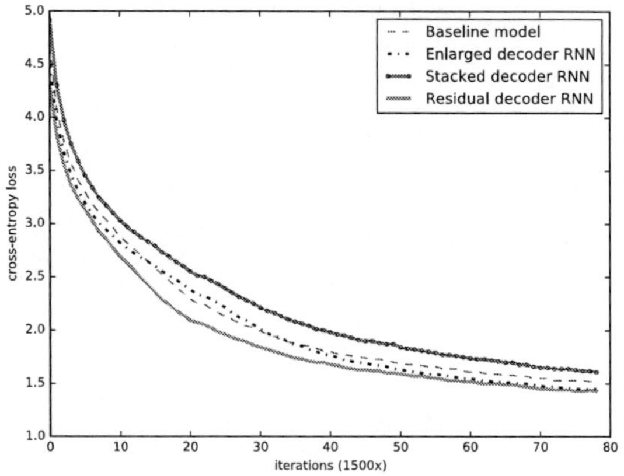

Figure 2: Validation loss (cross-entropy) of the first three epochs. The validation loss of the model with residual decoder RNNs is constantly lower than any other model variations, while stacking decoder RNNs naively slows down the training significantly.

is described in Section 3. *All RNNs in the network* are LSTM with 1200 hidden units. The pre-processing and training procedure is exactly the same as that in Section 4.2.

In order to test the performance with system combination, we trained a T2S transducer with Travatar (Neubig, 2013) on WAT2016 En-Ja dataset, but without forest inputs in the training phase. We used 9-gram language model with T2S decoding. We also evaluated the results of the T2S system with NMT reranking, where the reranking scores are given by the fore-mentioned NMT ensemble.

We tested performance of system combination in two approaches: GMBR system combination and a simple heuristics. The simple heuristics performs the system combination by choosing the result of NMT model ensemble when the input has fewer than 40 words, otherwise the result of reranked T2S system is chosen.

For GMBR system combination, we used 500 sentences from the development data for GMBR training. We obtain a 20-best list from each system, so our system combination task involves hypothesis selection out of 40 hypotheses. The loss function used for GMBR, the sub-components of the loss function are derived from n-gram precisions, brevity penalty, and Kendall's tau.

5.2 Official Evaluation Results in WAT2016

In Table 2, we show the automatic evaluation scores together with pairwise crowdsourcing evaluation scores for our submitted systems [1] in WAT2016. The first submission, which is a two-model ensemble of NMT models with residual decoder RNNs, achieved a comparably high RIBES (Isozaki et al., 2010) score.

For system combination, although we gained improvement by applying GMBR method[2], the naive method of system combination based on the length of input sentence works better in the evaluation with test data. Considering the scores of human evaluation, the system combination does make significant difference compared to the NMT model ensemble.

---

[1] We found a critical bug in our implementation after submitting the results. However, the implementations evaluated in Section 4.2 are bug-free. Hence, the results of NMT ensemble in Section 4.2 and the results of NMT model with residual decoder RNN in Section 5.2 are not comparable.

[2] We did not submit the result of GMBR system combination to human evaluation as the implementation is unfinished before the submission deadline.

Model	RIBES(%)	BLEU(%)	HUMAN
Online A	71.52	19.81	49.750
T2S system 1-best	77.87	32.32	-
T2S neural reranking	78.29	33.57	-
Ensemble of 2 NMT models with residual decoder RNNs (submission 1)	81.72	33.38	30.500
+ GMBR system combination with T2S results	80.90	34.25	-
+ System combination with a simple heuristics (submission 2)	81.44	34.77	29.750

Table 2: Official evaluation results of WAT2016

6 Related Works

Deep residual learning proposed in (He et al., 2015) learns a residual representation with a deep neural network. As stacking new layers does not lengthen the backprop path of early layers, residual learning enables the training of very deep networks, such as those with 1000 layers. Deep residual nets won the 1st place in ILSVRC 2015 classification task. The success of deep residual learning gives the insight of a better deep architecture of neural nets.

Beyond the success of residual learning, applying this technique to recurrent nets is a promising direction, which is researched in several previous works. Recurrent Highway Networks (Srivastava et al., 2015) enhance the LSTM by adding an extra residual computation in each step. The experiments show the Recurrent Highway Networks can achieve better perplexity in language modeling task with a limited parameter budget. (Liao and Poggio, 2016) achieved similar classification performance when using shared weights in a ResNet, which is exactly a RNN. Pixel Recurrent Neural Networks (van den Oord et al., 2016) demonstrates a novel architecture of neural nets with two-dimensional recurrent neural nets using residual connections. Their models achieved better log-likelihood on image generation tasks. Remarkably, the neural network architecture described in a lecture report [3] is similar to our models in spirit, where they applied stochastic residual learning to both depth and horizontal timesteps, which leads to better classification accuracy in Stanford Sentiment Treebank dataset.

7 Conclusion

In this paper, we demonstrates the effects of several possible approaches of enhancing the decoder RNN in NMT models. Surprisingly, Stacking multi-layer LSTMs in the decoder hinders the training and results in low performance in our experiments. Through empirical evaluation of several decoder architectures, we show that applying residual connections in the deep recurrent nets leads to superior results with same parameters as Stacked LSTMs. The advantage of the using of residual RNN in the decoder provides insights on the correct ways of enhancing NMT models.

8 Acknowledgment

We thank Weblio Inc. for financial support of this research.

References

Dzmitry Bahdanau, Kyunghyun Cho, and Yoshua Bengio. 2014. Neural machine translation by jointly learning to align and translate. *arXiv preprint arXiv:1409.0473*.

Kevin Duh, Katsuhito Sudoh, Xianchao Wu, Hajime Tsukada, and Masaaki Nagata. 2011. Generalized minimum bayes risk system combination. In *IJCNLP*, pages 1356–1360.

Kaiming He, Xiangyu Zhang, Shaoqing Ren, and Jian Sun. 2015. Deep residual learning for image recognition. *arXiv preprint arXiv:1512.03385*.

---

[3] https://cs224d.stanford.edu/reports/PradhanLongpre.pdf

Felix Hill, Kyunghyun Cho, Sebastien Jean, Coline Devin, and Yoshua Bengio. 2014. Embedding word similarity with neural machine translation. *arXiv preprint arXiv:1412.6448*.

Hideki Isozaki, Tsutomu Hirao, Kevin Duh, Katsuhito Sudoh, and Hajime Tsukada. 2010. Automatic evaluation of translation quality for distant language pairs. In *Proceedings of the 2010 Conference on Empirical Methods in Natural Language Processing*, pages 944–952. Association for Computational Linguistics.

Diederik Kingma and Jimmy Ba. 2014. Adam: A method for stochastic optimization. *arXiv preprint arXiv:1412.6980*.

Qianli Liao and Tomaso Poggio. 2016. Bridging the gaps between residual learning, recurrent neural networks and visual cortex. *arXiv preprint arXiv:1604.03640*.

Thang Luong, Hieu Pham, and D. Christopher Manning. 2015. Effective approaches to attention-based neural machine translation. In *Proceedings of the 2015 Conference on Empirical Methods in Natural Language Processing*, pages 1412–1421. Association for Computational Linguistics.

Toshiaki Nakazawa, Hideya Mino, Chenchen Ding, Isao Goto, Graham Neubig, Sadao Kurohashi, and Eiichiro Sumita. 2016a. Overview of the 3rd workshop on asian translation. In *Proceedings of the 3rd Workshop on Asian Translation (WAT2016)*, Osaka, Japan, December.

Toshiaki Nakazawa, Manabu Yaguchi, Kiyotaka Uchimoto, Masao Utiyama, Eiichiro Sumita, Sadao Kurohashi, and Hitoshi Isahara. 2016b. Aspec: Asian scientific paper excerpt corpus. In *Proceedings of the Ninth International Conference on Language Resources and Evaluation (LREC 2016)*, pages 2204–2208, Portoro, Slovenia, may. European Language Resources Association (ELRA).

Graham Neubig. 2013. Travatar: A forest-to-string machine translation engine based on tree transducers. In *Proceedings of the ACL Demonstration Track*, Sofia, Bulgaria, August.

Shiqi Shen, Yong Cheng, Zhongjun He, Wei He, Hua Wu, Maosong Sun, and Yang Liu. 2015. Minimum risk training for neural machine translation. *arXiv preprint arXiv:1512.02433*.

Rupesh Kumar Srivastava, Klaus Greff, and Jürgen Schmidhuber. 2015. Highway networks. *arXiv preprint arXiv:1505.00387*.

Ilya Sutskever, Oriol Vinyals, and Quoc VV Le. 2014. Sequence to sequence learning with neural networks. In *Advances in neural information processing systems*, pages 3104–3112.

Aäron van den Oord, Nal Kalchbrenner, and Koray Kavukcuoglu. 2016. Pixel recurrent neural networks. In *ICML*.

Will Y Zou, Richard Socher, Daniel M Cer, and Christopher D Manning. 2013. Bilingual word embeddings for phrase-based machine translation. In *EMNLP*, pages 1393–1398.

Author Index